Sizes

Sizes

The Illustrated Encyclopedia

John Lord

HarperPerennial
A Division of HarperCollins *Publishers*

The author has tried to make this publication a reliable source of general information. Portions acquaint the general reader with the existence and tenor of various technical documents, but this work is not offered as a substitute for, as examples, the building code, the standards or recommended practices of the various international, national, and industrial standards organizations, or other information sources generally relied on in the various trades and professions. Neither the publisher nor the author guarantee the accuracy or completeness of any information published herein, nor will they be responsible for any errors, omissions or damages arising out of use of this information. Readers are urged to consult original documents and appropriate professionals as necessary.

HarperCollins books may be purchased for educational, business, or sales promotional use. For information, please write to: Special Markets Department, HarperCollins Publishers, Inc., 10 East 53rd Street, New York, New York 10022.

FIRST EDITION

Library of Congress Cataloging-in-Publication Data

Lord, John.
    Sizes : the illustrated encyclopedia / by John Lord. —1st ed.
       p.   cm.
    ISBN 0-06-273228-5
    1. Physical measurements—Encyclopedias. 2. Units—Encyclopedias. I. Title.
    QC82.L67 1994
    530.8'1'03—dc20   94-25381

95 96 97 98 99 ♦/RRD 10 9 8 7 6 5 4 3 2 1

TO CAROL

Thanks for bearing with me

Contents

Abbreviations and Acronyms in This Book

'	foot, 1/3rd of the International Yard
"	inch, 1/36th of the International Yard
°	degree
=	exactly equal to (by definition)
≈	approximately equal to
…	the ellipsis is used to indicate a repeating decimal, e.g., 1.818…
abbr	abbreviated, abbreviation
ANSI	American National Standards Institute
approx	approximately equal to
ASTM	American Society for Testing and Materials
av	avoirdupois
c	century, as in 19TH C
cgs	centimeter-gram-second
CGPM	General Conference on Weights and Measures
CIPM	International Committee for Weights and Measures
cm	centimeter
cu	cubic
FR	Federal Register
g	gram
IAU	International Astronomical Union
IEEE	Institute of Electrical and Electronic Engineers
ISO	International Organization for Standardization
kg	kilogram
lb	pound
m	meter
mks	meter-kilogram-second
MKSA	meter-kilogram-second-ampere
mm	millimeter
NIST	National Institute of Standards andTechnology
no	number
oz	ounce
SAE	Society of Automotive Engineers
SI	International System of Units
UK	the United Kingdom
USA	the United States of America

Thanks

We thank the following persons for generously sharing their expertise; they are not, of course, responsible for any remaining errors. Organizations are mentioned only to identify individuals, and not to imply the organization has approved this publication.

Tim Dillon, The Crow's Nest; Gene Freeze, County Saddlery; Stephen Freitas, Patrick Media Group; Rick Guise, Osram Sylvania; Tom Gunnerson, U. S. Ultralight Assn; Joy and Loren Hannan; Phyllis Horowitz, Amer. Whitewater Affiliation; Richard Martinson, U. S. Coast Guard; Harry Miles; Seth Miller, Carl Zeiss Inc.; Dan Patterson, Amer. Symphony Orchestra League; Beverly Simmons, Early Music America; Joyce E. Taubitz; Macmillan Thompson; Amer. Sportfishing Assn.; Chris Verdegaal, M. van Waveren & Sons.

Dear Reader:

A book of this type is bound to contain some errors of fact or interpretation. If you find such a mistake, the author and future readers will be grateful if you call it to our attention. If you expected to find certain information in this book and were disappointed, we'd appreciate hearing about that, too. Mail may be sent in care of the publisher, and E-mail to the author at 73300.1200@compuserve.com.

A

abalone

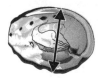

Size limits for these succulent, one-shelled molluscs are based on the shell's smallest diameter.

In California, the limits are:

Species	Commercial not less than	Sport not less than
Red	7 3⁄4"	7"
Green	7"	6"
Pink or White	6 1⁄4"	6"
Black	formerly 5 3⁄4"	formerly 5" (taking blacks is illegal)
All other	4"	4"

Over the years the average size of the abalone taken has tended to decline, but the largest red abalone ever measured by the California Department of Fish and Game was taken in September 1993; its shell had a minimum diameter of 12".

Big abalone are not tougher than little abalone; they are all tough until pounded.

abrasives

Abrasives are very hard, brittle substances that have been crushed to create particles with cutting edges, much as breaking a glass produces shards with sharp edges. Hardness and sharp edges give abrasives the

1

ability to grind and polish. As with a knife edge, the hardness helps retain sharpness, but with sufficient use the cutting edges of any abrasive, even diamond, become rounded over.

The size of the particles is important. Abrasive particles cut away the higher areas of a surface as they travel over it, but in doing so they leave behind scratches whose depth depends on the size of the particles. To remove these scratches, one must switch to a smaller particle size, and then to a still smaller size to remove the scratches produced by the new particles, and so on until the scratches are so small they don't matter. Many processes depend upon using progressively finer grits, whether grinding a mirror for the Hubble Space Telescope or finishing furniture. Abrasives are, therefore, almost always sold by the size of the grit.

A Highly-Idealized View of What Happens during Sanding

original surface

after #80

after # 120

after # 220

A common mistake in using products like sandpaper is using too fine a grade too soon, in the mistaken belief that this will produce a smoother end result. Starting with a grit much finer than the original surface imperfections will simply require more time sanding. So can skipping grades, depending on how long it takes to change grades. In changing grades, all traces of the previous grit must be removed. Otherwise, the very effort exerted to grind scratches out will cause rogue particles to dig more large scratches.

The usual way of grading grains of abrasive is to pass them through a series of ☞sieves with ever-smaller holes. The names of the abrasive grades are taken from this means of grading, although grades finer than about 240 are actually sorted, not with sieves, but by the speed with which they settle in a liquid or a current of air.

An abrasive must be at least as hard as the substance it is to abrade. Today most abrasives are synthetic. Sandpaper has not been made with sand for a long time. The principal materials used today are, in order of increasing hardness:

✓ Flint. Its only virtue is cheapness. It is used when the sandpaper will quickly become clogged, for example, in removing paint.

✓ Garnet. A step up from flint, garnet is also a natural mineral. The abrasive is made from the garnet species almandine, which is typically dark red—thus the orange color of the paper. Many woodworkers prefer garnet paper for sanding raw wood because it seems "sharper" than other papers. Garnet particles break more easily than those of aluminum oxide or silicon carbide, so fresh edges are exposed more often.

✓ Emery. A natural mixture of iron oxides and corundum, a form of aluminum oxide (rubies and sapphires are also aluminum oxide;

in fact precious sapphires are found in deposits of emery in North Carolina and Georgia). For centuries emery was mined at Cape Emeri on the Greek island of Naxos. It is used to polish metal, and is only coated on cloth, not paper.

✓ Aluminum oxide. All-around sandpaper, long-lasting, and can be used on wood or metal.

✓ Silicon carbide. Sandpaper made with this abrasive is black; wet-or-dry sandpaper is an example. Hard enough to sharpen tool steel, but mostly used for finish sanding.

✓ Alumina-zirconia. A newly available combination of aluminum oxide and the diamond substitute advertised late at night on shopping channels. Very hard, very tough, expensive; used to reduce thickness rather than to smooth surfaces.

✓ Diamond.

Abrasive Pads

Various makers sell pads consisting of abrasive particles embedded in a net of plastic fibers, under trade names like Scotch-Brite and Bear-Tex. These pads have the disadvantage of steel wool (they round over nubs, instead of shaving them off as sandpaper would) and also its advantage (they don't clog), as well as an additional advantage: they do not leave behind tiny steel particles. Steel particles rust when coated with water-based finishes, which are increasingly common due to air pollution regulations.

The grades are color coded, but the coding varies from manufacturer to manufacturer. The packaging usually gives a corresponding grade of steel wool. In 3M's colors and grades, blue (coarse) corresponds to a #2 or #3 steel wool, green to #0, gray to #00, and white to #9/0.

Sandpaper

Composition of the grit. The abrasive may be any of those listed above except diamond.

Density of the grit. On *closed-coat* sandpaper, the grit covers 100% of the surface; on *open-coat* paper it covers 50% to 70% of the surface, the advantage being that the paper doesn't clog as easily. Some paper is treated with a soap-like substance to reduce clogging ("stereated" or "nonclog" sandpaper). Because such paper leaves a deposit, it should not be used if a water-based finish is planned.

Adhesive. The adhesive used in light duty papers is not waterproof.

Backing. The backing of an abrasive "paper" may be either paper or cloth. Paper backings are made in grades A through F, with F being heaviest. The A and B weights are used for finishing papers, C and D are general purpose weights, D and E are suitable for machine sanding, and F is used for belts. Cloth backings are made in J, X, and Y weights, with Y the heaviest. The J weight is used when the sandpaper must conform to curved surfaces, and the Y weight usually found only in heavy duty industrial applications.

Sizes. Sandpaper is available in a wide variety of forms:

✓ Sheet: 9" × 11"; and quarter sheets, 4 1/2" × 5 1/2"; one-third sheets, 3 2/3" × 9"; and half sheets, 4 1/2" × 9".

✓ Discs: Diameters of 6", 8", 9", 10", 12", and 15".

✓ Sleeves: These are cylinders that fit over rubber drums used, for example, on drill presses.

✓ Belts: Some of the commoner sizes are 1" × 30", 42" or 44"; 2 1/2" × 16"; 3" × 18", 21", 23¾" or 27"; 4" × 21", 21 ¾", 24" or 36"; and 6" × 48".

✓ Tape: In widths from 1/16" to 1/4", with grades of 150 and 180 in aluminum oxide and silicon carbide. Crocus cloth is also available as tape.

✓ Cord: The abrasive is coated on a round cord from 0.012" to 0.093" in diameter, in grades from 120 to 280, in the same materials as tape.

Sandpaper Grades

Grade	Grit	Description	Uses
16	4	very coarse	Removing rust, paint, etc.
20	3 1/2	very coarse	
24	3	very coarse	
30	2 1/2	coarse	
36	2	coarse	
40	1 1/2	coarse	
50	1	coarse	
60	1/2	medium	
80	1/0	medium	Coarsest grade needed in finishing surfaced lumber.
100	2/0	medium	
120	3/0	fine	
150	4/0	fine	
180	5/0	fine	Many workers feel 180 is as fine a grade as need be used on raw wood that is to be varnished or lacquered.
220	6/0	very fine	
240	7/0	very fine	
280	8/0	very fine	
320	9/0	extra fine	Coarsest grade used to sand grain raised by stain.
360		extra fine	
400	10/0	extra fine	Finest grit available in stearated paper.
500		super fine	
600		super fine	

The remaining grades are used mainly in finishing metal and are most easily found at automotive supply stores.

800
1000   1000 to 1500 are used in rubbing out lacquer
1200   finishes on wood.
1500
2000

Grinding Wheels

Grinding wheels consist of abrasive particles bonded by some other substance, which may be anything from rubber to a kind of glass. The bond is meant to fail. As a particle becomes worn, the drag on it increases and friction makes it hotter, just as a plane with a dull blade requires more force than one with a sharp blade. The increased drag either fractures the particle, exposing a new cutting edge, or tears the worn particle out of the wheel, exposing fresh abrasive grains with unused cutting edges. The bonding should be such that, under the conditions in which the wheel is meant to be used, worn particles come out and unworn ones don't. The grade of a grinding wheel ("hard," "soft") refers to the tenacity with which the particles of grit are held, not to the hardness of the abrasive particles themselves.

Grinding wheels are marked with a specification that consists of alternating letters and numbers separated by dashes. Large wheels carry at least four and as many as six terms, but small wheels are marked only with grain size and grade—the other information is on the packaging. In order, the terms refer to:

1. Abrasive type (letter). A is aluminum oxide; C is silicon carbide.
2. Grain size (number). This corresponds to the grades of sandpaper.
3. Grade (letter). On a scale from A to Z, with A being softest.
4. Structure (number). This term is optional. Structure refers to the spacing between the grains of abrasive. The higher the number, the wider the spacing; ordinarily between 0 and 16.
5. Bond type (letter). Describes what holds the grains together. V, vitrified; R, rubber; S, silicate; E, shellac or elastic; B, resinoid (synthetic resins); O, oxychloride.
6. (optional) Manufacturers may use this position for lot numbers or other private information.

Sizes typically used on home bench grinders are (first dimension is the diameter of the wheel, the second the wheel's thickness): 5" × 1/2"; 6" × 3/4"; 8" × 1". The special wheels used for side grinding are thicker, e.g., 6" × 1". Aluminum oxide wheels cannot be used to sharpen carbide bits and blades.

Oilstones

Both natural and synthetic oilstones are available. Most benchstones are now silicon carbide, sold in fine, medium, and coarse grades (grade meaning particle size); Crystolon is a common brand. Aluminum oxide stones are also available, often called "india stones."

In the United States, the best-known natural oilstones are Arkansas stones. The best Arkansas stones have a fine, smooth, white surface. An even finer grade are the Black Hard Arkansas. Washita stones, often streaked with brown, are coarser than Arkansas stones.

In recent years Japanese "waterstones" have reached American woodworkers. The natural ones are available only in coarse grits and are absurdly expensive, but the synthetic stones have distinctive and useful properties—above all, a wide range of grits, from 100 to 8000, much finer than the "fine" silicon carbide and aluminum oxide benchstones. An 800 grit waterstone is approximately equivalent to a Washita or Soft Arkansas; 1000 to a Hard Arkansas; and 1200 is somewhat coarser than a Black Hard Arkansas. The grits beyond that have no natural equivalents. Waterstones have an open texture and soft bond and wear rapidly, but they also cut rapidly.

Silicon carbide sandpaper makes a satisfactory "oilstone" if it is backed with something flat, such as a piece of iron plate or plate glass.

Diamond

Consumers are just now getting their hands on "stones" made of industrial diamonds bonded to metal surfaces. These "stones" are more than twice as expensive as oilstones, but they are long-lasting, cut rapidly, never need dressing, and don't require oil or water in use. (The "stone" can be unclogged by rinsing it in soapy water.) They are usually sold in fine, medium, and coarse grits, which typically approximate grades of 600, 270, and 180 respectively. Being harder than carbide, diamond can sharpen carbide edges on bits and saws. Unlike other abrasives, diamond grains don't break to expose fresh cutting edges, but simply gradually become rounded over.

---

acre

1 hectare

1 acre

1) In the English-speaking world, BEFORE 8TH–20TH C, a unit of land area, now = 0.0015625 sq. miles = 160 sq. rods = 4840 sq. yards = 0.40468564 hectares. But see below.

The acre began as the amount of land that could be plowed in a single day with oxen—actually what could be done by midday, for refuelling took all afternoon: the oxen had to be put out to pasture. (Similar units are found wherever animals are used for plowing; the German *morgen* had much the same meaning). Like many units of land area, the acre was first conceived as having specific dimensions: 40 perches long

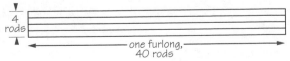

4 rods

one furlong,
40 rods

and 4 perches wide. (The king's perch was 5½ yards or 16½' long.) Forty perches was roughly the distance a team of oxen could plow before needing a breather (this furrow-long became the furlong, 220 yards). Not until much later (the 16TH C, according to R. D. Connor) did the acre began to be conceived in geometric terms, as so many square feet or square rods.

A strip 40 perches long and 1 perch wide was a *rood*, not to be confused with the *rod*, a name (from the Saxon *gyrd*) used by the 13TH C for the perch.

The width of the acre, 4 perches or rods, was itself used as a unit of length, also called an acre, 11TH–13TH C. In the 17TH C it became the length of the surveyor's ☞chain. It is the distance between wickets in cricket, and the width of the strip of land that might be acquired as public domain for a road, in the less-developed parts of the British Commonwealth.

In actuality the size of the acre used to vary greatly, generally being larger in poor land than good. In some contexts it is almost synonymous with "small holding." Another complication was the variety of perches; a 13TH C writer mentions perches of 18, 20, 22, and even 24 feet, and an official report of 1820 found in use, besides the 16 ½' perch or rod, others of 18', 21', 24', and 25'. The king's rod or perch, however, remained constant for centuries at 16 ½'.

In the United States, since the acre is a land measure it is currently based on the U.S. survey foot and not on the international foot.

2) As late as the 20TH C, several other acres were in use in Ireland: the Cunningham acre, ≈ 5,226 square meters ≈ 1.2913 acres; and the Irish acre, ≈ 6,555 square meters ≈ 1.6198 acres.

acre-foot

A unit used to measure volumes of water, typically for use in irrigation. One acre-foot is a volume of water sufficient to cover 1 acre of land to a depth of 1 foot, = 43,560 cubic feet ≈ 325,851 U.S. gallons ≈ 1,233.48 cubic meters. At current American rates of consumption, on average one acre-foot of water is enough to meet the industrial and municipal demands of four people for a year.

The *acre-inch*, the volume of water needed to cover 1 acre to a depth of 1 inch, 1/12th of an acre-foot, is ≈ 27,154.25 gallons ≈ 102.79 cubic meters.

air conditioners

The cooling capacity of residential air conditioners is given in Btu (☞British thermal units), and is the number of Btu (of heat) the unit can move out of the cooled space in one hour. Central air conditioning is usually installed by specialized contractors who calculate how much cooling capacity is required. The sizing suggestions below are for consumers selecting a room air conditioner.

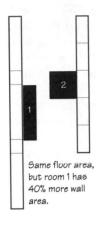

Same floor area, but room 1 has 40% more wall area.

As a first guess, a room requires about 10,000 Btu for every 500 square feet of floor space. But many other factors can increase that:

- Narrow rooms often require more capacity than squarish rooms, since they have more square feet of (possibly warm) wall surface for each square foot of floor space.
- Large windows. They are poor insulators, compared to walls. If they face south or west, sunlight streaming through them will warm the room. (Consider awnings, trellises, and blinds, before relying on air conditioning.)
- Heat sources such as appliances, the kitchen being the obvious example. A kitchen exhaust fan should be installed prior to air conditioning. (In bathrooms, exhaust fans can reduce the load on an air conditioner by removing humid air.) Water heaters are another common heat source; even a large chandelier with many incandescent bulbs may need to be taken into account.
- People themselves. The more people in a room the greater the need for cooling. A dining room that is fine for two, for example, may become a sauna during a dinner party. (Allow an extra 500 Btu per occupant.)

Simply buying the largest available unit isn't a good solution to the sizing problem; it may give less satisfaction than a smaller one. An oversize unit typically cycles on and off more frequently, so room air circulates through it for fewer minutes during a day than it would through a smaller unit. As a result, the room air may not be satisfactorily dehumidified.

Rooms that are long and narrow, L-shaped, or have other peculiarities that impede the circulation of air may be better served by two small air conditioners than by a single large one.

Will the Wiring Handle It?

Ordinary 115-volt house circuits are usually 15-ampere, sometimes 20-ampere. The capacity of the circuits can be determined by checking the fuse box or circuit breaker panel. The National Electrical Code limits the size of the largest appliance that can be plugged into a 15-amp circuit to 12 amperes. The largest available units that will operate on 115 volts, 12 amps, have cooling capacities between 12,000 and 14,000 Btu. For larger units, an electrician must install a separate circuit. Today many homes are built with 208-volt or 230-volt single-phase circuits for air conditioners already in place; such circuits can be spotted as unusual receptacles near windows, such as the one illustrated. The National Electrical Code requires room air conditioners that run on voltages above 240 volts to be wired in, not plugged in.

Energy Efficiency

In the USA, the average air conditioner runs 750 hours each year. Since air conditioners use a lot of electricity, their efficiency became a public issue. The Energy Policy and Conservation Act (December 1975, Public Law 94-163) requires all room air conditioners to carry a tag comparing that unit's efficiency with other units of the same general type. The EER (for Energy Efficiency Rating) is the ratio of the Btu's per hour to the number of watts the unit draws. (The EER has been criticized on the grounds that the test conditions don't fairly represent the real world, so the federal government devised a second test giving another figure of merit, dubbed the SEER, for Seasonal Energy Efficiency Rating. Generally it's about 1 point lower than the EER.)

The 1987 National Appliance Energy Conservation Act provided for minimum efficiency standards for various types of appliances, including room air conditioners. (This act preempted minimums previously established by some states, including New York and California.) Regulations under the Act divide room air conditioners into 12 classes and set a minimum EER for each class, typically 8 or 9, which is required of all units built after January 1, 1990.

aluminum

Aluminum alloys are identified by a four-digit number, followed by a suffix consisting of a letter and numeral identifying treatment. T, for example, indicates heat treatment, and "T0" means fully annealed. The first digit of the four-digit number classifies the alloys by the principal alloying element: 1 is reserved for alloys that are at least 99% aluminum by weight. If the first digit is 2, the main ingredient other than aluminum is copper; 3, manganese; 4, silicon; 5, magnesium; 6, magnesium and silicon; 7, zinc; and 8, none of the above. A decimal point between the third and fourth digits indicates a casting alloy. Some examples with typical uses:

1350   electrical conductors
2219   rocket fuel tanks (strong when cold)
3003   cooking utensils
3004   beverage cans
5182   beverage can ends
6061   trailers, trucks
390.0   automobile engines (cylinder blocks)

ampere

The unit of electric current in SI, one of the base units. One ampere is that constant current which, if maintained in two straight parallel conductors of infinite length, of negligible circular cross section, and placed 1 meter apart in a vacuum, would produce between these conductors a force equal to 2×10^{-7} newton per meter of length (CIPM 1946 Resolution 2, approved by the NINTH CGPM, 1948).

Almost every electrical appliance in a home has a measurement in amperes on its rating plate. These ratings indicate how much current the appliance draws. If two appliances run on the same voltage, ampere ratings are also a way of comparing the amount of power the appliances use. But see ☞watt.

Fuses and circuit breakers are rated in amperes. If the total of the ampere ratings of the appliances that are plugged into a circuit is greater than the rating of the fuse or circuit breaker for the circuit, the fuse will blow or the circuit breaker will trip.

Almost all appliances draw more current in starting than they do while running, and this may be greater than the ampere rating on the name plate. Most electric motors need two to three times their name plate amps to start. Fuses and circuit breakers are designed to accommodate such temporary overloads. But when power goes off and then comes back on, the combined load of all appliances starting at once may be enough to trip circuit breakers.

When extension cords are used, the amperes required determines the required wire gauge of the extension cord. If too small a cord is used, the voltage will be less than the appliance was designed for, and some types of appliance may be damaged.

Recommended Gauge of Extension Cords		
	Length	
Amps	50'	100'	150'
≤3	18	18	18
≤5	16	16	16
≤6	16	16	14
≤10	16	14	12
12	14	14	12
14*	14	12	10
16*	12	12	10
*Only for use on a 20-ampere circuit.		

History

Early investigators of electricity tried to measure electric phenomena, including the strength of an electric current, in terms of length, mass, and time. W. E. Weber succeeded in doing this in 1851.

In 1872 a committee on standards of electrical resistance of the British Association for the Advancement of Science made an influential recommendation advocating the use of the centimeter-gram-second (cgs) system of units (reversing an earlier recommendation for meter-gram-second), but the unit of resistance they defined, the ohm, was made 10^9 times larger than the cgs absolute unit of resistance. Such units were needed because the size of the units that fell out of the electric equations in cgs units were much too small for everyday use.

The First International Conference of Electricians (Paris, 1881) adopted the British Association definition of the ohm and added definitions for the volt, ampere, coulomb, and farad. Thus was born the absolute practical system of electrical units: absolute, because the units were defined solely in terms of mechanical units (length, mass, and time); and practical, because the sizes were much more convenient than the cgs units. The ampere was a derived unit, defined as the current produced in a conductor with a 1-ohm resistance when there was a potential difference of 1 volt between its ends.

The international ampere. The 1881 definitions had a serious deficiency as far as most workers in the field were concerned: they were not easily reproducible outside highly specialized laboratories. The Fourth International Conference of Electricians (Chicago, 1893) addressed the problem of producing definitions that were more "workable" with a new set of "international" units, corresponding as closely as possible to the absolute practical units, but better suited to replication in ordinary laboratories. For electric current, the *international ampere* was defined as that unvarying current that would deposit 0.001118000 grams of silver per second from a solution of silver nitrate in water. (Public Bill 105, passed July 12, 1894, made this the legal definition of the ampere in the USA.) Symbol, A_{int}. It was sometimes called the *silver ampere*. The amount of silver was chosen to make the international ampere equal to the absolute practical ampere within the limits of precision of the day. Today experimental evidence shows that one international ampere ≈ 0.99985 abamperes ≈ 9.9985 amperes.

The conference also defined an international volt and international ohm in similarly practical ways. Tying down all three units was a mistake, however. As standards laboratories in Germany, Britain, and America made ever more precise measurements, they found that the definitions were inconsistent with one other; volts did not equal amperes × ohms. An international conference in London in 1908 decided to leave the international ampere and the international ohm as they were, and to make the international volt a derived unit, its value set by its relation to the other two.

Back to the absolute. With the development of more sophisticated laboratory techniques, measuring electric units in terms of mass, length, and time became much easier, and there was less need to define electrical units in such terms as an amount of silver deposited. In 1948 the CGPM abandoned the international ampere and reverted to an absolute definition. The 1948 definition is identical to the one used today, except that they used "MKS unit of force" for what would today be called a newton. Investigation showed the new definition led to a new value for the ampere that was 1.00015 times the mean international ampere as previously realized in the various national standards laboratories. For the ampere of the U.S. National Bureau of Standards, the factor was 1.000165.

anchors

The big anchors displayed on lawns at ports and shown on insignia are a design that originated with the British Admiralty. Because the stock (the bar at the top, at right angles to the flukes at the bottom of the anchor) makes it impossible to draw such an anchor up into the hawsepipe, today few ocean-going ships use this design, although it holds very well.

The U.S. Navy, for example, uses stockless anchors, a type invented in 1821 that relies almost entirely on mass for its holding power. U.S. aircraft carriers use the Navy Mark 2 anchor, made in one size only, 60,000 pounds. This is too large for your average pleasure craft, which use anchors whose holding power depends mostly on their ability to dig into the bottom.

Anchors have a big job to do. The American Boat and Yacht Council estimated that in a 30-knot wind, a boat 35' long with a beam of 10' exerts a horizontal pull of *at least* 1,800 pounds.

Three of the most popular types of anchor are described below. Each type is available in a number of weights; as an aid in comparing the types, an estimate is given of the weight that a 35' cruiser might need, assuming the anchor is attached to the craft by 1/2" nylon line and 5/16" chain. These estimates should not be used to choose an anchor type and weight for a particular boat; to do that, consult anchor manufacturers' literature and ask owners of the same model boat what anchors they are using and under what conditions those anchors have held.

✓ The yachtsman's or fisherman's anchor is a smaller version of the admiralty anchor, often made with a stock that can be collapsed or detached for stowing. Various versions are made, some with narrow flukes good on rocky bottoms, and others with wide flukes designed for muddy bottoms. [45-pound]

✓ The plow or CQR anchor (a trademark, "secure") was introduced in 1938 in England. It is good on soft bottoms and in weeds. [25-pound]

✓ The very popular Danforth (a trademark) or light-weight anchor, invented in 1939 by R. S. Danforth. In this anchor the stock is at the base of the flukes, where the Chinese had it about 4,000 years ago, but arranged so that the whole thing folds flat for stowage. [18-pound]

The anchor is attached to the craft by the rode, which in small craft consists of chain attached to the anchor, followed by nylon line. As a rule of thumb, the chain should be long enough that its weight at least equals the weight of the anchor. Chain serves two purposes: its weight helps to keep the pull on the anchor more nearly horizontal, and it resists abrasion on rocky bottoms. The nylon line is easier to handle than chain, and its elasticity makes it a shock absorber. Paradoxically, a line can be too thick, when it is so strong the shock-absorbing action is reduced.

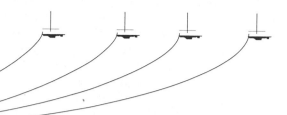

The greater the scope, the more nearly horizontal the pull on the anchor is.

The length of the rode is called the scope. As a rule of thumb, the scope should be 5 to 7 times the depth in which the ship is anchoring. A greater ratio of scope to depth is needed in shallow water than in deep.

angle, slotted

Generally made of 12- or 14-gauge galvanized, cold-rolled steel, slotted angle is available with a variety of perforations, and with equal or unequal legs. Lighter angle takes ¼" bolts and the heavier takes 5/16". Commonly available sizes are 1 ¼" × 1 ¼" (sometimes called "125 angle"); 2 ¼" × 1 ½"; and 3" × 1 ½".

Commonly available lengths are 3', 4', 10', and 12'. Many large cities have firms that produce slotted angle to order.

angstrom

A metric unit of length used mainly by spectroscopists and others studying light, defined by the CGPM in 1960 as exactly equal to 10^{-10} meter. Symbol, Å. The angstrom is obsolete; the nanometer should be used instead. One Å = 0.1 nm.

The *international angstrom* was defined in 1907 by the IAU by making the wavelength of the red line of cadmium in air equal to 6438.4696 Å. This particular value was chosen so that, within the limits of measurement at the time, the angstrom would be 10^{-10} meter. In 1961 the IAU accepted the 1960 CGPM definition.

Apgar score

A rating on a scale of 1 to 10 given a newborn baby by the delivering obstetrician or midwife at one minute after birth and again five minutes after birth, with 10 representing the apparently healthiest baby. The rating is based on well-defined characteristics, including color, heart rate, breathing, reflexes, and muscle tone, and is a way of capturing the obstetrician's initial impression as well as alerting the nursery staff to newborns who may require special attention. Anxious mothers should note that a rating of 10 is almost never given.

apothecaries' measure

In contrast with apothecaries' weight, apothecaries' measure is a system both recent and brief. It seems to have arisen with the UK's defining of the new imperial gallon in 1824, and is fully described at least by 1878 in the Weights and Measures Act. Pharmacists in the USA adopted a similiar system, but instead of subdividing the imperial fluid ounce, they subdivided the U.S. fluid ounce. In the USA, apothecaries' measure was gradually overtaken by milliliters, though even today if a prescription for a liquid is actually compounded by the pharmacist, it may be supplied in a bottle embossed with a scale marked with the symbol for drams. In the UK, the minim, scruple, and fluid drachm, already obsolete, were abolished by the 1976 Weights and Measures Act.

UNITED STATES, TO PRESENT

				gallon
			liquid pint	8
		fluid ounce	16	128
	fluid dram	8	128	1024
minim	60	480	7680	61,440
0.062 mL	3.97 mL	29.57 mL	473 mL	3.785 L

BRITISH, 1878–FEB. 1, 1971

				imperial gallon
			fluid ounce	160
		fluid drachm	8	1280
	fluid scruple	3	24	3840
minim	20	60	480	76,800
0.059 mL	1.18 mL	3.55 mL	28.41 mL	4.546 L
0.96 U.S. minim	19.09 U.S. minims	0.96 U.S. fl. dram	0.96 U.S. fluid ounce	1.20095 U.S. gallons

apothecaries' weight

A system of units of mass used by druggists, BEFORE 15TH–19TH C. The pound, ounce, and grain of apothecaries' weight have the same magnitudes as the corresponding units in ☞troy weight, but the scruple and dram are not found in troy weight. The division of the pound into 12 ounces is undoubtedly modelled on the Roman *libra*, but how the apothecaries' pound got its present value is controversial.

				pound
			ounce	12
		dram	8	96
	scruple	3	24	288
grain	20	60	480	5760
0.0648 g	1.296 g	3.888 g	31.10 g	0.373 kg

By the middle of the 18TH C, English druggists were using avoirdupois weight instead of apothecaries' weight, at first to measure what they sold, and then for compounding medicines as well. By the middle of the 19TH C apothecaries' weight had largely disappeared. In the UK the Medical Act of 1858 prescribed the use of avoirdupois weight; the

Weights and Measures Act of 1878 retained only the apothecaries' ounce, and that merely permissively.

are

The special name for the unit of land area in the metric system = 100 square meters = a square dekameter ≈ 119.599 square yards. In practice, the *hectare* (100 ares) is almost always used.

arpent

1) In Canada's province of Quebec, two units, 17TH–20TH C, one of length, ≈ 5.847 meters ≈ 191.835 feet, and one of area ≈ 3,419 square meters ≈ 0.845 acre. These units were applied to land granted under the French Seigneurial Tenure, prior to the British conquest, and were in use up to the 1970s.

2) In the state of Louisiana, USA, two units of length, 19TH–20TH C. In urban areas the arpent ≈ 5.847 meters ≈ 191.835 feet; that is, it is the linear *arpent de Paris* = 10 *perche de Paris*, the same as the Canadian unit. But in the rural portions of Louisiana the arpent ≈ 5.8504 meters ≈ 191.944 feet.

astronomical unit

A unit of distance, roughly equal to the average distance from the earth to the sun. Abbr, A, or formerly, AU. In 1976 the IAU at its 16TH General Assembly defined the *astronomical unit of length* (as part of the International System of Astronomical Constants) as "that length for which the Gaussian gravitational constant (k) takes the value 0.01720209895 when the units of measurement are the astronomical units of length, mass and time." The astronomical unit of time is the day, defined as 86,400 seconds (the second as defined in SI), and the astronomical unit of mass is the mass of the sun, by definition 1.9891×10^{30} kg. The value given for the gravitational constant makes A approximately the earth-sun distance; expressing the definition in meters makes one A = $1.49597870 \times 10^{11}$ meters. In the preparation of ephemerides, it was found necessary to use the value 1.4959787066.

atmosphere

A unit of pressure = 101,325 pascals, approximately the value of atmospheric pressure at sea level. Abbr, atm. Also called the *standard atmosphere* or *physical atmosphere*. It was defined in the International Practical Temperature Scale of 1948 and subsequently adopted by the 10TH CGPM (1954, Resolution 4). Currently its use is discouraged in favor of the pascal.

The *technical atmosphere* is a unit of pressure equal to one kilogram-force per square centimeter. One technical atmosphere ≈ 0.967841 atm ≈ 98,066.5 pascals.

atomic mass unit

A very, very small unit of mass equal to one-twelfth the mass of the nucleus of a carbon-12 atom, used to express the mass of atoms and molecules. Abbr, u, or formerly, amu. One u ≈ $1.6605655 \times 10^{-27}$ kg.

For many years chemists used a unit of atomic weight that was based on taking 16 as the atomic weight of oxygen. Oxygen was chosen because it combines with many other elements, which simplified research into their atomic weights, and 16 was the lowest whole number for oxygen that made the atomic weight of hydrogen greater than 1. (The pioneer in this field, Stanislao Cannizzaro (1826–1910), used the hydrogen atom as his standard, setting its atomic weight at 2. Others accepted his ideas but rejected his standard, because using a bigger mass—an oxygen atom—as the standard decreases experimental error.)

In nature, however, pure oxygen is composed of a mixture of isotopes: some oxygen atoms have more mass than others. This was no problem for the chemist's calculations as long as the relative abundance of the isotopes in the reagents remained constant. It did mean, however, that oxygen's atomic weight was the only one that was a whole number. Hydrogen's, for example, was 1.0008. Physicists, however, preferred an atomic mass unit equal to a sixteenth of the mass of the oxygen-16 atom.

In the years 1959–1961 the chemists and physicists resolved this difference by agreeing to use carbon-12 as the standard, setting its atomic mass at 12.

automobiles

In the automotive industry, the terms describing size have roughly the following meanings:

Size	Weight in lbs	Wheelbase	Overall length
Subcompact	—	<100"	<175"
Compact	<3,000	100–105"	175"–185"
Midsize	<3,500	105–108"	185"–200"
Full size	3500+	110"+	195"+

For its fuel economy tests, the U.S. Environmental Protection Agency developed a classification of sizes based on a car's interior volume:

Sedans (based on passenger and luggage volume): Minicompact, less than 85 cu. ft; Subcompact, 85–99 cu. ft; Compact, 100–109 cu. ft; Mid-size, 110–119 cu. ft; Large, 120 or more cu. ft

Two-seaters: cars designed to seat primarily two adults.

Station Wagons (based on passenger and cargo volume): Small, less than 130 cu. ft; Mid-Size, 130–159 cu. ft; Large, 160 or more cu. ft.

Trucks: Vans; Small Pickups, trucks having a Gross Vehicle Weight Rating less than 4,500 lbs.; Large Pickups, trucks having a Gross Vehicle Weight Rating of 4,500–8,500 lbs.

B

backpacks

Three types of recreational backpack are made:

1) Packs with an external frame. A cloth sack is attached to one side of a rigid frame, usually made of aluminum tubing. Straps on the other side of the frame rest against the back. External frame packs typically sport a variety of outside pockets sized to handle water bottles, fuel containers, and so on.

Airport baggage handling equipment tends to mangle these packs' exposed tubing. They have a high center of gravity, which makes it easy to lose your balance if you perform any gyrations on the trail. The open space between frame and sack allows air to circulate between pack and back, which can be very welcome in warm weather. External frame packs can have tremendous carrying capacity; in fact the "cubic inches of capacity" figures given for them understate their capacity, since backpackers usually strap items like sleeping bags and small tents directly to the frame. External frame packs are a good choice when great capacity is needed and travel will be over open, well-maintained trails.

2) Packs with an internal frame. The frame in these packs is within the cloth sack. Instead of holding the load off the hiker's back and isolating the hiker from it, an internal frame is designed to keep the load as close as possible to the hiker and make it move with him or her.

The form of the pack is maintained by a "framesheet" or frame stays, often made of molded nylon. This system is usually not rigid, but bends to accommodate changes in posture while walking and climbing. Form-fitting is accomplished by a formidable system of adjustable and interchangeable straps, which can be intimidating at first. Internal frame packs typically don't come with a lot of outside pockets, though they can often be added as accessories.

One disadvantage of these designs is that mispacked items can jab you in the back. Internal frame packs are a good choice for activities like skiing and for off-trail use. They are increasingly popular.

3) Rucksacks, including daypacks. Cloth sacks with shoulder straps, these are stiffened only by what you put in them. They are the lightest of all packs, have the smallest capacity, and are intended for light loads. Most people find rucksacks less comfortable than packs with frames for carrying heavy loads for more than a day.

Purchasing a Pack

The advice below concerns the fitting of an internal frame pack, but much of it applies to all types of packs.

As with clothing, some people are just lucky: a manufacturer's product seems to have been custom-made for them. Everyone else must choose an appropriate size, then alter the pack's out-of-the-box fit by adjusting straps and replacing hip belt and shoulder straps, if necessary and possible. As a last resort the fit can be altered by bending the frame.

Before shopping, measure your torso length (shoulder to crotch). At the store, check manufacturer's tags to find a pack with the capacity you need. Most tags also suggest the range of torso lengths and waist/hip sizes the model will fit.

After selecting a pack you are seriously considering buying, load it so that it has about the same weight *and weight distribution* as it will have when you use it. In a good store the sales personnel will be cooperative about this; after all, a good backpack is a substantial purchase.

Loosen all the straps. Then put it on and make the following checks and adjustments.

   ✓ **Hip belt**. If the hip belt pads meet, the belt should be exchanged for a shorter one. But the belt should not be so short that taut unpadded webbing rubs against your tummy as you walk.

   ✓ **Frame stays**. In the mirror, compare the frame stay profile with the profile of your back. The framesheet or frame stays should extend two to four inches above your shoulder; if they don't, you need a larger size.

   ✓ **Shoulder straps.** The point where the upper end of a shoulder strap is anchored to a stay should be two to three inches below the crest of your shoulders, so that the straps come from below and wrap over the shoulder. In many models, this anchor point is adjustable.

✓ **Load lifters.** These straps stretch from the top part of the frame to the shoulder straps; not all packs have them. The point of attachment to the frame should be at ear level. The point of attachment to the front of the shoulder straps should be lower than the shoulder crest but not lower than the collarbone.

✓ **Hip compressors** (sometimes called the waist belt stabilizer straps). Tighten.

✓ **Sternum strap.** In packs that have one, this strap joins the shoulder straps. Tighten, but not so much that the shoulder straps rub your neck.

Now that all the straps are adjusted, check the fit. Does the pack interfere with normal head movement? How does it feel? Walk around and climb some stairs.

The fit of a pack can be refined by bending the frame, which may be the only way of fitting some individuals. Bending a frame, however, is best left to an experienced packfitter. Whoever does it, before doing any bending it is a good idea to make a tracing of the original profile so that you have a chance of restoring it.

The magazine *Backpacker* prints a comprehensive annual listing of currently-marketed backpacks.

bacteria

Since experts disagree about whether viruses are "alive," or much more controversial, whether prions are alive, the smallest indisputably living things are bacteria. Many of the spherical bacteria are about 1 micrometer in diameter, which is about a hundred times the size of the virus that causes poliomyelitis, and about two and a half times the size of the virus that causes parrot fever.

Many bacteria are shaped like a gelatin medicine capsule. One such organism, *Haemophilus influenzae* (it was once thought to cause influenza) is among the smallest bacteria: 0.2–0.3 by 0.5–2.0 micrometers, which is about the smallest object that can be seen through a light microscope. *Escherichia coli*, the bacteria used in testing water for fecal contamination, has a similar shape and is about 7 µm long and 1.8 µm in diameter. Many bacteria are long and slender, only 1 or 2 µm wide but 10 to 20 µm long. For comparision, a human red blood cell is 8 µm in diameter.

Among the largest bacteria is *Schaudinnum bütschlii*, 50 to 60 µm long and 4 to 5 µm thick. In 1993, DNA testing showed that *Epulopiscium fishelsoni*, an organism living in the guts of the surgeonfish, is an extraordinary kind of bacteria. It is as long as half a millimeter, and is visible to the naked eye.

badminton

Shuttle. The ordinary shuttle contains 14 to 16 feathers, secured with thread. National associations may authorize substitutes, such as plastic, provided they do not materially alter the shuttle's behavior in play. Its mass is 73–85 grains (4.74–5.50 g). Surprisingly, the shuttle in competition badminton is claimed to be the fastest object in sports.

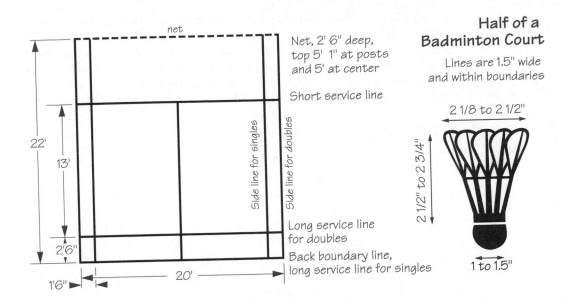

Half of a Badminton Court

Lines are 1.5" wide and within boundaries

net

Net, 2' 6" deep, top 5' 1" at posts and 5' at center

Short service line

Side line for singles

Side line for doubles

Long service line for doubles

Back boundary line, long service line for singles

22'

13'

2'6"

1'6"

20'

2 1/8 to 2 1/2"

2 1/2" to 2 3/4"

1 to 1.5"

Court. Dimensions of the singles and doubles courts are shown in the drawing. The net is dark-colored. If the posts are not at the boundary line, thin vertical posts at least 1.5 inches wide should be placed at the boundary line, rising to the top of the net.

Racket. Players may use any racket they like.

bag

In the USA, a bag of cement contains 1 cubic foot, and weighs 94–96 pounds. Bags of feed, flour, and so on typically weigh 100 lbs.

In the United Kingdom, until recently the bag was a unit of capacity = 3 imperial bushels.

bar

1) A unit of pressure, = 10^6 dynes per square centimeter = 10^5 pascal. The bar is not an SI unit, but the CIPM has sanctioned continued use of the millibar in meteorology, for the time being. The microbar is often used in calibrating microphones and loudspeakers. **2)** In the centimeter-gram-second absolute system of units, the unit of pressure = 1 dyne per square centimeter.

barleycorn

The barleycorn has been the basis of units of length and mass in a number of systems of units. In England and Scotland, at least as early as the 12TH C an inch was thought of as 3 barleycorns laid end to end. A document of 1474 states: "III barley corns take out of the middes [middle] of the Ere make an Inche and XII inches makith a foote and III fote makith a yarde." Occasionally "barleycorn" was used to mean one-third of an inch. It is still true that 36 barleycorns laid end to end closely approximate a foot, but legally the inch was always derived by subdividing such prototypes as the "king's iron yard."

Ibn Khurrâdadhbih, writing in the 9TH C, reported that the smallest unit of length in Islamic measure, the *aasbaa*, literally "finger," was the width of 6 barleycorns laid side by side.

The barleycorn has also been used as a standard of mass. The ☞grain, 1/5760th of the troy pound and the apothecaries' pound, and 1/7000th of the pound avoirdupois, is traditionally the weight of a barleycorn. Before the development of the modern strains of wheat and barley, the ratios 3 barley corns = 4 grains of wheat, 4 grains of wheat = 1 carob seed (siliqua) were used in many systems of weight. For example, as the *se*, the barleycorn was a standard of mass in ancient Sumeria.

barrel

1) The barrel of petroleum, LATE 19TH–20TH C, = 42 U.S. gallons ≈ 158.987 liters, originated in the Pennsylvania oilfields. It is the same size as the English *tierce* prior to 1824.

The barrel consumers are most likely to encounter today is the barrel of beer. In the USA, it holds 31 U.S. gallons; more familiar is the keg, half a barrel, 15 1/2 gallons. In Europe, the beer barrel holds 50 liters.

In 1912 Congress defined the *apple barrel* (Aug 3, 1912, c 273 § 1, 37 Stat. 250) as having staves 28 1/2" long, heads 17 1/8" in diameter and 26" apart, a circumference at the bulge of 64" and "as nearly as possible" a capacity of 7,056 cubic inches. Apple barrels with other capacities were to be marked on the ends, in 72-pt gothic letters, with the fraction of the standard apple barrel that they contained.

Three years later Congress defined a *dry goods barrel* for all dry goods except cranberries (March 4, 1915 c 168 § 1, 38 Stat. 1186), repeating the dimensions given in the earlier act, with the addition that the staves were to be no thicker than 1/4". The capacity continued to be 7,056 cubic inches = 105 U.S. dry quarts ≈ 115.627 liters. Any shape was acceptable, provided the capacity was 7,056 cubic inches. Third-barrels, half-barrels, and three-quarter barrels were made illegal in domestic trade.

The same law defined a smaller barrel, the *cranberry barrel*, with staves 28 1/2" long, heads 16 1/4" in diameter and 25 1/4" apart, a circumference at the bulge of 58 1/2", and staves no thicker than 1/4". The capacity is not specified in the act, but regulations defined it as 5,826 cubic inches, ≈ 95.471 liters.

In 1916 Congress defined the *lime barrel* as a measure of mass, not capacity (August 23, 1916, c 396 § 1, 39 Stat. 530). The *large lime barrel* was to contain a net weight of 280 pounds of lime, and the *small lime barrel* 180 pounds. In interstate commerce, smaller quantities of lime were to be marked with the fraction of the small lime barrel that they contained, together with the net weight in pounds.

Among traditional and commercial barrel sizes not defined in federal law were the flour barrel of 3 bushels (in U.S. Dept of Agriculture statistics, a barrel is 196 pounds of wheat or rye flour or 200 pounds of cornmeal); the barrel of sugar, 5 cubic feet; and the barrel of Portland cement, 4 cubic feet (4 bags to a barrel), equivalent to 376 pounds. The Revenue Service considered the whiskey barrel held 31 gallons, but the actual barrels seem to have held 50 gallons.

Steel drums, typically holding 55 gallons, are often called barrels, but not by those in trades that use them.

baseball

Ball. The mass is between 5 and 5 1/4 oz.; the circumference from 9 to 9 1/4". This is only slightly smaller than the 1861 ball, which had 5 3/4 oz and 9 3/4" maximums. It is covered by two pieces of white leather, formerly horsehide, but cowhide has also been permitted since 1975.

Bat. A round, solid wood stick no more than 42" long; maximum diameter 2 3/4". The first 18" may be covered with material which improves the batter's grip. A curved indentation is permitted on the end of the bat, not deeper than 1 inch, with a diameter no greater than 2 inches and not less than 1. Bats may not be colored. Designs for solid laminated bats may be approved, but such a bat's performance must be no better than that of a solid wood bat.

Gloves. The regulations on the size of gloves are extensive; for example, 17 measurements are taken of a fielder's glove.

Field. See illustration.

basket

In the first half of the 20TH C Congress defined a number of standard baskets.

In 1916 Congress prescribed dimensions for 2-quart, 4-quart, and 12-quart "Climax baskets" for grapes, other fruits and vegetables and mushrooms, and required that the capacities of any baskets used for berries, small fruits, and so on, be one dry half pint, one dry pint, one dry quart, or multiples of the dry quart.

In 1928, they passed a law requiring "hampers and round stave baskets" to contain either 1/8, 1/2, 5/8, 3/4, 1 1/4, 1 1/2, or 2 bushels, while splint baskets had to contain either 4, 8, 12, 16, 24, or 32 dry quarts. In 1954, 3/8-bushel baskets were added, and in 1964, 1/16-, 7/8-, and 1 1/8-bushel baskets, and 11-quart and 14-quart splint baskets.

Finally deciding nothing was gained by regulating basket sizes, Congress repealed all of the above laws in 1968.

basketball

Several slightly different sets of standards are current for basketball: one for high schools and colleges, one for women, one for professionals, and one for international matches. The biggest difference is the international standards for the court.

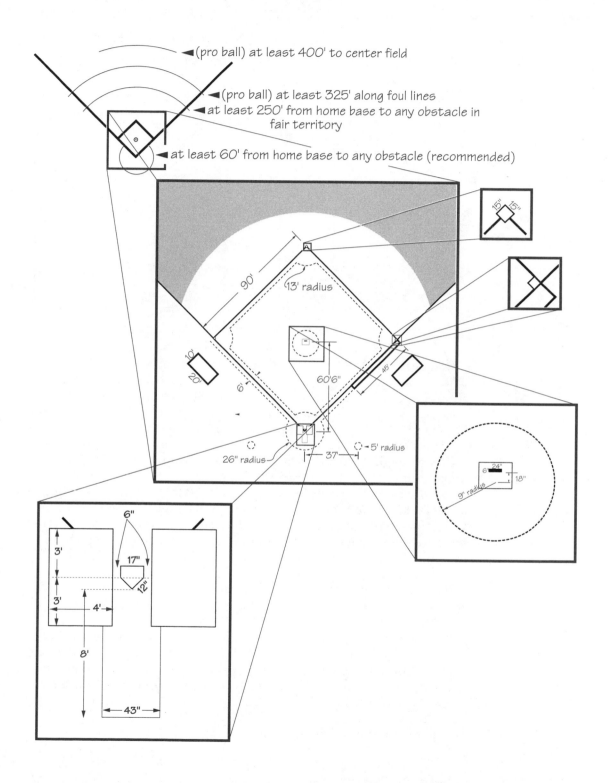

◄(pro ball) at least 400' to center field

◄(pro ball) at least 325' along foul lines
◄at least 250' from home base to any obstacle in
fair territory

◄at least 60' from home base to any obstacle (recommended)

90'

13' radius

15"   15"

10'
20'

6'

45'

60'6"

26" radius

37'

5' radius

24"

6'   18"

9" radius

6"

3'

17"

3'   12"

4'

8'

43'

Half of an FIBA Basketball Court

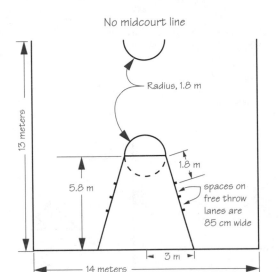

No midcourt line

Radius, 1.8 m

13 meters

5.8 m

1.8 m

spaces on free throw lanes are 85 cm wide

3 m

14 meters

Half of a U.S. Collegiate Basketball Court

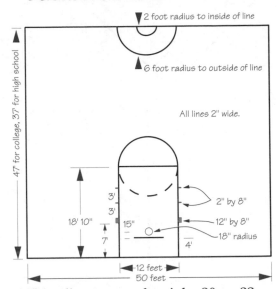

2 foot radius to inside of line

6 foot radius to outside of line

47 for college, 37 for high school

All lines 2" wide.

3'
3'

18' 10"

15"

7'

2" by 8"

12" by 8"

18" radius

4'

12 feet

50 feet

Ball is molded, 29 ½" to 30" in diameter and weighs 20 to 22 oz. when inflated. Dropped from a height of 6 feet to a solid wood floor, it should bounce to a height of from 49" to 54". The National Basketball Assn. considers the official ball to be size 7. Size 6 is a women's ball, 72.39 cm in diameter, weighing between 496 g and 553 g. Size 5, for youth, is 69 to 70 cm in diameter, weighing from 470 to 500 grams.

Before 1930, the ball was larger, with a maximum mass of 23 oz. and a maximum circumference of 32".

Playing court for adults is, ideally, 94 by 50 feet; for high schools, 84 by 50 feet. The boundary lines (and all other lines on the court) are 2" wide (international court, 5 cm). The size of the court is measured from the inside edges of the boundary lines. If the court is less than 74 feet long, it should be divided by two parallel lines, each parallel to and 40' from the end line farthest from it.

Basket is a ring with an inside diameter of 18", made of metal rod 5/8" in diameter. Its rim is mounted 10 feet above and parallel to the floor, with the nearest inside point 6" from the surface of the backboard.

Backboard may be rectangular, 4' high x 6' wide, with its surface 4' from the end lines and its top 13' above the floor. Or the backboard may be fan-shaped. Originally the backboard was on the end line; in the 1939–40 season it was moved in four feet to reduce the number of out-of-bounds calls.

bassinet

Inside measurements are generally 13" by 28".

batteries

Automobile Batteries

The physical dimensions and some other characteristics of an automobile battery are specified by its group number. Stores that sell batteries have tables showing what group number a given make of automobile, model and year requires. Battery groups are established by the Battery Council International, who publish the *BCI Replacement Battery Data Book*.

For each group the SAE specifies two minimum CCA (cold-cranking amps) ratings, one at a temperature of 0°F and the other at −20°F. After the battery is brought to the test temperature it is discharged at the rated CCA current for 30 seconds. To pass the test, each cell must then still have a voltage of at least 1.2 volts. Because starting an engine on a cold morning is one of the most severe demands placed on a battery, these ratings are a good indication of the battery's capacity.

A special class of automobile batteries are deep-discharge batteries, which are designed to be repeatedly drained completely, on electric trolling motors for fishing, for example. Such use would quickly destroy an ordinary car battery. Instead of a CCA rating, these batteries have an MCA (for marine cranking amps) rating.

Terminal posts may be threaded or unthreaded. If they are unthreaded, they have a 1:9 taper, are at least 0.625" high, and the positive terminal is slightly larger (0.688") than the negative terminal (0.625"). If they are threaded, the thread is 3/8-16 UNC 2A.

Dry Cells

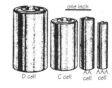

one inch

D cell   C cell   AA cell   AAA cell

Dry cell sizes were first designated by single letters. The system ANSI uses today is more complicated, but many of the letter names survive as the sizes of flashlight batteries, even some that consumers no longer use, such as "F"—inside the common 6-volt lantern battery are four F cells.

Battery capacity is rated in ampere-hours, but manufacturers don't usually provide such an estimate because the amount of current that can be drawn from a dry cell depends on such factors as the weather, the age of the cell, the cut-off voltage, the size of the load, and how quickly the power is withdrawn. If you put new batteries in a flashlight, turn it on and let it run until the batteries expire, you will have received fewer ampere-hours from them than if they were used for an hour a day until exhausted. Nonetheless, an estimate of the capacity in ampere-hours of the various sizes of carbon-zinc cells is: AA, 0.4; C, 1.5; D, 3.4; F, 5.2; G, 6.1. Alkaline-manganese cells have capacities roughly 1.5 to 2.5 times higher.

The chart gives typical maximum recommended current draw in milliamperes. The batteries described here are those most often encountered, such as those used in flashlights. Different types of batteries may be produced in the same cell size. For example, a C cell made for clocks is optimized for a much lower current draw but a much longer life than a C cell made for flashlights.

Cylindrical Dry Cells						
Designation		Nom.		Capacity, mAh		
				Carbon Zinc	Alkaline	Nickel cadmium
U.S.	IEC	dia.	Height	1.5v	1.5v	1.25v
AAA	R 03	13/32"	1 3/4"	20	100	600
AA	R 6	9/16"	1 31/32"	25	150	1,000
C	R 14	1 1/32"	1 13/16"	80	480	3,000
D	R 20	1 11/32"	2 13/32"	150	650	10,000†
F	R 25	1 1/4"	3 7/16"	—	—	
G	R 26	1 11/32"	4 5/32"	300	—	—
No. 6	—	2 5/8"	6 1/16"*	1500	—	—
N		0.445	1.180	20	85	300

* Height does not include height of terminals.
† Many consumer D-cell ni-cads are simply C-cells in a D-cell package. These have a capacity of around 1800 mAh.

bearings, ball Because the best ball bearings in early 20TH C were made by German manufacturers, ball bearings have usually been sized in millimeters, even those made in the USA—but the balls themselves were frequently sized in inches. The Anti-Friction Bearing Manufacturers Assn. adopted a classification of ball bearings according to their construction, with each type identified by a symbol (such as "BA"). Symbols that include the letter "I" identify types that are nominally sized in inches; of ten types, only two have an "I."

Embedded in the manufacturer's model number for most ball bearings is a three-digit code that gives its dimensions in millimeters. The first digit refers to the series. There are four principal series: 100, extra light; 200, light; 300, medium; and 400, heavy. The table below shows the sizes up through a bore of 50 mm, but much bigger sizes are defined. In the medium series, for example, a 356 bearing takes a shaft with a diameter of 280 mm—more than eleven inches.

Desig-nation	Bore	Series 100 (x = 1)		Series 200 (x = 2)		Series 300 (x = 3)		Series 400 (x = 4)	
		OD	Width	OD	Width	OD	Width	OD	Width
x00	10	26	8	30	9	35	11	—	—
x01	12	28	8	32	10	37	12	—	—
x02	15	32	9	35	11	42	13	—	—
x03	17	35	10	40	12	47	14	62	17
x04	20	42	12	47	14	52	15	72	19
x05	25	47	12	52	15	62	17	80	21

Desig-nation	Bore	Series 100 (x = 1)		Series 200 (x = 2)		Series 300 (x = 3)		Series 400 (x = 4)	
		OD	Width	OD	Width	OD	Width	OD	Width
x06	30	55	13	62	16	72	19	90	23
x07	35	62	14	72	17	80	21	100	25
x08	40	68	15	80	18	90	23	110	27
x09	45	75	16	85	19	100	25	120	29
x10	50	80	16	90	20	110	27	130	31

becquerel

The unit of activity (of a radioactive substance) in SI. Symbol, Bq. A substance is radioactive if the nuclei of its atoms are unstable, spontaneously changing into nuclei of another element and emitting radiation in the process. One becquerel is one such spontaneous nuclear transition per second.

The CGPM adopted the becquerel in 1975 (15TH CGPM, Resolution 8) on the advice of the International Commission on Radiation Units and Measurement and the International Commission on Radiological Protection. It replaced the ☞curie, whose continued use was temporarily sanctioned. One curie = 3.7×10^{10} Bq. The primary reason for the change was to make SI coherent.

bells, tolling of

Funeral. It was the custom in England to toll the funeral bell in spells of 3 for a child, 6 for a woman, and 9 for a man. In some areas the bell also tolled the number of years the person had lived.

Ship's. The ship's bell is tolled every half hour. A single stroke is struck a half hour after the beginning of each watch, at 12:30, 4:30, and 8:30 (both AM and PM). An additional stroke is added at each tolling, every half hour, so that 8 bells is struck at the end of the watch: 4:00, 8:00, and 12:00 (again, both AM and PM). Ship's bells are no longer rung on merchant ships, but the custom is maintained on passenger, training, and naval vessels.

Bible, units in the

A number of units of measurement occur in the Bible, and sometimes it is necessary to understand a unit's meaning to understand the significance of the passage in which it occurs. For good reasons, translators have sometimes rendered a number of different units by the same word in English. In the Revised Standard Version the word "measure," for example, is used for the *batos, koros,* and *saton,* units that differ in magnitude by a factor of 30. Sometimes a particular word in the Hebrew or Greek is translated by different English words in different contexts, e.g. *pechus* is sometimes translated as "cubit" and sometimes converted to the equivalent in yards.

How do we know how big Biblical units were? We can only guess at the size of some units (e.g., a "gomedh", the length of Ehud's sword in Judges 3:16) The value of other units during certain periods is fairly well known because of archeological discoveries. For example, archae-ologists have found the tunnel dug by Hezekiah (2 Kings 20:20). In the tunnel is an inscription stating that the tunnel is 1,200 cubits long. Measuring the tunnel and dividing by 1,200 gives the size of a cubit, at least on the date when the inscription was made. This value can then be checked by measuring other structures built at the time, since people tend to build in round numbers. (A visitor from another planet wandering around an American lumber yard could soon figure out we had a foot unit and another one-twelfth its size.) And in fact, structures were found with dimensions that were a whole number (such as 50) of the tunnel cubit. Sometimes, too, archeologists recover actual stand-ards of weight and capacity, such as pots marked with the name of a unit, just as someone thousands of years from now might find a glass measuring cup from some farmer's kitchen. Even these, however, do not necessarily provide a final word on the size of a unit.

Because the Old Testament touches such a vast sweep of time, geography and culture, a word naming a unit may represent many different magnitudes. Today a gallon in Canada is not the same size as a gallon in the United States, and neither is the same as an English ale gallon in 1600. The people of the Old Testament were themselves aware of the variability of weights and measures; think of Ezekiel's attempt at restandardization after the Babylonian Exile (Ezek. 45). It is hardly surprising that the meaning of many of the units is still debated. Among Jewish scholars, for example, there are two schools regarding measures: the "Na'eh" interpretation, by which, for exam-ple, the fingerbreadth is 2 cm, and the "Hazon Ish" interpretation, which takes it to be 2.4 cm. The sizes of such units figure in present-day religious observances; to play it safe, the observant generally choose whichever interpretation is most onerous under the circumstances.

In general, we can be more certain of the meaning of the units in the New Testament, since it covers a much shorter and more recent period of time. Some of the New Testament units were widely used Greek or Roman units. Others are hellenized versions of long-established He-brew units, for example, saton for seah.

Units in the Old Testament					
Word in the translation		unit in Hebrew & transliterated		Conversions	
King James	R.S.V.		Examples	SI	U.S.
Units of Length					
reed	reed	קנה kanneh = 6 ammah	Ezekiel 40:5	2.67 m	8' 9"

Units in the Old Testament

Word in the translation		unit in Hebrew & transliterated	Examples	Conversions	
King James	R.S.V.			SI	U.S.
"cubit of a man"	cubit	אמה ammah = 6 tophach	Deuteronomy **3**:11		
cubit			1 Samuel **17**:4 Genesis **7**:20 Esther **7**:19 2 Kings **14**:13 Nehmiah **3**:13 Jeremiah **52**:21	444 mm	17.47"
"the cubit is a cubit and an hand breadth"			Ezekiel **40**:5, **43**:13	518 mm	20.38"
cubit	cubit	גמד gomedh	Judges **3**:16	?	?
span	span	זרת zeres = 3 tophach (some say 2)	1 Samuel **17**:4 Ezekiel **43**:13 Isaiah **40**:12	22.2 cm	8.75"
hand breadth	handbreadth	טפח tophach = 4 etzbah	Ezekiel **40**:5; **43**:13	7.4 cm	2.9"
finger	finger	אצבע etzbah	Jeremiah **52**:21	1.9 cm	3/4"

Units of Area

"an half acre of land, *which* a yoke of *oxen might plow*"	acre	צמד tzemed, lit. "yoke"	1 Samuel **14**:14	0.2 ha	around 1/2 acre
acre			Isaiah **5**:10		
homer	homer	חומר chomer	Lev. **27**:16	2.4 ha	6 acres

Units of Dry Capacity

homer	homer	חומר chomer	Numbers **11**:32 Isaiah **5**:10 Ezekiel **45**:11, 13, 14* Hosea **3**:2	230 L	6.5 bushels
measure	measure		1 Kings **18**: 32		
cor	cor	כור kor	Ezekiel **45**:14	230 L	6.5 bushels
measure	cor		1 Kings **5**:11		
	lethech	לתך lethekh = 1/2 chomer		115 L	3 1/4 bushels

Units in the Old Testament

Word in the translation		unit in Hebrew & transliterated	Examples	Conversions	
King James	R.S.V.			SI	U.S.
ephah	ephah	א י פ ה ephah = 1/10 chomer	Exodus **16**:36 Lev. **5**:11, **6**:20; **19**:36 Ezekiel **45**:10, 11*, 24; **46**:5 Numbers **5**:15 Judah **6**:19 Ruth **2**:17 1 Sam **1**:24, **17**:17 Isaiah **5**:10 Amos **8**:5 Zechariah **5**:6–10	23 L	21 dry quarts
measure	measure	ה א ס ח seah = 1/3 ephah	Genesis **18**:6 Isaiah **40**:12	7.6 L	7 dry quarts
omer	omer	ע מ ר omer = 1/10 ephah	Exodus **16**:16, 18, 22, 32, 33, 36*	2.2 L	4 dry pints
a tenth deal of flour	tenth part	ע ש ר ו ן issaron = 1/10 ephah	Exodus **29**:40 Lev. **5**:11; **6**:20 Numbers **28**:13 Ezekiel **45**:11	2.2 L	4 dry pints
cab	kab	ק ב kav	2 Kings **6**:25	1.2 L	2 2/9 dry pints

Units of Liquid Capacity

		ש ר ך kor same vol. as dry kor			
bath	bath	מ ך bath = 1/10 kor	1 Kings **7**:26, 38 2 Chr **2**:10; **4**:5 Ezekiel **7**:22 Isaiah **5**:10 Ezekiel **45**:10, 11, 1614	22 L	5.8 gallons
hin	hin	ט ו ח hin = 1/6 bath	Exodus **29**:40 Lev. **19**:36 Numb. **15**:4, 5, 6, 9; **28**:5, 7, 14 Ezekiel **4**:11; **45**:24; **46**:5, 7, 11, 14	3.66 L	3.86 quarts
		qabh = 1/3 hin		1.3 L	1.35 qts
log	log	ל ו ג log = 1/12 hin	Lev. **14**:10, 12, 15, 21, 24	320 mL	0.67 pint

SIZES

Units in the Old Testament					
Word in the translation		unit in Hebrew & transliterated	Examples	Conversions	
King James	R.S.V.			SI	U.S.
Units of Mass					
talent	talent	כיכר kikkar	2 Kings 18:14		75.6 lbs
maneh	mina	מנה maneh	Ezekiel 45:12*	571 g	20.15 oz
shekel	shekel	שקל sheqel	1 Samuel 17:5, 7	11.4 g	176.3 grains
shekel of the sanctuary	shekel of the sanctuary	הקודש בשקל bishekel hachodesh	Exodus 30:13 Lev. 5:15; 27:25 Num. 3:47; 18:6 Ezekiel 45:12		
not translated	pim	לפים pim	1 Samuel 13:21		
bekah	beka	בקע beka	Exodus 38:26	5.7 g	88.1 grains
	gerah	גרה gerah	Exodus 30:13 Lev. 27:25* Numbers 3:47; 18:16 Ezekiel 45:12	570 mg	8.8 grains

*Starred passages contain a definition of the unit.

Units in the New Testament

Word in the translation		unit in Greek & transliterated	Examples	Conversions	
King James	R.S.V.			SI	U.S.
cubit	cubit	πῆχυς pechus	Matthew 6:27 Luke 12:25 Rev. 21:17	44.5 cm	17.5"
	"a 100 yards" (= 200 cubits)		John 21:8		
fathom	fathom	ὀργυιά orguia	Acts 27:28	180 cm	70"
furlong	"7 miles" (= 60 stadia) "3 or 4 miles" (= 25 or 30 s.)	στάδιον stadion	Luke 24:13 John 6:19, 11:18	185 m	202.5 yds
	furlong		Matthew 14:24		
	stadia		Rev. 14:20, 21:16		
measure	measure	βάτος batos	Luke 16:6	23 L	6.1 gals
measure	measure	κόρους koros	Luke 16:7	231 L	61 gals
measure	measure	σάτον saton	Matthew 13:33 Luke 13:21	13 L	7 dry quarts
"2 or 3 firkins"	"20 or 30 gallons" (= metretes)	μετρητής metretes	John 2:6	39.4 L	10 gals
measure	quart	χοινιξ choinix	Rev. 6:6	1.1 L	1 dry qt
bushel	bushel	μόδιος modios	Matthew 5:15 Mark 4:21 Luke 11:33	8.7 L	7.68 dry qts
pot	pot	ξέστες xestes	Mark 7:4, 8	0.3 L	1 dry pint
talent	hundredweight	τάλαντον talenton	Rev. 16:21 (Mt. 18:24; 25:15ff)	41 kg	90 lbs
pound	pound	λιτρα litra	John 12:3; 19:39	0.33 kg	0.72 lb
pound	pound	μνα mna	Luke 19:13ff	0.57 kg	1 1/4 lbs

bicycles

Children's Bicycles
Bicycles for children under 12 should be strong enough to withstand abuse, reliable, simple to maintain, and safe—not necessarily the priorities one would set for an adult's bike. Strength means weight;

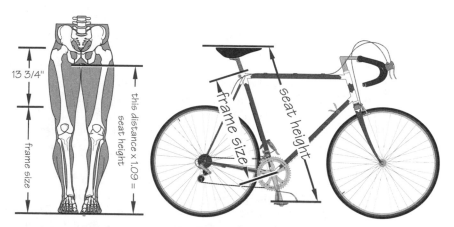

reliability and low maintenance rules out finicky mechanisms like sophisticated derailleurs. Children's hands are not as strong as adults', so a coaster brake is preferable to hand brakes. Do not put accessories like levers on the top tube of a child's bicycle, because in an accident they can injure a boy's testicles. When children, no matter how young, are given a bicycle, they should also be given a helmet and expected to wear it—just as their parents do.

Road Bicycles

Like cars, bicycles are made in different models for different purposes. A touring bike differs from a road racing bike much as a touring car differs from a sports car; the latter is more responsive and less comfortable. The information below is meant for adults buying their first serious bicycle, to help them recognize what sort of bicycle they are being sold so that they can avoid models that don't fit them or suit the intended use.

Frame Size. The frame size is the distance between the top of the seat tube and the axis around which the cranks rotate, measured along the seat tube. Frame sizes generally run from 19" to 25" in increments of 1".

To find a good frame size for a rider, have the person stand in bare feet on an uncarpeted floor. Measure the vertical distance from the floor to the head of the femur (see drawing). Subtract 13.75".

Adjusting saddle height is the second step in fitting a bike to a rider. With the rider standing in bare feet on an uncarpeted floor, measure the vertical distance from floor to crotch. Rotate the pedals so that the cranks are parallel to the seat tube. Adjust the height of the saddle until the distance from the top of the bottom pedal to the top of the saddle is equal to the rider's crotch height times 1.09 (a factor developed by Vaughn Thomas at Loughborough University, England). Try this for a few weeks; if it feels wrong, it can always be adjusted.

If adjusting the saddle height results in less than 2.5" of seat post inside the seat tube, you need to purchase a longer seat post. Seat posts are manufactured in diameters from 26.2 mm to 27.2 mm, in steps of 0.2 mm.

Sometimes the problem is that the seat cannot be lowered far enough. If a smaller frame size is not available, it may be possible to lower the seat by inverting the clamp, or, if the saddle is leather, by switching to a plastic saddle (they're not as deep).

Opinions about saddle tilt differ. Some say nose down, at a 10° angle; some prefer horizontal.

Gears. Cycling enthusiasts have a peculiar way of stating gear ratios: a gear ratio is given as the diameter of an imaginary driven wheel directly connected to the pedals that would move the bicycle the same distance as one rotation of the pedals using a particular gear ratio does. This system comes from the days of the high-wheeler bicycle when the pedals actually were directly connected to the front wheel, and a higher "gear ratio" could only be had by using a bigger wheel.

To find the "gear" for any combination of sprockets, divide the number of teeth on the chainwheel by number of teeth on the rear sprocket (which gives you the real gear ratio), then multiply by the diameter of the rear wheel. For example, suppose the chain passes over a chainwheel with 40 teeth and a rear sprocket with 20, on a bicycle with a 27" wheel. The gear would be $(40 \div 20), \times 27 = 54$.

Pedals. Pedals are sold in pairs; the one on the rider's right has a left-hand thread (tightens as it is turned counterclockwise) and the one on the left an ordinary thread. In this way drag in their bearings tightens, rather than loosens them. In a pair, the one with a "D" or an "R" stamped on the end of the axle is the right pedal; the other one is a left.

Inexpensive bicycles often have one-piece cranks; these are tapped $1/2" \times 20$. English, Japanese and Italian pedals are $9/16" \times 20F$, though the Italian pedals have a slightly different thread. French cranks and pedals are 14 mm × 1.25.

Saddles are attached to the seat post by a clamp that grasps two parallel rails under the saddle. On most saddles the distance between the rails is 36 mm and the flat stretch on which the clamp can be placed is 60 mm long. A much less common type is made for riders who need a greater range of back and forth adjustment: it has a flat stretch 120 mm long. Its rails, however are 20 mm apart, so the two types are not interchangeable.

Typical characteristics that distinguish a road bike intended for touring from one designed for a racer:

	Touring	Racing
hubs	low-flange	high-flange
wheelbase	long	short
number of spokes		
front wheel	36	often 28 or 32
rear wheel	36 (40 for a heavy rider or lots of luggage)	36 or less
frame angle	71°–73°	72°–74°
saddle	relatively wide	relatively narrow

Mountain Bicycles

Mountain, or off-road, bicycles have heavier tires and more robust frames than road bicycles, and the frames are a different shape. They often have suspension systems, on the front fork, the rear fork, or both. An individual requires a frame size two to four inches smaller than his or her road bicycle frame size.

Compare the lengths of the seat tubes.

Mountain bike   Road bike

big game

A system for calculating a figure of merit for North American big game trophies was devised by James L. Clark in 1935, and another by Grancel Fitz in 1939. Having two systems is confusing, so in 1949 the Boone and Crockett Club appointed a committee to develop a scoring system that incorporated the best features of the two existing systems with such corrections, additions, and simplifications as they thought necessary. The system the committee produced is the one now used for North American game trophies. The record keeping continues to be done by the Boone and Crockett Club (250 Station Dr., Missoula, MT 59801).

The scoring system is a point system, and varies with the species. For whitetail deer, for example, it is entirely based upon measurements of the antlers: inside spread, the length of each tine, the circumference at various locations, and so on. Boone and Crockett publishes a report form for each species, somewhat resembling an income tax form. A hunter who has shot what he or she believes to be a trophy animal submits the completed and signed form to the club.

binder clips

Width	Capacity
3/4"	3/8"
1 1/4"	5/8"
2"	1"

binders, ring

The length of the side along which the holes are punched is given first.

Page Size	Hole dia.	No. of holes	Distance between centers
11" × 8½	¼" or 5/16"	3	3½"
8½" × 5"	¼"	3	2¾"
8½" × 6"	¼"	3	3½"

A series of small ring binders called "memo books" have six rings. The paper is punched with 3/16" holes.

5" × 3"
6" × 3 1/2"
6 3/4" × 3 3/4"
7 1/4" × 4 1/4"

Metals. Those with locks at top and bottom (double-lock rings) are generally of higher quality than those with only one or no lock.

Three styles of ring are used: round, elliptical, and D-ring. Elliptical rings are used in binders for a large number of pages: their advantage is that tabs are easier to read than they are with round rings. A D-ring metal is mounted on the back cover of the binder; it will hold about 25% more pages than round rings of the same size.

binoculars

Power. The figure before the "×" is the power: the amount things will appear to be magnified. With a pair of either 7×50 or 7×35 binoculars, for example, things 1000' away would appear as large as they would if the viewer were standing (1000 ÷ 7 =) 143' away. Beyond about 8 or 9 power, a tripod may be necessary.

Aperture. The number following the "×" is the diameter of the objectives in millimeters. The larger the aperture, the greater the light-gathering power. Other factors, however, may prevent some of this light from reaching the viewer's retina.

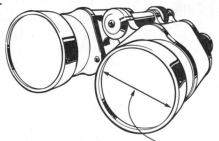

The "50" in the "7 x 50" marking on this pair of binoculars indicates that the diameter of this lens is 50 millimeters.

Field width. Sometimes this is given in degrees, sometimes as a field of view: "300 feet at 1,000 yards" or "120 meters at 1,000 meters." To convert "feet at 1,000 yards" to degrees with a calculator with trigonometric functions, divide the number of feet by 6,000, take $\tan^{-1}$, multiply by 2. Meters at 1,000 meters can be converted by dividing by

2,000, take $\tan^{-1}$, multiply by 2, e.g., 120 m at 1,000 m is the same as 6.9 degrees. The optical design of some binoculars gives them a wider-than-usual field of view.

Exit pupil. The diameter of the exit pupil is sometimes given; if not, it can be found by dividing the aperture by the power; thus the exit pupil of a pair of 7×50 binoculars is 50 ÷ 7 = 7.1 mm. The bigger the exit pupil, the less critical the alignment of the binocular and the eye.

In dim light, another effect of the size of the exit pupil becomes more important. Assuming two binoculars are the same power, the one with the bigger aperture will have the bigger exit pupil. As the size of the exit pupil increases, the image appears brighter, up to the point at which the exit pupil is the same diameter as the pupil of the eye and the entire area of the pupil is illuminated. After that, further increases produce no gain in brightness.

As people age the maximum opening of the pupil diminishes. The pupil of a healthy young person's eye has a diameter of about 2 mm in bright light, 5 mm in dim, and 7 mm in the dark. People in their thirties typically have a maximum pupil diameter of about 6 mm, which shrinks to 4.5 to 5 mm in their forties. (See the chart on page 119.) Thus, at dusk, people in their twenties would see a brighter image through 7×50 (exit pupil dia. 7 mm) binoculars than through 7×35 (exit pupil dia. 5 mm) binoculars, but persons in their sixties would perceive no difference.

Some manufacturers give a "relative brightness index," found by squaring the size of the exit pupil in millimeters. The highest number allowed in this index is 49, since human pupils open no more than about 7 mm.

Eye relief is the distance between the eyepiece and the point of focus of the exit pupil. Currently marketed binoculars have eye reliefs ranging from 1 mm to 23 mm. The former is outlandishly small; eyelashes will dirty the lens. Large eye reliefs—around 15 mm is enough—are needed by persons who wear eyeglasses while using binoculars. Although the focusing adjustments of binoculars can compensate for most near- and farsightedness, they cannot compensate for astigmatism. Many who aren't astigmatic prefer to wear their glasses while using binoculars, simply because they don't like putting them on and off.

No figures of merit are given for some of the most important characteristics of a binocular; above all, the tolerance permitted in aligning the two halves. Collimation is critical, but there is no easy way for the consumer to check it. Other features, such as the quality of the lens coating and the effectiveness of internal baffling, can also be important.

birds

Not surprisingly, the biggest birds can't fly. The heaviest bird of all time was the elephant bird, *Aepyornia titan*, which lived in Madagascar as late as the 17TH C. Built somewhat along the lines of an ostrich, it was much heavier and not made for running (the ostrich is the fastest thing on two feet). *Aepyornia* stood 10 feet tall, weighed a thousand pounds, and laid 2-gallon, 20-pound eggs a foot long. (The yolks of these eggs are the largest known cells.) New Zealand had a remote relative called *Dinornis maximus* which became extinct around 1800. It was the tallest bird that ever existed, at around 11' 6".

The bird the author would least like to meet in a dark alley is *Phorusrhacus inflatus*, which lived in Patagonia from the Early to Middle Miocene. Ten feet tall with a heavy, flesh-tearing beak like that of an eagle, this fellow was definitely a meat-eater.

New Jersey had some big birds in the Early Eocene. *Diatryma gigantea* stood 7' tall. (Its fossils are also found in New Mexico, Wyoming, and parts of Europe.) We don't know what it ate.

Among living birds, the wandering albatross has the greatest wingspread, about 12 feet. But a vulture-like South American bird of the Late Miocene, *Argentavis magnificens*, had a 24-foot wingspread.

The smallest bird is found in Cuba: the bee hummingbird, *Melisuga helenae*. Two inches long, it weighs less than 2 grams and its eggs are only 0.3 inches long. More than 30,000 *Melisuga helenae* eggs would fit in a single *Aepyornia titan* egg.

bit

The smallest possible unit of information in a binary digital computer: an amount of memory that can lead to recollection of one of only two possible states, which might be interpreted as "yes" or "no," "off" or "on," "0" or "1," "true" or "false," etc. Such features of computer hardware as the size of the gulps a microprocessor takes (an "8-bit microprocessor") or the width of address busses ("The first IBM PC had an 8-bit bus.") are described in bits. Not to be confused with ☞byte.

blankets

The usual sizes in the United States are:

twin	66" × 90"
double	80" × 90"
queen	90" × 90" to 100" × 90"
king	108" × 90" to 108" × 100"

Stadium blankets are 50" × 60" to 54" × 72".

blood, human

A man has approximately 69 milliliters of blood per kilogram of body weight (so a 150-lb man has about 4.7 liters of blood), and a woman 65 mL per kg. Of this, in men 39 mL per kg of body weight is plasma, and 40 mL per kg in women.

The surface of a red blood cell carries molecules known as antigens. Certain cells release into the blood susbstances called antibodies. An antibody in the blood which matches an antigen, like a key matches a lock, can bind to the antigens and in doing so initiate an immune reaction which leads to the death of that red blood cell. Blood can be classified by the antibodies with which it will react, and such classification is essential for transfusion. More than 20 different blood group systems are recognized in medicine. Of these, the best known are the ABO system and the Rh system.

Using tests for the three blood systems shown, a randomly chosen person has about a 50% chance of demonstrating he or she is not the child's biological parent. Most courts in the United States admit the results of tests for blood group systems ABO, MN, and Rh as evidence in paternity cases (see box). They haven't, however, accepted such results as sufficient to prove paternity.

Parent	Baby	Other parent can't be
A	B	O or A
	AB	O or A
	O	AB
B	A	O or B
	AB	O or B
	O	AB
AB	AB	O
O	A	O or B
	B	O or A
	O	AB
M	MN	M
N	MN	N
Any group	M	N
Any group	N	M
Rh+	Rh-	Rh+
Rh-	Rh+	Rh-

The Major ABO Blood Groups

One parent's blood type	Other parent's blood type	Person's blood type	Americans of Western European descent	Americans of African descent (NY, 1955)	West Africans (Ewe, 1951)	Native Americans (pure Cherokee, 1958)
A^1	A^1	A^1	35%	21%	19%	4%
A^1	A^2					
A^1	O					
A^2	A^2	A^2	10%	6%	2%	
A^2	O					
B	B	B	8%	17%	29%	1%
B	O					
A^1	B	A^1B	3%	1%	4%	0%
A^2	B	A^2B	1%	3%	4%	
O	O	O	43%	51%	43%	96%
h	h	O_h	very rare	very rare	very rare	very rare

blood pressure

In the USA, blood pressure is usually measured in millimeters of mercury. Two measurements are made, the first of the pressure as the heart pumps (systolic pressure), and the second while the heart is between beats (diastolic pressure). High blood pressure (hypertension) is associated with various diseases.

Formerly the stages of hypertension were described as mild, moderate, and severe. Unfortunately, describing a condition as "mild" encourages people to do nothing about it. In 1992, the National High Blood Pressure Education Program released the staging shown in the table below.. The numbers 1 to 4 represent increasingly greater risk.

Average Dia-stolic	Average systolic blood pressure						
	<120	120-129	130-139	140-159	160-179	180-209	>209
<80	optimal*	normal	high normal	1	2	3	4
80-84	normal	normal	high normal	1	2	3	4
85-89	high normal	high normal	high normal	1	2	3	4
90-99	1	1	1	1	2	3	4
100-109	2	2	2	2	2	3	4
110-119	3	3	3	3	3	3	4
>120	4	4	4	4	4	4	4

*Although readings of less than 80/120 are described as optimal, it is possible for blood pressure to be too low. Since very low blood pressure could be a sign of a problem, people with very low readings should consult a physician.

board foot

A unit of volume used to measure sawn lumber, = 144 cubic inches. Abbr, bd ft. In calculating board feet for boards, it is customary to assume that they are 1" thick, even if after surfacing they are thinner than that. Similarly, the number of board feet in two-by-fours and similar pieces of wood (which are not "boards," but dimension lumber) is calculated on the basis of their nominal size (as if they were 2" by 4"). Like many American lumber terms, the board foot has spread around the world.

boccie

Boules are spherical, 11 cm in diameter, and weigh between 0.7 and 1.3 kg. They are made of metal or synthetic materials and must not contain nails, lead weights, etc.

Jack. The jack is the ball used as a target. It is spherical, made of wood, and has a diameter of 3.7 cm. It must have no ridges, weighting, nails, etc.

Unique to the game is an instrument called a *baguette*, an L-shaped metal rod which is used to trace out the lines of the pitch and to trace an arc in front of the designated target (either the jack or an opponent's boule). The rod is 6 mm in diameter and pointed on both ends.

Boccie Pitch

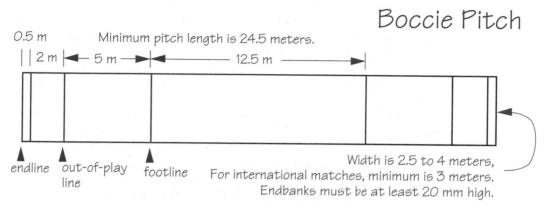

0.5 m   Minimum pitch length is 24.5 meters.

| | 2 m |←— 5 m —→|←————— 12.5 m —————→|

endline   out-of-play   footline   Width is 2.5 to 4 meters,
          line   For international matches, minimum is 3 meters.
                                      Endbanks must be at least 20 mm high.

The longer leg is 50 cm long and the shorter 50 mm. The competing teams' baguettes must be identical.

body armor

"Bulletproof" vests and similar garments are not, of course, proof against *every* bullet. More protection requires more weight and less comfort.

National Institute of Justice Standard 0101.03 sets standards for six body armor "threat levels": I, IIA, II, IIIA, III, and IV, in increasing order of effectiveness. A parallel but slightly different set of standard "protection levels" is defined by the Personal Protective Armor Assn.; their levels run from A to E, with A offering the least protection. In both sets of standards the levels are defined in terms of rounds of ammunition: caliber, type and mass of the bullet, and muzzle velocity.

The NIJ advises all law enforcement officers to wear some type of body armor at all times. Many do not because they find it uncomfortable, although continued improvements in the aramid fiber from which the armor is made (almost always, Dupont's Kevlar) have made today's armor lighter and less bulky than the original product. Type II can be uncomfortable in hot, humid climates. Most people don't consider Type III-A suitable for routine wear in any climate, while Types III and IV are definitely primarily for wear in especially dangerous situations.

Below, for each type, are examples of rounds against which it is intended to offer protection:

I: .22 long rifle high velocity, 40 grain round nose lead bullet, 1050 f/s +50/-0. .38 special, 158 grain round nose lead bullet, 850 f/s +50/-0.

II-A: Low velocity .357 magnum and 9 mm, .45 mm auto.

II: Higher velocity .357 magnum and 9 mm.

III-A: .44 Magnum, submachine gun 9 mm, most handgun rounds.

None of the preceding types offer protection against rifle fire.

III: high-powered rifle, 7.62 mm NATO rounds, 12-gauge rifled slug, 30 caliber full metal jacket.

IV: armor-piercing rifle, 30 caliber.

According to the standard, every ballistic panel must bear a label that, among other information, gives the rated level of protection and the edition of the standard used to define the level.

bolts

For bolt heads, see ☞screw drive systems; for threads, see ☞screw threads.

What is a bolt? An engineer's definition is that a bolt is held on by a nut, while the identical object, screwed into a threaded hole in a casting, would be a screw. In the local hardware store big threaded fasteners are bolts and the small ones are machine screws. The U.S. Customs Service has even issued a pamphlet on the subject for its inspectors, since the tariff on a bolt differs from that on a screw.

In the USA, standards for bolts have been set by the Society of Automotive Engineers and by the military/aerospace industry.

Special Types of Bolts

Carriage bolts have a wide, domed head without a recess (so they can't be driven with a screwdriver), and most have a shank which is square for about ¼" from the head. As the name suggests, this style of bolt was originally used to build carriages. When the bolt is driven into a hole in wood, the square shank prevents the bolt from turning while a nut (with washer) is spun on to the other end. Today they are used to assemble things like picnic tables.

Stove bolts with square heads and nuts were very common as late as the 1950s, and even had their own series of threads. They can be replaced with ordinary bolts.

Lag screws are often referred to as "lag bolts," though they are tapered and aren't used with nuts.

Studs are headless bolts, threaded on both ends, sometimes with different threads.

Cap screws. Currently manufactured cap screws are SAE grade 8.

SAE Standards

The SAE has established a sequence of grades from 0 to 8 for steel bolts, on the basis of the metal from which the bolt is made and the manner of manufacture. Available grades run from 2 to 8, with 8 the strongest. Higher grade numbers almost always mean increased

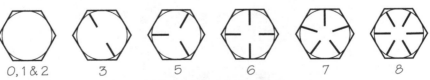

SAE grades on bolt heads

strength (an exception is that some grade 6 bolts are stronger than grade 7). The heads of steel bolts are marked to identify their grade.

In the 1980s, large numbers of counterfeit bolts appeared in the USA, almost all imports. For this reason, the SAE grade markings can no longer be trusted unless one knows exactly who made and graded the bolt. Aerospace-grade bolts are also being counterfeited (even NASA has been duped, to the tune of one million dollars to disassemble the Astro 1 space lab to remove counterfeit and defective fasteners).

As a rule, when a bolt is installed the nut (over a washer) should be turned and not the bolt's head. Unless a torque wrench is used the tendency is to undertighten large bolts and overtighten small ones. Suggested torques are given below for the three most common grades. These suggestions do not apply if the bolt or nut has been specially lubricated.

Suggested Torque Settings (Ft-lbs)			
Bolt dia.	grade 2	grade 5	grade 8
1/4"	5	7	10
5/16"	9	14	22
3/8"	15	25	37
7/16"	24	40	60
1/2"	37	60	92
9/16"	53	88	132
5/8"	74	120	180
3/4"	120	200	296
7/8"	190	302	473
1"	282	466	714

Aerospace Standards

The bolts used to assemble aircraft are made to higher standards than those used for cars; the Federal Aviation Administration does not permit aircraft to be assembled with SAE-graded bolts. There are three aerospace standards for bolts: AN (for Air Corps-Navy), MS (Military Specification), and NAS (National Aerospace Standard). Some of these are truly superbolts.

Metric Standards

Standards for metric bolts are set by the ISO. In metric bolts, a grade is called a "property class." A property class designation consists of two numbers separated by a decimal point. The number before the decimal point is one-hundredth of the nominal tensile strength of the bolt in newtons per square millimeter. The number after the decimal point is the ratio between the nominal yield stress and the nominal tensile strength, times ten. Bolts in property classes 4.6, 5.6, and 8.8 and above *must* have the property class marked on the head

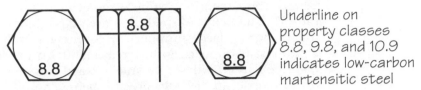

Underline on property classes 8.8, 9.8, and 10.9 indicates low-carbon martensitic steel

of the bolt. Property class 6.8 roughly corresponds to SAE grade 2; 8.8 to SAE 5; and 10.9 to SAE 8.

bond ratings

In the USA, municipal and corporate bonds are rated by a number of services, notably Standard and Poor's, Fitch, and Moody's Investors Service. The highest rating given by Standard and Poor's and Fitch is "AAA", followed by "AA", "A" and "BBB". Bonds with any of these four ratings are considered "investment grade," or "bank grade" or "bank quality," phrases which have legal meaning in many jurisdictions. A person with certain fiduciary responsibilities (investing for an orphan, for example) is often prevented by law from purchasing bonds that are below investment grade.

Below the investment grade bonds are the "BB", "B", "CCC", and "CC" ratings, which, in the words of Standard and Poor's, "are regarded, on balance, as predominantly speculative." Bonds receiving these ratings are sometimes referred to as "junk bonds."

The rating "C" is reserved for income bonds, those whose interest payments, if any, are contingent upon the issuer's earnings. A "D" rating indicates a bond is in default.

Ratings "AA" through "BB" may be followed by a "+" or "-", a refinement that ranks that particular bond in relation to other bonds with the same letter rating.

A "p" (for provisional) attached to a rating indicates that the rating applies only if the project for which the bond was issued is successfully completed. It might be applied, for example, to a bond issue meant to be repaid out of income from sales of electricity from a nuclear power plant. If the power plant is not successfully completed, repayment is jeopardized.

Moody's ratings differ somewhat from those described above. Their highest rating is "Aaa", followed by "Aa", "A," "Baa," "Ba," "B," "Caa," "Ca," and "C." A "1" added to the "A" and "Baa" indicates issues within the group that the service believes have the strongest "investment attributes." A "Con" rating corresponds to Standard and Poor's "p;" the rating when the condition is removed may follow in parentheses.

books

Today the sizes of books are usually given in inches or centimeters. The American mass market paperback, referred to as "rack size," is 7" × 4 1/8" or 4 1/4", larger than the typical 1950s 6 3/8" × 4 3/16". Trade paperbacks are generally 8" × 5 1/4".

In the 18TH AND 19TH C the sizes of books had names. Most of these names included the size of a signature. A book consists of a number of folded sheets of paper. A printed sheet of paper can be folded in half to make 4 pages; this is a folio. If it is folded in half, and then folded in half again, it will have 8 pages, and so on. The number of pages on a folded sheet is always a power of 2.

One or more folded sheets are nested together to make a signature; in a hard-bound book they are sewn together through the crease. A book's signatures can be seen by viewing the spine from above. In modern printing 32-page signatures are common.

Nowadays even duodecimo is often pronounced "twelve-mo."

Double Elephant Folio	25"+
Atlas Folio	25"
Elephant Folio	23"+
Folio (F)	13" +
Quarto (4to)	11" – 13"
Small Quarto (Sm. 4to)	10"
Octavo (8vo)	8" – 9"
Small Octavo (Sm. 8vo)	7½" – 8"
Duodecimo (12mo)	7" or slightly more
Sextodecimo (16mo)	6" – 7"
Vigesimoquarto (24mo)	5" – 6"
Trigesimosecundo (32mo)	4" – 5"
Fortyeightmo (48mo)	less than 4"
Sixtyfourmo (64mo)	about 3"
Miniature	less than 3"

box

In New England, 19TH and early 20TH C, a box of green vegetables was the quantity sufficient to fill a box 17½" × 17½" × 7".

boxing

The weight classes for amateur (including Olympic) and professional boxing in the United States are:

	Maximum Weight in Kilograms	
Class	Amateur	Professional
Light Flyweight	48	49
Flyweight	51	51
Bantamweight	54	53.5
Super Bantamweight	—	55
Featherweight	57	57
Junior Lightweight	—	59
Lightweight	60	61
Light Welterweight	63.5	63.5
Welterweight	67	66.5
Light Middleweight	71	70
Middleweight	75	72.5

Maximum Weight in Kilograms (cont.)		
Class	Amateur	Professional
Light Heavyweight	81	79
Cruiserweight	—	88.45
Heavyweight	91	>88.45
Super Heavyweight	> 91	—

A boxer must weigh more than the maximum weight for the previous class and no more than the maximum weight for his class. A boxer cannot compete in more than one weight class in a single tournament.

Weigh-in begins at 8 AM. A boxer who is no more than 2 pounds overweight has until 10 AM to work off the excess weight and be reweighed. A boxer who is more than 2 pounds overweight is immediately disqualified.

Interestingly, though the weight classes are defined in kilograms, in the United States the weighing of boxers is done in customary units, which leads to one of the last survivals of the dram. For example, a Super Heavyweight must weigh more than 200 pounds, 9 ounces, and 15 drams.

braille

In the English-speaking world, braille comes in two flavors: grade 1 and grade 2. Each character in the braille alphabet is formed by a combination of raised dots in six possible positions, for a total of 63 possible characters. In grade 1 braille, only the letters of the alphabet are represented.

In grade 2 braille, as defined by a conference in London in 1932 and revised in 1957, certain common combinations of letters, such as "ch," "gh," "sh," "th" and "wh" are also represented by single characters, as are common short words such as "the," "and," "with" and "for." This saves a vast amount of space and makes reading faster. The U.S. laws requiring braille lettering on elevator control panels, for example, specify grade 2.

A	G	L	N	Z	wh	sh	and	with	for

brassieres

In the USA, bra sizes take the form "34B," where the number is the band size and the letter is the cup size.

To find band size, measure around the rib cage just below the bust, in inches. Add 5". If the result is an odd number, add 1.

To find cup size, measure around the fullest part of the bust while wearing a bra, again in inches. Subtract the band size. If the result is 1", the cup size is A; 2" = B; 3" = C; 4" = D; 5" = DD; and 6" = DDD.

bricks

Bricks are usually sold in "cubes" of 500 bricks. A cube weighs about a ton.

Non-modular Brick Sizes

Dimensions given are nominal; *they include the thickness of the mortar joint.* The actual physical dimensions of a brick would be smaller; when the brick is laid the mortar brings it to the size of the module. So for example a "standard" brick intended to be laid with 3/8" mortar joints might have actual dimensions of 3 3/4" × 1 7/8" × 7 5/8", while a standard brick for 1/2" joints might be 3 3/4" × 1 3/4" × 7 1/2".

Type	Depth × height × length
standard	3 3/4" × 2 1/4" × 8"
jumbo	3 3/4" × 2 3/4" × 8"
3-inch	3" × 2 3/4" × 9"

The following are considered oversize bricks.

8" square	3 5/8" × 8" × 8"
12" square	3 5/8" × 12" × 12"
high brick	4" × 8" × 16"

Modular Brick Sizes

Modular bricks were introduced to make it easier to insert standard sizes of doors and windows into walls. Modular doors and windows, and courses of modular bricks, all fit into a 4" by 4" grid. For bricks, the 4" module includes the thickness of the mortar joints.

1 course = 1 module (4")

jumbo closure	4" × 4" × 8"
jumbo utility	4" × 4" × 12"
6" jumbo	6" × 4" × 12"
8" jumbo	8" × 4" × 12"

2 courses = 1 module (4")

Roman	4" × 2" × 12"

3 courses = 2 modules (8")

standard	4" × 2 2/3" × 8"
1" veneer	1" × 2 2/3" × 8"
Norman	4" × 2 2/3" × 12"
SCR	6" × 2 2/3" × 12"

jumbo closure

Roman

Standard

3 courses = 4 modules (16")
double   4" × 5 1/3" × 8"
triple   4" × 5 1/3" × 12"

5 courses = 4 modules (16")
engineer   4" × 3 1/5" × 8"
Norwegian   4" × 3 1/5" × 12"
6" Norweg.   6" × 3 1/5" × 12"

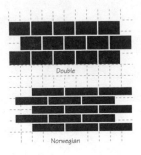

Double

Norwegian

Grades

Building brick (per ASTM C62): SW, for severe weather; MW, for moderate weather; NW, no weather, brick that will not be exposed to weather.

Face brick (per ASTM C216) FBS: general use; FBX: mechanically perfect; FBA: a grade permitting considerable non-uniformity, to give architects some variety in design.

Sand-lime brick (per ASTM C73): SW, severe weather; MW, moderate weather.

British gravitational system of units

A system of units used by engineers in the English-speaking world, 19TH–20TH C, having the same relation to the foot-pound-second system that the meter–kilogram-force–second system has to the meter-kilogram-second system. Since engineers deal with forces, instead of mass, it's convenient for them to use a system that has as its base units length, time, and force, instead of length, time and mass. In the British gravitational system, the three base units are the foot, the second, and the *pound-force.*

Pound-force. A unit of force, approximately the force which a mass of 1 pound exerts on whatever it is resting on on the Earth; that is, the weight of a mass of 1 pound. Abbr, lbf. The weight of a mass of 1 pound, however, varies from place to place; it weighs less on the equator than at the poles, and is lighter at high altitudes than at sea level. The pound-force, however, is unvarying; it is defined as the weight (a force!) that a body with a mass of 1 pound would exert at a location where the acceleration due to gravity was exactly 32.1740 feet per second per second, which is about the value at sea-level at a latitude of 45°. So 1 pound-force = 32.1740 poundals. Later a standard value of 9.80665 meters per second per second was adopted for the acceleration due to gravity, and 1 pound-force ≈ 4.4482216152605 newtons.

Slug. The unit of mass, also called the *geepound.* One slug is a mass such that 1 pound-force acting on it will produce an acceleration of 1 foot per second per second. This unit, rather than the pound (mass!), is used as the system's unit of mass in order to make the system coherent. The slug was never used much outside of textbooks, which in one respect was unfortunate because using either it or the poundal would have helped to dispel the confusion between the pound as mass and the pound as force. One slug = 32.1740 pounds (mass!) ≈ 14.594 kilograms.

See also ☛foot-pound-second system of units.

| British thermal unit | A unit of energy, usually referred to as a Btu (pronounced "bee tee u"). Symbol, Btu, but in Britain it was formerly abbreviated B.Th.U.. Originally defined as the quantity of heat needed to raise the temperature of 1 pound av. of air-free water 1°F under a constant pressure of 1 atmosphere, at the temperature at which water is most dense, 39.1°F. One btu is about the amount of energy released when the tip of a kitchen match burns. |

International Table Btu (1956)	≈ 1055.05585262 joules
thermochemical Btu	≈ 1054.350 joules
mean Btu	≈ 1055.87 joules
39°F Btu	≈ 1059.67 joules
59°F Btu	≈ 1054.80 joules
60°F Btu	≈ 1054.68 joules

| bucket | A North American unit used to describe the size of a "sugar bush," a grove of sugar maple trees producing sap from which maple syrup is made, e.g, "a 1000-bucket grove." It is the number of taps that the grove can sustain. |

| bushel | A measure of capacity in the English-speaking world, dating from the Norman Conquest. In the USA, the bushel is a unit of dry capacity = 2,150.42 cubic inches ≈ 35.239 liters. It derives from the Winchester bushel as confirmed by William III in 1696 (8 and 9 William III c. 22 s 9 and s 45.): "Every round bushel with a plain and even bottom being eighteen inches and a half wide throughout and eight inches deep shall be esteemed a legal Winchester bushel according to the standard in His Majesty's Exchequer." The U.S. bushel has no relation to the U.S. gallon. A heaped bushel for apples of 2,747.715 cubic inches was established by the U.S. Court of Customs Appeals on Feb. 15, 1912, in United States *v* Weber (no. 757). A heaped bushel = 1 1/4 stricken bushels is also recognized. |

In British imperial measure, 1824–1976, the bushel = 8 gallons ≈ 36.3687 liters. By the act establishing imperial measure, (Act 5 George IV chap. 74), from May 1, 1825 the bushel was to be eight gallons each "containing ten pounds Avoirdupois of distilled water weighed in air at the temperature of sixty-two degrees of Fahrenheit's thermometer the barometer being at thirty inches." That made the bushel 2218.19 cubic inches.

SIZES

In the UK, the Winchester bushel was specifically abolished by the Acts of 4 and 5 William IV c 49 (1834) and 5 and 6 William IV c 63 (1835). Nonetheless, it continued to be used for such purposes as customary procedures for setting land rents.

buttons

In the USA, buttons are now often sized by the diameter in inches. In an older system still used by button makers but rarely by those who sew garments, the diameters of buttons are given in "lines." There are 40 lines to the inch; thus a line 20 button is half an inch in diameter. (The line also survived as the measure for watchglasses in the USA long after it was no longer used elsewhere.)

These lines should not be confused with the premetric French unit, the *ligne*, which was one-twelfth of a *pouce* or ≈ 2.2558 mm, almost 4 times larger.

buttonholes

As a rule of thumb, the length of a buttonhole should equal the diameter of the button plus the button's greatest thickness. The best way of determining buttonhole length, however, is to make a slit in a scrap of cloth or paper and try buttoning the button through it.

byte

A unit of information in a binary digital computer = 8 ☛bits. An example of a byte, written as a binary number, would be "10101011." A byte is enough to store, for example, any whole number from 0 to 255, or a single character of the alphabet in the ASCII code.

Although the term was first used to refer to units of 6 bits, 7 bits and other values, depending on the machine, it was inexorably drawn to a value that was a power of 2. According to Eric Raymond (in his wonderful *New Hacker's Dictionary*), the byte began to become standardized at 8 bits around 1956, and was fixed at 8 bits by the introduction of the IBM/360 computer.

The kilobyte (symbol, K, KB, or Kb) is not equal to 1,000 bytes, but rather to 1,024 (i.e., 2^{10}) bytes. Present-day electronic computers represent information in binary notation; the signals can have only one of two values. The number that is 1,024 in decimal notation is a round number in binary notation, 10,000,000,000. The decimal number 1,000 (which is 111,110,100 in binary) is not.

The term megabyte (symbol, MB, M or Mb) is used with three different meanings. Usually, it = 1,024 kilobytes, or 1,048,576 bytes (= 2^{20}). A few vendors of hard disc drives like to consider one megabyte = 1,000,000 bytes, a definition which is easier to understand and incidentally makes their drives look bigger. Finally, in giving the capacity of floppy disks, the megabyte has been taken to be 1,000 kilobytes.

Half of a byte, four bits, is sometimes called a nibble (sometimes spelled nybble), but this was never a common term.

50

caballería

A unit of land area in Texas, South America, and the Caribbean, 16TH–20TH C. The first law granting land in the Americas to Europeans was a decree of Ferdinand V on June 18, 1513, by which Ferdinand extended to the New World a system Castile had already used for conquered areas in Europe: retired foot soldiers were given a *peonia* of land, and retired cavalrymen a *caballería* ("caballería" means cavalry). A caballería was four to five times the size of a peonia; the actual area of a peonia or caballería depended on the productivity of the land and the merit of the recipient. One caballería = 12 *fanegas*. Later a caballería was sometimes thought of as a rectangle 552 × 1104 varas.

In Texas, a *caballería* is 107.948 acres. In South America and the Caribbean it is generally around 45 hectares, but is as large as 75.46 ha in the Dominican Republic, and as small as 11.29 ha in Ecuador and 13.420 ha in Cuba.

cable

1) In the USA, 19TH–20TH C, a unit of length, = 240 yards ≈ 219.456 meters.   2) In the UK, a unit of length used on ships, = 200 yards ≈ 182.88 m.

calendar

The central problem all earthly calendar makers face is how to combine three incommensurable intervals: the time from sunrise to sun-

51

rise, the time from full moon to full moon, and the time from summer to summer. Because day, month, and year have no common factor, all calendars are approximations requiring periodic correction.

It doesn't take long for errors to accumulate. For example, suppose a calendar uses a 365-day year. In four years, the seasons will be one day off; in 100 years, 25 days; and in 730 years winter will arrive when summer used to. If we make the year 366 days, the seasons will reverse in only 244 years, but instead of winter coming later each year it will be earlier.

The quality of fit of the calendar to the solar year was of more than astronomical interest in pre-modern times. In regions with pronounced seasons, a farmer prospers who plants as early as possible but after the last killing frost. If the traditional date of the last killing frost shifts in relation to the equinoxes, something is wrong; an error of 25 days would be disastrous. Wandering seasons negate the whole purpose of the calendar to some of its users.

The day is the basic unit in all calendars, since it is very hard to legislate a change in the length of the day. Although the month is obviously derived from the cycle of the moon's phases, one such cycle (a lunar month, or lunation) is about 29½ days. If the year is taken to be 12 lunar months, it will have 354 days, 11.4 days shorter than a solar year. Month and year have been reconciled in one of two ways: One approach is to make the months longer than a lunar month, as our civil calendar does, or add an extra 11- or 12-day month. The date of the full moon then falls where it may, but in July it will always be summer. The other approach keeps the lunar month (as, for example, the Islamic calendar does), so that the full moon falls on the same day of the month every month, but the relation between months and seasons changes each year. Herders and cultures in the aseasonal tropics have often preserved calendars with accurate months (lunations), while planters in the temperate zones have gravitated toward accurate solar years.

The Roman and Julian Calendars

The first Roman calendar appears to have been lunar, with ten months: Martius (31), Aprilis (30), Maius (31), Iunius (30), Quintilis (31), Sextilis (30), September (30), October (31), November (30), December (30). According to tradition, in 509 BC the king Numa Pompilius replaced that calendar with one more like that of the Greeks: a year of 12 months and 355 days. Those months which had 30 days in the old calendar now had 29. The two added months were Januarius (29), named after the god of gates, added to the beginning of the year and, Februarius (28), added to the end. In 450 BC, Januarius was moved from before Martius to before Februarius, which established the order of months we still use.

The year, however, began on Martius 1, the day on which new consuls were inaugurated. In 154 BC a rebellion broke out in Spain. To avoid changing consuls in the middle of a war, New Year's was shifted up two months, to January 1, beginning January 1, 153 BC.

Since the total number of days in a year of months was less than a solar year, an extra month 22 or 23 days long, called *mensis intercalaris*, was added every two to four years after Februarius 23, followed by the last five days of Februarius. This addition had to be called for by the chief priest, the Pontifex Maximus.

The problem with the Roman calendar was that it was highly adjustable, like the present-day Jewish calendar, but unlike the Jewish calendar, the adjusters did not show any sense of astronomical discipline. Politicians, for example, sometimes succeeded in lengthening months to prevent their term of office from expiring at a critical point, or the chief priest failed to add the necessary *mensis intercalaris* at the right time. The result was that by the time Julius Caesar overthrew the Republic the calendar was three months out of whack with the seasons. With the advice of the Alexanderian astronomer Sosigenes, Caesar instituted the following reforms in 46 BC:

✓ A one-time addition of 67 days between November and December in 46 B.C. This unique 445-day year returned the vernal equinox to its traditional date, March 25.

✓ Beginning January 1, 45 BC, the length of the year was to be 365 1/4 days. The months were lengthened; most got their present number of days. The fractional day was provided by adding an extra day every four years, inserted where the *mensis intercalaris* had been, that is, between February 23 and 24, which is why on leap year we add our extra day to February.

In 44 BC the month Quintilis was renamed Julius in honor of the calendar reformer. At some later point the month Sextilis was lengthened by one day and renamed Augustus, in honor of Augustus Caesar, probably by the consuls Asinius Gallus and Marcius Censorinus. Later attempts by the emperors Caligula and Domitian to name months after themselves were annulled after their deaths.

Gregorian Calendar

The Julian calendar assumes the solar year is 365.25 days long, but it is actually more like 365.2422 days, about 11 minutes 14 seconds shorter. In 384 years the annual eleven-minute error adds up to about three days, and to about 7.8 days in a millennium. By the 8TH C people were already noticing that the vernal equinox was coming early. By the 13TH C the error was more than seven days and Roger Bacon was urging reforms on the pope.

Three hundred years later Pope Gregory XIII decided to do something about it, enlisting the help of Aloysius Lilius (?–1576) and

Christopher Clavius (1537–1612). By a papal bull of February 24, 1582, Gregory made the following reforms:

✓ Some of the accumulated error was removed by making the day following October 4, 1582, October 15. This change was not enough to return the vernal equinox to March 25, where it had been in Caesar's time, but rather to March 21, where it had been during the Council of Nicea in AD 325. That Council had fixed the date of Easter in relation to the vernal equinox (the first Sunday after the 14th day of the moon that occurs on or after March 21).

✓ To prevent error from accumulating in the future Gregory and his advisors added a new rule: no century year is a leap year if it is not evenly divisible by 400. This rule leads to alternately eight and seven fewer leap days per millennium than in the Julian calendar, and made the calendar agree with earth's revolution about the sun within one day in 3,323 years.

In modern times an additional rule has been suggested: years evenly divisible by 4,000 (AD 4000, AD 8000, etc) will not be leap years. Such a change would make the Gregorian calendar correct to one day in 20,000 years.

The Gregorian calendar was adopted in 1582 by the Italian states, Spain, Portugal, and France (where the day after December 9, 1582 was December 20), and a year later by the Catholic states of Germany. The Protestant states held out. In 1700, the imperial diet at Regensberg adopted the Gregorian calendar for the Protestant states of Germany; Denmark adopted it at about same time; and Sweden, which had briefly adopted it much earlier, readopted in 1753. Many states that now use this calendar did not adopt it until the 20TH C.

At first, the difference between the Julian and Gregorian calendars was 10 days; 1700, however, was a leap year in the Julian calendar but not in the Gregorian, increasing the difference to 11 days. Dates in the Julian calendar that occur after the introduction of the Gregorian calendar are termed "old style." The initials "O.S." appearing after a date indicate it is in the Julian calendar.

In Great Britain, the Gregorian calendar was adopted in 1751 by Act of Parliament. To make a day's date the same in Britain as in its neighbors, the day following September 2, 1752, was made September 14, 1752. Riots broke out in London as people protested the government's snatching two weeks from their allotted threescore and ten. The same act made January 1 the first day of the year; it had been March 25. (In Scotland the year had begun on January 1 since perhaps 1600.)

A second wave of adoptions occurred in Eastern Europe in the early 20TH C: Bulgaria, April 1, 1916; Russia, February 14, 1918; Yugoslavia, 1919; Romania, 1919; Greece, February 1923; Turkey, December 26,

1925. In Asia, Japan adopted the Gregorian calendar on January 1, 1873, and China in 1949.

Jewish Calendar

The current Jewish calendar is only a few centuries older than the Gregorian, though it incorporates many ancient elements. The names of the months are mostly Babylonian; they were all established by the 1ST C AD. Its complexity is almost overwhelming; it seems a full-employment program for those responsible for ascertaining when significant religious events should occur, which is the calendar's primary purpose.

The era is that of the biblical Creation, which is placed in 3761 BC; since the 9TH C AD the years in this calendar have been styled A.M., for *anno mundi* (*lizira* or *libri' ath 'olam*). The year consists of 12 lunar months of either 30 days (*male*, a full month) or 29 days (*haser*, a defective month). Two of the months vary in length from year to year. The 11-day difference between 12 lunar months and one solar year is compensated for by inserting an additional 30-day month in the 3rd, 6th, 8th, 11th, 14th, 17th, and 19th years of a 19-year cycle (derived from the 19-year lunar cycle). Consequently the number of days in a year varies from year to year.

Types of Years in the Jewish Calendar Number of days in the month						
	common years			leap years		
Month	complete (*shelema*)	normal (*sedura*)	defective (*hasera*)	complete (*shelema*)	normal (*sedura*)	defective (*hasera*)
Tishri	30	30	30	30	30	30
Heshvan	30	30	29	30	30	29
Kislev	30	29	29	30	29	29
Tebet	29	29	29	29	29	29
Shebet	30	30	30	30	30	30
*Adar**	29	29	29	30	30	30
II Adar or *Veadar*	—	—	—	29	29	29
Nisan	30	30	30	30	30	30
Iyyar	29	29	29	29	29	29
Sivan	30	30	30	30	30	30
Tammuz	29	29	29	29	29	29
Ab	30	30	30	30	30	30
Elul	29	29	29	29	29	29
days in year	355	354	353	385	384	383

*Called *I Adar* in leap years.

By altering the pattern of years within the 19-year cycle, it is possible to prevent holidays from falling on days that would be religiously unacceptable. For example, the Day of Atonement (Yom Kippur, Tishri 10) must not fall on a Friday or Sunday, so New Year's (Rosh Hashana, Tishri 1) must not fall on a Wednesday or Friday. These adjustments are made, however, in such a fashion that it all comes out in the wash at the end of every 19-year cycle, and over the long haul the seasons remain in place.

calorie

Various units of energy, specifically defined for heat flows. In principle, the amount of heat necessary to raise the temperature of 1 gram of water 1°C at a pressure of 1 atmosphere. Abbr, cal.

A problem arises because the amount of heat required differs depending on the initial temperature of the water. Different choices of starting temperature have led to different calories, usually identified by subscripts. The most common calorie, in which the water temperature is raised from 14.5°C to 15.5°C, is sometimes called the 15°C calorie. Abbr, cal_{15}. One cal_{15} = 4.1855 joules, a value adopted by CIPM in 1950.

Other calories have been based on initial temperatures of 0°C, 3.5°C, and 19.5°C. Still another definition made the calorie 1/100th of the quantity of heat needed to raise the temperature of a gram of water from 0°C to 100°C. The values produced by the various definitions differ by somewhat less than 1%.

The thermochemical calorie (cal_{th}), used in some branches of chemistry, is defined as = 4.184 joules.

The International Steam Table calorie. In 1929, the International Steam Table Conference (London) defined the international calorie as 1/860 of the international watt hour, = 4.1860 international joules. The adoption of the absolute system of electrical units changed these values to 1/859.858 watt hours ≈ 4.18674 joules. At present, one cal_{IT} = 4.1868 joules (Fifth International Conference on the Properties of Steam, London, 1956).

An associated unit is the *Celsius heat unit* (abbr, CHU) = 453.59237 cal_{IT}, which is about the quantity of heat needed to raise the temperature of a one-pound mass of pure water 1°C at a pressure of one atmosphere.

The dieter's calorie. All of the above calories are based on heating one gram of water, and are sometimes called the "gram-calorie". The calorie used by physiologists and dieters is based on raising the temperature of a kilogram of water 1°C, and is about a thousand times bigger. It is called a "kilogram calorie" or kilocalorie, = 1,000 cal_{15}, and abbreviated "C," capitalized to distinguish it from the lowercase "c" for the other calories.

Activity	Kilocalories per hour
Sleeping, men over 40	66
Lying fully relaxed	72
Sleeping, men aged 15–20	78
Sitting at rest	102
Sitting writing	108
Standing relaxed	108
Riding in an automobile	120
Standing, peeling potatoes	126
Sitting typing	138
Polishing	144
Seated, playing musical instrument	174
Seated, taking lecture notes	180
Slow walking	230
Standing, ironing	260
Standing, scrubbing	280
Rowing for pleasure	300
Playing golf	320
Cycling, 8–11 mph	340
Playing table tennis	350
Gardening, standing	350
Chopping wood	370 – 450
Playing tennis	380
Baseball pitching	390
Shoveling sand	410 – 460
Swimming crawl at 1 mph	420
Army drill	430
Trotting on horseback	430 – 590
Cycling rapidly, own pace	500
Swimming backstroke at 1 mph	500
Playing soccer	500
Digging	530
Skiing 3 mph on level	540
Climbing stairs, 116 steps/min	590
Cycling in race (100 miles in 4.4 hr)	590
Cycling at 13.2 mph	600
Fencing	630
Playing squash	630
Rowing, two oars, 3.5 mph	660
Galloping on horseback	680
Playing basketball	680
Sculling, 97 strokes/min	760
Wrestling	780
Marching at double time	800

| Endurance marching | 890 |
| Harvard Step Test | 970 |

candela

The unit of luminous intensity in SI, one of the base units. Roughly speaking, it is used to measure how bright a beam of light is. Symbol, cd. Since October 1979, the candela has been "the luminous intensity, in a given direction, of a [light] source that emits monochromatic radiation of frequency 540×10^{12} hertz and that has a radiant intensity in that direction of 1/683 ☞watt per ☞steradian."

The candela began life as the "new candle" (*bougie nouvelle*), a unit defined by the International Commission on Illumination (CIE) and the CIPM before 1937, but because of World War II the CIPM did not promulgate it until 1946 ("the brightness of the full radiator at the temperature of solidification of platinum is 60 new candles per square centimeter"). This definition was ratified by the NINTH CGPM (1948), which changed the name to candela.

In 1967 the 13TH CGPM altered the definition to correct possible ambiguities, and the candela became "the luminous intensity, in the perpendicular direction, of a surface of 1/600,000th square meter of a blackbody at the temperature of freezing platinum [2042°F] under a pressure of 101,325 newtons per square meter." The same session (Resolution 7) formally did away with the name "new candle."

Eventually the 1967 definition was discarded because it was too hard to realize in practice. While the technology of photometry was struggling with molten platinum at the temperature at which it solidifies, great advances were being made in radiometry. In 1977, the CIPM adopted a definition relating photometric and radiometric quantities: the spectral luminous efficacy of monochromatic radiation of frequency 540×10^{12} hertz would, by definition, be 683 lumens per watt. In October 1979, noting that "despite the notable efforts of some laboratories there remain excessive divergences between the results of realizations of the candela based upon the present blackbody primary standard" (i.e., some people's candelas were bigger than other people's), the 16TH CGPM (Resolution 3) turned the 1979 equivalence around, adopting the definition of the candela first given above.

candle

One of several obsolete units of luminous intensity. In the English-speaking world it was the luminous intensity of an actual standardized candle, made from spermaceti, 7/8" in diameter, weighing 1/6th of a troy pound, and burning at a rate of 120 ☞grains per hour. But the extent of the variation in light output from such a source became significant as precision improved, and whales becoming scarce, the candles were eventually replaced by various standardized lamps burning a pure gas.

The *international candle*, adopted in 1909, is one lumen per steradian, 1/60th of the intensity of one square centimeter of a blackbody radiator at the temperature at which molten platinum solidifies. It is sometimes known by its French name, *bougie decimale* (decimal candle).

candle (English) = 0.96 international candle
candle (German) = 0.95 international candle
candle (pentane) = 1.00 international candle

The candle has been superseded by the ☞candela.

candles

Candle sizes are not standardized by any official body; still, most new candlesticks have holes 7/8" or 1/2" in diameter.

Tapers are candles with the shape characteristic of hand-dipped candles. The larger tapers have a base 7/8" or 9/16" in diameter, and may be as short as 6" and as long as 18". They are sometimes referred to as "dinner candles." A smaller size, often called tapers to distinguish them from dinner candles, are 10" long with a 1/2" base (metric, 260 mm × 12 mm). Still smaller are *flower tapers*, which are usually 12 3/8" long with a 1/4" base. Flower tapers are the candles inserted into flower arrangements and held by the frog that holds the flowers; they are the only candles intended to be burned while tilted.

Candelabra candles are cylindrical; otherwise they came in sizes like those of the larger tapers.

Pillars are thick and usually cylindrical, though sometimes tapered with straight sides, or with a hexagonal cross section. Diameters are usually in whole inches, 2", 3", or 4". Some of these are designed to "exfoliate," an effect some people enjoy in which the unburned sides of the candle soften and droop, forming "angel wings." For best results, such candles should only be burned for about three hours at a time. If the candle comes with this advice, it is an exfoliating type.

Plumber's candles are the inexpensive utility candles kept on hand for blackouts (but which should not be lit in case of earthquake, because of the possibility of broken gas mains!).

Jar lites. Found in taverns and cathedrals, these candles are made or burned in glass containers. The larger votive candles are made to burn for at least 6 1/2 days and contain about 600 grams of wax. It is difficult to make satisfactory votive candles in containers with an inner diameter of more than about 3".

Of course, novelty candles exist in as many sizes and forms as their makers can imagine.

cans

The can industry describes the dimensions of cylindrical cans by three-digit numbers: the first digit is the number of whole inches, and the second two the number of sixteens. So, for example, a 303 × 407 can would be 3 3/16" in diameter and 4 7/16" high.

The table below lists some common can sizes.

Traditional name	Capacity in fluid oz.	Dimensions in inches	Can industry
202	4	2 1/8 × 2 7/8	202 × 214
Tall 202	5	2 1/8 × 3 1/2	202 × 308
8-Z short	7	2 11/16 × 3	211 × 300
No. 1	10	2 11/16 × 4	211 × 400
Tall no. 1	12	2 11/16 × 4 13/16	211 × 413
300	14	3 × 4 7/16	300 × 407
303	16	3 3/16 × 4 3/8	303 × 406
Short no. 2	14	3 7/16 × 3 3/8	307 × 306
No. 2	19	3 7/16 × 4 9/16	307 × 409
Tall no. 2	24	3 7/16 × 5 9/16	307 × 509
No. 2 1/2	28	4 1/16 × 4 11/16	401 × 411
No. 3	32	4 1/4 × 4 7/8	404 × 414
Tall no. 3	46	4 1/4 × 7	404 × 700
2 lb coffee	66	5 1/8 × 6 1/2	502 × 608
No. 10, same as 3-lb coffee can	105	6 3/16 × 7	603 × 700

Cans of milk were formerly sealed by drops of lead, a process abandoned in the 1980s because of lead's toxicity. Sweetened condensed milk cans now hold 14 ounces av. (formerly 15); of evaporated milk 5 or 12 fluid ounces (formerly 6 or 14 1/2).

carat

For the measure of the fineness of gold, see ☞karat.

A unit of mass used for weighing precious stones, currently = 200 milligrams ≈ 3.086 grains. Adopted by the FOURTH CGPM in 1907, for "diamonds, fine pearls, and precious stones." Sometimes called the *metric carat*. In the USA, the value 205.3 milligrams was used prior to July 1, 1913; thereafter the metric carat has been used. In the United Kingdom, the metric carat was made legal for precious stones and pearls by the Weights and Measures of Act of 1963.

The carat is an ancient unit, originally the weight of a seed of the carob tree (*Ceratonia siliqua*, also known as St. John's Bread), from whose pods the familiar chocolate substitute is made. In classical times the seed was known as the siliqua or keratia, and one siliqua = three barley corns = four wheat grains. Twelve hundred years later, Johnson's *Dictionary* (1755) defined a carat as four grains.

By the middle of the 19TH C various values were being used for the carat as a measure of the mass of precious stones: in Amsterdam 205.1 milligrams, in London 205.3 mg, in Lisbon and Rio de Janeiro (the *quilate*) 199.1 mg, in Venice 207.0 mg, and so on. In 1877, principal merchants in the gem trade in London, Paris, and Amsterdam met and agreed on a standard value of 205 milligrams.

Carnegie unit

In the USA, a unit of credit for college preparatory coursework, established in 1907 under the aegis of the Carnegie Foundation for the Advancement of Teaching, implementing recommendations of committees of the National Education Association. To persuade colleges to require 14 of these units from every candidate for admission, the Foundation let it be known that colleges that did not require the units would not be eligible to participate in a pension program the Foundation was then setting up for college faculty.

Each unit represents a year's course in a recognized subject, normally a minimum of about 130 hours of instruction. In the 1990s the Carnegie unit came under severe criticism as a "babysitting unit," since it is largely based on time spent, rather than mastery of any defined course content.

carpets

Wall-to-wall carpeting is now sold in widths from 12' to 15' ("broadloom" simply means the rug is at least 12' wide).

Most of the numbers given to describe carpet's construction concern how densely yarn has been packed into the pile, which, other things being equal, determines service life.

Pitch is the number of warp lines of yarn in a 27-inch width. Twenty-seven inches was a standard width for woven carpeting in the 19TH C. The greater the pitch the better.

Stitch rate, which applies to tufted carpet, is the number of yarn tufts in one lengthwise inch. Sharply bending the carpet reveals the tufts for counting. Seven to eight tufts per inch is pretty good; three or four is poor. The distance between the centers of tufts is called the gauge.

Pile height is measured from the surface of the backing to the top of the pile. High pile does not wear as well as low pile, but a high-density high pile wears better than a low-density one, because the fibers support one another. Modern heat-set twists, used on synthetic yarns, are also helpful.

The amount of yarn in a carpet can be summed up by its weight, usually given as ounces per square yard. The *total weight* includes everything, backing and all. Since the backing may include heavy coatings that might not influence the wearability of the carpet, a much better measure of quality is *face weight*. Unfortunately, many stores and manufacturers now refuse to reveal the face weight. A face weight of 40 to 50 ounces is a serviceable carpet, although lower face weights might be appropriately used in low-traffic areas such as bedrooms. Below 30 ounces, beware.

Area Rugs

A figure of merit for oriental rugs is the number of knots per square inch. An ordinary rug may have 50 knots per square inch, and a fine rug 250 or so. Rugs with as many as 600 knots per square inch are known; though they are beautiful objects, it is hard to admire them without recalling that tying such rugs destroyed the eyesight of many children.

The knot density of modern Chinese rugs is sometimes described in lines. A 90-line rug has 8,100 knots per square foot, the "90" being the square root of the number of knots in a square foot. Dividing by 144 square inches in a square foot shows that 90-line is equivalent to 56.25 knots per square inch.

cental

A unit of mass = 100 lbs av ≈ 45.359237 kg. The term was mostly used in Britain (where a hundredweight = 112 pounds), and was first suggested in the Report of 1841 by the commission studying how to proceed after the fire that destroyed the UK's prototypes. By 1859 the cental was in use for grain. An Order in Council in 1879 legalized it. With many other units, it had to be abandoned when the United Kingdom became part of the European Economic Community (Statutory Instrument No. 484, 1978).

centimeter-gram-second systems

The principal systems of units used in scientific work, LATE 19TH–EARLY 20TH C. Abbr, cgs or CGS or cm-gm-sec. Endorsed by a committee of the British Association in 1872, gradually superseded by meter-kilogram-second-ampere (MKSA) systems, and finally rendered obsolete in 1960 by the CGPM's adoption of SI, which is a MKSA system. Many cgs units, however, are still in daily use; for example, in the controversy concerning the effect of electromagnetic fields on health, the field strengths have almost always been reported in milligauss.

Besides the centimeter, gram, and second, some of the other nonelectromagnetic units in cgs systems were:

Dyne. The unit of force, 1 dyne being the force which imparts an acceleration of 1 centimeter per second squared to a body having a mass of 1 gram, Symbol, dyn. In SI units, one dyne = 10^{-5} newton.

Erg. The unit of work, 1 erg being the work done by a force of 1 dyne acting through a distance of 1 centimeter, = 10^{-7} joules. Symbol, erg.

Barye. A unit of pressure, 1 dyne per square centimeter. Never a common term. One barye = 0.1 pascal.

Phot. The unit of illuminance. Symbol, ph. One phot = 10,000 lux.

Poise. The unit of absolute viscosity. Symbol, P. Viscosity is the property of a liquid that resists flowing, sort of internal friction; for example, molasses has a higher viscosity than water. One poise is the viscosity of a fluid that requires a shearing force of 1 dyne moving a square centimeter area of either of two parallel layers of fluid 1 centimeter apart with a velocity of 1 centimeter per second relative to the other layer, the space between the layers being filled with the fluid. One poise = 0.1 pascal-second.

This unit was defined around 1924, and named for Jean Louis Marie Poiseuille (1799–1869). Its pronunciation reflects its French origin:

not like the poise in "she showed great poise," but pwäz. It is almost always encountered as the *centipoise*.

Stokes. The unit of kinematic viscosity. Symbol, St (formerly S). A fluid with a dynamic viscosity of 1 poise and a density of 1 gram per cubic centimeter has a kinematic viscosity of 1 stokes. In SI units, 1 stokes = 1 centimeter squared per second.

The mechanical units are the same in all cgs systems. Length, mass, and time, however, are not sufficient to define electric and magnetic quantities; something else must be included. The different cgs systems arose from differing choices of a fourth base unit.

The cgs electric units were much too small for practical use in engineering, which lead to the creation of the international system of units (not be confused with SI!), which is not a cgs system. All of these systems share certain names, such as volt and ampere, but with different meanings. To avoid confusion, the prefix "ab-" was often added to cgs electromagnetic units (especially by Americans) and "stat-" to cgs electrostatic system units. Many workers did not use the special names, but simply referred to, for example, the "esu unit of charge" or "the emu unit of resistance."

CGS Electrostatic System of Units

Symbol, esu. Imagine two bodies with electric charges, Q_1 and Q_2 respectively. Coulomb's Inverse Square Law for electrostatic charges describes the force between them:

$$F \propto \frac{Q_1 Q_2}{\varepsilon r^2}$$

where F is the force, r is the distance (which has to be considerably larger than the bodies themselves), and epsilon is what is called the permittivity of the medium between the charges.

In the cgs system force is in dynes. The dyne has the dimensions $\frac{g \cdot cm}{s^2}$, and r is in centimeters. To define the unit of charge in the cgs electrostatic system of units, ε (epsilon) is disposed of by defining its value as equal to 1 for a vacuum. Inserting the other dimensions into Coulomb's law, the dimensions of the unit of charge are seen to be:

$$\frac{\sqrt{g \cdot cm^3} \text{ (unit of } \varepsilon)}{s}$$

This unit is referred to as the esu unit of charge, the electrostatic unit of charge, or the statcoulomb. All the the other esu units are defined in terms of the unit of charge and the centimeter, gram, and second.

Statampere. The unit of electric current. One statampere is a flow of charge equal to 1 statcoulomb per second, $\approx 3.3356 \times 10^{-10}$ ampere. Abbr, statA.

Statvolt. The unit of electric potential and electromotive force. One statvolt is the potential difference between two points such that the work needed to transport 1 statcoulomb of electric charge from one to the other is equal to 1 erg, $\approx 2.9979 \times 10^2$ volts. Symbol, statV.

Statfarad. The unit of capacitance. One statfarad is the capacitance of a capacitor such that a charge of 1 statcoulomb increases the potential difference between its plates by 1 statvolt, $\approx 1.1126 \times 10^{-12}$ farad. Symbol, statF.

Stathenry. The unit of inductance. One stathenry is the self-inductance of a circuit or the mutual inductance between two circuits if there is an induced electromotive force of 1 statvolt when the current is changing at a rate of 1 statampere per second, $\approx 8.9876 \times 10^{11}$ henry. Symbol, statH.

Statmho. The unit of conductance, admittance, and susceptance. One statmho is the conductance between two points in a conductor when a constant potential difference of 1 statvolt applied between the points produces in the conductor a current of 1 statampere, the conductor not being the source of any electromotive force, $\approx 1.1126 \times 10^{-12}$ mho. Symbol, stat℧. Also called statsiemens (statS).

Statohm. The unit of resistance, reactance, and impedence. One statohm is the resistance between two points in a conductor when a constant potential difference of 1 statvolt applied between the points produces in the conductor a current of 1 statampere, the conductor not being the source of any electromotive force, $\approx 8.9876 \times 10^{11}$ ohm. Symbol, statΩ.

Statweber. The unit of magnetic flux. One statweber is the magnetic flux which, linking a circuit of one turn, produces in it an electromotive force of 1 statvolt as it is reduced to zero at a uniform rate in 1 second, $\approx 2.9979 \times 10^2$ weber. Symbol, statWb.

Stattesla. The unit of magnetic flux density. One stattesla is the a magnetic flux density of 1 statweber per square centimeter, $\approx 2.9979 \times 10^6$ tesla. Symbol, statT.

CGS Electromagnetic System of Units
Symbol, emu. The units in this system are formed in manner similar to that of the cgs electrostatic system of units: the unit of electric current was defined using the law that describes the force between current-carrying wires, and the fourth base unit was a unit for the permeability of free space (the magnetic constant, relating the magnetic flux density in a vacuum to the strength of the external magnetic field), again set at 1 for a vacuum.

In the discussion equivalents in SI units are given. Strictly speaking, though, cgs electromagnetic units cannot be converted to SI units, because cgs has three dimensions and SI (for mechanics and electric quantities) has four.

Abampere. The unit of electric current. Symbol, abA. That current which, if maintained in two straight, parallel conductors of infinite length and placed 1 centimeter apart in a vacuum, would produce between these conductors a force of 2 dynes per centimeter of length. One abampere = 10 amperes.

Abcoulomb. The unit of electric charge. Symbol, aC. One abcoulomb of charge passes a point in a circuit in one second when a 1-abampere current is flowing. One abcoulomb = 10 coulombs.

Abfarad. The unit of capacitance. Symbol, aF. One abfarad is the capacitance of a condenser such that a charge of 1 abcoulomb produces a potential difference between the terminals of 1 abvolt. One abfarad = 10^9 farads.

Abhenry. The unit of inductance. Symbol, abH. A circuit has an inductance of 1 abhenry if a current changing at the rate of 1 abampere per second induces an electromotive force of 1 abvolt in it. By the 1940s the use of this unit was being discouraged. One abhenry = 1×10^{-9} henry.

Abmho. The unit of electric conductance. A conductor has a conductance of 1 abmho when there is a potential difference of 1 abvolt between the ends of the conductor while an unvarying current of 1 abampere flows through it. Symbol, ab℧ or ab$(\Omega)^{-1}$. Renamed the absiemens (abbr, aS). One abmho = 10^9 siemens.

Abohm. The unit of electric resistance in the centimeter-gram-second electromagnetic system of units. A conductor has a resistance of 1 abohm when the potential difference between the 2 ends of the conductor is 1 abvolt when a current of 1 abampere flows through it. Symbol, abΩ. One abohm = 10^{-9} ohm.

Maxwell.The unit of magnetic flux. Symbol, Mx. The magnetic flux which, linking a circuit of 1 turn, produces in it an electromotive force of 1 abvolt as it is reduced to zero in 1 second. Sometimes called a *line* or *abweber* (abbr, abW). One maxwell corresponds to 10^{-8} ☞weber in SI.

Gauss. The unit of magnetic flux density. Symbol, Gs, sometimes G, especially in the abbrevaition for milligauss, mG. One gauss is a magnetic flux density of 1 maxwell per square centimeter. One gauss corresponds to 10^{-4} tesla in SI, although strictly speaking, the two units cannot be compared. Usually encountered as milligauss. Sometimes called the abtesla; symbol, abT.

In the first half of the 20TH C, the gauss was frequently also applied to magnetic field strength, because in the cgs electromagnetic system of units magnetic field strength and magnetic flux density are numerically equivalent in free space, since the permeability of free space is set equal to 1. In 1930 the International Electrotechnical Commission created a separate unit for magnetic field strength, the oersted, to eliminate this ambiguity. (Earlier the term oersted had been used for the unit of magnetic circuit reluctance.)

Oersted. The unit of magnetic field strength. Symbol, Oe. In a vacuum, the value of the magnetic intensity in oersteds is equal to the force in dynes exerted on a unit magnetic pole placed at the point. The unit magnetic pole was conceived of as a magnetic pole such that two of them, of the same sign, will repel each other with a force of 1 dyne if they are placed 1 cm apart in a vacuum. Later the oersted was redefined as the strength of the magnetic field at a distance of 1 cm from a straight conductor of infinite length and negligible circular cross section which carries a current of 0.5 abamperes. One oersted corresponds to $\dfrac{1000}{4\pi}$ (≈ 79.577) amperes per meter.

Gilbert. The unit of magnetic potential difference and magnetomotive force in the centimeter-gram-second electromagnetic system of units, the magnetomotive force around a closed path enclosing a surface through which flows a current of $\dfrac{1}{4\pi}$ abamperes. Symbol, Gb. One gilbert ≈ 0.79577 amperes (or ampere-turns).

Stilb. The unit of illuminance. Symbol, sb. One stilb corresponds to 1 candela per square centimeter in SI units.

Abvolt. The unit of electric potential difference and electromotive force. Symbol, abV. The difference in electric potential between two points in a conductor carrying a constant current of 1 abampere when the power dissipated between them is equal to 1 erg per second. One abvolt = 10^{-8} volt.

CGS Gaussian System of Units

Sometimes called the symmetrical system; its only connection with Gauss is the name. The electric units come from the cgs electrostatic system and the magnetic units from the cgs electromagnetic system. A characteristic of this system is that the velocity of light pops up in many of the equations relating electric and magnetic units. By Maxwell's equations, the product of the permittivity of free space and the permeability of free space is the reciprocal of the speed of light (c). As a result, taking the speed of light in cm/sec, the ratio between an "ab-" unit and the corresponding "stat-" unit is c, $\dfrac{1}{c}$, or some power of c.

Generalized CGS Systems

During the period of transition from cgs to MKSA it was frequently necessary to convert data expressed in units in a cgs system to units in MKSA. However, there is no easy way to do this, as the cgs systems are based on three fundamental quantities and the MKSA on four. If a cgs system could be created which had four dimensions and in which each unit in the cgs system corresponded to a unit in the four-dimensional cgs system, and physical quantities had the same numerical values, then values in this "generalized cgs system" could be converted to values in MKSA units by simple conversion factors.

At a meeting in Copenhagen in 1951, the International Union of Pure and Applied Physics approved the introduction of two such generalized cgs systems (Resolution 5):

The CGS-Franklin System of Units

This system is a four-dimensional generalization of the cgs electrostatic system, adding as a fundamental unit a unit of electric charge and electric flux that became known as the franklin (abbr, Fr). Proposed in 1941, the franklin is a special name for the electrostatic unit of electric charge in the cgs system for use within the cgs-f system, and is defined as that charge which exerts a force of one dyne on an equal charge at a distance of 1 centimeter in a vacuum. By this definition, 1 franklin = $10/c$ coulombs, where c is the velocity of light in a vacuum in cm/s. One franklin of charge $\approx 3.33564 \times 10^{-10}$ coulombs; of flux, $\approx 2.654 \times 10^{-11}$ coulombs.

The CGS-Biot System of Units

This system is a four-dimensional generalization of the cgs electromagnetic system of units, adding as a fundamental unit a unit of electric current later named the biot (abbr, Bi). The biot is defined as that constant current intensity which, when maintained in two infinitely long parallel rectilinear conductors of negligible cross section, 1 cm apart in a vacuum, would produce a force of 2 dynes per centimeter of length between them. One biot = 10 amperes.

chain

Various units of length used by surveyors in the English-speaking world. In the USA, the unit is Gunter's chain (17TH C–PRESENT), = 1/10 furlong = 22 yards = 66 feet $\approx$ 20.1168 meters. A chain is subdivided into 100 *links*, each 7.92 inches long in the case of Gunter's chain.

The square link is a unit of area, = 62.75 square inches $\approx$ 404.686 square centimeters. A square chain = 4,356 square feet $\approx$ 404.686 square meters.

Gunter's chain had other lengths in Scotland and Ireland; a link was 8.928" in Scotland and 10.08" in Ireland.

A second chain is Ramden's chain = 100 feet. One link of Ramden's is 12 inches. Ramden's chain is sometimes called the "engineer's chain."

Preceding both of these chains was the *Rathborn chain*, 17TH C, which was two perches long (that is, 33 feet), and was subdivided into ten *primes*, each 19.8 inches, and 100 *seconds* or *links*, each 1.98 inches long. It is only of historical interest.

SIZES

champagne

The types of champagne reflect their sugar content, roughly as follows:

Type	Sugar per liter
brut	15 g
extra sec *or* extra dry	12–20 g
sec or dry	17–35 g
demi sec	33–50 g
doux	50 g

Nowadays champagne is bottled in the same sizes as other wines, in the USA, by order of the federal government. The traditional bottle sizes were:

Split	¼ bottle
Pint	½ bottle
Quart	800 mL, the old "bottle of champagne"
Magnum	2 bottles
Jeroboam	4 bottles
Rehoboam	6 bottles
Methuselah	8 bottles
Salamanzar	10, sometimes 12 bottles
Balthazar	16 bottles
Nebucandnezzar	20 bottles

cheese

French

Each label bears two percentages, one marked ES and the other MG. The ES figure gives the percentage of dry matter in the cheese. If a cheese is marked "60% ES" 40% of the cheese, by weight, is water.

"40% MG" means that 40% of the dry matter in the cheese is fat. So, for example, a cheese marked 60% ES, 40% MG would be (0.6 x 0.4 = .24) 24% fat by weight. The fat content of the cheese may also be described in words:

Description	Percentage Fat by Weight
skim-milk cheese	under 20%
cream cheese	40–45%
double-cream cheese	46–60%
triple-cream cheese	60–75%

Swiss

The real name of the holey cheese Americans call "Swiss" is Emmental, when it is really from Switzerland. Genuine Emmental is made in wheels as large as 110 kg, though they can be as small as 85 kg. A typical wheel is 80 to 90 cm in diameter and 17–24 cm thick; mild Emmental is made in a "flat type" 17–19 cm thick and a "high type" 20–24 cm thick.

The large size of the Emmental wheel has affected the production process. To make a single wheel requires about 1,000 liters of milk no more than a half day old (milk from the evening's milking is held overnight and combined with the morning's). To produce 1,000 liters of milk a day requires about 80 Swiss cows, averaging output over the year. Since the Swiss hill farmer typically owns 10 to 15 cows, it takes the output of at least six to eight farms to make Emmental cheese. Cooperation is essential. Farmers deliver their milk to a local village cheese dairy, of which there were about 600 in the 1980s. If anyone delivers off-taste or otherwise poor quality milk, the value of everyone's milk is destroyed. Some of the alpine cooperatives go back to the early Middle Ages.

cholesterol

The results of the finger-prick test indicate "total blood cholesterol." The reading is in milligrams per 100 milliliters. According to generally-accepted guidelines, less than 200 is considered normal, 200 to 239 is borderline, and greater than 240 suggests a high risk of peripheral, cerebral and cardiovascular disease.

More sophisticated tests can determine the composition of the blood cholesterol, which is a mixture of low-density lipoprotein (LDL, the "bad cholesterol" that clogs arteries), high-density lipoproteins (HDL, the "good cholesterol" that protects against coronary artery disease), and very low-density lipoprotein (VLDL).

chopine

In Canada, 20TH C, a unit taken as the equivalent in French to the U.S. dry pint. The chopine is an old and widespread French unit of liquid capacity, first recorded in the 13TH C, ≈ 23.475 cubic *pouces* (of Paris), 0.465 liters. In the *Système Usuel*, 1812 to 1840, the chopine was set = 0.5 liters.

Two chopines make a *pinte*; it was equivalent to the *setier*. The chopine has been especially associated with wine since medieval times, and today in France the word usually means a drink of wine.

chopsticks

Chinese chopsticks are about ten inches long, with blunt ends. Japanese chopsticks are pointed on one end and come "his and hers;" the men's are about eight inches long and the women's seven.

cigars

Cigars are sized by the length in inches (often indicated by the traditional name), the diameter measured by a ring gauge calibrated in 64ths of an inch (that is, a ring gauge 32 cigar has a diameter of 1/2"), and the shape, for which there are a number of traditional names such as Lonsdale, Toro, Churchill, and Robusto (also called Rothschild).

clothing, children's

The table below shows the dimensions in inches of typical ready-to-wear childen's clothing. Toddler hip sizes are measured over diapers. The H and S suffixes in boy's sizes indicate husky and slim sizes.

Size	Height	Chest	Waist	Hip
Toddler				
2T	33	21	20	21–22*
3T	36	22	20 1/2	22–23*
4T	39	23	21	23–24*

*Measured over diapers

Size	Height	Chest	Waist	Hip
Girl				
4	39	23	21	23
5	42	23 1/2	21 1/2	24
6	45	24 1/2	22	25–26
6X	47	25 1/2	22 1/2	26
7	49	26	22 1/2	27
8	52	27	23	28–29
10	55	28	24	30
12	58	30	25	32
14	60	32	26	34
16	62 1/2	33 1/2	27	36

Size	Height	Chest	Waist	Hip
Boy				
4	39	23	21	23
4S		22	19	22
5	42	23 1/2	21 1/2	24
5S		22 1/2	19 1/2	23
6	45	24 1/2	22	25
6S		23 1/2	20	24
7	49	25 1/2	22 1/2	26
7S		24 1/2	20 1/2	25
8	52	27	23	27
8S		25 1/2	21	25 1/2
8H		29 1/2	26	30
10	55	28	24	30
10S		26 1/2	22	26 1/2
10H		30 1/2	27	31
12	59	30	25	29
12S		28 1/2	23	27 1/2
12H		32 1/2	28	32
14	62	32	26	31
14S		30 1/2	24	29 1/2
14H		34 1/2	29	34

Size	Height	Chest	Waist	Hip
16	64	33	27 1/2	33
16S		31 1/2	25 1/2	31 1/2
16H		35 1/2	30 1/2	36
18	66	34 1/2	28 1/2	34 1/2
18S		33	26 1/2	33
18H		37	31 1/2	37 1/2
20	68	36	29 1/2	36
20S		34 1/2	27 1/2	34 1/2
20H		38 1/2	32 1/2	39

clothing, women's

The mix of sizes a store receives is determined by the garment manufacturer. Patterns are laid out to minimize waste of fabric, and pieces for the smaller sizes are more easily fit in here and there than pieces for larger sizes. As a result, when a store marks down an item, the remaining garments are often in smaller sizes.

The distribution of demand for the various sizes varies by income—women in low-income areas buy larger sizes than women in wealthier areas—and by region. Large sizes sell well in Michigan and Minnesota while San Francisco takes more small sizes.

Dresses, Knitwear, Lingerie

The table gives dimensions in inches for ready-to-wear misses and misses petite (P) sizes, which fit most American women. Dimensions for these sizes in patterns are smaller, often by as much as 2".

Bust	Waist	Hip	US	UK	Continental
32 1/2	24	34	2	4	
33–33 1/2	24 1/2–25	35–35 1/2	4	6	
32	24	34 3/4	4P		
34–34 1/2	25 1/2–26	36–36 1/2	6	8	
33	25	35 3/4	6P		
35–35 1/2	26 1/2–27	37–37 1/2	8	10	38
34	26	36 3/4	8P		
36–36 1/2	27 1/2–28	38–38 1/2	10	12	40
35	27	37 3/4	10P		
37 1/2–38	29–29 1/2	39 1/2–40	12	14	42
36 1/2	28 1/2	39 1/4	12P		
39–39 1/2	30 1/2–31	41–41 1/2	14	16	44
38	30	40 3/4	14P		
40 1/2–41	32–32 1/2	42 1/2–43	16	18	46–48
39 1/2	31 1/2	42 1/4	16P		
42 1/2–43	34–34 1/2	45	18	20	50
41 1/2	33 1/2	44 1/4	18P		
44 1/2–45	36–36 !/2	47	20	22	

coherent system of units

A coherent system of units is one in which all units are either base units or are derived from the base units without using any numerical factors other than 1. The International System of Units, SI, is a coherent system. The foot-pound-second system is not; for example, the factor 550 occurs in the definition of the unit of power, horsepower (550 foot-pounds per minute).

cognac

In France, the labelling of cognac is regulated by the Bureau National Interprofessionel du Cognac. In the Bureau's way of counting cognac's age, year zero begins on April 1 of the year after the grapes were grown; year one begins on April 1 of the year after that, and so on. For a cognac to be labelled Three Star, the youngest cognac in the blend must be at least one year old. To be labelled V.S.O.P., it must be at least four years old.

In the USA and the UK, the age of cognac is reckoned in the same way as human birthdays. In the USA, a three-star cognac must be at least two years old. In the UK, a three-star must be at least three years old and (since 1955) a "V.O.," "V.S.O.P.," or "Réserve" is at least four years old and "Extra," "Napoléon," or "Vielle Réserve" is at least five.

comforters

twin	66" × 86"
full	78" × 86" to 81" × 86"
queen	86" × 92" to 86" × 96"
king	102" × 92" to 104" × 96"

Comforter Covers

twin	66" × 90" to 68" × 86" or 66" × 99"
full	81" × 86" to 81" × 90
queen	88" × 92" to 86" × 100"
king	107" × 92" to 104" × 100"

computers

Personal computers have been made in a variety of sizes:

	Weight (lbs)	Typical dimensions (inches)
Tower	any	18" H × 7" W × 18" D
Desktop	any	3.5" or 7" H × 16" W × 16" D
Portable (obsolete)	25+	18" H × 16" W × 7" D
Laptop (obsolescent)	10+	4" H × 13" W × 8.5" D
Notebook	4.5 – 8	2" H × 8.5" D × 11" W
Subnotebook	2 – 4	1.2" H × 8" D × 11" W
Palmtop	1	1" H × 3.4" D × 6.3" W

A keyboard-input computer can't get much smaller than today's palmtop. On traditional keyboards, keys are ¾" (19 mm) apart, center to center. When they get much smaller, typing becomes difficult. (An easy test for key sizes is to place U.S. cents, which are 19 mm in diameter, on the keys. Any overlap reveals how much smaller than standard the keyboard is.)

condoms

Condoms are made in sizes, but they are not standardized, and in the United States the sizing is indicated only obliquely, if at all. According to a spokesperson for Condomania, a retail outlet that stocks as large a variety as might be found anywhere, a few brands carry designations like "slender," "snug fit," or "large," but in many cases a particular model may be larger or smaller than usual without stating so on the packaging. Only the buyer knows for sure.

The ISO specifies condom measuring procedures: the diameter is determined by draping the condom over a ruler.

cord

In the USA, a unit of capacity used for fuelwood, a pile 4 feet deep, 8 feet long, and 4 feet high, = 128 cubic feet ≈ 3.62 cubic meters. A *face cord* is also 8 feet long and 4 feet high, but only 2 feet deep, sometimes even less. A *cord-foot* = 16 cu. ft = ⅛ cord.

cotter pins

American standard cotter pin sizes are in nominal fractional inches, starting at a 1/32" and advancing from 3/64" to 5/32" in steps of 1/64", from 3/16" to 1/4" in steps of 1/32"; from 1/4" to 1/2" in 1/6" steps, and finally 5/8" and 3/4". The sizes below 5/16" are intended to fit a hole 1/64" larger than the pin size; for pins larger than that the pin and hole size are the same.

Lengths are not standardized. The way the length of a cotter pins is measured depends on the style of the points. The measurement begins at the point where the large end meets the hole into which the pin is inserted. It ends at the end of the farthest point of both prongs for pins with miter or bevel point ends; or the farthest point of the longer prong, for hammerlock ends; or in all other styles, to the end of the shorter prong.

coulomb

The unit of electric charge in SI. Symbol, C. The amount of charge transported through any cross section of a conductor in one second by a constant current of one ampere. In equations, the symbol for charge is Q. The dimensions of the coulomb, in terms of base units, are ampere-second.

cradle

The standard size in the USA is 18" by 36". If the cradle has slats, the openings between them should be no wider than 2 3/8".

crib

The standard full-size crib mattress is 27 1/4" by 52", and the crib 30" by 54". Compact and portable cribs are 26 1/4" by 39 1/2". Voluntary standards set by the ASTM and the Juvenile Products Manufacturers Assn.

require that the openings between slats be no greater than 2 3/8", so that babies' heads can't be caught. The cornerposts also may not rise more than 1/16" above the side unless they rise at least 16"; a baby could hang by catching clothing on protruding posts.

Safety standards for cribs assume a child less than 35" high, and under the age of 2. If cribs are used for taller or older babies, they run the risk of falling out. Cribs should not be placed near dangling window cords (to avoid hanging). Mattress covers should not be improvised out of plastic film (to avoid suffocation). Loose teething rails should be replaced.

Crib sheets are 28" × 52" (because nowadays they are usually fitted sheets), and crib blankets, about 45" × 60".

The 30" × 54" size was established before 1900, but at that time a larger size, 40" × 60", was also sold.

crochet hooks

Five-inch long steel crochet hooks are sized from number 00, the largest, to number 15, the smallest, made for use with #250 thread. Steel hooks are usually used with cotton. Bone hooks are 4 1/2" or 5" long and made in sizes 1 through 6.

In all other hooks, "1" or "A" is the smallest size, and manufacturers use a variety of systems. Letter sizes run from A (thinnest) to K, the thickest. The numbered sizes run to 16. Plastic and aluminum hooks are sized in various ways. Wooden hooks are 9" or 10" long, and come in sizes from 7 through 16.

Afghan hooks are distinguished by a lack of a flat fingergrip.

crocodile

A unit of electric potential = 1,000,000 volts. It bites.

curie

A unit of specific activity, used to express the rate at which a unit weight of a radioactive substance decays. Its value was originally set in a fashion that gave radium-226 a specific activity of approximately 1 curie per gram. The unit is usually encountered as the millicurie (a thousandth of a curie) or microcurie (a millionth of a curie).

The curie was first defined (at a Radiology Congress in Brussels in 1910) as the quantity of "radium emanation" (i.e., radon) in equilibrium with 1 gram of radium, which requires some explanation. Imagine some radium is put in a sealed bottle. When a radium atom undergoes radioactive decay, an atom of the radioactive gas radon is produced. Since the gas is also radioactive, eventually the radon atom will decay to produce some third substance. The amount of radon in the bottle will continue to increase until the number of radon-destroying disintegrations per second among the radon atoms in the bottle equals the number of radon-producing disintegrations among the radium atoms in the bottle. The radon and radium are then said to be in equilibrium. In 1930, the International Radium Standard Commission made the curie the equilibrium quantity of any decay product of radium.

In practice, however, workers in the field had begun to use a different definition for the curie, applying it to any radioactive substance. To them, a curie was that quantity of any radioactive substance in which 3.7×10^{10} disintegrations occur each second (which is the number of disintegrations per second in 1 gram of radium). In 1948, the Committee on Standards and Units of Radioactivity of the National Research Council (USA) recommended that this unofficial definition be made the official definition of the curie.

The curie is typically used in working with radioactive isotopes that are used, for example, as tracers. If a substance has a specific activity of 41 millicuries per gram, in a milligram of it will there will be $41 \times \frac{1}{1,000} \times 3.7 \times 10^7$ nuclear disintegrations per second.

The curie has been replaced by an SI unit, the ☛becquerel; 1 curie $= 3.7 \times 10^{10}$ becquerel.

---

cut

1) For glass or asbestos yarn, a yarn number system, in which the cut number is equal to the number of 100-yard lengths needed to make up one pound avoirdupois.   2) A unit of length of wet-spun linen yarn = 300 yards.   3) A standard length of woven cloth, ≈ 60 yards in the unfinished state.   4) A measure of the concentration of shellac solution. The cut number is equal to the number of pounds of shellac flakes dissolved in each gallon of solvent. Prepared liquid shellac is usually three-, four-, or five-pound cut.

darts

Board is made of coiled paper or bristles. It is hung with the center 5' 8" above the floor. The thrower stands behind a toe line 7' 9¼" from the board.

Darts cannot be longer than 12" or weigh more than 50 grams.

dash

The dash is a unit of liquid capacity now mostly met in recipes for mixed drinks. It is usually taken as ⅛ teaspoon, but according to Trader Vic (Victor Berguon), the famous saloonkeeper, in mixed drinks a dash is ⅛ teaspoon when applied to bitters; otherwise (for sugar syrup, orgeat, grenadine, lemon juice, etc.) it is ¼ U.S. fluid ounce = 1½ teaspoons.

day

When Does a Day Begin?
In the Western civil calendar, the day begins at midnight local time. For astronomers, the day begins at noon, which conveniently avoids dividing the night's events between two dates. Astronomers' dates are 12 hours ahead of the civil date; an occurrence on the afternoon of May 8 would have happened on May 9 as astronomers see it.

In many cultures the day begins at sunset, a division observed for religious purposes by Jews and Moslems.

The Length of the Day

The simplest definition of a day's duration, and the one used in most sciences, including astronomy, is that it is 86,400 seconds as the second is defined in SI. The rotation of the earth is not explicitly mentioned in this definition, but of course that is where the "86,400" comes from.

The apparent motion of the sun defines a day for most people. A good way of timing its coming and going (sunsets and sunrises are messy because light is bent more near the horizon) is to imagine a line running from north to south and passing through the point directly overhead. Such a line is called a meridian. Start your stopwatch when the sun crosses the line and stop it at the instant when it next crosses it again (such a crossing is called a transit). You have recorded the length of an *apparent solar day*. If you did this for an entire year, you would find that some days—remember, we are talking about 24-hour days here—are longer than others. To even things out, we can average all the apparent solar days during a year and get the *mean solar day*.

Imagine however, that instead of using the sun, we begin timing when some particular point on the celestial sphere, say the star Sirius, crosses the meridian, and stop when it crosses again. To our surprise, we would find that the duration is shorter than the mean solar day. What we have measured is the *apparent sidereal day*. The sidereal day is subdivided in the same way as the solar day, into 24 *sidereal hours*; each sidereal hour into 60 *sidereal minutes*, and each sidereal minute into 60 *sidereal seconds*. As with solar days, the length of sidereal days is subject to irregularities in the earth's rotation (see below), and so there is both an apparent sidereal day and a *mean sidereal day*.

Actually, the point on the celestial sphere that it used for measuring sidereal time is not a star, but the true vernal equinox, the point where the sun crosses from the southern celestial hemisphere into the northern celestial hemisphere each year. The true vernal equinox is one of two points where two great circles on the imaginary celestial sphere cross: one circle (the true Equator) found by projecting the plane of the earth's equator onto the celestial sphere, and the other (the ecliptic) by similarly projecting the plane of the earth's orbit. The true sidereal day is the time interval between two transits of the true vernal equinox.

In 1991, one mean solar day = 1.00273790935 mean sidereal days. The mean sidereal day is 23 hours, 56 minutes, 4.09054 seconds long, about 3 minutes 55 seconds shorter than the mean solar day. In other words, the stars rise about four minutes earlier each day.

Why do the solar and sidereal day differ? Try this: Place a cent and quarter face up on the table before you, with the penny on the left. Abe and George will be facing each other. The penny represents earth and the quarter the sun. Abe is our observer on the earth; he sees the sun directly in front of him.

Move the penny around the quarter in a clockwise direction. When the penny is above the quarter, the quarter passes out of Abe's view and remains hidden until it appears overhead when the penny is below the quarter. The sun has risen and set, but the penny hasn't rotated at all; Abe has continued to look at the same point on the wall all this time. In other words, the number of solar days in a year is one more than the number of sidereal days.

Because the vernal equinox itself moves (due to the precession of the earth's axis), the sidereal day is not quite the same as the period of earth's rotation with respect to a fixed direction in space. That period is 0.0084 seconds longer than a sidereal day. Oddly enough, this, the true period of the earth's rotation, has no special name or use.

The Erratic Earth

One of the great frustrations of 19TH C astronomy was that it could predict the motion of everything but the Moon. Using Newtonian mechanics, astronomers should have been able to predict exactly where the Moon would be at a given moment, but the predictions were repeatedly wrong. Towards the end of the century, it began to dawn on them that it wasn't the Moon's motion that was irregular, but the clock they were using: the rotation of the earth, which affects the length of the apparent solar and sidereal days and the time assigned to observations. The problem showed up first in studies of the Moon because the Moon moves more quickly against the background of distant stars than anything else. As a result, smaller intervals of time are visible in its motion than in that of slower moving objects. Several different causes for irregularities in the earth's rotation have been discovered:

By the 1860s astronomers generally agreed that over the very long term, days are getting longer as the Earth's spin slows due to tidal friction and the transfer of some of its energy to the moon. The length of the day increases by about 0.001 second each century.

In the 1930s it was discovered that days in March are about 0.001 second longer than days in July. The pattern more or less repeats each year. This seasonal variation is thought to be due to the action of winds and tides.

Recently abrupt, irregular changes of several thousandths of a second have been discovered, which are thought to be due to interactions between motions in the earth's outer layers and core.

day, Julian

Calculating with dates is easier if they are numbered consecutively instead of being identified by year, month and day. In order to number them, some date must be picked as day number one. A proposal made in 1582 by an Italian scholar, Joseph Scaliger (1540–1609), is still the basis of the way we number days.

In Scalinger's time, every year bore three major designations:

1. In any year the days fall on the same day of the week as they did 28 years ago. This is called the *solar cycle*, and is the basis of perpetual calendars.

2. In any year the phases of the moon fall on the same days of the month as they did 19 years ago (the lunar or Metonic cycle). Each year was given a "golden number" that identified its place in this cycle, gold because the number was crucial in establishing the date of Easter and was painted gold in manuscripts. (To find the golden number for any year *anno domine*, add 1 to the year, then divide by 19. Any non-zero remainder is the golden number; a zero remainder indicates a golden number of 19.)

If every year is described by its place in the lunar and solar cycle (e.g., "this year is the 23rd year of the solar cycle and the 7th year of the lunar cycle"), 532 years can pass before two years will have the same description ($19 \times 28 = 532$). This period has been variously called the *Victorian period* (after Victorius of Aquitaine, a 5TH C advisor to Pope Hilarius), the *Dionysian period* (after Dionysius Exiguus, the 6TH C monk who established the Christian era by specifying the year of Christ's birth) and the *Great Paschal period*.

So the 532-year period was old news in Scaliger's time. He added a third cycle, of fiscal instead of astronomical significance:

3. The Roman emperor Diocletian (245?–313?; reigned AD 284–305) established a practice of taking tax censuses every 15 years, a period that became known as the *cycle of indiction*. In the early Middle Ages these cycles were taken to have begun with the accession of Constantine in AD 312, and until the 13TH C were widely used to date correspondence, charters, and other documents—even later for public documents in Spain. (To find the year of indiction for a year *anno domine*, add 3, then divide by 15. A non-zero remainder is the year of indiction; a zero remainder indicates year 15.)

Combining the three cycles ($19 \times 28 \times 15$), Scalinger got a period of 7,980 years in which no two years would have identical numbers for all three cycles. Unlike the 532-year Great Paschal period, this period was long enough to take in all of human history as then conceived, and then some. Scaliger named the period the *Julian period* (after his father, not after Julius Caesar or the Julian calendar) and proposed it be used to keep track of such things as astronomical occurrences.

To set day one of the first Julian period, Scaliger calculated backwards to find the date on which all three of the cycles began on the same day (the beginning of the world?). The day he come up with was January 1, 4713 BC, which conveniently is about the time medieval Christians believed the Creation occurred, and before any historical events one might wish to date. Not surprisingly, Scaliger missed: the three cycles don't start on that date, since, among other complications, the lunar cycle is not exactly 19 years. And Scaliger had no computer.

However, by convention Julian period 1 began on New Year's 4713 BC and will end on January 23, AD 3268.

Today astronomers define the Julian date as the number of days since Greenwich mean noon of 1 January 4713 BC. The Julian date of 1 January 1995 is 2,449,718.5.

The *modified Julian date* is the Julian date described above, less 2,400,000.5, which resets the count to begin at 0h on November 17, 1858, and makes the day begin at midnight instead of noon. Using the modified Julian date for contemporary records saves having to record two digits that will always be the same. Space programs and timekeeping laboratories use modified Julian dates.

Computer programmers are now the most extensive users of the Julian day. The modified Julian day figures in the calculation of monthly bank statements, mortgage payments, and so forth. Unfortunately, some of the algorithms that have been published for computing Julian dates are not accurate.

decibel

One-tenth of a bel. Symbol, dB. A dimensionless unit used to express the ratio between two powers, voltages, currents, or sound intensities. It is 10 times the common logarithm of the power ratio.
See also ☞sound, ☞noise.

degree-day

Two units, the heating degree-day and the cooling degree-day, used by utility companies and heating, ventilating, and air conditioning personnel to express the demand for heating or cooling created by the weather over a given period of time. When the term "degree-day" is not qualified, the heating degree-day is meant.

The concept originated with the observation that demand for natural gas for heating does not pick up until the average daily temperature falls below 65°F. Instead of the average daily temperature, in practice the highest and lowest outside temperatures during a 24-hour day are averaged. The result, subtracted from 65, is the number of heating degree-days for that day. The degree-days for longer periods are found by adding the degree-days for the individual days.

In Great Britain, where interior temperatures are not kept as high as they are in North America, the heating degree-day is based on 60°F instead of 65°F.

The cooling degree-day is less used and less firmly defined. In National Oceanic and Atmospheric Adminstration statistics, the number of cooling degree-days for a day is the average of that day's high and low temperatures minus 65.

derived units

In a system of units, derived units are those that can be defined by algebraic relations between ☞base units. For example, in SI the unit of force, the newton, is a derived unit, because it is defined as meters times kilograms divided by seconds squared, all of which are base units.

diamonds

The largest diamond thus far discovered is the Cullinan, found in 1906 at the Premier Mine in South Africa. It weighed 3,106 ☞carats, about 1 1/3 pounds, and was roughly 2" × 2 1/2" × 4". Cut, it made nine important gems and 96 smaller brilliants, with 9 1/2 carats of leftovers. The largest of the gems, weighing 530.2 carats, was named the Great Star of Africa and mounted in the British Royal Sceptre. The next biggest, 317.4 carats, became part of the Imperial State Crown.

The largest diamond ever found in the United States is the Uncle Sam Diamond, 40.23 carats, found in the "Crater of Diamonds" near Murfreesboro, Arkansas.

In addition to weight, diamonds are sized by the size of the table, the flat surface on the top of a cut diamond. On a round brilliant, table size is measured from opposite corners. On fancy shapes, it is measured from corner to corner across the narrowest diameter; on step cuts, from side to side across the narrowest dimension.

The cut which produces the most fire in a diamond is the Tolkowsky theoretical brilliant cut, worked out by Marcal Tolkowsky. Its proportions are shown in the drawing. Today a slightly larger table than is optimal is usual; instead of 53% of the diamond's diameter, 57% or even 60%.

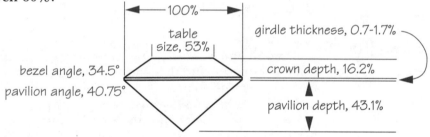

diaphragms

These contraceptive devices are made in several styles and in a range of diameters; the largest and smallest sizes differ in diameter by about two inches (50 mm–105 mm).

To achieve a leak-free fit, wearers must be fitted individually. The fitter (a doctor or nurse) first makes a preliminary measurement, then tries several sizes until the best fit is found.

More than one fitting may be necessary. Many people are especially tense during the first fitting, and that can result in their getting a size that doesn't fit when they are relaxed. Women who were fitted as virgins should have the size rechecked later, since sexual activity can change the shape of the vagina, as can large weight gains or losses.

dinosaurs

The dinosaurs were the biggest ever in many ways. The Carnosauria were the biggest carnivores that ever walked the earth. Even bigger were their vegetarian relatives (though some of today's whales are bigger). The Ceratopsids had the largest skulls of any terrestrial animal, and so on.

But not all dinosaurs were big. A full-grown *Wannanosaurus yansiensis* (late Cretaceous, central Asia) was only 60 cm long. Elmisaurids averaged only 35 to 65 kg.

Dobson unit

A unit expressing the concentration of ozone in the earth's atmosphere. Abbr, DU. Imagine that all the ozone in a column reaching from the earth's surface to the top of the atmosphere were concentrated in a single layer of pure ozone at a temperature of 0°C and a pressure of 1 standard atmosphere. The thickness of that layer, measured in hundredths of a millimeter, would be the concentration of ozone expressed in Dobson units.

The lowest level measured before 1994 was 90 Dobson units, measured on October 6, 1993 by a balloon flown from the U.S. research station at the South Pole. The previous record low was 105 Dobson units, recorded in 1992.

dollhouses

In the USA, by far the most common scale among dollhouse hobbyists is 1:12; that is, one inch represents one foot. Miniatures are also made for dollhouses within 1:12 dollhouses; the scale for these is 1:144.

Another, much larger scale is used for dollhouses meant to be used by children playing with "fashion dolls" like Mattel's Barbie and Ken. The scale is approximately 2" to a foot, but for this class of dollhouse (referred to as Playscale), appearance is considered more important than strict adherence to scale.

Additional scales used are 1:24, sometimes called "H-scale" (1/2" represents one foot), and 1:48 (1/4" represents one foot). Miniature buildings are also made to match various model railroad scales, but these don't usually interest the miniaturists who specialize in dollhouses.

down

The insulating power of down is described by "fill power." To measure fill power, one ounce avoirdupois of down is placed in a cylinder, shaken, and allowed to settle. The number of cubic inches occupied by the settled down is its fill power, which is generally stated in increments of 50. Down with fill power as high as 800 is known, but never seen in commerce. In the consumer market, down with a fill power of 650 is excellent, and 500 is good.

Sellers often specify how many ounces of down are in a garment or comforter. A higher number is better (warmer) only if one is comparing downs with the same fill power.

dram

1) A unit of mass = 1/16 ounce avoirdupois = 27.34375 grains = 1.771845195 grams. Symbol, dr. The dram continues in current use in such activities as reloading ammunition. Not to be confused with the

British drachm, ≈ 3.88793 g.   **2)** In England and the USA, a system for specifying the fineness of thrown silk yarn, such as silk sewing thread, = weight in drams of 1,000 yards. "Number 1 dram silk."

duck

The numbering system used to describe grades of the unsized cotton cloth called duck is calculated as 19 minus the weight in ounces of a piece a yard long and 22" wide, although duck is also woven in other widths.

If the piece weighs less than 19 ounces the cloth is called *numbered duck*. For example, a piece of #5 numbered duck 1 yard by 22" would weigh 14 ounces (19 − 14 = 5). Numbered duck is nominally made in weights from 1 to 12, but numbers 7, 9, and 11 are no longer used. Some typical uses of various weights are: #1, hammocks, sand bags; #2, hatch paulins; #4, sea bags; #6, large boat covers; #8, clothes bags; #10, shower curtains.

If a 1 yard × 22" piece weighs 19 ounces or more, the cloth is called *naught duck*. A 1 yard × 22" piece of 1/0 naught duck weighs 19 oz; 2/0 naught duck weighs 20 oz, and so on; with each extra ounce of weight another naught is added. Thus a piece of 6/0 duck 1 yard by 22" would weigh 24 ounces.

earthquakes

Each year instruments record about 800,000 "earthquakes" so small people can't feel them. On the other hand, between 1945 and 1986 earthquakes caused half of all the deaths due to natural disasters–about 1,198,000 fatalities. Of all the types of natural disasters (hurricanes, typhoons, volcanic eruptions, and so on), major earthquakes caused more deaths per disaster (6,272) than any other type. Little ones we don't even notice; the big ones are catastrophic.

Intensity

One way of describing the size of an earthquake is by the amount of shaking at some particular location. A seismometer is needed to measure ground motion directly, but the results of the shaking, such as various kinds of damage to buildings, can serve as a substitute. So can events that people who experience a 'quake tend to remember, such as the ringing of church bells, or even whether they felt the earthquake at all (seated persons typically notice earthquakes that people moving around do not). A scale can be constructed whose steps are defined by the kinds of damage and events that typically occur together. With such a scale, scientists arriving at the scene of an earthquake can put a number on its intensity by gathering witnesses' impressions.

In 1883 M. S. de Rossi and F. A. Forel published a 10-step intensity scale which was widely used in the 19TH and early 20TH C. Measurements on this scale are stated as the initials "R.F." followed by a roman numeral. Its steps roughly correspond to those of the Mercalli scale, described below, except "R.F. X" lumps together steps 10 through 12 on the Mercalli scale.

In 1902, Giuseppe Mercalli greatly improved the scale, later increasing the number of steps to 12, and the intensity scale has since been known as the Mercalli Scale. Further improvements were made by A. Sieberg in 1923, Harry O. Wood and Frank Neumann in 1931, and Charles Richter in 1956. All of these are "Modified Mercalli scales;" often the initials "M.M." are used before the step number. The improvements have made the descriptions less regional and more precise (instead of "buildings fall," the newer scales say what kind of buildings fall), and have refined the groupings to be sure they include events that actually occur together.

The Modified Mercalli Scale is a good way of saying how bad it was at some particular location, but it isn't a good way of saying how strong the earthquake was in general. For example, intensity depends a great deal on the nature of the ground. An earthquake's intensity will be much greater in a town built on fill than in one built on granite. In 1985, an earthquake 300 km away caused catastrophic damage in Mexico City, but mainly in 15- to 25-story buildings. The buildings had a natural resonance at a period of around two seconds, and the geological conditions beneath the city picked up such waves from the quake and amplified them. If an earthquake's "size" is to be described without reference to location, some other technique must be used.

Modified Mercalli Scale, 1956 version		
Intensity value	Characteristics	Rich-ter†
I	Only detectable by seismographs.‡	<3.5
II	Felt by persons at rest on upper floors or favorably placed.	3.5
III	Felt indoors. Hanging objects swing. Vibration like passing of light trucks. Duration estimated. May not be recognized as an earthquake.	4.2
IV	Hanging objects swing. Vibration like passing of heavy trucks. Windows, dishes, doors rattle. Parked cars rock. Glasses clink. Crockery clashes. In the upper range of IV, wooden walls and frames creak.	4.5
V	Felt outdoors; direction estimated. Sleepers awakened. Liquids disturbed, some spilled. Small unstable objects displaced or upset. Doors swing, close, open. Shutters, pictures, move. Pendulum clocks stop; start, change rate.	4.8
VI	Felt by all. Many frightened and run outdoors. Persons walk unsteadily. Windows, dishes, glassware broken. Knickknacks, books, etc. fall off shelves. Pictures fall off walls. Furniture moves or overturned. Weak plaster and masonry D* cracked. Small bells ring (church, school). Trees, bushes sway visibly or are heard to rustle.	5.4

	Modified Mercalli Scale, 1956 version	
Intensity value	Characteristics	Rich-ter†
VII	Difficult to stand. Noticed by drivers. Hanging objects quiver; furniture breaks; damage to masonry D, including cracks. Weak chimneys broken off at roof line. Fall of plaster, loose bricks, stones, tiles, cornices, unbraced parapets and architectural ornaments. Some cracks in masonry C*. Waves on ponds, water turbid with mud. Small slides and caving in along sand and gravel banks. Large bells ring. Concrete irrigation ditches damaged.	6.1
VIII	Steering of cars affected. Damage to masonry C and partial collapse; some damage to masonry B*, none to masonry A*. Fall of stucco and some masonry walls. Twisting, fall of chimneys, factory stacks, monuments, towers, elevated tanks. Frame houses moved on foundations if not bolted down; loose panel walls thrown out. Decayed piling broken off. Branches broken from trees. Changes in flow or temperature of springs and wells. Cracks in wet ground and on steep slopes.	6.5
IX	General panic. Masonry D destroyed; masonry C heavily damaged, sometimes with complete collapse; masonry B seriously damaged. General damage to foundations. Frame structures, if not bolted down, shift off foundations. Frames racked. Serious damage to reservoirs. Underground pipes break. Conspicuous cracks in ground. In alluviated areas sand and mud ejected, earthquake fountains, sand craters.	6.9
X	Most masonry and frame structures destroyed with their foundations. Some well-built wooden structures and bridges destroyed. Serious damage to dams, dikes, and embankments. Large landslides. Water thrown on banks of canals, rivers, lakes, etc. Sand and mud shifted horizontally on beaches and flat land. Rails bent slightly.	7.3
XI	Rails bent greatly. Underground pipelines completely out of service.	8.1
XII	Damage nearly total. Large rock masses displaced. Lines of sight and level distorted. Objects thrown into the air.	>8.1

Masonry A shows good workmanship, mortar, and design; reinforced, especially laterally, and bound together using steel, concrete, etc.; designed to reduce lateral forces.
Masonry B. Good workmanship and mortar; reinforced, but not designed in detail to resist lateral forces.
Masonry C. Ordinary workmanship and mortar; no extreme weaknesses like failing to tie in at corners, but neither reinforced nor designed against horizontal forces.
Masonry D. Weak materials, such as adobe; poor mortar; low standards of workmanship; weak horizontally.
From: *Elementary Seismology,* by Charles F. Richter. Copyright © 1958 by W. H. Freeman and Company. Reprinted with permission.
†Though a Richter scale equivalent is shown, it is approximate at best, since the two scales measure different things. It applies only to Mercalli intensities experienced at or near the epicenter of the earthquake.
‡Intensity I is also assigned to some quakes even though they were detected by people, if the people were very far from the epicenter and could feel the quake only because of exceptionally favorable circumstances. Some people in the Space Needle in Seattle, for example, felt the 1964 Alaska earthquake, and some in Houston skyscrapers the 1985 Mexican earthquake.

Notice that intensities on the Mercalli scale are usually shown in Roman numerals, a convention worth preserving because it helps to distinguish intensity ratings from magnitude ratings.

Magnitude
A typical earthquake begins when bent rock stops sticking and starts slipping. The unbending of the rock releases energy, much as releasing a coiled spring would, and this energy spreads out from the place where the earthquake began in the form of waves. Ideally, there

should be a way of describing the "strength" of an earthquake in terms of the energy released, independent of the location of the observer.

Instruments that record the waves made by earthquakes are called seismographs. Each contains a mass that is free to move. Because of inertia, the mass tends to stay where it is when the ground and the rest of the seismograph move during an earthquake. A pendulum is a simple example. The relative movement of the mass in relation to everything else is magnified (by levers, in the simplest case) and makes a record, for example, by moving a pen that is marking moving paper. The farther the ground moves, the greater the back and forth movement of the pen. Although earthquake  detecting devices have been built for more than a thousand years, it was not until the last half of the 19TH C that instruments comparable to modern seismographs were widely deployed. Many of these devices were installed in California.

In 1931 the Seismological Laboratory in Pasadena, California decided to publish an annual list of local earthquakes. The list, however, contained two or three hundred earthquakes, and it was felt it would be too scary for general consumption without some indication that most of the quakes were small. Intensity estimates were not available; all the data came from seismographs. So Charles Richter decided to define some "rational," as he put it, way of describing the size of these earthquakes. The method he chose resembled one used by K. Wadati in Japan.

As a basis for his comparisons, Richter decided to use the extent of the pen movement on a particular type of seismograph that all the stations in southern California had: torsion seismographs with an 0.8 second period and a magnification of 2,800. The scale would have to be logarithmic; Richter chose log to the base 10. To provide a set point on the scale, Richter 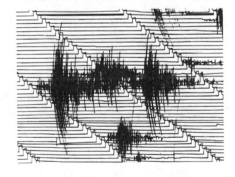 said an earthquake would be magnitude one if it made the pen of one of his seismographs, located 100 km from the quake, move a maximum of one-thousandth of a millimeter. This value was chosen to ensure that any earthquake a person could feel would have a positive magnitude. Given the above assumptions, the magnitude of any quake can be described by the $\log_{10}$ of the ratio of the maximum trace amplitude of that quake (at a distance of 100 km) to the maximum trace amplitude of the magnitude one quake, i.e., one-thousandth of a millimeter. So a pen movement of one millimeter indicated a magnitude three earthquake—if the quake was 100 km away.

Since earthquakes do not conveniently occur at 100-km distances from seismographs, Richter devised an empirical method for correcting the trace amplitude for distance.

Richter's original scale of earthquake magnitudes had a number of limitations. Almost all California earthquakes are shallow, so the scale got by without taking into account the depth of an earthquake. Only relatively local quakes were on the list, so the scale didn't need to deal with distant quakes. But for its purpose, the original scale was a great success, and that success prompted Richter, Beno Gutenberg, and many other workers to devise more general measures of magnitude.

The more sophisticated scales now used take into account differences in the types of waves generated by earthquakes; M_b magnitudes reflect waves that have traveled through great depths, and M_S magnitudes, waves that travel along the surface (the symbol for magnitudes on Richter's scale is M_L). The new scales (including many used only in a particular area) have been defined so that their values are consistent with those of the original scale, and these too are popularly called magnitudes "on the Richter scale."

Each whole number step in the Richter scale represents a ten-fold increase in magnitude, but roughly a 32-fold increase in released energy. The annual frequency of big earthquakes, at least in a recent 47-year period, has been as follows:

M_S	Earthquakes per year
8.5–8.9	0.3
8.0–8.4	1.1
7.5–7.9	3.1
7.0–7.4	15
6.5–6.9	56
6.0–6.4	210

Unlike the Mercalli scale, the Richter scale has no defined "highest reading." But in fact the highest readings recorded on the M_b scale have been about 6.5–6.8, and on the M_S scale, about 8.3–8.7. There is a problem: all the magnitude scales described so far underestimate the size of very large earthquakes because their definitions assume all earthquakes generate the same mixture of waves. In very large quakes the rock ruptures across a very large underground surface, and the resulting waves have a greater proportion of waves with very long periods than smaller earthquakes do. So workers looked for a way of describing earthquake size that reflect even more closely the geological reality.

Seismic Moment

By analyzing the waveforms recorded by a number of seismographs, each seeing the earthquake from a different angle, researchers can reconstruct what happened where the earthquake occurred, such as the direction and tilt of the fault and the direction the rock moved. From these they can calculate a quantity called the seismic moment, the product of the fault surface area over which movement occurred, the strength of the rock, and the average displacement. A new magnitude scale (symbol, M_W) has been defined based on the seismic moment. Unlike the other scales, the M_W scale takes into account the geometrical relationships between the fault's orientation and the observers. Magnitudes based on seismic moment give a truer picture of large earthquakes than the other scales do; the 1960 Chile quake, for example, was M_S 8.5 but M_W 9.6; the 1964 Alaska earthquake, M_S 8.3, but M_W 9.2.

Some memorable big quakes:

7.5	Kanto, Japan	1923
8.2	Tangshan	1976
8.25	San Francisco	1906
8.5	Chile 22 May	1960
8.5	Alaska	1964

eggs, chicken

In the United States, traffic in eggs is regulated under the federal Egg Products Inspection Act (1970). Both grades and sizes are defined, and the two are not related; Peewee eggs can be Grade AA and Jumbos can be Grade B.

Grades. A "grade shield" on the packaging indicates the eggs have been graded under federal supervision, as most have. Some states do their own grading. In order of decreasing quality, grades are AA, A, and B. All ungraded eggs sold to consumers must meet B standards. "Restricted eggs" do not meet B standards; their disposition is regulated to prevent them from reaching consumers, although two types of restricted eggs, checks (the shell is cracked but the membrane beneath is not broken), and dirties, may be sold to factories equipped to process them properly.

All graded eggs must be clean and have sound, whole shells. Grade B may show some staining, provided it covers less than 25% of the shell, and the shell may be misshapen or have a thin spots, ridges, and other textural defects. There are no color requirements.

The main difference between the grades is internal, and mostly reflects the freshness of the egg. The air cell in a grade AA egg must not be more than 1/8" deep; in a grade B egg it is over 3/16" deep. The egg white should be thick and clear; the yolk firm and well-defined.

Candling—placing a very strong light behind the egg—can reveal more about the egg than one might think. For example, if the egg white is thin, twirling the egg will make the yolk move nearer to the shell than it would if the egg white were thicker.

Quality is more obvious once the egg is broken. The yolk of a grade AA egg is tall; the white doesn't spread out much, and there is more thick white than thin white. The yolk of a grade B egg is flattened, it has more thin white than thick white and will spread out to cover a larger area. The USDA has developed a test of egg quality based, for example, on measurements of yolk height on a flat plate; the results are stated in Haugh units.

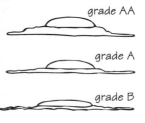

Sizes are defined by the weight of a dozen eggs.

Size	Oz. per dozen
Jumbo	30
Extra Large	27
Large	24
Medium	21
Small	18
Peewee	15

About 11% of a chicken egg's weight is shell.

Recipes that call for a certain number of eggs usually mean Large eggs. The chart below (courtesy of the American Egg Board) may be used to convert a number of Large eggs to an approximate equivalent in other sizes.

Large	Jumbo	Extra-Large	Medium	Small
1	1	1	1	1
2	2	2	2	3
3	2	3	3	4
4	3	4	5	5
5	4	4	6	7
6	5	5	7	8

electric power Almost all the electricity sold in the United States is been 60-Hz alternating current. In homes, the voltage is approximately 120 volts, but it may be brought into the house at a higher voltage, and high voltages are used for some power-hungry appliances, such as kitchen ranges, air conditioners and water heaters. (The higher voltage makes it possible to supply the same amount of power with smaller wires.) Three-phase power is rarely found in residences.

The appearance of the receptacle usually indicates what voltage and amperage is available, since the National Electrical Manufacturers Assn. (NEMA) and the NEC specify what type of current each design is to be used for.

Some Electrical Receptacles in the United States

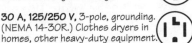

15 A, 125 V, 2-pole. (NEMA 1-15 R, Fed. Spec Style A.) Used only to replace existing ungrounded receptacles.

15 A, 125 V, 2-pole, grounding. (NEMA 5-15 R, Fed Spec. Style D.) The standard household receptacle.

20 A, 125 V, 2-pole, grounding. (NEMA 5-20 R, Fed. Spec Style X.) Used for room air conditioners, in kitchens, other locations where heavy-duty appliances might be used.

15 A, 250 V, 2-pole, grounding. (NEMA 6-15 R.) Used for room air conditioners, commercial appliances, heavy-duty portable tools.

20 A, 250 V, 2-pole, grounding. (NEMA 6-20 R.) Same uses as 6-15 R.

15 A, 277 V, 2-pole, grounding. (NEMA 7-15 R.) Used for commercial lighting fixtures.

20 A, 125/250V, 3-pole. (NEMA 10-20 R, Fed. Spec. Style L.) Commercial and industrial. Note lack of grounding.

30 A, 125/250 V, 3-pole. (NEMA 10-30 R, Fed. Spec. Style S.) Clothes dryers in homes; commercial and industrial equipment.

50 A, 125/250 V, 3-pole. (NEMA 1-50 R, Fed. Spec. Style T.) Kitchen ranges in homes. Commercial and industrial heavy-duty equipment.

30 A, 125 V, 2-pole, grounding. (NEMA 5-30R.) Office copying machines, commercial air conditioners, other heavy equipment.

30 A, 250 V, 2-pole, grounding. (NEMA 6-30 R.) Same uses as 5-30R at a higher voltage.

30 A, 125/250 V, 3-pole, grounding. (NEMA 14-30R.) Clothes dryers in homes, other heavy-duty equipment.

50 A, 125 V, 2-pole, grounding. (NEMA 5-50 R.) Commercial air conditioners, office copying machines, other heavy equipment.

50 A, 250 V, 2-pole, grounding. (NEMA 6-50 R.) Same as 5-50 R, but higher voltage.

50 A, 125/250 V, 3-pole, grounding. (NEMA 14-50 R.) Kitchen ranges and similar high-amperage equipment, with grounding protection.

60 A, 125/250 V, 3-pole, grounding. (NEMA 14-60 R.) House trailers. High amperage commercial and industrial equipment.

20 A, 250 V, 3-phase (4-pole) (NEMA 18-20 R.) Mostly used for three-phase motors.

60 A, 250 V, 3-phase (4-pole). (NEMA 18-60 R.) Even larger three-phase motors and other equipment needing 3-phase power.

electric shock

Current in mA		Effect
60-Hz AC	DC	
0–1	0–4	Perception.
1–4	4–15	Surprise. Currents over 5 mA can be lethal.
4–21	15–80	Reflex action.
21–40	80–160	Muscular inhibition.
41–100	160–300	Respiratory block.
over 100	over 300	Usually fatal.

electronvolt

The energy acquired by one electron passing through a potential difference of one volt, = 1.602×10^{-19} joule. Abbr, eV.

envelopes

Announcement Text

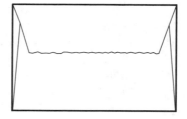

A-2	$4\frac{3}{8}" \times 5\frac{5}{8}"$
A-6	$4\frac{3}{4}" \times 6\frac{1}{2}"$
A-7	$5\frac{1}{4}" \times 7\frac{1}{4}"$
A-8	$5\frac{1}{2}" \times 8\frac{1}{8}"$
A-10	$6\frac{1}{4}" \times 9\frac{5}{8}"$
Slim	$3\frac{7}{8}" \times 8\frac{7}{8}"$

Baronial
Pointed flap on long dimension, diagonal seams.

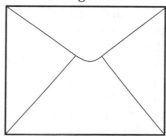

2	$3\frac{3}{16}" \times 4\frac{1}{4}"$
4	$3\frac{5}{8}" \times 4\frac{5}{8}"$
5	$4\frac{1}{8}" \times 5\frac{1}{8}"$
$5\frac{1}{4}$	$4\frac{1}{4}" \times 5\frac{1}{4}"$
$5\frac{1}{2}$	$4\frac{3}{8}" \times 5\frac{5}{8}"$
$5\frac{3}{4}$	$4\frac{1}{2}" \times 5\frac{3}{4}"$
6	$5" \times 6"$

Commercial

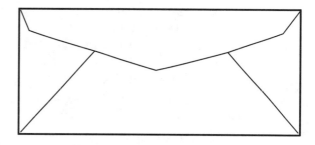

$6\frac{1}{4}$	$3\frac{1}{2}" \times 6"$
$6\frac{3}{4}$	$3\frac{5}{8}" \times 6\frac{1}{2}"$
7	$3\frac{3}{4}" \times 6\frac{4}{4}"$
$7\frac{3}{4}$	$3\frac{7}{8}" \times 7\frac{1}{2}"$
8	$3\frac{7}{8}" \times 7\frac{1}{2}"$
9	$3\frac{7}{8}" \times 8\frac{7}{8}"$
10	$4\frac{1}{8}" \times 9\frac{1}{2}"$
11	$4\frac{1}{2} \times 10\frac{3}{8}"$
12	$4\frac{3}{4}" \times 11"$
14	$5" \times 11\frac{1}{2}"$

Booklet

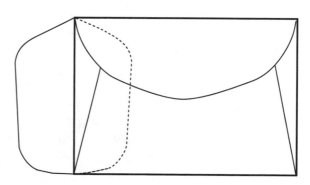

3	$4\frac{3}{4}" \times 6\frac{1}{2}"$
5	$5\frac{1}{2}" \times 8\frac{1}{2}"$
6	$5\frac{3}{4}" \times 8\frac{7}{8}"$
$6\frac{1}{2}$	$6" \times 9"$
$6\frac{5}{8}$	$6" \times 9\frac{1}{2}"$
$6\frac{3}{4}$	$6\frac{1}{2}" \times 9\frac{1}{2}"$
7	$6\frac{1}{4}" \times 9\frac{5}{8}"$
$7\frac{1}{4}$	$7" \times 10"$
$7\frac{1}{2}$	$7\frac{1}{2}" \times 10\frac{1}{2}"$
9	$8\frac{3}{4}" \times 11\frac{1}{2}"$
$9\frac{1}{2}$	$9" \times 12"$

10   9 1/2" × 12 5/8"
13   10" × 13"

Metal Clasp
Made of heavy paper: kraft or manila.

5   3 1/8" × 5 1/2"
10   3 3/8" × 6"
11   4 1/2" × 10 3/8"
14   5" × 11 1/2"
15   4" × 6 3/8"
25   4 5/8" × 6 3/4"
35   5" × 7 1/2"
50   5 1/2" × 8 1/4"
55   6" × 9"
63   6 1/2" × 9 1/2"
68   7" × 10"
75   7 1/2" × 10"
80   8" × 11"
83   8 1/2" × 11 1/2"
87   8 3/4" × 11 1/4"
90   9" × 12"
93   9 1/2" × 12 1/2"
94   9 1/4" × 14 1/2"
95   10" × 12"
97   10" × 13"
98   10" × 15"
105   11 1/2" × 14 1/2"
110   12" × 15 1/2"

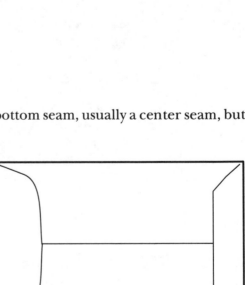

Catalog
Flap on the short dimension, bottom seam, usually a center seam, but sometimes a single side seam.

1   6" × 9"
1 3/4   6 1/2" × 9 1/2"
2   6 1/2" × 10"
3   7" × 10"
6   7 1/2" × 10 1/2"
7   8" × 11"
8   8 1/4" × 11 1/4"
9 1/2   8 1/2" × 10 1/2"
9 3/4   8 3/4" × 11 1/4"
10 1/2 9" × 12"
12 1/2 9 1/2" × 12 1/2"
13 1/2 10" × 13"

14 1/4	11 1/4" × 14 1/4"
14 1/2	11 1/2" × 14 1/2"
15	10" × 15"
15 1/2	12" × 15 1/2"

Remittance

Hug flap along the long dimension, suitable for printing a large amount of copy. The flap is sometimes perforated. Two side seams.

6 1/4	3 1/2" × 6"
6 1/2	3 1/2" × 6 1/4"
6 3/4	3 5/8" × 6 1/2"
3	3 1/2" × 6 1/2"
9	3 7/8" × 8 7/8"
10	4 1/8" × 9 1/2"

Ticket

3	1 15/16" × 4 7/16"

Drug

Rounded flap on longest dimension, diagonal seams.

1	1 3/4" × 2 7/8"
3	2 5/16" × 3 5/8"

Policy

Flap on the short dimension, bottom seam, center seam. The long shape accommodates an insurance policy securely.

9	4" × 9"
10	4 1/8" × 9 1/2"
11	4 1/2" × 10 3/8"
12	4 3/4" × 10 7/8"
14	5" × 11 1/2"

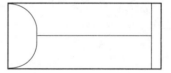

Coin

Flap on short dimension, center seam, bottom seam.

1	2 1/4" × 3 1/2"
3	2 1/2" × 4 1/4"
4	3" × 4 1/2"
4 1/2	3" × 4 7/8"
5	2 7/8" × 5 1/4"
5 1/2	3 1/8 × 5 1/2"
6	3 3/8" × 6"
7	3 1/2" × 6 1/2"

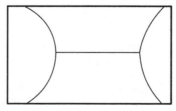

Window

On window envelopes a rectangle with rounded corners is cut out of the front of the envelope, to allow addresses printed on the letter within to show through. The hole is often covered with a patch of polyethylene, cellophane, or glassine. Only the most common sizes are listed below.

The window on the following sizes is $4\,3/4"\times1\,1/8"$ and is placed $3/4"$ from the left for the $6\,1/4$ size and $7/8"$ for all other sizes, and $1/2"$ from the bottom.

$6\,1/4$	$3\,1/2"\times6"$
$6\,3/4$	$3\,5/8"\times6\,1/2"$
7	$3\,3/4"\times6\,3/4"$
$7\,3/4$	$3\,7/8"\times7\,1/2"$

The $8\,5/8"$ window envelope comes in two versions. The window in the A Check is $4\,3/4\times1\,1/8$ and is located $5/8"$ from the left and $13/16"$ from the bottom. In the B check the window is $4"\times1"$ and is located $1"$ from the left and $3/4"$ from the bottom.

A Check	$3\,5/8"\times8\,5/8"$
B Check	$3\,5/8"\times8\,5/8"$

The window on the following sizes is $4\,1/2"\times1\,1/8"$, and is located $7/8"$ from the left and $1/2"$ from the bottom.

9	$3\,7/8"\times8\,7/8"$
10	$4\,1/8"\times9\,1/2"$
11	$4\,1/2"\times10\,3/8"$

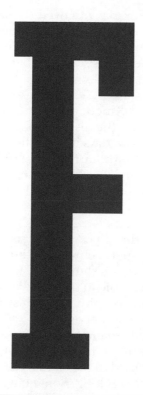

fabric

A fabric store today is likely to offer cloth in widths of 36", 41", 44", 45", 54", and 108". Some of these widths are very old. The width of 54" is 6 quarters, that is, 6 quarter-yards, which was a cloth width required by the Statute of Northhampton (2 Edward III s 14 1328). The legal width of the same type of cloth was later changed to 5 quarters, perhaps by 1373 and certainly by Henry V in 1405; 5 quarters is our 45" width and in the 14TH C was the length of the weavers' ell.

farad

In SI, the unit of capacitance. Abbr, F. A capacitor has a capacitance of 1 farad if a charge of one coulomb increases the potential difference between its plates by one volt. Its dimensions are $\dfrac{coulomb}{volt}$, or in terms of base units only, $\dfrac{second^4 \cdot ampere^2}{meter^2 \cdot kilogram}$

The reciprocal of capacitance is elastance. A unit sometimes used in the United States to measure elastance is the daraf (farad spelled backwards). Symbol, F^{-1}.

The farad is too big for most practical purposes; capacitors in electronic equipment are usually rated in microfarads, nanofarads, or picofarads. Use of the "micromicrofarad" (µµF), once common, is now discouraged.

faraday

A unit of electric charge. Michael Faraday discovered that in electrolysis, a given quantity of electricity always sets free the same mass of gas. The faraday is the quantity of electricity needed to liberate one gram-equivalent of any substance by electrolysis. It has been determined experimentally to be ≈ 96,487.0 ± 1.6 coulombs.

fathom

In the United States and the United Kingdom, 11TH C–20TH C, a unit of length = 6 feet. In original concept, the distance between the tips of the fingers of outstretched arms. Nowadays it is applied almost exclusively to the depth of water ("Full fathom five thy father lies"), but formerly it was also applied to timber and to the circumference of haystacks, which were measured by people putting their arms around the stack.

faucets, water

On kitchen sinks, the centers of the pipes to faucets are usually 8" apart. On lavatories, the pipes are on 4" centers. In the past almost all faucets were the compression type, which shut off the water by pressing a rubber washer against a seat with a hole in the middle. Now there are many other types that, though they require much less maintenance, require proprietary parts when they do need repair.

In compression faucets, the seal is made by a bibb washer which is usually neoprene. Bibb washers come in three styles: flat, beveled, and swivel-head. The first two types are held to the stem by a brass or monel machine screw, anywhere from ¼ to ½" long. Some have a 6-32 thread and some 8-32, but if the hole is #10 use caution! Three different #10 threads have been used in faucets: 10-24, 10-28, and 10-32.

In order of increasing size, neoprene washers come in sizes 00, 0, ¼S, ¼L, ⅜, ⅜M, ⅜L, ½. Fiber washers, which some prefer if the seat is worn, come in 0, ¼S, ¼, ¼L. Because householders almost always buy washers in a pack of assorted sizes and fit them by cut-and-try, the main purpose of these lists is to let you know if there is a larger or smaller size you don't have, when the size you've got doesn't fit.

Swivelhead washers are held to the stem by two prongs instead of screws. They are used when the screw has broken off (a new, unthreaded hole is drilled), or when the rim around the bottom of the faucet stem has been worn away.

femto-

In SI, the decimal submultiplier meaning one quadrillionth. One might wonder what such a small unit is good for; there are as many femtoseconds in one second as there are seconds in 30 million years. Yet by 1991, researchers working with lasers had succeeded in creating light pulses lasting only six femtoseconds, and were working on shorter pulses. Such short bursts of light can be used, for example, to investigate chemical reactions. This is the sort of work in which femto- is a convenience.

fertilizer

A fertilizer grade consists of three numbers, for example "10-3-10," sometimes called its N-P-K. The first figure is the percentage by weight of elemental nitrogen. The second is the percentage by weight of anhydrous phosphoric acid (P_2O_5), assuming all the phosphorus in the fertilizer were converted to phosphoric acid. The fertilizer need not actually contain any phosphoric acid; the phosphorus content may be provided by ammonium phosphate, superphosphate, or any number of other compounds. Converting all the phosphorus in them, conceptually, to P_2O_5 is just a convenient way of expressing the amount of phosphorus they contain. To convert to percentage by weight of elemental phosphorus, multiply by 0.830. Similarly, the last figure is the percentage by weight of potassium oxide, K_2O. Again, the fertilizer need not actually contain potassium oxide. To convert to elemental potassium, multiply by 0.436.

A 20-14-18 fertilizer and a 10-7-9 fertilizer have the same fertilizer ratios; other things being equal, they would have the same effect, provided twice as much of the 10-7-9 were applied. The advantage of the higher analysis 20-14-18 fertilizer is the saving in transportation costs.

Sometimes additional terms are added to the N-P-K string, especially for fertilizers made for soils with specific deficiencies. These additional terms contain the symbol for one of the chemical elements and a number that is the percentage by weight of that element. For example, a fertilizer marked "20-20-20-10S" would be 10% elemental sulfur by weight.

Fertilizer grades don't capture all the properties desirable in a soil amendment. Compost, for example, has a very low N-P-K grade.

file folders

Two sizes are standard in the United States: letter-size (11 3/4" wide) and legal size (14 3/4" wide). The standard height for both is 9 1/2", but letter-size folders are also available in a taller "guide height," 9 15/16" high. Shorter "interior folders," only 9 1/8" high, are made for use in hanging file folders, so that their tabs do not obscure the tabs of the hanging file folders.

The length of the tab on the top of the folder is indicated by the cut number. On a 1/3-cut folder, the most commonly used cut, the tab extends 1/3 of the way across the top of the folder, and may be in any of three positions. The 1/5-cut and 2/5-cut folders both have five possible positions. Half-cut come in two positions, and on "straight cut" folders the tab extends all the way across the top.

The thickness, or weight, of the paper from which the folder is made is indicated in points. A 9 1/2-points folder is for light-duty; 11-point is a typical weight. For a folder that will be in constant use much heavier weights are available, and even plastic.

End tab folders are made for shelf filing; the body sizes are the same, but the tabs extend from the right side of the folder. The front panel

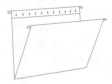

is the same height as the back and the right side of the front panel is cut away where the tab is on the back panel.

Hanging files are also made in letter (9 3/8" × 11 3/4") and legal (9 3/8" × 14 3/4") sizes. The tabs are not part of the folder but in movable plastic holders; 1/5-cut tabs are 2" wide and 1/3-cut are 3 1/2" wide.

filing cabinets

Vertical Files
Cabinets have 2, 3, 4, or 5 drawers, with typical heights of 29", 40", 52", and 60" respectively, and are made for either letter-size paper (8 1/2" × 11") or legal-size paper (8 1/2" × 14") paper; letter-size cabinets are typically 15" wide and legal size are 18 1/4".

The typical office vertical file cabinet is 28 1/2" deep and the drawer holds 27" of files. Shallower cabinets are also made: 26 1/2" deep cabinets with 25" drawer depth, 25" deep cabinets with 23 1/2" drawers. Naive buyers shopping for price often inadvertently compare units with shallow and deep drawers.

Lateral Files
Lateral files are wider than they are deep. Five-drawer files are 64"–66" high, three-drawer 40", four-drawer are 50"–53" high, and two-drawer are 28" or a little more. Typical depths are 18" or 19". Widths may be 30", 36" (33 1/4" of filing space, measured laterally), 38", 42", or 44" (the last with 39 1/4" of filing space). Drawers can be configured in different ways, for example, as one row of hanging folders running front-to-back, or as two rows side-by-side. An advantage of this flexibility is that a single drawer in a cabinet can be configured to hold data printouts or other odd sizes.

Open-Shelf Files
These files are simply shelves with fairly closely-spaced vertical supports, used with end tab folders. Besides being less expensive than cabinets with drawers, the tabs of all files are constantly visible. Most users of open-shelf systems use colored codes on the tabs. They are popular in, for example, medical offices. Whenever a file is used the tab for year is checked. If it isn't the current year it is updated by covering it with a colored adhesive label for the current year. Since each year has a distinctive color, it is easy to spot old files and move less active files to storage areas.

fire extinguishers

Extinguishers that are effective on one kind of burning material don't necessarily work well on another. To indicate the kinds of fire for which an extinguisher is suitable, it will usually be labeled with an Underwriters Laboratory (UL) rating using the code letters A, B, C, or D.

Class A Burning wood, paper, cloth, and other everyday materials. Enough water can extinguish such fires.

Class B Burning liquids, such as kitchen grease, gasoline, oil, and other flammable liquids. Putting water on such fires may simply spread them.

Class C Fires involving electrical equipment. Spraying such a fire with water might not be a good idea.

Class D Burning combustible metals, such as magnesium and sodium. This is not a problem in the home; D-class extinguishers are special items.

In front of the letters A and B are numbers, which are ratings indicating the relative size of the fire the extinguisher can deal with. For example, a 2-A extinguisher could put out a paper fire twice the size of the biggest fire a 1-A extinguisher could handle.

The UL ratings capture almost everything one needs to know about the extinguisher. The one exception is the extent of the damage done by the extinguisher itself. Most modern extinguishers spray powder, in many cases baking soda, in others ammonium phosphate. In most situations if the powder is promptly cleaned up afterwards no harm is done. But if the powder gets into a computer or other electronic gear, the equipment will probably be ruined. Halon extinguishers, formerly used for fighting fires in such circumstances, are no longer allowed except for very special circumstances (airplane cockpits), because Halon is a fluorocarbon that destroys the ozone layer. A carbon dioxide extinguisher might be a useful compromise.

A good size for each floor of a home is a 3-A:40-B:C, unless residents are too frail to use one this heavy (eight to ten pounds). The kitchen needs a small extinguisher of its own, one specifically designed for grease fires (that is, no A rating is needed). Inexpensive 5-B:C models are sold.

flooring, hardwood

In the USA, hardwood strip flooring is sold in face widths of 1 1/2", 2", 2 1/4", and 3 1/4". Flooring made of maple, beech, or birch is 25/32" thick. Each piece must be at least 2' long in First and Second grade flooring and at least 1 1/4' for third grade. There are also three special grades: Selected First grade light northern hard maple, Selected First grade amber northern hard maple, and Selected First grade red (made from northern beech or birch). In the Second grade, minor imperfections such as small tight knots are permitted. Third grade flooring must provide a good, serviceable floor.

Oak or pecan flooring comes in thicknesses of 25/32", 1/2", and 3/8". Pieces must be at least 2' long with a minimum average of 4 1/2' in a shipment.

Oak flooring is either quartersawed or plainsawed. Quartersawed comes in two grades, Clear and Select, and plainsawed in four: Clear, Select, No. 1 Common, and No. 2 Common. The only defect allowed in Clear is 3/8" of bright sap. Select permits some pinholes and small tight knots. Number 1 makes a sound floor without cutting. Number 2 is only required to provide a serviceable floor.

fly lines

The nature of the line is critical in fly fishing, because the line is more massive than the fly, and it is actually the line which is cast.

In the 17TH C the line was horsehair, but the fly was dropped on the water, not cast. Later fly lines were made of silk, and the sizes were identified by letters on a scale from A (0.060" in diameter) to I, decreasing in diameter by 0.005" with each step, so I was 0.020" in diameter.

The old system wasn't capable of describing all the ways the nylon and Dacron lines introduced after World War II differed. In particular, it didn't indicate density: nylon is less dense than silk, and Dacron denser. A new system was introduced in which letters indicated construction. "HCH", for example, was a double taper line and "HCF" was a weight-forward line. Descriptions were sometimes added to the designation, such as "HCH sinking Dacron".

In 1961, the American Fishing Tackle Manufacturers Assn. introduced a new system based on describing by a series of numbers the weight of the first 30' of the line, exclusive of any untapered tip on a tapered line.

No.	Grains	Permissable range in grains
1	60	54–66
2	80	74–86
3	100	94–106
4	120	114–126
5	140	134–146
6	160	152–168
7	185	177–193
8	210	202–218
9	240	230–250
10	280	270–290

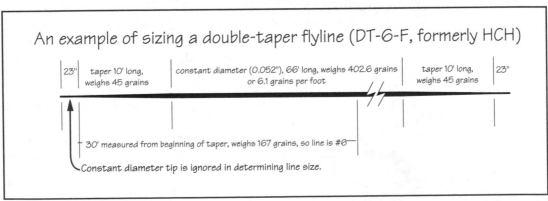

An example of sizing a double-taper flyline (DT-6-F, formerly HCH)

23" | taper 10' long, weighs 45 grains | constant diameter (0.052"), 66' long, weighs 402.6 grains or 6.1 grains per foot | taper 10' long, weighs 45 grains | 23"

30' measured from beginning of taper, weighs 167 grains, so line is #6

Constant diameter tip is ignored in determining line size.

| 11 | 330 | 318–342 |
| 12 | 380 | 368–392 |

Important characteristics were assigned code letters:
L   level line, constant diameter
DT   double taper
WF   weight forward
ST   single taper
F   floating
S   sinking
I   intermediate

A line is designated by giving the symbol for the taper, followed by the number for the weight, followed by the symbol for its sinking/floating characteristic. So, for example, a DT-9-F line would be double taper, the first 30' measured from the beginning of the taper would weigh between 230 and 350 grains, and it would float.

Notice that this system does not take into account the diameter, finish, composition, or braid of the line.

foot

A measure of length in the English-speaking world; since the 12TH C, the foot has been legally defined as one-third of a yard. Since 1959, one foot = 0.3048 meter exactly; see ☞yard and below.

The foot is only roughly the size of a human foot. The median foot of American males (as many smaller as bigger) is 10.4" long, and the female median is an inch smaller. Even 17-year old U. S. Army trainees have a median foot length of only 10.6", and 95% of them have feet smaller than 11.2".

The most recent change in the length of the foot was the result of an agreement among the English-speaking countries to eliminate discrepancies between their customary measures. The United States implemented the agreement by an announcement in the Federal Register on July 1, 1959 ("Refinement of Values for the Yard and the Pound"), and since then in the United States the foot has been the *international foot* = 0.3048 meter exactly. Since the United States is now almost the only country still using the foot, the name is now something of a joke.

The United States uses a different foot for one activity. The U.S. Coast and Geodetic Survey, mappers of the nation, objected that converting all their geodetic data to international feet would be a horrendous undertaking. They were allowed to continue to use the previous definition of the foot, that of the Mendenhall order (U.S. Coast and Geodetic Survey Bulletin 26, April 5, 1893), one foot = 1200/3937 meter. This foot is now known as the U.S. Survey foot, = 0.99999800 international foot, and is used only for land measurements.

football	The regulations of the National Collegiate Athletic Assn. (NCAA) and the National Football League (NFL) call for slightly different fields and balls, and very different goal posts.

foot-candle	A unit of illuminance in the foot-pound-second system of units, the illuminance at 1 foot from a 1-candela point source of light. Abbr, Ftc. One foot-candle ≈ 10.7639 ☞lux. Originally the foot-candle was the illuminance at 1 foot from a standard ☞candle, then at 1 foot from an international candle. It was then defined as the illuminance produced by 1 ☞lumen of "luminous flux" evenly distributed over a square foot. Though not an SI unit, foot-candles are still widely used to set lighting levels in architecture, in stage lighting, and in photography.

foot-pound second system of units	A coherent, absolute system of units based on the customary units in English. Between 1893 and 1959, the values of the foot and pound in the United States differed slightly from their values elsewhere, which were based on British prototypes. The British version is also known as the British absolute system of units. Major scientific work was done in this system in the 19TH century, but it was gradually eclipsed by various versions of the "metric system." In this system, the pound is a unit of mass. (For the system in which the pound is a unit of force, see ☞British gravitational system.) **Poundal**. The unit of force. Symbol, pdl. One poundal is the force that accelerates a mass of 1 pound at a rate of one foot per second per second. One poundal ≈ 0.138255 newton. The poundal should not be confused with the pound-force, a unit in the British gravitational system of units.

frames, picture	In the USA, ready-made frames are typically available in the following sizes:

4" × 5"	9" × 12"	16" × 20"
5" × 7"	10" × 13"	18" × 24"
6" × 8"	11" × 14"	20" × 28" or 30"
8" × 10"	12" × 16"	22" × 28"
8 1/2" × 11"	14" × 18"	24" × 36"

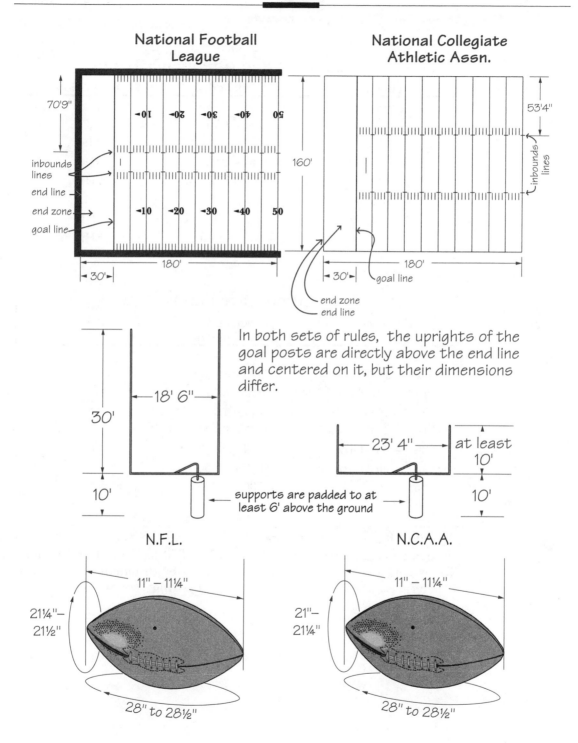

National Football
League

National Collegiate
Athletic Assn.

70'9"

53'4"

160'

inbounds
lines

end line

end zone

goal line

inbounds
lines

180'

30'

180'

30'

goal line

end zone
end line

In both sets of rules, the uprights of the goal posts are directly above the end line and centered on it, but their dimensions differ.

18' 6"

30'

10'

23' 4"

at least
10'

10'

supports are padded to at least 6' above the ground

N.F.L.

N.C.A.A.

11" – 11¼"

11" – 11¼"

21¼"–
21½"

21"–
21¼"

28" to 28½"

28" to 28½"

frequency

International Radiofrequency Bands		
Frequency	Wavelength	Designation
3 – 30 kHz	100 km – 10 km	VLF
30 – 300 kHz	10 km – 1 km	LF
0.3 – 3 MHz	1000 m – 100 m	MF
3 – 30 MHz	100 m – 10 m	HF
30 – 300 MHz	10 m – 1 m	VHF
0.3 – 3 GHz	1 m – 10 cm	UHF
3 – 30 GHz	10 cm – 1 cm	SHF
30 – 300 GHz	1 cm – 1 mm	EHF

Microwave Bands		
Frequency	Wavelength in centimeters	Band
0.225 – 0.390 GHz	133.3 – 76.9	P
0.390 – 1.550 GHz	76.9 – 19.3	L
1.55 – 5.20 GHz	19.3 – 5.77	S
5.20 – 10.90 GHz	5.77 – 2.75	X
10.9 – 36.0 GHz	2.75 – 0.834	K
36.0 – 46.0 GHz	0.834 – 0.652	Q
46.0 – 56.0 GHz	0.652 – 0.536	V
56.0 – 100.0 GHz	0.536 – 0.300	W

furlong

A unit of length in English-speaking countries, 13TH C–PRESENT, = 1/8 mile = 10 chains = 40 rods = 220 yards = 660 feet ≈ 201.168 meters. Today it is used almost exclusively to describe distances to be run in horse races. The word comes from "furrow long;" see ☞acre.

gallon

A unit of capacity used throughout the English-speaking world, 12TH C–PRESENT, the word coming into England with the Norman Conquest. In the United States, it is a unit of liquid capacity only = 231 cubic inches ≈ 3785.4118 cubic centimeters. Though this is the only nationally recognized gallon, it is not the only gallon that has been used in the United States; for example, in the late 19TH C some states had a 282-cubic-inch "milk gallon."

Some books provide conversion tables for a "U.S. dry gallon." There is no such unit; it is imagined by analogy with the British system, whose capacity units are used for both liquid and dry measure, and whose bushel holds eight gallons. United States dry measure includes a dry pint and a dry quart (which, like the English quart, is 1/32nd of a bushel), but the next dry unit is the peck, 1/4th of a bushel.

The U.S. gallon descends from the English wine gallon; see ☛United States, history of weights and measures.

The wine gallon itself has a peculiar history. Apparently it began (by the 14TH C?) as a unit used by wine merchants; R. D. Connor suggests that it was probably the volume occupied by eight *librae mercatoria* of wine. (The *libra mercatoria*, or London pound, of 15 troy ounces, didn't survive the development of avoirdupois weight.) From use by merchants to use by tax collectors was a short step, and for several hundred years the Excise collected duty on wine imports by the 231-cubic-inch gallon. Then in 1688 someone told the Commissioners of the Excise that a 224-cubic-inch gallon was the "true wine gallon." Of course the origins of the unit had been forgotten, but on looking into the matter, they found that the custodian of all legal standards, the Exchequer, had a standard for a 272-cubic-inch gallon but none for one of 231 cubic inches. Changing to a larger gallon would have meant a big drop in the King's revenues (since the tax was on the gallon), so the Commissioners carefully did nothing. But the idea was out. In 1700, a canny wine importer sued the government on the grounds that there was no legal definition for the gallon the customs agents were using. The Crown had to forfeit the case, and shortly thereafter the government legalized the wine gallon (5 Anne c 27, s 17, 1706, which took effect March 1, 1707).

Canada, the United Kingdom, and other nations formerly used the *imperial gallon,* created by legislation in 1824 (Act 5 George IV c 74) that defined the gallon as the volume of 10 avoirdupois pounds of water at 62°F, ≈ 277.274 cubic inches. The imperial gallon replaced both the wine gallon and the 282-cubic-inch ale gallon (from which, no doubt, the American states got their milk gallon).

General Conference on Weights and Measures

Acronym, CGPM, from the French, Conférence Générale des Poids et Mesures. The CGPM is an assembly of delegates from all the member states of the Meter Convention, at present 46 nations. The conference is held every four years. Its principal duty is to improve and spread SI, which it does by considering and approving recommendations made by the CIPM. The conference elects the 18 members of the CIPM, and also makes major decisions concerning the operation of the BIPM.

gill

1) In British imperial measure, 19TH–20TH C, a unit of capacity, ≈ 142.065 milliliters. Sometimes called a *noggin.* 2) In the United States, a unit of liquid capacity, ≈ 118.294 milliliters. Today the word "gill" is rarely used in the USA; the quantity is almost always referred to as a "half cup."

glass

Sheet glass and plate glass have now been almost entirely replaced by float glass, which is made by floating molten glass on a bed of molten tin, producing a very flat, high-quality surface, better than sheet glass, and almost as good as plate glass but without the expense of grinding. Float glass is made in five qualities, from best to worst: Mirror Select (q1), Mirror (q2), Glazing Select (q3); Glazing A (q4), Glazing B (q5), and Greenhouse (q5).

Metric designation, millimeters	Nominal decimal inch	Traditional designation
1	0.04	Micro-slide
1.5	0.06	Photo
2	0.08	Picture
(The sizes above are not used for glazing windows.)		
2.5	0.09	Single-strength
2.7	0.11	lami
3.0	0.12	1/8" or double-strength
4.0	0.16	5/32"
5.0	0.19	3/16"
5.5	0.21	7/32"
6.0	0.23	1/4"
8.0	0.32	5/16"
10.0	0.39	3/8"
12.0	0.49	1/2"
16.0	0.63	5/8"
19.0	0.75	3/4"
22.0	0.87	7/8"
25.0	1.00	1"
32.0	1.23	1 1/4"

The maximum size of pane that can be installed depends on the strength of the glass and on the load—mainly, how strong local winds are. The local building code may specify double-strength or even thicker glass.

Safety glass. Federal regulations prohibit the use of ordinary glass in certain locations where breakage might have life-threatening consequences, such as in sliding patio doors, doors on shower stalls and bathtubs, and glass panels near doors. Safety glass (or plastic) must be used for such purposes. There are several types of stronger glass:

✓ Fully Tempered Glass, after it has been cut to size, is heated to about 1,200°F and then rapidly cooled. The rapid cooling freezes internal stresses into the glass that make it four to five times stronger than untreated float glass, and that cause it to shatter into many small pieces when it breaks. (The lenses in eyeglasses, if glass, are tempered.) Glass cannot be cut, drilled or edged after tempering.

✓ Heat-Strengthened Glass has been heat-treated at a lower temperature than fully tempered glass. It breaks in much the same way, but it is only about twice as strong as ordinary float glass. It is not considered a safety glass, but may be used where extra strength is needed.

✓ Laminated glass is a sandwich, a layer of plastic between two sheets of glass. When it breaks, the glass remains adhered to the plastic.

Automobile windshields are laminated glass. Local dealers can cut laminated glass to size.

✓ Wired glass is rolled glass with welded wire mesh laminated in the middle. It is mainly used in locations where the glass, though cracked, must remain in position to block drafts during a fire; it was formerly very common in skylights. It is not as strong as float glass.

glass block

Inch Sizes (Actual Dimensions)	Metric Sizes (Nominal)
5¾" × 5¾" × 3⅞"	160 × 160 × 30 mm
7½" × 7½" × 3¼" or 4"	190 × 190 × 80 or 100
7¾" × 7¾" × 3⅞"	240 × 115 × 80
9½" × 9½" × 3⅛"	240 × 240 × 80
11¾" × 11¾" × 3⅞" or 4"	

Decorative
7¾" × 5¾" × 3⅛" or 3⅞"
4½" × 4½" × 3⅛"
4½" × 9½" × 3⅛"

Solid glass block is 7⅝" × 7⅝" × 3". Glass pavers, such as those inserted in sidewalks, are 5¾" × 5¾" × 1" or 7⅝" × 7⅝" × 1½".

glasses

Wine Glasses

The minimal wine glass is clear, has a stem, and holds at least four ounces. The usual all-purpose wine glass holds at least twice as much. In recent years, the sizes of wine glasses have increased—and so, perhaps, have the sizes of servings—but the extra capacity is better devoted to still air space that traps the wine's bouquet. Except for champagne glasses, the actual amount of wine poured is half or less

Cf   Cs   Co   W   R   Burg   RBurg   Sh   H2O

of the glass's capacity. All of the numbers in the descriptions are approximate.

Champagne flute (Cf): six, sometimes seven fluid ounces; 8 ½" high.

Champagne saucer (Cs): are lower than the flute (around 5 ½"), hold more (8 ¾ ounces) and are sneered at because the wine soon becomes flat. Still, it has festive associations.

Cordial (Co): Two ounces, 4". Cordials may also be served in larger glasses, say, Spanish-style sherry glasses.

White wine (W): The white wine glass has been growing, but remains smaller than the red. Older styles have capacities somewhat under eight ounces; newer designs somewhat under 12 oz. The traditional German glass for riesling, the *romer*, is much smaller.

Red wine (R): The smaller red wine glasses are now around nine ounces, which used to be an average size. More typical are 12- and even 14-ounce glasses.

Burgundy (Burg): The burgundy glass has a more balloon-shaped bowl and larger capacity than the red wine glass; it holds about 14 ounces and is 7" high. Next to the ordinary burgundy glass is the premiere example of the new generation of enormous glasses, the acclaimed 37-ounce glass for Burgundy (RBurg) developed by the Austrian firm Riedel, which has a program for designing the optimum glass for each type of wine, based on a theory that the size of the mouth of the glass and the shape of its bowl affects which part of the tongue (and hence which taste buds) the wine reaches first. Some scoff and some wine experts are believers.

Sherry (Sh): The Spanish-style sherry glass shown (a *copita*) is about 6" high and holds 6 ounces. Another type of sherry glass has a conical bowl; it deserves the reputation of the champagne saucer.

Port: The traditional port glass holds 6½ ounces and is 6" high. It is shaped like a small version of a red wine glass. Some people feel the traditional glass does not do justice to the wine's complexity, and that port should be served in a much larger glass.

Water (H20): The stemmed water goblet that accompanies wine service is about 7 ½" high and holds 13 ounces. This glass can be filled.

gloves

Gloves are sized by measuring around the hand at the point where thumb and palm meet. The following tables provide an approximate conversion if named sizes are used.

Men		Women	
XS	7"–7 ½"		
S	8"–8 ½"	S	6"–6 ½"
M	9"–9 ½"	M	7"–7 ½"
L	10"–10 ½"	L	8"–8 ½"
XL	11"–11 ½"		

The length of a glove is sized in "buttons," a measure that dates back to the time of Catherine di Medici. Buttons that closed the cuff of a glove were usually sewn on at one *pouce* (a French unit ≈ 1.0658 inch) intervals, from the base of the thumb to the edge of the cuff. A glove with five buttons would therefore be one pouce longer than a four-button glove.

golf

Club Heads

Lie is the angle between the shaft and the ground. Lie is called "upright" if the shaft is more vertical than usual; "flat" if less; the range of variation is about ±2°. A lie that is too great for the player can result in shots to the left of the target; if the lie is too flat for the player, shots may go to the right.

Loft is the angle between the face of the club and the vertical. A player with a low handicap will probably prefer several degrees less loft in a driver than the average golfer.

Face angle. Loft describes the vertical tilt of the club face; face angle describes a horizontal tilt in woods. The face angle is zero, or square, if the face "faces" straight ahead; it is "open" if it faces left, and "closed" (or "hooked") if it faces away from the golfer. To a person addressing the ball, the face appears to be about 2° more hooked than it really is.

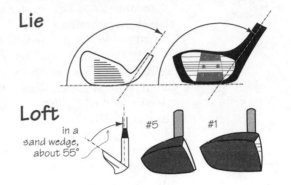

Lie

Loft

in a sand wedge, about 55° — #5 — #1

Face Angle (greatly exaggerated)

open — hooked

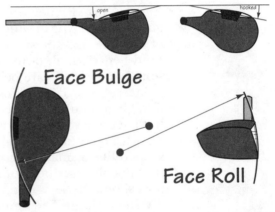

Face Bulge

Face Roll

Face bulge, face roll. The face of a wood is curved in two directions, like the surface on the rim of a doughnut. The amount of curvature is described by two radiuses. Face bulge is measured in a horizontal plane and face roll in a vertical plane. Values are from 7" to 20" in steps of 1/2"; a typical value for a #1 wood is 9 1/2 or 10".

Offset. In some clubs the shaft is ahead of the head; the hosel curves back to meet the head.

Grooves. USGA rules regulate the size of grooves on the club face. They may be no deeper than 0.020" and no wider than 0.035", and the flat area between grooves must be at least three times the groove width or 0.075", whichever is smaller.

The following tables give some idea of the ranges of values these parameters can take in a set of clubs. These are not ideal values; that depends on the player and his or her game. Golf pros and club shops are happy to take measurements, analyze swings, and make recommendations.

Woods		#1	#2	#3	#4	#5	#6	#7	#8	#9	#11
Loft		9°–12°	14°	15°–17°	20°	21°–24°	24°	26°	29°	32°	35°
L i e	Flat	53°		54°		55°					
	Std.	55°	54°	56°	56°	57°	56°	58°	58.5°	59°	60°
	Up.	57°		58°		59°					
Face Angle		+1°		+1°		+1°		+1°	±1°	±1°	±1°
Typ. head weight (gms)		200		210		220		228	231	240	240

Metal Woods		#1	#2	spoon	#3	#4	#5	#7	#8	#9	#11
L o f t	Flat	7°	12°-13°		16°	19°	22°	25°–26°	29°	32°	35°
	Std.	10°	12°	13°							
	Deep	12°	13°					28°			
L i e	Flat	53°			54°		55°				
	Std.	55°			56°	56.5°	57°	58°	58.5°	59°	60°
	Up.	57°			58°		59°				
Face Angle		+1°–2°	+1°	+1°	+1.5°	+1°	+2°	+2°	±1°	±1°	±1°
Typ. wt* (gms)		202			210		220	228	231	240	240

*Metal woods are also made in another sequence of sizes which are about 25 grams heavier in each size.

Irons		#1	#2	#3	#4	#5	#6	#7	#8	#9	pitch wedge	sand wedge*
Loft		16°–17°	18°–20°	21°–24°	24°–27°	28°–31°	32°–35°	36°–39°	40°–43°	44°–47°	48°–51°	54°–56°
L i e	Flat	54°	55°	56°	57°	58°	59°	60°	61°	62°	62°	62°
	Std.	56°	57°	58°	59°	60°	61°	62°	63°	64°	64°	64°
	Up.	58°	59°	60°	61°	62°	63°	64°	65°	66°	66°	66°
Offset		5	4.5	4	3.5	3	2.5	2	1.5	1	1	.5
Weight (g)		229	236	243	250	257	264	271	278	285	292	304

*Beyond the sand wedge lie other irons, often called lob wedges, with lofts of 60° or 64°.

Club Shafts

Flex. From most flexible to most rigid, the grades are L (ladies or light), A (average), R (regular), (some makers add F, firm, after R), S (stiff), and XS (extra stiff). The more powerful the player, the stiffer the required shaft.

Tip diameter. Shafts for woods have diameters of 0.270", 0.277", 0.286", 0.294", and 0.320", all of which are tapered, and a 0.335" parallel tip. For irons, shafts are available in a 0.355" taper tip and a 0.370" parallel tip.

Butt diameter. From 0.560" to 0.620" in 0.020" increments, and also 0.700".

Grip. Grips are sized by shaft diameters. Those for shafts with smaller diameters have thicker walls than those for thicker shafts, so that each shaft plus its matching grip comes out the standard size. If a grip is installed on a shaft larger than it was intended for, its installed diameter will be oversize. The club maker can also enlarge the grip by wrapping the shaft with masking tape before installing the grip. A very small increase—1/32" or even 1/64"—can make a difference. A grip that is too large can cause a player to slice; too small, to hook. Special grips are available for players with arthritis.

Swingweight. Total weight is important, but so is how the weight is distributed over the length of head and shaft. Swingweight describes this distribution. Two swingweight systems are in use, one using a fulcrum 12" from the butt of the shaft, and the other with the fulcrum at 14".

Balls

The maximum weight is 1.62 ounces. In the United States, the minimum diameter is 1.68"; but under the rules of the Royal and Ancient Golf Club of St. Andrews, Scotland, which apply in much of the world, the minimum diameter is 1.62".

Tees

The standard tee is 2⅛" long; 1⅝", 1⅞", and 2¾" tees are also made.

grain

The smallest unit of mass in the customary systems of units used in the English-speaking world, BEFORE 13TH C–PRESENT, since 1959 = 64.79891 milligrams exactly. Abbr, gr. Its subdivisions—see ☞moneyer's weight—are largely imaginary. The grain is the common element in ☞troy, ☞apothecaries', and ☞avoirdupois weight: the troy and apothecaries' pound are 5,760 grains, and the pound avoirdupois is 7,000 grains.

Traditionally, the grain was thought of as the weight of a barleycorn taken from the middle of the ear. In the United Kingdom the Weights and Measures Act, 1985, prohibited further use of the grain in trade. In the United States it remains the customary unit for expressing, for example, the weight of bullets.

gram

A metric unit of mass, one thousandth of a ☞kilogram, ≈ 15.4324 grains. Abbr, g. Sometimes spelled *gramme*.

A handy way of estimating the mass in grams of small objects is to compare them to U.S. coins, especially the cent and the nickel:

Coin	Since	Mass (grams)	Diameter (mm)
cent	1982	2.5 ± 0.100	19 mm
nickel	1938	5 ± 0.194	21 mm
dime	1965	2.268 ± 0.091	17.9 mm
quarter	1977	5.67 ± 0.227	24.3 mm
half dollar	1977	11.340 ± 0.454	30.6 mm

gray

The unit of absorbed dose in SI, used in studying and regulating ionizing radiation. Symbol, Gy. One gray is the quantity of ionizing radiation that, absorbed in a mass of 1 kilogram, would impart to it 1 joule of energy. In SI base units, it has the dimensions $\dfrac{meter^2}{second^2}$. The gray replaces the ☞rep.

The gray was adopted as the SI unit of absorbed dose by the 15TH CGPM in 1975 (Resolution 9). In 1976, the CIPM also approved the use of the gray as a unit of specific energy imparted, kerma, and absorbed dose index, by approving a report of the Consultative Committee for Units that adopted a recommendation of the ICRU.

grommets

Both the eyelet and ring type and the spur type of grommet are sized by the inner diameter of the grommet, which for practical purposes is the same as the diameter of the hole which is punched in cloth to insert the grommet. The eyelet type is commonly available in sizes 00 to 8, and the spur type in sizes 0 to 6. Sizes as large as 15 have been made.

Size	00	0	1	2	3	4	5	6	7	8
Hole dia.	3/16"	1/4"	9/32"	3/8"	7/16"	1/2"	5/8"	3/4"	15/16"	1 1/16"

hand

In English-speaking countries, 15TH–20TH C a unit of length, = 4", by the 18TH C used only to measure the height of horses. Abbr, hh ("hands high"). A writer in 1701 refers to "the measure called a handful used in measuring the height of horses, by 27 Henry VIII, Chap. 6, ordained to be 4 inches." Modern studies of the handbreadth of adult American males show a median (50th percentile) width of 3.4" at the knuckles, the metacarpal joint, while the breadth at the thumb is 4.1". So as a body measurement, it might have been taken toward the back of the hand, or at the metacarpal joint but including the thumb.

hats

In the USA, numerical men's hat sizes are the diameter of the sweat band inside the hat, if it were formed into a perfect circle. Women's hat sizes are simply the circumference of the inner band.

Size	Circum-ference	Size
6	19"	
6 1/8	19 3/8"	
6 1/4	19 3/4"	
6 3/8	20 1/8"	
6 1/2	20 1/2"	XS

Size	Circumference	Size (continued)
6 5/8	20 7/8"	XS
6 3/4	21 1/4"	S
6 7/8	21 5/8"	S
7	22"	M
7 1/8	22 3/8"	M
7 1/4	22 3/4"	L
7 3/8	23 1/8"	L
7 1/2	23 1/2"	XL
7 5/8	23 7/8"	XL
7 3/4	24 1/4"	XXL
7 7/8	24 5/8"	XXL
8	25"	

hectare

A unit of area = 100 ares = 10,000 square meters, ≈ 2.471054 ac. Symbol, ha. The *are, hectare*, and their symbols were adopted by the CIPM in 1879. In 1978 the CIPM decided it would be better to express all areas in square meters, and, while the are and hectare could continue to be used for the time being, they should not be introduced where not presently used. In the USA, however, the hectare is legally considered a unit within SI.

henry

The unit of inductance and permanence in SI. Symbol, H. The self- or mutual inductance of a closed loop is 1 henry if a current of 1 ampere gives rise to a magnetic flux of 1 weber. Its dimensions are $\frac{weber}{ampere}$, or in terms of base units, $\frac{meter^2 \cdot kilogram}{second^2 \cdot ampere^2}$.

hertz

The unit of frequency in SI. A measurement in hertz of a periodic phenomenon's frequency is the number of periods in 1 second. Symbol, Hz. The hertz was introduced by the 11TH CGPM (1960) in Resolution 12, which introduced SI. It replaced cycles per second.

hooks and eyes

These fasteners are made in a wide variety of styles. The sizes of the most common type, made of bent wire, run from 00 (the smallest) to 5 and are the same in the USA and UK. The dimensions below were obtained by measuring examples and not from a standard.

	00	0	1	2	3	4	5
A	1/8	5/32	1/8	11/64	13/64	7/32	9/32
B	1/4	5/16	13/32	16/32	17/32	21/32	25/32

horsepower

1) The unit of power in the British engineering system, = 550 foot-pounds of work per minute = 33,000 foot-pounds per hour, ≈ 745.6999 watts. Abbr. hp. Sometimes called British horsepower and abbr. B.H.P.

Prior to 1971, the figures American automobile manufacturers gave for engine horsepower were taken from tests of engines running on test stands without mufflers or other impediments. Nowadays the engine horsepower numbers are for the engine as installed in the car, which is roughly a third lower than the test stand figure.

2) Boiler horsepower = 9,809.50 watts.   **3)** Electric horsepower = 746 watts.   **4)** Metric horsepower = 75 meter kilograms-force per second = 735.49875 watts. Abbr, in French, ch (for *cheval-vapeur*); in German, PS (for *Pferdestärke*).   **5)** Water horsepower = 746.043 watts.

horseshoes

In the game of horseshoes, the steel stakes are an inch in diameter and 14" high, placed 40' apart (30' for women and juniors) and in the centers of squares 6' on a side. The stakes are tilted so that their tops are displaced 3" in the direction of the other stake.

The shoes are 7 5/8" long and have a maximum width of 7". At the open end of the U the clearance between the two sides is 3 1/2". The weight is 2 1/2 pounds. The shoes used in the game are not typical of those used on horses.

human beings

The figures given below are typical rather than normal. Where two figures are separated by a slash, the first is for an adult male and the second for an adult female.

Appendix   2"–6" long
Blood   1.6/0.875 gallons
Brain   1,300–1,500/1,200–1,350 cubic centimeters
Egg   0.1 mm in diameter. Newborn has 200,000–400,000; at puberty about 10,000; a mature woman has about 400.
Lungs   2 1/2 pounds, 800–1,000 square feet surface area capacity, 4.5–9/3.3–5.7 qt
        air intake: resting, 0.79/0.36
                light work, 1.77/0.91
                heavy work, 2.15/0.93
                maximum (vital capacity), 5.18, 3.17
Heart   Weighs less than a pound. Pumps 2,000 gallons per day, including 17 pints per minute through the lungs.
Intestine   28-30 feet long
        small intestine (1 1/2" diameter): duodenum 10–12", jejuneum 8–9', ileum 9'.
        large intestine (2 1/2" diameter), 6'.

Kidneys	4½" long, 2½" wide, 1½" thick. Weigh about 5 oz. The one on the left is longer and narrower.
Liver	The largest gland, 3–4 pounds (2.5% of body weight)
Ovaries	1¼" long, ½" thick
Pancreas	Second largest gland: 3 ounces.
Prostate	Size and shape of a walnut.
Skeleton	8/6 lb (dry, fat-free)
Skin	14 pounds, 2.2/1.9 sq. meters
Spleen	6 ounces, 6" long
Stomach	Capacity of 2½" pints
Sperm	Head 2.6 by 4.6 nanometers, tail 0.05 mm long. A man's daily production is about 200,000,000 sperm, which is also the number in a typical ejaculation.
Sweat glands	2,000,000 per person
Testicles	1¾" × 1" × 1"
Uterus	Size of a small pear; cervix is 1" long.
Vagina	2¾" to 3½" long

Effect of Aging on Pupil Size			
Age (years)	Diameter of pupil in millimeters		
	daylight	night	difference
20	4.7	8.0	3.3
30	4.3	7.0	2.7
40	3.9	6.0	2.1
50	3.5	5.0	1.5
60	3.1	4.1	1.0
70	2.7	3.2	0.5
80	2.3	2.5	0.2

hundred-weight

A unit of mass. Abbr, cwt. In the UK and several other Commonwealth countries = 112 lb, although other values have existed (including, centuries ago, 100 pounds). See ☞sack for an explanation of the origin of the 112-pound value. In the USA, when the term hundredweight is used at all, 100 pounds is meant, although sometimes, just to be sure, it is called a *short hundredweight*. It is also sometimes called a *cental*, a name proposed in the UK in the 19TH C for 100 pounds.

hurricanes

While a hurricane is being tracked in the United States, the National Weather Service provides frequently updated reports that include a force number. The number is a quick way of alerting local authorities to actions they should take, such as evacuations, and the scale of forces was devised with this in mind.

Saffir-Simpson Damage Potential Scale for Hurricanes					
Force	**Central Pressure**		**Winds (miles per hr)**	**Storm surge (feet)**	**Damage**
	kilo-pascals	**inches of mercury**			
1	98.0 or more	28.94	74 to 95	4 to 5	Minimal. Damage primarily to shrubbery, trees, foliage, and unanchored mobile homes. No real damage to other structures. Some damage to poorly constructed signs. Low-lying coastal roads flooded, minor pier damage, some small craft torn from moorings in exposed anchorage.
2	96.5 to 97.9	28.50 to 28.91	96 to 110	6 to 8	Moderate. Considerable damage to shrubbery and tree foliage; some trees blown down. Major damage to exposed mobile homes. Extensive damage to poorly constructed signs. Some damage to roofing materials of buildings; some window and door damage. No major damage to buildings. Coastal roads and low-lying escape routes inland cut by rising water two to four hours before arrival of hurricane center. Considerable damage to piers; marinas flooded. Small craft torn from moorings in unprotected anchorages. Evacuation of some shoreline residences and low-lying island areas required.
3	94.5 to 96.4	27.91 to 28.47	111 to 130	9 to 12	Extensive. Foliage torn from trees; large trees blown down. Practically all poorly constructed signs blown down. Some damage to roofing materials of buildings; some window and door damage. Some structural damage to small buildings. Mobile homes destroyed. Serious flooding at coast; many smaller structures near coast destroyed; larger structures near coast damaged by battering waves and floating debris. Low-lying escape routes inland cut by rising water three to five hours before hurricane center arrives. Flat terrain five feet or less above sea level flooded inland eight miles or more. Evacuation of low-lying residences within several blocks of shoreline possibly required.
4	92.0 to 94.4	27.17 to 27.88	131 to 155	13 to 18	Extreme. Shrubs and trees blown down; all signs down. Extensive damage to roofing materials, windows, and doors. Complete failure of roofs on many small residences. Complete destruction of mobile homes. Flat terrain 10 feet or less above sea level flooded inland as far as six miles. Major damage to lower floors of structures near shore due to flooding and battering by waves and floating debris. Low-lying escape routes inland cut by rising water three to five hours before hurricane center arrives. Major erosion of beaches. Massive evacuation of all residences within 500 yards of shore possibly required and evacuation of single-story residence on low ground within two miles of shore required.

Saffir-Simpson Damage Potential Scale for Hurricanes

For-ce	Central Pressure		Winds (miles per hr)	Storm surge (feet)	Damage
	kilo-pascals	inches of mercury			
5	91.9 or less	27.16 or less	156+	18.1+	Catastrophic. Shrubs and trees blown down; considerable damage to roofs of all buildings; all signs torn down. Very severe and extensive damage to windows and doors. Complete failure of roofs on many residences and industrial buildings; extensive shattering of glass in windows and doors. Some complete building failures. Small buildings overturned or blown away. Complete destruction of mobile homes. Major damage to lower floors of all structures less than 15 feet above sea level within 500 yards of shore. Low-lying escape routes inland cut by rising water three to five hours before hurricane center arrives. Massive evacuation of residential areas on low ground within five to 10 miles of shore possibly required.

Between 1900 and 1989 there were 57 class 1 hurricanes; 34 class 2; 44 class 3; 14 class 4; and 2 class 5.

hydrometer scales

Hydrometers measure the density of liquids. Generally they are floated in the liquid to be measured; the depth to which they sink indicates the density of the liquid. Many different scales have been developed for hydrometers, often for particular trades.

Baumé scale. A hydrometer scale used to indicate the density of liquids. Symbol, Bé. Usually one hydrometer is used for liquids denser than water and another for liquids lighter than water.

To calibrate a Baumé hydrometer for liquids denser than water, the hydrometer was immersed in distilled water, and the level at which it floats was taken as 0 on the scale (the 0 will be at the top of the scale). It was then immersed in a solution of 15 parts by weight sodium chloride (common salt) to 85 parts distilled water, and this point was marked 15. The rest of the scale was then marked off at intervals equal to one-fifteenth the distance between the 0 and 15 points.

In the Baumé hydrometer for liquids lighter than water, the 0 point is at the bottom of the scale and is the level at which the hydrometer floated when it was immersed in a solution of 10 parts common salt to 90 parts water by weight. The other fixed point is at 10, and is at the level at which the hydrometer floated in distilled water. The rest of the scale is marked off at intervals equal to one-tenth the distance between the marks for 0 and 10.

Unfortunately, early versions of the scale didn't take into account such factors as temperature, and they also didn't have very accurate values for the density of the salt solutions, with the result that 19TH C tables (including Baumé's) for converting Baumé degrees to density are not to be trusted.

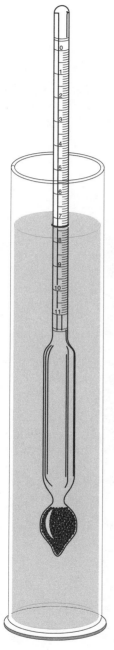

For liquids less dense than water, degrees Baumé $= \dfrac{140}{G} - 130$

For liquids denser than water, degrees Baumé $= 145 - \dfrac{145}{G}$

where "G" stands for the specific gravity of the liquid at 60°F in relation to water at 60°F.

Brix scale. A hydrometer scale calibrated so that readings at a specified temperature (in the USA, usually 20°C) equal the percentage by weight of sugar in the solution. Introduced in 1897 by Adolf F. Brix, an Austrian; often encountered on wine labels where it describes the sugar content of the grape juice from which the wine was made. Each two degrees Brix of the juice leads to about 1% alcohol by volume in the wine.

Balling scale. Similar to the Brix.

Öchsle scale. A German hydrometer scale used in the making of wine, which is simply specific gravity (with water = 1.000) in thousandths, minus 1000 (thus a specific gravity of 1.072 translates to 72 on the Öchsle scale, which is the average minimum reading required if a Kabinett wine is to be made. (Other average minimums are 86 for Spätlese; 95 for Auslese, 123 for Beerenauslese, and 150 for Trockenbeerenauslese.)

Dujardin scale reads in the potential percentage by volume of alcohol in the finished wine, assuming all the sugar were to be converted to alcohol.

Twaddell number. An arbitrary hydrometer scale for liquids denser than water, mostly used in England, 19TH–20TH C, for example in the leather industry to check tanning solutions. Abbr, °Tw. To convert a Twaddell number to a scale in which the specific gravity of water = 1, multiply by 0.005, then add 1. For example, 20°Tw is equivalent to a specific gravity of 1.100.

imperial measure

A system of weights and measures established for the British Empire in 1824 by "An Act for ascertaining and establishing Uniformity of Weights and Measures," (5 George IV chap. 74). The word "imperial" was first used in this connection in a committee report of March 31, 1821. Imperial measure was supposed to take effect on May 1, 1825, but it proved impossible to manufacture and distribute standards to the various cities and colonies by that date, so its implementation was delayed (by 6 George IV chap. 12, 1825) until January 1, 1826.

In a characteristically British fashion—especially in comparison to the French reforms 20-odd years before—the new system mainly redefined old measures instead of creating entirely new units, arguably with the exception of the gallon. For the changes made by imperial measure in a particular unit, see the entry for that unit.

The Weights and Measures Act of 1963 enjoined the Board of Trade not "to cause the exclusion from use for trade of Imperial in favour of metric units of measurement, weights, and measures," but in the 1970s and 1980s imperial measure was tentatively and gradually dismantled in favor of metric units, as the UK became more integrated with the European Community and its regulations. As a concession from the EC, the mile will be retained on road signs, and the pint in pubs.

inch

A unit of length in the English-speaking world = 2.54 centimeters exactly, in the United States since July 1, 1959 (see ☞yard), although that value had been recommended by, for example, the American Standards Assn. since 1933.

The inch is an old unit, used by the Saxons at least by the 7TH C, since a law of around 602 requires malefactors to give those they have stabbed one shilling for each inch of wound. The word comes from the Latin *uncia*, from which we also get "ounce." "Uncia" was the Roman name both for a 12th part of the *libra* (similar to a pound) and for a 12th part of a *pes* (similar to a foot). The division of the foot into 12", and of the troy pound into 12 ounces, is a legacy from the Roman invaders.

Legally the inch is defined as 1/36th of a yard. Traditionally it had two definitions: the length of three barleycorns from the middle of the ear, placed end to end, and the width of the thumb at the base of the nail. The "thumb inch" was especially common in the cloth trade; in 1711 Queen Anne finally explicitly forbade its use (10 Anne chap. 16 s 4).

index cards

Standard index card sizes in the United States are 3" × 5", 4" × 6", and 5" × 8". The cards in rotary files—those popularized by Rolodex—are 2 1/8" × 4".

International Bureau of Weights and Measures

English translation of the official name, *Bureau International des Poids et Mesures*, from which the acronym, BIPM. The BIPM was created by the Meter Convention signed by seventeen nations in Paris on May 20, 1875, during the last session of the Diplomatic Conference of the Meter. The following year the French government made available to the organization an estate at Sèvres, near Paris, where it is still located.

The International Prototype of the Kilogram, the sole remaining physical prototype of an SI unit, is kept at the Bureau, as well the International Prototype of the Meter. Since 1985 the Bureau has also been responsible for maintaining Atomic Time.

The Bureau is an intergovernmental organization supported by the member states in order to maintain and improve standards of measurement. For example, a national government might send its national standard of, say, the kilogram, to be checked against the International Prototype kept at the Bureau. In all likelihood, the national standard originated at the Bureau. The BIPM is supervised by the ☞International Committee for Weights and Measures.

International Committee for Weights...

International Committee for Weights and Measures; acronym, CIPM, from its official name, *Comité International des Poids et Mesures*. The committee consists of eighteen scientists elected at the previous CGPM, each from a different nation that is signatory to the Meter Convention. The committee receives reports, makes recommendations to the

CGPM, and has oversight of the ☞International Bureau of Weights and Measures.

International System of Electric and Magnetic Units

A system of electrical units defined by the International Electrical Congress at Chicago in 1893, with the object of arriving at definitions which would be more easily realized in the laboratory than the absolute cgs units. *(This system is not the current "metric system," known as SI, the Système International, or International System of Units.)* Its four fundamental units measure resistance, current, length and time. The units of length and time were the centimeter and second; the units of resistance and current were defined so that they would be approximately equal to the absolute practical ohm and the absolute practical ampere. The system was modified by the London Electrical Conference in 1908, and discarded by the CGPM in 1948.

International ampere. See ☞ampere.

International ohm. See ☞ohm.

International coulomb. A unit of electric charge: the quantity of electric charge which passes any point in a wire in one second when the wire carries a current of 1 international ampere. One international coulomb ≈ 0.99985 absolute coulomb.

International System of Units

The modernized metric system, what most people mean when they speak of "the metric system." Abbr, SI. It consists of seven base units, a number of derived units with special names, and two supplementary units (each of these has its own entry in this book). To any of these units may be attached one of 16 decimal multiplier or submultiplier prefixes.

Base Units

meter	length
kilogram	mass
second	time
ampere	electric current
kelvin	thermodynamic temperature
mole	amount of substance
candela	luminous intensity

Derived Units with Special Names

hertz	frequency
newton	force
pascal	pressure, stress
joule	energy, work, quantity of heat
watt	power, radiant flux
coulomb	electric charge, quantity of electricity
volt	electric potential, potential difference, electromotive force

farad	capacitance
ohm	electric resistance
siemens	electric conductance
weber	magnetic flux
tesla	magnetic flux density
henry	inductance
degree Celsius	Celsius temperature
lumen	luminous flux
lux	illuminance
becquerel	activity
gray	absorbed dose, specific energy imparted, kerma, absorbed dose index
sievert	dose equivalent, dose equivalent index

Supplementary Units

radian	plane angle
steradian	solid angle

Prefixes in the International System of Units

Prefix	Symbol	Meaning (using American names of numbers)	Example
yocto-	Y	10^{24} = 1 000 000 000 000 000 000 000 000 = 1 septillion	
zepto-	Z	10^{21} = 1 000 000 000 000 000 000 000 = 1 sextillion	
exa-	E	10^{18} = 1 000 000 000 000 000 000 = 1 quintillion	
peta-	P	10^{15} = 1 000 000 000 000 000 = 1 quadrillion	
tera-	T	10^{12} = 1 000 000 000 000 = 1 trillion	
giga-	G	10^{9} = 1 000 000 000 = 1 billion	gigajoule
mega-	M	10^{6} = 1 000 000 = 1 million	megawatt
kilo-	k	10^{3} = 1 000 = 1 thousand	kilowatt
hecto-	h	10^{2} = 100 = 1 hundred	hectare
deka-*	da	10^{1} = 10 = ten	
		10^{0} = 1 = one	
deci-	d	10^{-1} = .1 = a tenth of a	decibel
centi-	c	10^{-2} = .01 = a hundredth of a	centimeter
milli-	m	10^{-3} = .001 = a thousandth of a	milliliter
micro-	μ	10^{-6} = .000 001 = a millionth of a	microfarad
nano-	n	10^{-9} = .000 000 001 = a billionth of a	nanometer
pico-	p	10^{-12} = .000 000 000 001 = a trillionth of a	picofarad
femto-	f	10^{-15} = .000 000 000 000 001 = a quadrillionth of a	femtosecond
atto-	a	10^{-18} = .000 000 000 000 000 001 = a quintillionth of a	
zetta-	z	10^{-21} = .000 000 000 000 000 000 001 = a sextillionth of a	
yotta-	y	10^{-24} = .000 000 000 000 000 000 000 001 = a septillionth of a	

* The spelling "deca-" is often used (but not in the United States).

History

See ☞metric system for the early development and spread of the basic units.

The Conference on the Meter led to the formation of permanent international bodies (the CGPM, BIPM, CIPM) with a commitment to the meter and kilogram, and a mandate to standardize and improve the world's weights and measures. In the early years, the organizations' attention was focused mainly on units, rather than systems of units.

In the late 19TH and early 20TH C, most scientists used ☞centimeter-gram-second systems, which proliferated because there were various ways of handling electromagnetic quantities. Alongside these systems were others, also ostensibly "metric," which defined other electric and magnetic units for practical use. A subject which involved both electric and magnetic quantities required treatment in two and possibly three different systems of units. Furthermore, as new sciences developed they tended to extemporize new units, for example, the study of radioactivity led to nuclear physics and to curies, rads, rems, barns, and other units, all "metric."

In 1901, the Italian physicist G. Giorgi proposed a meter–kilogram-second–electrical unit system, presenting it to the International Electrotechnical Commission (IEC) in 1904. Giorgi originally suggested that the electric unit be a unit of resistance, but later that was replaced by a unit of current, the ampere. The great advantage of Giorgi's proposal was that it used familiar units of mass, length, and time and, with rationalized units (and the right choice of a value for the permeability of free space), it preserved the sizes of the practical electric units, even though they were defined in absolute rather than material terms. It was an absolute practical system. In 1935, the IEC passed a resolution adopting the Giorgi system (but without deciding whether the units should be rationalized or not) and recommending it be named after him. But it was too late; almost everywhere it was referred to as the MKSA system.

Also in 1935, the Commission on Symbols, Units and Nomenclature of the International Union of Pure and Applied Physics (IUPAP) recommended basing a system on the meter and kilogram, and proposed the name newton for the unit of force based on the kilogram, second and meter. The IEC confirmed their 1935 decision in 1938 (still without deciding the rationalization issue), and the IUPAP repeated their recommendation in 1948.

In 1948 the NINTH CGPM, prodded by the French government and noting that IUPAP had asked the CIPM "to adopt for international use a practical international system of units" and had recommended "the MKS system and one electric unit of the absolute practical system," formally requested the CIPM "to make recommendations on the establishment of a practical system of units of measurement suitable for adoption by all signatories" (Resolution 6).

In July, 1950, the IEC's Technical Committee No. 24 on Electrical and Magnetic Magnitudes and Units chose the ampere to be the fourth, electric, unit and finally recommended rationalized units.

The 10TH CGPM (1954) adopted as base units the meter, kilogram, second, ampere, degree Kelvin, and candela, thus adopting the Giorgi system. The remaining base unit, the mole, was added by the 14th CGPM in 1971 (Resolution 3).

The 11TH CGPM (1960) named the new system "International System of Units;" adopted the "international abbreviation" SI and the prefixes from tera- through pico-; and added two supplementary units and 27 derived units, 13 of which had special names. So 1960 may be taken as the birth year of SI. Since then, one base unit, 11 derived units (including five with special names) and eight prefixes have been added; the second, meter and candela have been redefined; the liter and micron have been discarded, and the "degree Kelvin" changed to "Kelvin."

Written Usage in SI

The following recommendations are based on those of the United States' National Institute of Standards and Technology:

Capitalization. When written out, the names of units start with a lower-case letter, except at the beginning of a sentence or in a title. The sole exception is "degree Celsius."

Symbols for units are lower-case unless they come from a person's name, in which case the first letter of the symbol is capitalized. The exception, in the United States, is L for liter. See ☞liter.

Symbols for numerical prefixes are lower-case, except for those representing factors of 10^6 or more: mega- (M), giga- (G), tera- (T), peta- (P), exa- (E), zepto- (Z), and yocto- (Y). When written out, all prefixes are lower-case.

Plurals. When the names of units are written out, they should be made plural when the number to which they refer is greater than one. Fractions are always singular. Symbols are never made plural. So "3 kilograms" and "3 kg" are correct, but "3 kilogram" and "3 kgs" are not.

Periods. A period is not used after a symbol, except at the end of a sentence.

Numerals. In newspapers, it is usual to write out the numbers from one to nine and use numerals for everything else. In ordinary magazines and books, whole numbers from one through ninety-nine, and any of these followed by "hundred," "thousand," "million," etc., are written out. If the unit is represented by an abbreviation or symbol, the associated number should be written as numerals. Only the last of these conventions applies to scientific and technical writing, in which all numbers expressing physical quantities should be represented by numerals.

Decimal marker. In the USA, the dot is used as the decimal marker and is placed on the line. In the rest of the world, the comma is used as the decimal marker. (A centered dot was formerly used in Great Britain, for example "0·14".)

Grouping of digits. Digits should be separated by spaces into groups of three, counting from the decimal marker. The use of a space, and not a comma, is necessary because in the USA, in nontechnical writing a period is used as the decimal marker and a comma is used to separate groups of three digits, while in other countries the comma is used as the decimal marker. Using a space avoids crosscultural confusion. So "3.141 592" and "176 000." not "176,000." No space should be put in a number that has only 4 digits: not "1 568" but "1568".

Spaces. A prefix should not be separated from the name of the unit by a space or hyphen.

A space should be left between a symbol and the number to which it refers ("3 kg", not "3kg"), with the exception of the symbols for degree, minute, and second of angles: "3° 27' 59"."

Mathematical operations. When symbols for mathematical operations are used, the SI units should also be represented by symbols, not by their written-out names. So "joules per mole", "J/mol" and "J·mol^{-1}" are acceptable, but "joules/mole" and "joules·mol^{-1}" are not. This principle also applies to compound units, such as the newton meter. "N·m", "newton meter", and "newton-meter" are all correct; "newton·meter" is not.

Spoken Usage

Reading numbers aloud is simplified by the written usage rule that numbers are to be broken into groups of three digits, starting from the decimal point. Read aloud, a group of three digits consists of the name of the first digit; followed by "hundred," followed by the name of the number represented by the last two digits; followed by (for numbers greater than 999) the name of the order of magnitude for that group of three, such as thousand, million, and so on. For example, the number "123 456" is read aloud as "one hundred twenty-three thousand four hundred fifty-six." Expressions like "fifteen hundred" should not be used, nor should "a hundred twenty-three."

Decimal fractions. In numbers with a decimal fraction, the digits after the decimal point are to be spoken as a series of the names of the individual digits. For example, "123.456 millimeters" would be read aloud as "one hundred twenty-three point four five six." It should not be read as "one hundred twenty-three and four hundred fifty-six thousandths."

The decimal prefixes in SI greatly simplify, and hence clarify, verbalization of numbers. A number that contains many trailing zeros can usually be simplified by choosing a larger unit, e.g., not "one million two hundred thirty thousand centimeters" but "one point two three kilometers." Of course, this cannot be done when the trailing zeros indicate significant figures.

international units

Various units of biological potency used in pharmacology. Abbr, IU. For example, a dose of 200 IU of an antibiotic has a certain amount of bacteria-fighting ability, but it might have a mass of 20 milligrams from one manufacturer and 40 from another. The size of the unit varies with the substance and is presently set by the Expert Committee on Biological Standardization of the World Health Organization (WHO). An International Unit is standardized by defining a test method and providing a reference standard, an actual preparation of the substance having a known activity. Suppose, for example, one wants to determine how many IUs are in a given amount of a preparation of an antibiotic, and that WHO says one gram of the reference standard for that antibiotic has an activity of 500 IU. The amount of the preparation being tested that inhibits the growth of bacteria in the test to the same extent as one gram of the reference standard will contain 500 IU of the antibiotic. The assay is biological, not chemical.

In the United States, the reference standards are produced and released under the authority of the United States Pharmacopeia Convention. USP Units and the International Units of potency are usually identical.

Measuring the size of a dose in terms of its biological effect rather than as a specific weight of pure substance solved a number of problems: sometimes it wasn't known exactly which chemical had the effect; sometimes the preparation (for example, material produced by fermentation) contained a number of chemicals each of which produced the effect but in varying degrees; sometimes the amount was so small it could not be assayed quantitatively by the methods of the day.

In the 1950s quantitative analysis of pharmacologicals became much more precise and sensitive. With new methods it was possible to detect and determine the actual mass of chemicals in very small concentrations. Once the substance responsible for an effect has been isolated, identified, and prepared in a form that allows it to be completely characterized by chemical and physical properties, the biological assay is no longer needed and the International Unit for that substance is generally discontinued. For a decade or more stating the actual weight has been preferred to using IU; for example, they are no longer used in the *U.S. Pharmacopeia*. Some examples of old international units and their modern equivalents are:

One IU of vitamin A = 0.3 micrograms of retinol or 0.6 micrograms of beta-carotene. Quantities of vitamin A are also measured in "retinol equivalents." One retinol equivalent = 3.33 IU of retinol, or 10 IU of beta-carotene.

One IU of vitamin E = 0.91 milligrams of synthetic *dl*-alpha-tocopherol, or about 0.67 milligrams of *d*-alpha-tocopherol.

jackets, men's

In casual outerwear like parkas fit is not as important as it is in sports jackets or overcoats, as long as the garment is not too small. Alterations are rarely done. Far fewer sizes are manufactured and they are identified by letters, not numbers. The sizes are not standardized; each manufacturer uses its own judgment in choosing the "builds" it believes make up its market.

To illustrate the nature and extent of the variations, reproduced here with their permission is a recent size table from Eddie Bauer, a highly reputable supplier of outdoor wear.

Size	Chest	Waist	Neck	Sleeve
XS	34–36	26–27	13–13 1/2	31–32
S	37–39	28–31	14–14 1/2	32–33
M	40–42	32–35	15–15 1/2	33–34
L	43–45	36–39	16–16 1/2	34–35
XL	46–48	40–43	17–17 1/2	35–36
XLL	49–51	44–46	18–18 1/2	36–37

Tall men's sizes 1 1/2"–2" longer in sleeves and body (3/4" longer if short sleeved). XXL, larger all over.

If we compare these sizes with those of another outdoor clothing supplier, we find that the two company's XL sizes are virtually identical. For a person with a 34" chest, however, the second company offers size

133

S, specified for a 28–30" waist, 14–14 1/2" neck, and 32–33" sleeve; in other words, the waist, neck, and sleeve length are each an inch bigger than Bauer's XS size. The sizes describe two very differently shaped bodies.

The example shows that one should not rely on suit size in choosing jackets, and that despite the limited number of sizes and lack of alterations, the alert shopper does have a choice of fits.

joule

The unit of energy in SI. Symbol, J. The work done when the point of application of a force of 1 newton is displaced 1 meter in the direction of the force. A watt-second is equal to 1 joule. In terms of derived units, the joule's dimensions are *newton* times *meter*, or in terms of only base units, $\dfrac{meter^2 \cdot kilogram}{second^2}$.

Average heat flow in one second from earth's interior out through 1 sq. meter of the earth's surface	60 millijoules
Heat content of a gallon of gasoline	131 megajoules
Heat content of 1,000 cubic feet of natural gas	1.09 gigajoules
Heat content of a barrel of crude oil	6.1 gigajoules
Heat content of a cord of wood (U.S. avg.)	21 gigajoules
Heat content of a short ton of anthracite	26.78 gigajoules
Average annual household energy consumption in U.S., 1987	106.5 gigajoules
Average annual per capita energy consumption in U.S., 1991	340 gigajoules
Energy released by sun in one second	390 yoctojoules
Energy released by one of the brightest stars in one second	390 million yocto-joules

karat

A unit of proportion indicating what part of an alloy is precious metal. Pure, unalloyed gold is 24 karat; 12-karat gold is ¹²/24, or 50% gold, and so on. In the USA it is spelled with an initial "k," to distinguish it from the carat, a unit of mass, but in much of the world it is spelled with a "c."

The word is from the Arabic *qirat*, which represented the ratio ¹/24 much as in English the word "nail" used to represent ¹/16 of a larger unit, sometimes ¹/16 of a yard and sometimes ¹/16 of a hundredweight. In Lebanon today, for example, one *kirat* is ¹/24th of a *drah*.

Pure gold is quite soft and not suitable for objects like rings; a ring is made of 18-karat gold alloy to improve performance, not to save on the cost of materials. Alloys below 14 karat, however, are liable to crack.

kelvin

The unit of thermodynamic temperature and the unit of temperature interval in SI, defined by the 13TH CGPM, 1967, as ¹/273.16 of the thermodynamic temperature of the triple point of water (the temperature at which water can exist simultaneously as solid, liquid, and gas). Abbr, K.

When the kelvin was originally established in 1948 (NINTH CGPM, resolution 7), it was as the "degree absolute" with the symbol °K. In 1960 the 11TH CGPM changed the name to "degree Kelvin," with the same symbol. Seven years later, the 13TH CGPM decided to change the name to simply "kelvin" (note the switch to lowercase) and the abbreviation to K, but allowed the older usage to continue for the time being. In 1980, the CIPM withdrew that permission. Consequently, no degree mark is used with this abbreviation, and it is read as, for example, "four hundred kelvin," not "four hundred degrees kelvin." The temperature in kelvin can be found by adding 273.15 to the temperature in degrees Celsius. See ☞temperature.

kilogram

The unit of mass in SI, equal to the mass of the International Prototype of the Kilogram, a platinum-iridium cylinder kept by the BIPM at Sèvres, France ≈ 2.2046 pounds avoirdupois. Abbr, kg. The kilogram is one of SI's seven base units, the only SI unit still defined by a physical prototype, and the only one that incorporates one of the decimal multiplier prefixes in its name. To be completely consistent, the gram should have been the unit of mass.

History

The kilogram originated in the reforms of the French Revolution. Conceptually, it was to be the mass of a cubic decimeter of water at water's maximum density, and was originally called a *grave*, but the name was changed to kilogram in 1795, the same year that Lefèfre-Gineau was given the job of determining just how massive a cubic decimeter of water was. In the meantime, a provisional kilogram was made which was expected to be close enough to the final value for commercial purposes.

The method that Lefèfre-Gineau chose depends on the principle that the difference between the weight of an object in air and its weight immersed in water is the weight of the water it displaces. He made a hollow brass cylinder, just heavy enough to sink in water, whose dimensions were measured repeatedly. After corrections were made for changes in size due to thermal expansion, the cylinder's volume was calculated to be 11.28 cubic decimeters at 0°C. To weigh the cylinder, special weights were made of brass of the same density as the brass of the cylinder, to compensate for the buoyancy in air of the weights.

After months of subtle and precise work, the researchers concluded that the mass of a cubic decimeter of water at its maximum density was 99.92072% of the mass of the provisional kilogram.

To create platinum standards for the new system of weights and measures, the former royal jeweller, Marc Etienne Janety (Janetti), was recalled to Paris (he had fled when the trouble started). By 1796 he was making kilogram masses. One of these, a cylinder 39.4 millimeters in diameter and 39.7 millimeters high, was legally declared the official prototype of the kilogram in 1799. Since then it has been called the Kilogramme des Archives.

In the 1870s the French government sponsored a series of conferences (1870, 1872) to discuss how metric standards ought best be designed, produced and distributed. One of the conference's conclusions was that new standards ought to be made of a platinum-iridium alloy rather than pure platinum. The first attempts to do so were failures. The Metric Convention (1875), which led to the estab-

lishment of the BIPM, gave fresh impetus to the work, and preparation of the alloy was entrusted to the London firm of Johnson, Matthey, who specialized in precious metals. They did succeed in casting the alloy, the French produced standards from it, and the new standards were ready for distribution before the FIRST CGPM in 1889. This conference recognized one of the new platinum-iridium standards—the one whose mass most closely matched that of the Kilogramme des Archives—as the new prototype of the kilogram. It is that object, made in the 1870s, which is referred to as the International Prototype Kilogram.

Modern measurements of the mass of water have shown that a cubic decimeter of water has a mass that is about 28 parts per million less than a kilogram—but that doesn't matter, because the mass-of-a-cubic-decimeter-of-water definition hasn't applied since the Kilogramme des Archives was accepted.

Future

The continued dependence of the kilogram on a physical prototype makes some metrologists uneasy. The prototype's mass may be changing by as much as 50 parts per billion per century. Besides, because of the risk of damaging it, the unique prototype can't be used very often—the use being comparisons with the various national standards laboratories' standard kilograms. Although currently the prototype meets all needs for accuracy, physicists have been searching for a way of defining the kilogram in terms of fundamental physical constants.

A means of defining the kilogram in terms of electric units has been proposed by B. P. Kibble at the National Physical Laboratory in Teddington, England, and explored there and at NIST. The method uses a movable coil of wire in a magnetic field and exploits the precision with which the volt and ohm can now be defined using quantum effects. From measurements of the coil's velocity, the acceleration due to gravity, the coil's velocity, and the current and voltage in the coil, the mass of the coil can be calculated. As of 1993, the accuracy was not as good as that obtained with the Prototype Kilogram, but in the future this or some similar technique is bound to lead to a definition that will supplant the Prototype Kilogram.

kip

In the USA, a unit of force = 1,000 pounds-force, $\approx 4.44822 \times 10^3$ newtons. Used by architects and structural engineers to describe deadweight loads. From "**ki**lo" + "**p**ound".

kitchen

An old rule of residential kitchen design is that the "work triangle", a triangle connecting the range, sink, and refrigerator, should have a perimeter of more than 12' but less than 22'.

Horizontal levels in kitchens are described by height above the finish floor (a.f.f.).

The tops of base cabinets are 34 1/2" a.f.f.. The countertop adds another 1 1/2", so the height of the finished counter is conventionally 36" a.f.f. Ideally, however, a countertop should be 3" below the height of the elbow of the person who will be using the counter.

The depth of the counter is usually 24". Single door and drawer base cabinets range in length from 12" to 24", on 3" modules. Double door and other types can be as wide as 48", again on 3" modules. Base units for sinks and ranges range from 54" to 84" on 6" modules.

Wall cabinets are usually either 30" or 42" high, although 12", 18", and 24" cabinets are also available. The depth is usually 12". The level for the top of 30-inch cabinets is 83 1/2" a.f.f. with a soffit, or 84" a.f.f. without. The tops of 42-inch cabinets are 95 1/2" a.f.f.. Available lengths range from 24" to 48" in steps of 3".

Cabinets 84" high are made for refrigerators (in widths of 36", 39", and 42"), for such tools as brooms (18" to 36" in steps of 6"), and to hold ovens at eye level (24" or 27" wide).

Dishwashers require a 24" opening (European models require 60 cm). Ranges are 30", 36" and 48" wide.

kitchen measure

In the United States, following a convention established by the Boston Cooking School in the 19TH C, recipe quantities are measured by volume and spoonfuls are always level spoonfuls unless otherwise stated. Measurement by weight is more common in Europe.

In the United States, the cup is a definite quantity, one half of a U.S. fluid pint, even when it is used to measure dry materials like flour. The distinction maintained elsewhere between U.S. dry and U.S. liquid quarts, pints, etc. does not apply in the kitchen; liquid capacity is used for everything.

Two important but unofficial units of liquid and dry measure are the tablespoon (abbr, T or tbl) and the teaspoon (abbr, t or tsp). In the USA, 1 tablespoon = 3 teaspoons. There are 16 tablespoons in a cup, so a tablespoon is ½ U.S. fluid ounce ≈ 14.787 mL, and the teaspoon ≈ 4.929 mL. (A study several decades ago by the U.S. Bureau of Standards found that the typical silver teaspoon and measuring teaspoon held 1½ fluid drams (≈ 5.5 mL), not the 1 fluid dram (≈ 3.7 mL) often given in reference works.) For practical purposes, today the U.S. teaspoon is 5 mL and the U.S. tablespoon is 15 mL.

Another spoon measure, the barspoon, = ½ teaspoon, is only used in mixing drinks.

Many sources define the drop as a sixtieth of a teaspoon, but the size of drops is very dependent on the dropper and the nature of the liquid.

							quart
						pint	2
					cup	2	4
				half cup	2	4	8
			US fluid ounce	4	8	16	32
		tablespoon	2	8	16	32	64
	teaspoon	3	6	24	48	96	192
milliliters	4.9	14.8	29.6	118.3	236.5	473	946

Cooking with British Recipes

As the saying has it, the British and Americans are separated by a common language. In recipes from British cookbooks (before metrification), the words are the same but the meanings are different, a trap for the unwary.

The cup is not a well-defined quantity in the UK. The imperial half pint may be referred to a breakfastcupful or, sometimes, as a British Standard Cup. A teacupful is a quarter pint.

Between the teaspoonful and the tablespoonful lies the dessertspoonful, such that 1 tablespoonful = 2 dessertspoonfuls, 1 dessertspoonful = 2 teaspoonfuls, and 1 teaspoonful = 2 saltspoonfuls. Thus 4 (instead of 3) British teaspoons = 1 British tablespoon. However, in British recipes a spoonful of a dry ingredient traditionally means a rounded spoonful, with as much heaped above the spoon edge as lies within it. (A rounded spoonful is not a heaping spoonful, which would be as much as the spoon could hold.)

An English pharmacopeia of 1618 defined the tablespoon as the volume of distilled water weighing 3 drachms, which would be about

12 mL. Pharmacists, and following them such respected sources as *The Economist*, say the British tablespoon = ½ imperial fluid ounce ≈14.21 mL, so that there would be 10 tablespoons in an imperial gill and 20 in a half pint.

Cooks, however, don't seem to agree. Mrs. Beeton, the great survivor among British cookbook authors, says under the heading Liquid Measure that a quarter pint contains "6 large tablespoonfuls." Since an imperial quarter pint (a gill) contains 5 imperial fluid ounces, that would make the "large" tablespoon ⅚th of an imperial fluid ounce ≈ 23.7 mL, and the teaspoon about 6 mL.

Irma Rombauer and Marion Becker mention in their perennial *The Joy of Cooking* the grief they suffered in exploring British recipes before realizing the measures differed. They settled on taking 1 British tablespoon as 1 ¼ U.S. tablespoons, and 1 British teaspoon ≈ 1 ¼ U.S. teaspoons as well. Clearly this cannot be right, since the two countries' teaspoons to a tablespoon ratios differ, but whatever works....

On purely theoretical and un-kitchen-tested grounds, we would suggest trying this as a first approximation:

For liquid ingredients, let 1 British teaspoon = 1 U.S. teaspoon, and let 1 British tablespoon = 1 ¼ U.S. tablespoon.

For dry and solid ingredients, let 1 British teaspoon = 2 U.S. teaspoons, and let 1 British tablespoon = 1 U.S. tablespoon plus 2 U.S. tablespoons.

Let us know how it comes out.

labór

In Texas, 19TH–20TH C, a unit of land area, ≈ 71.67 hectares ≈ 177.136 acres. A labór is one million square varas, often specifically a square 1000 varas on a side. For its history, see ☞vara.

lamps, electric

The key component in most lamps is threaded steel tube, often brass-plated, called "lamp pipe." The standard size is ⅛ IP; the IP stands for "iron pipe;" the sizes belong to the 19TH C Briggs Standard of Wrought-Iron Pipe Dimensions, to which seamless brass and copper tubing was also made. Although ⅛ IP tube is by far the most common size in lamps, three IP and one non-IP size are used:

✓ ⅛ IP, 0.405" outer diameter, fits in a 7⁄16" hole, threaded 27 threads to the inch.

✓ ¼ IP, 0.540" outer diameter.

✓ ⅜ IP, 0.675" outer diameter. This was the size of the outlets for gas lighting; the system of sizes used for the pipes that brought gas to gas lights was adopted for electric lights. In older ceiling fixtures (the outlet box is perfectly round instead of square) the light is attached to a ⅜ IP stud, just as a gas light was. Today an adapter, called a "hickey," is used to get from the ⅜ IP stud to the fixture's ⅛ IP.

In addition to the IP sizes, a smaller tube is available,

✓ 1⁄4-27. Unlike the IP sizes its outer diameter actually is 1⁄4", but its screw thread is not standard (National Fine is 1⁄4-28). The standard thread for 1⁄8 IP pipe, however, is 27 threads per inch.

The locknuts, reducers, adapters, and so on for use with lamp pipe are speciality items; ordinary nuts won't work. Fortunately many hardware and craft stores carry a large selection of lamp parts.

Harps are made in heights from 7" to 12" in steps of 1⁄2", and then by whole inches to 15". The stud at the top of the harp, onto which the finial is screwed to hold down a shade, has a 1⁄4-27 thread.

Machine screws in lamps are almost always 8-32.

lamp shades

When only one number is given as the size of a round lamp shade, it is the diameter of the bottom of the shade. If the shade is oval, the diameter is taken to be the longest distance across the bottom. If the shade is polygonal—square or hexagonal, for example—it is the distance from one point on the bottom of the shade to the opposite point.

When the size is stated as "$a \times b \times c$," a is the diameter of the top, b is the diameter of the bottom, and c is the depth.

The top fitting of most shades is a washer with a 5⁄16" hole, to fit over the 1⁄4-27 stud on a harp. "Uno" shades have a threaded 1 1⁄2" hole that is meant to screw onto the threads on a socket. Shades with large unthreaded rings are meant to sit on a glass chimney.

land area units

At least in the industrialized world, today's land measures are strictly geometric: the units are defined by squaring units of length. Most of the world uses the hectare (though the NINTH CGPM discouraged the use of that term, preferring plain square meters) and the United States uses the acre. For most of human history, however, land area has been the intense concern of peasant farmers rather than developers, and land units reflected a farmer's experience of the land. Several types of non-geometrical units recur worldwide:

Seed measures of land. Units based on the amount of land that could be sown with a certain quantity of some type of seed. These units of area usually have the same name as the unit of capacity used for the seed. For example, Leviticus XXVII specifies that land should be "estimated according to the seed thereof, an homer of barley seed shall be valued at 50 shekels of silver." A homer is about 6 1⁄4 bushels, but it is not that much barley seed which is worth 50 silver shekels (a lot of money), but the "homer of barley seed," namely the amount of land (roughly 6 acres) that could be sown with 1 homer of barley seed. Other examples include the *seterée, estrée,* and *boisselée* in France, the *kula* in India, the *fanegada* in Spain, the *bu* in Japan, the *matomana* in Nepal, the *diesyatina* in Russia, the *mud* in Holland, and the *sáa* in Libya. Many of these later evolved into units that were defined geometrically.

Seed measures of land have several advantages. First, they are easily understood by people who are good farmers but do not have the notions of measurement a surveyor does. Second, they adjust automatically to the quality of the land. Seed is sown less densely on poor land than it is on fertile land, so a seed-based unit will be a larger area on poor land than on good land. It is fairer to fix taxes on farmers by a seed-measure of land than by a geometrical unit like the hectare, and so also for rents, land grants, and inheritances.

Person-day measures of land. Units representing the amount of land that could be cultivated in 1 day by hand, that is, without horse, oxen, or mules. Such units are often specific to a particular type of agricultural land. For example, in France one *ouvrée* is 20 square rods of vinyard. Person-day measures are seldom applied to fields where grain is raised. Examples are the *daieswork*, about 10 square rods, and the *hommée*.

Plow-day measures of land. Units representing the amount of land that could be plowed in a day. The ☞acre was originally such a unit. Other examples are the Roman *jugerum*, the Italian *giornata*, the French *journal* and *arpent*, the German *morgen*, the *joch, acker, bouw, bigha, feddan,* and *ardagh*.

Farmstead measures of land. Units representing the amount of land that a farmer owning a yoke of oxen could keep in cultivation. Typically these units are about 7 acres. Examples are the English *yard-land* and the *oxgang*.

Feudal measures of land. Unlike the previous units, these reflect society's requirements and not the efficient use of the farmer's tools and time; they take into account only the land's yield and not cultivation practices. Typically the smallest such unit is that amount of land just large enough to produce a surplus sufficient to support a knight in service to the king. An example is the English *hide*.

langley

Various units used in measuring the amount of solar energy falling upon a surface, used, for example, in designing solar water heaters. Abbr, ly. In some early work it is a unit of power, cal_{15} per square centimeter per minute ($\approx$ 698 watts per square meter). Later it is defined as calories per square centimeter ("surface density of radiant energy"), but the precise value depends on which calorie is used. One langley can be:

1 $calorie_{IT}/cm^2$	$\approx$ 41,868 joules per square meter, or
1 $calorie_{15}/cm^2$	$\approx$ 41,855 joules per square meter, or
1 $calorie_{TH}/cm^2$	$\approx$ 41,840 joules per square meter.

league

In England, a unit of distance, probably introduced by the Norman invaders and derived from the Gallic *lieus*. In the 12TH–13TH C it was equal to 12 furlongs, not much bigger than the Gallic unit, but lengthened in the 14TH C to 2 miles. From the 15TH–19TH C it grew to = 3 (statute) miles, which is the present value in the USA and many other countries.

The nautical or geographical league, 18TH–19TH C = 3 nautical miles. The various nautical miles have led to different nautical leagues: the international nautical league = 5.556 kilometers; the British nautical league = 18,240 feet ≈ 5.559552 km.

In Texas, the league is a unit of land area, an anglicization of the Spanish *legua*, = 25,000,000 square varas ≈ 4428.4 acres. For its history, see ☞vara.

lens, photographic

Focal Length

Conventionally, the focal length of a camera's "normal" lens is equal to the length of the diagonal of the image on the negative. The lengths of the diagonals of some common formats are: 35mm, 43 mm; 2 1/4 × 2 1/4, 81 mm; 4 × 5, 151 mm; 5 × 7, 207 mm; 8 × 10, 311 mm; and 11 × 14, 436 mm. In practice, though, the normal lens is often a little longer: 50 mm in 35mm photography (inherited from the Leica) and 210 mm in 4 × 5 (up from 150 mm in the days when press photographers used 4 × 5, probably because most of today's 4 × 5 photographers use the front and back movements and want a lens that covers a bigger area in the film plane).

Lenses with focal lengths shorter than normal are called "wide angle." "Telephoto," which originally referred to a long focus lens physically shorter than its focal length, thanks to a particular optical design, now generally refers to any lens with a significantly longer-than-normal focal length. A common misconception is that wide angle lens have more depth of field than normal lenses. With minor exceptions, all focal lengths give the same depth of field at the same magnification and aperture.

The table below shows the focal lengths most often offered for four camera formats with which interchangeable lenses are used and the angle of view for the longer side of the image. The normal focal lengths are in boldface.

Angle of View of Lenses in Several Formats							
35mm		2 1/4 × 2 1/4		2 1/4 × 3 1/4		4 × 5	
14, 15mm	104°, 100°	30mm	87°	47mm	82°	58mm	92°
18	90°	40	71°	58	71°	65	85°
20, 21	84°, 82°	50	59°	65	64°	75	77°
24	74°	60	51°	75	57°	90	67°
28	65°	**80**	39°	90	49°	100	62°
35	54°	120	27°	**100**	45°	120	53°

Angle of View of Lenses in Several Formats								
35mm		2 ¼ × 2 ¼		2 ¼ × 3 ¼		4 × 5		
50	40°	135	24°	120	38°	135	48°	
85, 90	24°, 23°	150	22°	135	34°	150	44°	
100, 105	20°, 19.5°	180	18°	150	31°	180	37°	
135	15.2°	250	13°	180	26°	**210**	32°	
180, 200	11.4°, 10.3°	350	9°	210	22°	240	28°	
300	6.9°	500	7°	240	19°	300	24°	
400	5.5°	1000	3.2°	300	16°	360	19°	
500	4.1°					400	17°	
600	3.4°					450	15°	
800	2.6°					500	14°	
1000	2.1°					600	11°	
2000	1.0°							

Aperture

Almost all consumer lenses have iris diaphragms. Changing the size of the hole made by the diaphragm adjusts exposure. This adjustment is calibrated in f-stops or f-numbers, which, roughly speaking, are the diameter of the glass at the front of the lens divided by the diameter of the hole made by the iris diaphragm. The smaller the f-number, the more light will be admitted. The great advantage of f-stops is that they apply equally to lenses of any focal length; f/8 at ¹⁄₅₀th of a second will produce the same exposure with a 24mm lens as it will with a 200mm lens.

Because shutter speed scales are chosen so that the duration of every shutter speed is either twice or half the durations of the settings next to it, it is convenient if adjacent "whole stops" (the marked f-stops) also represent a doubling or halving of the amount of light reaching the film. That way a photographer who increases the shutter speed by one click can compensate by opening the aperture by one click. To double the amount of light passing through the lens, the *area* of the aperture must double, and for that the new diameter of the aperture must be the square root of 2 (1.414…) times the old diameter, because the area of a circle varies as the square of its radius.

With the steps defined, a set point must be chosen to establish a scale. After World War II, standards groups decided the set point would be f/2. An earlier standard sequence, (3.2, 4.5,…) was often used in continental Europe before World War II.

All the f-stops that aren't a multiple of 2 are rounded off, which leads to a curious effect. F/11, for example, would be f/11.3 if the calculation were carried out to one more decimal place. Two stops farther on, f/22 would be f/22.6, which rounds off to 23. But that spoils the instructive pattern of the numbers doubling every second stop. As a result, f-stop numbers are conventional, not calculated.

The table below shows, in the first four lines, conventional f-numbers in quarter stops. On each line, a number differs from those next to it on the same line by a whole stop, and from those next above and below it by a quarter stop. The final three lines depict the third-of-a-stop f-numbers. Numbers in boldface are those that differ from the calculated values.

```
0.5    0.71    1    1.4    2    2.8    4    5.6    8    11    16    22    32    45    64
  0.55   0.77   1.1   1.5   2.2   3    4.4   6.2   8.7   12   17   25   35   49
   0.59   0.84   1.1   1.6   2.3   3.3   4.7   6.6   9.5   13   19   26   38   54
    0.65   0.92   1.3   1.8   2.6   3.8   5.2   7.3   10.4   15   21   29   41   59

0.5    0.71    1    1.4    2    2.8    4    5.6    8    11    16    22    32    45    64
  0.56   0.79   1.1   1.5   2.2   3.1   4.4   6.3   8.9   12   17   25   36   51
   0.63   0.89   1.2   1.7   2.5   3.5   5    7.1   10   14   20   28   40   57
```

A lens has its maximum possible resolution at its widest aperture, but in practice, as a rule of thumb a lens is sharpest about 2 whole stops below its widest aperture.

Instead of f-stops, many old American-made lenses are marked in the Uniform System (U.S.), which was one of the first attempts to establish a standard, by the Britain's Royal Photographic Society in 1881. It only caught on in the United States, where Eastman Kodak used it extensively on roll film cameras that nowadays often turn up in antique shops and garage sales.

f stop	4	4.5	5.6	6.3	8	11	16	22	32	45
U. S.	1	1.26	2	2 1/2	4	8	16	32	64	128

Another system, T-stops, is mostly used on lenses for professional cinematography, in which shots taken with different lens must match so that they will cut together smoothly. At any given f-stop, less light is transmitted through a lens with many elements, such as a zoom or extreme wide angle, than would be transmitted through a simpler lens. Instead of being calculated geometrically as f-stops are, T-stops are determined by actually measuring the amount of light transmitted through the lens (the "T" stands for transmission). The numbers and the relationships between them are the same as for f-stops. There is no fixed relationship between f-stops and T-stops.

lightning

Five microseconds after the average lightning stroke begins it reaches its maximum value of current, 20,000 amps; the whole stroke lasts 40 microseconds.

lights

Incandescent Household Light Bulbs

Bases. Most light bulbs screw into a socket. Almost all household bulbs have a medium screw base, sometimes called an edison screw, 1 1/16" in diameter with 7 threads per inch. Bulbs with a base that looks like a medium base but isn't are made to defeat bulb thieves in public places. Some have a left-hand thread; others are the size called "ad-medium," used in signs, just a bit bigger (1 5/32") so they won't fit a residential socket. Other common screw bases, in order of decreasing diameter, are:

✓ Mogul, 1 19/32" diameter. High-wattage bulbs: some overhead fixtures, modern outdoor security lights, and old-fashioned sun lamps. Screw-in adapters are readily available to convert mogul sockets to medium screw.

✓ Intermediate, 5/8" diameter. Refrigerators and some other appliances. Intermediate base light bulbs found in the home are almost always tubular.

✓ Candelabra, 1/2" diameter. Seven-and-a-half-watt Christmas tree lights, the kind often used outdoors.

✓ Min-can, 7/16" diameter. In the home it is found only on some special high-intensity lights.

✓ Miniature, 3/8" diameter. Night lights, Christmas tree lights and some flashlights.

✓ Midget, still smaller. Signal lights.

Size. Householders usually describe bulb size by wattage, but the industry has a system for describing the actual dimensions of the bulb. Bulb shapes are identified by letters: "A" is the shape of a typical household bulb; "B" is the shape of a candelabra base Christmas tree bulb; "C" is the shape of a miniature screw night light bulb, and so on. The bulb size is then given by a letter for shape followed by the bulb's maximum diameter in eighths of an inch. For example, a T-8 bulb would be a tubular bulb 1 inch in diameter. Ordinary 40-watt and 75-watt bulbs are A-19, with a few A-21.

The size of the base or the shape and size of the bulb aren't sure signs of the bulb's wattage or voltage. For example, A-19, medium base lamps are made for 12 volts, 100 volts, 115 volts, 130 volts and 250 volts.

Incandescent Bulbs for Audiovisual Uses

Lamps for slide, movie and overhead projectors must often meet special requirements; for example, the lamp's filament may need to be very precisely positioned. To identify lamp types used in audiovisual applications, ANSI assigns three-letter codes. A "DDB," for example, is a 750-watt bulb used in 16mm movie projectors. Several hundred of these codes have been assigned. Most of these lamps have strange shapes or bases, but some of the codes cover photoflood bulbs that have the same shape and medium screw base as an ordinary household bulb, for example, BBA, ECA, and ECT.

Many types are now difficult or impossible to obtain; lamp dealers have tables which may be able to suggest workable substitutes.

Fluorescent

To start a fluorescent lamp a high-voltage pulse must be sent through it. Once the lamp lights, the stuff inside the tube becomes a good conductor of electricity—too good—and then some means of preventing too much current from flowing must be provided. The initial surge and the later current limiting is done by the ballast, a black box in the lamp housing. Originally ballasts were magnetic, constructed something like a transformer, of many thin sheets of special steels. A side effect as alternating current passes through the ballast is that the sheets move a very small amount; magnetic ballasts, not the lamps themselves, are the source of the hum associated with fluorescents. Electronic ballasts, though somewhat more expensive, do not hum and use less energy than a magnetic ballast. In addition, they can raise the frequency of the current going to the lamp, which eliminates the flicker which annoys some people. Old fixtures can be retrofitted with electronic ballasts.

Brightness. A new fluorescent lamp may not reach maximum brightness for several hours. After that its brightness slowly declines. A four-foot, 40-watt cool white tube, the typical home workshop light, has an initial brightness of 3250 lumens. Six thousand hours later (40% of its rated life of 15,000 hours) its brightness will have declined to 2960 lumens, on average.

Color. The visible light given off by a fluorescent comes from a powdery coating of phosphors on the inside of the tube, somewhat like the phosphors on the inside of the face of a color TV tube. The color of the light given off by the tube is manipulated by changing the mixture of phosphors. The color balance is described by terms like those below, shown with their correlated color temperature and color rendering index.

Name (abbreviation)	CCT	CRI
"Warm" (correlated color temperatures below 3200 kelvin)		
Incandescent Fluorescent (IF)	2750	89
Deluxe warm white (WWX)	2950	74
Warm white (WW)	3000	52
In-between (3200 kelvin to 4000 kelvin)		
White (W)	3450	57
Natural white (N)	3600	86
"Cool" (correlated color temperatures above 4000 kelvin)		
Deluxe cool white	4100	89
Cool white (CW)	4200	62
Daylight (D)	6300	76

Starters. Some older fluorescent fixtures and those under 20 watts often require starters, which are the small aluminum cans in a socket near one end of the lamp. When its starter fails the lamp won't ignite, but starters are easily replaceable. Twisting a starter less than a quarter turn frees it from its socket. Starter types are numbered, with the prefix FS (fluorescent starter); the designation can be found stamped on the end of the can. The type must match the wattage of the lamp.

Starter	Wattages served
FS-2	14, 15, 20
FS-4	13. 30, 40
FS-12	32
FS-25	22, 25
FS-40/400	40
FS-85	90, 100

Most fluorescent fixtures installed today are either rapid-start or instant-start types that do not require starters. Some low-wattage desk fixtures require a person to be the starter by holding down a push button until the lamp ignites.

Life. The more often a fluorescent is switched on and off, the shorter its life and the faster it dims. Manufacturer's ratings of lamp life are based on operating the lamp for 3 hours each time it is started.

Shapes, Sizes and Sockets. The most common form of fluorescent lamp is a tube with two pins on each end. The diameter of the tube is described in eighths of an inch, as it is for incandescent lamps, so a fluorescent lamp 1 1/2" in diameter is a T-12. The 2-pin bases (called bi-pin bases) come in several sizes, but by far the most common in homes is the medium bi-pin.

Medium bi-pin base lamps that are 1 1/2" in diameter don't require a starter. They come in 24", 36" and 48" lengths, of 30, 25, and 40 watts respectively.

Pre-heat style lamps require starters. Lamps 15" long are 14-watt and 18" lamps are 15-watt; they may be either T-8 or T-12. The 12", 13-watt lamps are made only in T-8 and 24", 20-watt bulbs only as T-12.

Miniature bi-pin sockets are used in lanterns, mobile home and automobile fixtures, and similar settings. Lamps made to fit these sockets are 5/8" in diameter and 6", 9", 12" or 21" long, and the wattage will be 4, 6, 8 or 13 watts respectively. They need a starter, but this usually takes the form of a push button.

Mogul bi-pin bases are rare. They are found on 60" T-17 preheat lamps, usually of 90 watts, but 82 watts in energy-efficient versions. They are also used on 40-watt instant start lamps, 48" T-12's and 60" T-17.

Lamps in the form of circles (Circline is a trademark for a popular version) are 8" or 12" in diameter and have a special 4-pin connector.

Compact Fluorescents Compared with Incandescents

Compact fluorescents were designed to overcome householders' resistance to fluorescent lights, with the goal of saving large amounts of electricity. Compact fluorescents are no more efficient than their tubular cousins, but they screw into medium screw sockets and their light has a more pleasing color than that of most tubular fluorescents. Some have electronic ballasts.

The table below compares the light output in lumens of typical medium screw base incandescent bulbs (without reflectors) with compact fluorescents.

Inside Frosted Incandescent			Compact Fluorescent		
wattage	life (hrs)	initial lumens	lumens	life (hrs)	wattage
15	2500	125	575	10,000	11
25	2500	190	720	9000	15
40	1000	505	900	10,000	16
60	870	1000	1100	10,000	18
75	750	1190	1200	10,000	20
100	750	1750	1500	10,000	23
150	750	2850	1650	10,000	27
300	750	6360			

line

1) In the USA, 19TH–20TH C, a unit of length, = 0.025 inches (40 lines = 1 inch). Nowadays used only for the diameters of buttons, formerly also used for the diameters of watchglasses.   2) In the UK, 17TH–20TH C, 0.0833… inches (12 lines = 1 inch).   3) A synonym for the maxwell, see ☞centimeter-gram-second systems of units.

liter

In SI, a special name for the cubic decimeter, and thus a unit of capacity. Abbr in the United States, L; in some other countries, l (see below). One milliliter equals a cubic centimeter. The use of the liter in scientific work is discouraged.

History

In 1901 the THIRD CGPM resolved that "the unit of capacity, for high accuracy determinations, is the volume occupied by a mass of 1 kilogram of pure water, at its maximum density and at standard atmospheric pressure; this volume is called 'liter.'" Since the kilogram had originally been conceived as the mass of a cubic decimeter of water under those conditions, one might expect that one milliliter would equal one cubic centimeter. However, the mass of the kilogram is actually defined by the mass of the platinum prototype, which was based on an 18TH C determination of the mass of a cubic decimeter of water.

The 1901 definition, although defining a volume, made its size depend, not on a standard of length (the International Prototype of the Meter), but on a standard of mass (the International Prototype of the Kilogram). Its volume expressed in meters thus had to be determined experimentally, which led to the conversion factor 1 liter = 1.000027×10^{-3} cubic meters (see Guillame, *La Création du Bureau International des Poids et Mesure et son Oeuvre*, Paris, 1927, pp. 256–258). In 1950, the CIPM declared that 1 liter = 1.000028 cubic decimeters was the best conversion.

In 1964 the 12TH CGPM (Resolution 6) abrogated the 1901 definition and declared "that the word 'liter' may be used as a special name for the cubic decimeter," and recommended that it not be used to present the results of high accuracy volume measurements.

In the United States and a few other countries, the abbreviation for liter is "L", with the intention of avoiding confusion with the numeral "1." The existence of two abbreviations was reluctantly sanctioned by the 16TH CGPM in 1979 (Resolution 6), although it expressed the hope of suppressing one of them in the future.

lumber

When the dimensions of a piece of lumber are given as $a \times b \times c$, a is the thickness, the smallest dimension of the end, the surface perpendicular to the direction in which the tree grew; b is the width, the other dimension of the end; and c is the length, measured with the grain.

Wood as it comes from the tree is a very variable commodity. A large piece of pine may fetch a hundred dollars from a cabinetmaker; another exactly the same size may be good only for firewood. These differences are captured in grades, which reflect the value to users of different sets of wood characteristics. Originally each sawmill established its own grades, which might be no more than which pile a plank was put in. As transportation improved, regional associations set standards dealing with the local economically important species; many of these associations, or their descendants, are still active. Despite government efforts in the first quarter of the 20TH C, today there are hundreds, perhaps thousands of wood grades in the USA alone.

A buyer can save money by understanding grades, mainly by not paying for characteristics he doesn't need. Remember, however, that a grade represents the state of the lumber at the time it was graded; it may have changed from improper storage conditions, for example. Simply cutting a board in two can change its grade.

Hardwood Grades

In the USA, standards for grading hardwood are set by the National Hardwood Lumber Assn. The standards are voluminous, replete with exceptions, special rules for certain species, and many details. Here we will only try to illustrate the principles behind the grading, with a few indications of how the home woodworker can use them. For details, contact the association.

Unlike softwood, most hardwood is used in applications where appearance is crucial, such as furniture. Hardwood being a natural product, no two boards are alike, and almost all contain defects like knots that would be unacceptable in a piece of fine furniture. In most cases, however, only one side of the board will show. The grading of hardwood reflects that; it is based on the number and size of the "clear face cuttings"—rectangular pieces free of defects on the graded side—that could be cut from the board being graded. The other side of a clear face cutting may contain defects, as long as they don't affect the strength of the cutting. The fewer and bigger the clear face cuttings, the higher the board's grade. Grading a board doesn't involve actually sawing the clear face cuttings from it; they are purely conceptual.

The three top grades are:

FAS. Although the NHLA defines grades called "Firsts" and "Seconds," in practice the best boards are almost always sold as a combined grade, FAS (which stands for "firsts and seconds"). From 20 to 40 percent of the boards in a lot graded FAS must be Firsts; the actual percentage required depends on the species. Boards must be at least 6" wide and from 8' to 16' long; in a lot no more than 30% of the boards can be shorter than 11', and only half of those can be 8' or 9' long.

FAS grading is based on the poorest side of the board. The clear face cuttings must be no smaller than 4" by 5', or 3" by 7'. As many as 4 cuttings are allowed, depending on the board's area. For a 4 sq. foot board to qualify as a Firsts, for example, only 1 cutting can be made, but 3 cuttings are allowed in a board with an area of 15 square feet or more. For larger boards, a choice of two numbers of cuttings is offered, but the larger number must take in a greater percentage of the board's area. For example, if the grading of a particular 12 sq. foot board as Seconds is based on getting 3 clear face cuttings out of it, those cuttings must include 83 1/3% of the board; but if 4 cuttings are planned, they must take in 91 2/3% of the board's total surface.

Selects. Unlike the other hardwood grades, Selects are graded on the basis of the *best* side. Minimum width is 4" and lengths run 6' to 16'. In a lot, 30% of the boards may be 6' to 11' long, but only one-sixth of those may be 6' or 7' long. Except for those restrictions, Selects over 4 square feet are graded by the same criteria as Seconds. Since Selects are cheaper than FAS, the home woodworker should seriously consider them for any use in which only one side of the board will be seen.

No. 1 Common. A No. 1 Common board need only be at least 3" wide; the minimum clear face cuttings size drops to 4" by 2', or 3" by 3'. In a lot, 10% of the boards may be 4' to 7' long, and half of those may be 4' or 5' long. Even in the larger boards, where as many as 5 cuttings are permitted, the clear face cuttings will take in at least 66⅔% of the board.

The remaining grades—2A, 2B, 3A and 3B—rarely reach the retail market; manufacturers make flooring, pallets and similar products from them.

The best way of grasping the puzzle-like nature of grading hardwood is to consider a real example. Here is one from the *Wood Handbook*, by the Forest Products Laboratory of the U. S. Department of Agriculture (Washington, 1974).

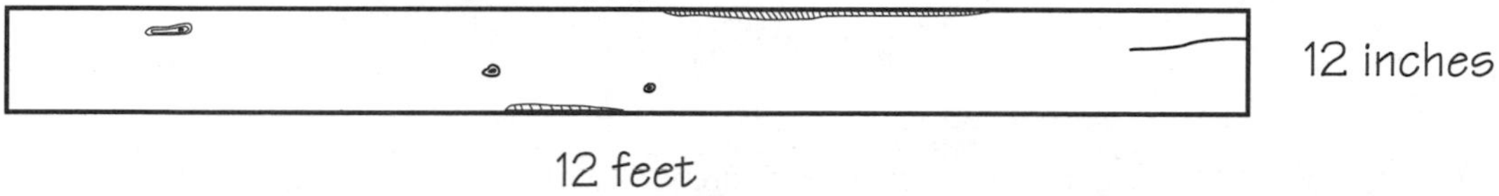

12 inches

12 feet

In this case, the grader gets a board 12' long and 12" wide. He examines both sides and senses it will make No. 1 Common, so he turns to the poorer side, pictured above. One end is cracked, bark shows along both edges, and there are several knots. According to the standard for No. 1 boards between 11 and 13 square feet, a maximum of 4 clear pieces may be cut, which, if 3" wide, must be at least 3' long, and if 4" wide at least 2'—and the cuttings must take in 66⅔% of the area of the board. Can the grader do it?

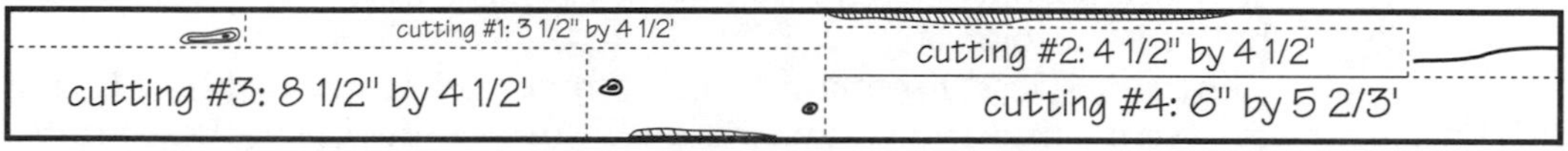

cutting #1: 3 1/2" by 4 1/2'
cutting #2: 4 1/2" by 4 1/2'
cutting #3: 8 1/2" by 4 1/2'
cutting #4: 6" by 5 2/3'

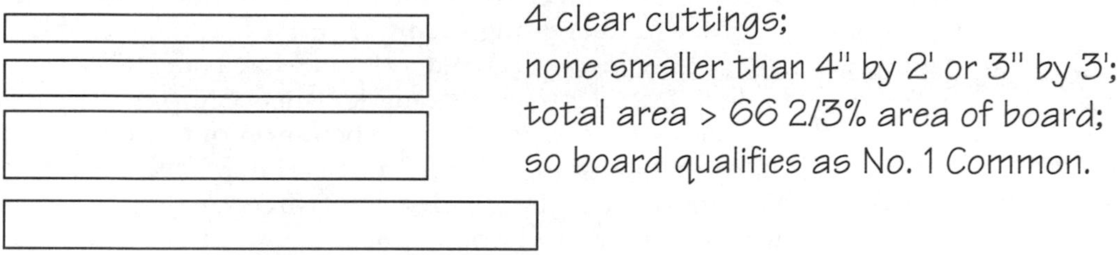

4 clear cuttings;
none smaller than 4" by 2' or 3" by 3';
total area > 66 2/3% area of board;
so board qualifies as No. 1 Common.

Hardwood Sizes

Hardwood lumber comes in random widths, but not less than the minimum specified in the grades. The length may be any number of whole feet from 4 to 16, but no more than 50% of the boards in any shipment may be odd lengths.

The standard hardwood thicknesses are:

Rough	Surfaced 2 Sides
3/8"	3/16"
1/2"	5/16"
5/8"	7/16" (continued)

Rough	Surfaced 2 Sides (continued from previous page)
3/4"	9/16"
1"	13/16"
1 1/4"	1 1/16"
1 1/2"	1 5/16"
1 3/4"	1 1/2"
2	1 3/4"
2 1/2"	2 1/4"
3"	2 3/4"
3 1/2"	3 1/4"
4"	3 3/4"

Softwood Grades

The various grades can first be divided into two broad categories: construction and remanufacture.

Remanufacture grading is applied to wood used in industry. There are, for example, pencil stock, barrel stave, ladder rail, and stadium seat stock grades, each emphasizing particular qualities needed by a certain industry. Many such grades are encountered only in a particular part of the country, and in any case you won't find them in the average lumber yard. A second class of remanufacture grades is industrial clears, used for kitchen cabinets, for example. Because appearance is important, the grading of industrial clears somewhat resembles that of hardwood.

The final class of remanufacture grades is Factory or Shop Grades, which may find their way to a retail lumber yard. The best grade is called Factory Select or Select Shop; the remaining grades are usually numbered in order of decreasing quality, No. 1, No. 2, and No. 3. To know what the grades mean you need to know what association's rules are being applied, but as a typical example, Select Shop might mean cutting 70% clear both sides or 70% B or better on one side, with the percentage clear dropping to 50% for No. 1 and to 33 1/3% for No. 2.

Construction grades can be divided into three categories: Stress-graded, Nonstress-graded, and Appearance.

Appearance grade is mainly for board and moldings. The grades are designated by letters, A, B, C, D, and combination grades such as "B

MILL 3 ROSEBURG
(WWP®) CONST S-DRY [D FIR]

grade, in this case, "construction."

tree species, in this case, Douglas fir.

surfaced-dry, an American Lumber Standard indication of moisture content of 19% or less when the lumber was surfaced.

Association by whose standards the grading was done, in this case, the Western Wood Products Association.

and better" (B&BTR, sometimes called B&B) and "C and better" (C&BTR) are usual. Appearance grades may also be called "Select," "Clear" or "Prime," depending on the species. Special designations are used with certain species, such as "all-heart redwood." Not all grades are available. Like hardwood grading, appearance grades emphasize the appearance of the best side. As a general rule, even D contains no defects that would detract from the appearance after the wood is painted. C is considered appropriate for "high-quality exterior and interior trim, panelling, and cabinet work, especially where these are to receive a natural finish." B has minor defects like pin knots, depending on the species.

Nonstress-graded lumber is used where structural failure is unlikely or its consequences not catastrophic. Not that strength is unimportant, but grading is based on size and appearance. The grades may be numbered or terms like "construction," (equivalent to No. 1) "standard," (No. 2) and "utility" (No. 3) may be used. Typical uses for No. 1 are as siding, shelving and panelling. The lower grades are used for wall and roof sheathing, subfloors, and concrete forms. The lower the grade, the more knots, knotholes, and other defects. Certain products have their own nonstress-graded grades; for lath, for example, there is a No. 1 and a No. 2 lath grade.

Stress-graded. The goal of these grades is that all the lumber in a single grade will have similar mechanical properties; it is principally used for dimension lumber such as two-by-fours. Unlike the grades discussed so far, a single set of standards for stress-graded lumber, the National Grading Rule, applies across the USA—which helps to ensure that a wood-framed house built to a particular set of plans won't collapse no matter where in the country it's built. Stress grades are either visual or mechanical. The visual grades are assigned by visual inspection; the inspector assesses how much the defects that can be seen detract from the strength the wood would have if it was defect-free. The mechanical grades are assigned by testing the wood in a machine; lumber so graded may be marked MSR (machine stress rated).

The table below gives the names of the visual stress-graded grades and some idea of their mechanical properties. The bending strength ratio compares the strength requirement for the grade with that of a piece of wood of the same size and species having no visible strength-reducing characteristics. The Light Framing classification applies to wood 2" to 4" thick and 4" wide and the Structural Joist and Planks classification to wood 2" to 4" thick and 6" or more wide; all the others are for wood 2" to 4" thick and 2" to 4" wide.

Classification	Grade Name	Bending strength
Light Framing	Construction	34%
	Standard	19%
	Utility	9%
Structural Light Framing	Select Structural	67%
	1	55%
	2	45%
	3	26%
Studs	Stud	26%
Structural Joists & Planks	Select Structural	65%
	1	55%
	2	45%
	3	26%
Appearance	Appearance	55%

So if you're putting up a shelf in the garden shed to hold that old VW engine you're planning to restore some day, it's probably not a good idea to use Utility grade two-by-fours, even though you don't care what the shelf looks like.

Softwood Sizes

Softwood lumber is categorized by the piece of wood's smallest dimension: **boards**, which are less than 2" thick; **dimension lumber**, from 2" up to but not including 5"; and **timbers**, whose least dimension is 5" or more.

Seasoning. The American Lumber Standard requires softwood to have a moisture content of 19% or less, which is indicated by the mark S-DRY, for surfaced dry. Some other markings are KD, kiln dried (in southern pine, KD indicates 15% maximum moisture); S-GRN, surfaced green, moisture content of more than 19% when the lumber was surfaced; and PAD, partially air dry.

Surfacing. Lumber grades often indicate which sides have been surfaced. S4S, for example, means surfaced 4 sides and S&E means surfaced on 1 side and 1 edge.

American Standard Board Lumber Sizes		
Nominal size	Green	Dry
*1 × 2	25/32" × 1 9/16"	3/4" × 1 1/2"
*1 × 3	25/32" × 2 9/16"	3/4" × 2 1/2"
*1 × 4	25/32" × 3 9/16"	3/4" × 3 1/2"

American Standard Board Lumber Sizes		
Nominal size	Green	Dry
1 × 5	25/32" × 4 5/8"	3/4" × 4 1/2"
*1 × 6	25/32" × 5 5/8"	3/4" × 5 1/2"
1 × 7	25/32" × 6 5/8"	3/4" × 6 1/2"
*1 × 8	25/32" × 7 1/2"	3/4" × 7 1/4"
1 × 9	25/32" × 8 1/2"	3/4" × 8 1/4"
*1 × 10	25/32" × 9 1/2"	3/4" × 9 1/4"
1 × 11	25/32" × 10 1/2"	3/4" × 10 1/4"
*1 × 12	25/32" × 11 1/2"	3/4" × 11 1/4"
1 × 14	25/32" × 13 1/2"	3/4" × 13 1/4"
1 × 16	25/32" × 15 1/2"	3/4" × 15 1/4"
1 1/4 × 2	1 1/32" × 1 9/16"	3/4" × 1 1/2"
1 1/4 × 3	1 1/32" × 2 9/16"	3/4" × 2 1/2"
1 1/4 × 4	1 1/32" × 3 9/16"	3/4" × 3 1/2"
1 1/4 × 5	1 1/32" × 4 5/8"	3/4" × 4 1/2"
1 1/4 × 6	1 1/32" × 5 5/8"	3/4" × 5 1/2"
1 1/4 × 7	1 1/32" × 6 5/8"	3/4" × 6 1/2"
1 1/4 × 8	1 1/32" × 7 1/2"	3/4" × 7 1/4"
1 1/4 × 9	1 1/32" × 8 1/2"	3/4" × 8 1/4"
1 1/4 × 10	1 1/32" × 9 1/2"	3/4" × 9 1/4"
1 1/4 × 11	1 1/32" × 10 1/2"	3/4" × 10 1/4"
1 1/4 × 12	1 1/32" × 11 1/2"	3/4" × 11 1/4"
1 1/4 × 14	1 1/32" × 13 1/2"	3/4" × 13 1/4"
1 1/4 × 16	1 1/32" × 15 1/2"	3/4" × 15 1/4"
1 1/2 × 2	1 9/32" × 1 9/16"	3/4" × 1 1/2"
1 1/2 × 3	1 9/32" × 2 9/16"	3/4" × 2 1/2"
1 1/2 × 4	1 9/32" × 3 9/16"	3/4" × 3 1/2"
1 1/2 × 5	1 9/32" × 4 5/8"	3/4" × 4 1/2"
1 1/2 × 6	1 9/32" × 5 5/8"	3/4" × 5 1/2"
1 1/2 × 7	1 9/32" × 6 5/8"	3/4" × 6 1/2"
1 1/2 × 8	1 9/32" × 7 1/2"	3/4" × 7 1/4"
1 1/2 × 9	1 9/32" × 8 1/2"	3/4" × 8 1/4"
1 1/2 × 10	1 9/32" × 9 1/2"	3/4" × 9 1/4"
1 1/2 × 11	1 9/32" × 10 1/2"	3/4" × 10 1/4"
1 1/2 × 12	1 9/32" × 11 1/2"	3/4" × 11 1/4"
1 1/2 × 14	1 9/32" × 13 1/2"	3/4" × 13 1/4"
1 1/2 × 16	1 9/32" × 15 1/2"	3/4" × 15 1/4"

*The most commonly available sizes.

Two-by-fours were originally two inches by four inches, unsurfaced. Surfaced, in the 1950s they were 1 5/8" × 3 5/8", and have now shriveled to $1\frac{1}{2}" \times 3\frac{1}{2}"$. The table below gives the most common "two by" sizes. (The dimensions are slightly different for some species.)

American Standard Dimension Lumber Sizes		
Nominal size	Green	Dry
2×3	$1\frac{9}{16}" \times 2\frac{9}{16}"$	$1\frac{1}{2}" \times 2\frac{1}{2}"$
2×4	$1\frac{9}{16}" \times 3\frac{9}{16}"$	$1\frac{1}{2}" \times 3\frac{1}{2}"$
2×6	$1\frac{9}{16}" \times 5\frac{9}{16}"$	$1\frac{1}{2}" \times 5\frac{1}{2}"$
2×8	$1\frac{9}{16}" \times 7\frac{9}{16}"$	$1\frac{1}{2} \times 7\frac{1}{4}"$
2×10	$1\frac{9}{16}" \times 9\frac{9}{16}"$	$1\frac{1}{2}" \times 9\frac{1}{4}"$
2×12	$1\frac{9}{16}" \times 11\frac{1}{2}"$	$1\frac{1}{2}" \times 11\frac{1}{4}"$

Dimension lumber can be as large as $4\frac{1}{2}" \times 16"$. Sizes not listed above can be figured out from the green and dry equivalents for nominal sizes in the table above and that below.

Nominal dimension	Green	Dry
$2\frac{1}{2}$	$2\frac{1}{16}"$	$2"$
$3\frac{1}{2}$	$3\frac{1}{16}"$	$3"$
$4\frac{1}{2}$	$4\frac{1}{16}"$	$4"$
14	$13\frac{1}{2}"$	$13\frac{1}{4}"$
16	$15\frac{1}{2}"$	$15\frac{1}{4}"$

lumen

In SI, the unit of luminous flux, the rate of flow of light energy. Abbr, lm. One lumen is the luminous flux emitted within a solid angle of 1 steradian by a point source with an intensity of 1 candela. In terms of base units, the lumen is *candela·steradian*.

A typical use for the lumen is in describing how much light ordinary household light bulbs give off. The packaging usually gives the bulb's light output in lumens; a new 75-watt incandescent bulb puts out about 1,180 lumens.

lux

In SI, the unit of illuminance—how brightly a surface is illuminated. One lux is 1 lumen per square meter. (One lux $\approx$ 0.09 foot-candles.) In terms of base units, the lux's dimensions are $\dfrac{candela \cdot steradian}{meter^2}$

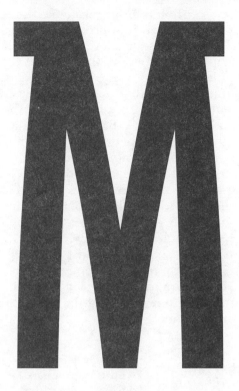

Mach number

A unit of speed used to describe the speed of aircraft and spacecraft within the atmosphere. Mach 1 is the speed of sound; Mach 2, twice the speed of sound, and so on. In dry air at 0°C, the speed of sound is 1,193.3 kilometers per hour (741.5 miles per hour).

Nonmilitary aircraft are not permitted to reach Mach 1 over the United States. The British-French Concorde airliner does reach supersonic speeds on its transoceanic flights, and has a Mach meter on the forward bulkhead of its passenger cabin.

magnitude (astronomy)

Visual Magnitude. Abbr, m. Our system for describing the apparent brightness of stars began with Hipparchus (*fl* 146–127 BC), a Greek astronomer who compiled the first star catalog, over objections that cataloging the gods' abodes was an outrageous impiety. Completed in 129 BC, his catalog gave position and brightness for about 850 stars. Hipparchus called the brightest stars "stars of the first magnitude." Stars just noticeably dimmer than first magnitude stars were stars of the second magnitude, those noticeably dimmer than stars of the second magnitude were stars of the third magnitude, and so on. Five such steps took Hipparchus down to the faintest stars he could see: sixth magnitude stars.

The human eye's perception of brightness, like the ear's perception of loudness (compare ☞decibel) is approximately logarithmic. Imagine three light levels (or three sound levels), A, B, and C, such that B is just perceptibly brighter (or louder) than A, and C just perceptibly brighter than B. If the amount of energy at levels A, B, and C are measured by instruments, it will be found that they don't differ by a constant amount, but by a constant factor, that is, the ratio between adjacent steps is always the same. A, B, and C differ as 2, 4, and 8 do, and not as 2, 3 and 4. Since Hipparchus' system of magnitudes was based on human perception, his scale is logarithmic.

The invention of the telescope made it possible to see stars fainter than the sixth magnitude, and these stars were also assigned magnitudes. Through a telescope with a 3-inch aperture (the aperture is the diameter of the front objective in a refractor, or of the main mirror in a reflector), stars of magnitude 11.5 are visible (even 13 under the best conditions); 13.0 through a six-incher; and 14 through a ten-incher.

In 1856 Norman R. Pogson suggested a mathematical definition of magnitude. Like Herschel and other early observers, Pogson had noticed that if two stars differed in brightness by 5 magnitudes (for example, a first magnitude and a sixth magnitude star, or a 10th magnitude and a 15th magnitude star), the brighter one was about 100 times brighter than the fainter one. Observers had reached this conclusion through a fairly simple technique. The amount of light a telescope gathers depends on its aperture. If part of the aperture is covered up, faint stars seem to disappear, as the amount of light the eye is receiving from them becomes too little to be perceptible. Suppose we choose a star and, while observing it, cover up more and more of the aperture until that star can no longer be seen. Repeat the procedure with another star. The ratio of the brightness of the two stars will be the ratio between the areas of the apertures at the point at

Some Visual Magnitudes	
Sun	−26.5
Full Moon	−12.5
Venus (at brightest)	−4.74
Jupiter (at brightest)	−2.1
Sirius (the brightest star)	−1.4
Vega	0.1
Deneb	1.3
Aldebaran	1.0
Altair	1.0
Halley's Comet (at its brightest in 1986)	2.0
Naked eye limit (urban areas)	2.5
Andromeda galaxy	5.0
Orion nebula	6.0
Naked eye limit (dark sky)	6.2
(About 6000 stars have magnitudes greater than 6.2.)	
Naked eye (experienced, gifted observers under ideal conditions)	7.0
Naked eye (laboratory tests with artificial stars)	8.5
Limit of 8" telescope	14.0
Limit of largest earth-based telescopes	25

which each star became too faint to see.

Pogson proposed that successive magnitudes differ by some constant multiplier. Call it x. **The ratio of the brightness of a first magnitude star to the brightness of a second magnitude star will be 1:x; the ratio of a second to third is also 1:x, and so on. What is the ratio of the first magnitude star to a third magnitude star? 1:(x times x), or 1:x^2.** Extending this, the ratio between the brightnesses of magnitude 1 stars and magnitude 6 stars must be 1:x^5. Since observations had shown that this ratio is 1:100, $x^5 = 100$. So, Pogson suggested, the ratio between successive magnitudes should be set at 1:the fifth root of 100, which is about 1:2.512. ($2.512 \times 2.512 \times 2.512 \times 2.512 \times 2.512 \approx 100$)

Pogson's definition determines the size of the steps between magnitudes, but not how bright any particular magnitude is. To do that, astronomers at first assigned magnitudes to a group of stars around the north celestial pole. With the development of more sensitive photoelectronic instrumentation this original definition was no longer good enough. Today, zero magnitude is defined by the magnitudes of ten rather average, non-variable stars fairly evenly distributed over the celestial sphere.

By defining the ratio between magnitudes as Pogson did, and by the magnitudes assigned to the ten stars, astronomers have largely preserved the ratings Hipparchus gave the stars in his catalog 20 centuries ago.

Photographic Magnitudes. Photography extended the range of magnitudes far beyond that of the eye, because in a time exposure a photographic plate can soak up light for hours on end, which the eye cannot. All stars except the sun are so far away that they appear as points, with no diameter; but on a photographic plate, the brighter the star, the bigger the image. Magnitudes can be determined by measuring the diameters of star images on the plate. Magnitudes determined in this way are called photographic magnitudes.

Most astronomical photographs are taken on types of film that are not equally sensitive to light of all colors. *Blue magnitude* or *photovisual magnitude* refers to a photographic magnitude that has been measured using photographic plates whose sensitivity to various colors is similar to that of the human eye.

Bolometric magnitude. Bolometric magnitude takes into account all the radiation emitted by the star, whatever its wavelength. (There are even stars that shine entirely in the infrared, outside the band of visible light.) Because earth's atmosphere blocks some wavelengths, determining bolometric magnitudes is extremely difficult, and they have been found for only a few stars.

Integrated magnitude. To assign a magnitude to objects that are not point sources, such as galaxies and nebulas, astronomers treat them as if all the light from them came from a point. So the Orion nebula, whose integrated magnitude is 6, doesn't look as bright as a magnitude 6 star.

If light from all the stars (excluding the sun) were combined in a single star, it would have an apparent magnitude of −6.7, much less than the full moon. The range of brightness of everything we have seen in the sky can be summed up in two gigantic leaps of apparent magnitude: the sun is about 25 magnitudes (10^{10}) brighter than the brightest star, Sirius, and Sirius is 25 magnitudes brighter than the faintest star that can be photographed by the 200" telescope on Mt. Palomar.

Absolute Magnitude. Abbr, M (in contrast to the lowercase "m" for apparent magnitude). A big, bright star that is far off can easily be fainter than a dimmer star that is near us—such as the sun. To compare stars' real brightnesses, they would all have to be at the same distance. The measure that does this is *absolute magnitude*, the apparent magnitude a star would have if it were 10 ☞parsecs away, an arbitrarily chosen distance. Absolute magnitude is calculated from the star's apparent magnitude and distance. The absolute magnitude of the sun is about 4.8. Most stars have absolute magnitudes between 0 and 15; the extreme range is −10 to +19.

The *absolute bolometric magnitude* of a star is the bolometric magnitude it would have if it were at a distance of 10 parsecs.

magnum

1) A size of wine bottle which has twice the capacity of the usual wine bottle; nowadays, = 1.5 liters. A double magnum has four times the usual bottle's capacity. 2) Applied to ammunition, the word suggests a powerful round, but it is largely a term of hype without any exact meaning. It cannot even be relied upon to distinguish a more powerful from a less powerful round; for example, when the .357 magnum was introduced, there was no other .357 round. According to Jan Libourel, Executive Handgun Editor at *Guns and Ammo*, the word "express" was used for the same purpose in the past, and may be making a comeback.

mattresses

In the United States, the standard mattress sizes are: twin, 39" × 75" or 76"; long twin, 39" × 80"; full or double, 54" × 75" or 76"; queen, 60" × 80"; king, 78" or 79" × 80"; and California king, 72" × 84". (The people in the drawing are 6' tall.)

Twin   LT   Double   Queen   King   Cal King

The top of the mattress should be about 18" above the floor and, in a bunk bed, at least 30" below the bottom of the mattress above.

Words such as "extra firm," "firm" and so on may be helpful in comparing different mattresses within a line, but they have no meaning in comparing mattresses from different manufacturers. In general, mattresses and box springs should be more than 6" thick. A double bed innerspring mattress should have more than 300 coils, a queen size more than 375, and king size more than 450. The gauge of the wire from which the springs are made is also significant; 13-gauge springs are sturdier than 16-gauge. A foam mattress should have a density of more than two pounds per cubic foot. In all types of mattresses, the edges and corners in particular should not feel flimsy.

When you try out the mattress—if it is for two people, both of you simultaneously—note whether your hips and shoulders are supported comfortably when you lie on your side. Roll around and listen for strange noises; there shouldn't be any.

meter

The unit of length in SI, one of the seven base units. Since 1983 the meter has been defined as the distance light travels in a vacuum in exactly 1/299,792,458th of a ☛second (17TH CGPM, Resolution 1).

This definition of the meter makes the length of the meter depend on the duration of the second; by definition the speed of light is now *exactly* 299,792,458 meters per second. A measurement of the time it takes light to travel between two points in a vacuum can no longer indicate the speed of light; it indicates the distance between the points!

Most of the English-speaking world spells meter "metre." The American spelling is due to Noah Webster, who condemned the "-re" ending in his influential speller and dictionary. Compare "liter" and "litre."

History

In the 1780s, French weights and measures were a mess, with dozens of units, each with dozens or even hundreds of local values. No other nation suffered from such a disparity between the demands of an industrializing economy and the capabilities of its system of weights and measures. Long before the French Revolution, persons of all political persuasions were calling for metrological reform. There was also a feeling, consonant with the Rousseauistic spirit of the times, that units should be, somehow, "natural."

The seconds pendulum. Jean Picard, Olaus Rømer and other astronomers had suggested that a unit of length be defined as the length of a pendulum with a period of 1 second. (A pendulum's period is the time it takes to make one complete swing, back and forth). It was already known that identical pendulums set up in different places had different periods, so any such a definition would have to specify a location for the standard pendulum.

In 1790 Talleyrand, then Bishop of Autun, made a report to the Constituent Assembly on the state of French weights and measures, in which he suggested a new measure of length based on the length of the seconds pendulum at the latitude of Paris, 45° N. He also suggested that the Academy of Sciences in Paris collaborate with the Royal Society of London in defining the new unit, a proposal the Assembly and subsequently Louis XVI approved, though nothing came of it.

By the end of 1790 the Academy had placed the matter in the hands of as illustrious a scientific commission as has ever existed: Lagrange, Laplace, Borda, Monge, and Condorcet. In their report to the Academy on March 19, 1791, the commission recommended scrapping the seconds pendulum. Instead, they suggested the new unit of length be one ten-millionth of the distance at sea level from the pole to the equator.

The quadrant of the earth. From a metrological point of view, taking a quadrant of the earth as a standard makes no sense at all. Any two surveys of such a distance are bound differ by much more than the amount of precision demanded of the unit. Nor is there some special relation between the definition and the unit's use, as there is, say, for the nautical mile in marine navigation or the astronomical unit in astronomy. But the idea that the basic unit was to be a definite fraction of 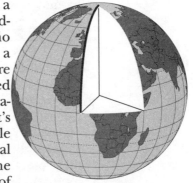 the earth's size appealed to the Enlightenment's desire to trace standards back to Nature, much as the idea that a food contains only natural ingredients appeals to some of today's consumers. And there were other reasons.

Enormous meridian measuring projects were to the science of the late 18TH C as space programs or the construction of large particle accelerators have been to ours. They challenged the limits of the day's technology and tested the predictions of the new physics—in the 18TH C, Newtonian predictions that the earth was not a sphere. Preeminence in such projects was a matter of national pride, at least among "natural philosophers." Borda, for example, a member of the commission, had constructed extremely precise graduated circles for measuring angles, just what would be needed for this sort of work. (His circles were graduated in a new unit, the "grade," rather than degrees, which he sneered at as "Babylonian.")

The Assembly approved the proposed unit on March 26, 1791, and work on realizing it began. To replace the hated "royal foot" until the results of the survey were in, a provisional meter was defined, two of which equalled 6 *pied*, 1 *pouce*, 10 22/25 *lignes* of the *toise du Perou*.

Measuring the quadrant. Obviously it would be impossible to survey the distance between the North Pole and the equator, the whole 90°. No one had ever been to the North Pole. But if one could measure a significant piece of a meridian, the rest could be calculated. The two ends of the line to be measured had to be at sea level, and somewhere near the middle of the pole-to-equator quadrant. As it happens, there is only one such meridian on earth: from Dunkirk to Barcelona, which covers about a tenth of the distance from the pole to the equator. The distance lies almost entirely in France, which did not escape the French, nor indeed such impartial observers as Thomas Jefferson.

The survey was put in the hands of P. F. A. Méchain and J. B. J. Delambre. In the summer of 1792, Delambre began working his way south from the coast near Dunkirk, while Méchain started north from the Mediterranean. They would meet at Rodez, 300 miles south of Paris. Méchain's share was shorter, but more difficult, for it crossed the Pyrenees Mountains that separate Spain and France. In September the Republic was declared.

The revolution was in full swing. Within a few months France was at war with Great Britain, Austria, Prussia, Holland and Spain; Louis XVI had been executed, and Parisian mobs were massacring various groups. The Terror was not far off. In such a climate the surveyors were regularly arrested. The flags on their survey poles were white—the color of the royalists! They were from Paris. All they had going for them was that their story—we are measuring the distance from Dunkirk to Barcelona—was so unbelievable in the midst of war and revolution that no real spy would have used it.

Once when Delambre was seized his captors compelled him to make his explanations in the most republican way, to an audience of volunteers on their way to the war. The troops did not find the trigonometry lecture entertaining. Delambre was saved from the crowd by an official who took him into protective custody, and was eventually released only because the National Convention ordered it.

On August 8, 1793, the National Convention abolished the Academy of Sciences as unrepublican. The Committee of Public Safety, however, remained intent on doing away with the old feudal measures and needed the help of the Academicians to do it, so it persuaded the Convention to create a new, independent temporary commission (Commission temporaire des poids et mesures républicains) with the same members. In November Lavoisier was arrested; the commission asked for his release; the Committee of Public Safety responded by kicking five more members off the commission, including Delambre. Seeing which way the wind blew, the commission then devoted itself to preparing revolutionary denunciations of the old weights and measures. Delambre thought they should kill the whole meridian-measuring project and just accept the provisional meter.

But war requires maps. A military cartographer who was also a Jacobin was put in charge of map-making. Needing trained people, he brought Delambre and Méchain back to Paris. (Méchain had prudently withdrawn to Genoa, narrowly escaping pirates.)

On April 7, 1795 an order establishing the names now in use (meter, liter, gram) also reestablished the commission (except for Lavoisier, who had been guillotined the previous year) and ordered resumption of the survey.

Delambre finished his portion in the fall of 1797. But Méchain had yet to reach Rodez. Sick, with winter coming, he wrote to his colleague, "I will sacrifice everything, give up everything, rather than return without completing my part." And so the survey stalled. But Méchain recovered and resumed work; in September, 1798, he reached Rodez.

To this point, except for the sides of two triangles, only angles had been measured, the angles of contiguous triangles stretching all the way from Dunkirk to Barcelona. If any side of only one of these triangles were known, the dimensions of all the others could be calculated, and from them the distance along the meridian. While Mechain labored in the south, Delambre measured one of the baselines with a special ruler. It took him 33 days.

On November 28, 1798 the French convened an international meeting of experts from friendly powers and puppet states. One of the meeting's committees consisted of four persons, each of whom independently calculated the length of the meter from the measurements made by Delambre and Méchain (and from certain assumptions about the shape of the earth). Their calculations agreed. The meter was established at 0.144 lignes of the *toise de Perou* shorter than than the provisional meter.

Today the length of the earth's quadrant can be measured relatively easily by the use of satellites. Such measurements show that the meter is actually about 1/5 mm shorter than one ten-millionth of the earth's quadrant. The startling thing about this fact is not that the meter does not conform to its original conception, but that two 18TH C surveyors should have come so close.

The meter as a bar. Since 1795 the former royal jeweller had been producing bars of platinum 4 mm thick, 25.3 mm wide and about a provisional meter long, with plane parallel ends. The lengths of these bars were compared with the length of the meter as determined by the survey. The one nearest that length (at 0°C) was deposited in the National Archives on June 22, 1799, and has since been known as the Mètre des Archives. The metric system itself was legalized on December 10, 1799.

The Mètre des Archives was, by definition, a meter long, from end to end. Metrologists call such a standard an end measure. End measure standards are not a good idea, because any simple way of measuring their lengths requires touching the ends, which causes wear and shortens the standard. A much better form for a standard of a unit of length is a pair of scratches on a metal bar, because the lines' locations can be determined visually. Such a standard is called a line measure.

International interest in the meter and the French proselytizing spirit led to two international conferences (Commission Internationale du Mètre) in 1870 and 1872 to discuss international standardization of the meter. The attendees favored replacing the Mètre des Archives with a new prototype which would be a line measure and made of a harder, platinum-iridium alloy (10% iridium, to within 0.0001%). They also suggested that the meter be taken as the length of the Mètre des Archives, "in the state in which it is found," without reference to the quadrant of the earth.

In 1875, twenty countries attended the third conference. Eighteen subscribed to a treaty (the Convention du Mètre), which set up the Bureau International des Poids et Mésures. Production of the meter standard, however, proved very difficult. Besides having an extremely high melting point (2,443°C), iridium had not yet been produced in purities greater than 50%. The bars from the first casting of the alloy, in 1874, were rejected in 1877, and the problem was turned over to the London firm of Johnson, Matthey and Co. They succeeded, and one of the resulting bars was made the provisional standard, even though it was 0.006 mm shorter than the Mètre des Archives. In 1882 France ordered thirty more bars, one of which (No. 6) turned out to be, as nearly as could be ascertained, exactly the length of the Mètre des Archives. This bar is the standard which was declared to be the International Prototype of the Meter by the First General Conference on

Weights and Measures (FIRST CGPM) in 1889: "This prototype, at the temperature of melting ice, shall henceforth represent the metric unit of length." The International Prototype continues to be preserved by the BIPM.

As a way of distributing this standard to the countries signing the treaty, "national Meters" were made, which were copies of the International Prototype plus or minus 0.01 millimeter, supplied with a correction factor obtained by comparing that particular national meter with the International Prototype.

The meter defined by light. The idea of defining a unit of length in terms of the wavelength of light had been floated early in the 19TH C (J. Babinet, 1827), before there was any way of realizing the idea in practice. By the end of the century this was no longer so.

"White" light is a mixture of light with different wavelengths. To define a unit of length in terms of wavelength, one needs light that is all of the same wavelength. Light consisting of only one wavelength—any wavelength, provided it is visible—appears to a human to be colored, and is called monochromatic.

Fortunately it doesn't seem hard to produce monochromatic light: sprinkle some salt on the gas flames of a kitchen range. When the sodium atoms in the salt get excited, they give off a yellow light which is pretty much all the same wavelength. It is the same yellow as the light from sodium vapor street lamps. The wavelength is characteristic of the sodium atom.

In 1892–3 A. A. Michelson and J. R. Benoit succeeded in measuring the meter in terms of the wavelength of red light given off by excited cadmium atoms. Benoit and others refined the measurement in 1905–7, and in 1907 the International Solar Union (which is now the IAU) defined the international angstrom, a unit of distance to be used in measuring wavelengths, by making 6438.4696 international angstroms equal to the wavelength of the red line of cadmium. This value was taken from Benoit's experiments, and was chosen so that one angstrom $\approx 10^{-10}$ meter. (In 1927, the SEVENTH CGPM provisionally sanctioned measuring distances in terms of the red line of cadmium, taking its wavelength to be 0.64384696 μm.)

Meanwhile, much had been learned since 1892. Even in the best of spectroscopes, the red line of cadmium was somewhat fuzzy. In fact, it turned out to be composed of many lines (physicists refer to its "hyperfine structure"), which affected how precisely the light's wavelength could be determined. When the existence of isotopes was discovered, it became clear that part of the reason for the fuzziness was that the light was not coming from a single kind of atom, but from a mixture of isotopes: cadmium atoms with the same number of protons, but different numbers of neutrons. Investigating light from pure isotopes, it was found that if an atom had an even number of protons, and the sum of the numbers of protons and neutrons it contained was also even, the light from it had no hyperfine structure. (Such atoms have no nuclear spin, hence no coupling of nuclear spin to electron spins—and the light comes from the electrons.)

The NINTH CGPM (1948) allowed as how the meter might eventually be defined in terms of light from such an isotope. Three isotopes were intensively investigated to see which would be most suitable as the basis for a standard of length: krypton-86 (36 protons), mercury-198 (80 protons), and cadmium-114 (48 protons). The committee in charge of following these developments recommended that any new definition be stated in terms of the wavelength in a vacuum instead of in air, and that the length of the wavelength should be specified by comparing it with the already determined wavelength of the red line of cadmium, not with the International Prototype of the Meter. The 10TH CGPM (1954) accepted these recommendations, in effect making the angstrom exactly equal to 10^{-10} meter and defining the meter in terms of light, although this was not formally acknowledged until 1960.

The advisory committee declared krypton-86 the winner in 1957, and in 1960, the 11TH CGPM (Resolution 6), noting that "the international Prototype does not define the meter with an accuracy adequate for the present needs of metrology," redefined the meter as "the length equal to 1 650 763.73 wavelengths in vacuum of the radiation corresponding to the transition between the levels $2p_{10}$ and $5d_5$ of the krypton 86 atom."

Defined this way, it proved impossible to realize the meter with an accuracy better than 4 parts in 10^9, and eventually that was not accurate enough. In the meantime, however, the laser had been invented, and the light it produced—not only all one wavelength, but all in phase—opened up new possibilities for metrology.

In 1983 the 17TH CGPM (Resolution 1) redefined the meter in terms of the speed of light in a vacuum. The value for the speed of light, 299,792,458 meters per second, had already been recommended in 1975 by the 15TH CGPM, (RESOLUTION 2). ITS USE IN THE METER'S DEFINITION MADE THE SPEED OF LIGHT FALL WITHIN THE LIMITS OF UNCERTAINTY OF THE BEST EXISTING MEASUREMENTS.

Thus the second, rejected as too arbitrary in 1791, has become the basis of the meter. We have probably not seen the last redefinition of the meter; the current definition may need tuning if even more accuracy becomes necessary. For example, the speed of light is affected by the strength of the gravitational field, and the 1983 definition does not take such factors into account.

meter-kilogram-second-systems of units

Systems of units that take the meter, kilogram, and second as their units of length, mass, and time. SI is such a system. Units for these three properties are enough to do Newtonian mechanics, a branch (some would say the trunk) of physics.

In the last half of the 19TH C, when the "metric system" was beginning to gain worldwide acceptance, most of the scientific community decided to use a system of units based on the centimeter and gram (see ☞centimeter-gram-second systems). Such a system had been recommended by the great German physicist Wilhelm Weber and seconded by a committee of the influential British Assn. for the Advancement of Science, influenced by the equally great J. Clerk Maxwell. During the same period, because the cgs electric units were much too small for everyday use, a separate system of much larger practical electric units arose. (See ☞International System of Electric and Magnetic Units.)

Their electric and magnetic units were the undoing of the cgs systems. Agreement was never reached on a satisfactory way of reconciling the electric and magnetic units with each other or with the practical units, which made life difficult for anyone who needed to use both electric and magnetic units in the same problem. Further, because some of the units had been defined by different parties at different times (unit electric flux, for example, or the gauss), there was some confusion about what they really meant. Many wanted units that would be numerically equivalent to the practical units, and many objected to the fact that, in their usual form, the cgs systems were not rationalized.

To see what a rationalized unit is and why some scientists wanted them, consider the following example, which was suggested by B. A. Massey. Suppose that our unit for measuring area was not the square foot (the area of a square 1 foot on a side), but the area of a circle with a radius of 1 foot. Call it a "circfoot." The area of a circle with a radius of 2 feet would be 4 circfeet. But the area of a rectangle 2 feet by 3 feet would be $6/\pi$ circfeet. In fact, π would appear as a factor in the area of every rectangle, and not in that of any circle (assuming the radius or side length wasn't a multiple of π). There is something very disturbing and unnatural about such a state of affairs. One expects π to come up when one is dealing with circles, but why should it come up with rectangles?

Much the same thing happened with the electrical and magnetic units in the centimeter-gram-second and meter-kilogram-second systems; π kept popping up where it made no sense.

The Giorgi System

One of the critics of the cgs systems was an Italian physicist, Giovanni Giorgi (1871–1950), who as early as 1895 condemned cgs in a letter to the English magazine *Electrician*. In October 1901, in a talk given before the Italian Electrical Engineering Assn. ("Razionali di elettromagnetismo"), Giorgi proposed a system that resolved most of the failings of the cgs systems. It used the meter, kilogram, and second, and in a slightly later revised form, set the permeability of free space at 10^{-7} henry/meter (for the significance of permeability, see ☞centimeter-gram-second systems of units). This choice gave the ampere the same value that it had as a practical unit, and in fact the value for the permeability of free space is realized through the definition of the ampere. Over the following decades, the Giorgi, or MKSA, system gradually caught on.

In a plenary session in 1935 the IEC adopted the Giorgi system. In 1950 it decided to increase the value for the permeability of free space by a factor of $4\,\pi$ (the surface area of a sphere of radius 1), thus rationalizing the system. Expressions concerning spheres would contain "$4\,\pi$"; those concerning coils, "$2\,\pi$"; and those dealing with straight wires would not contain π at all. The resulting "rationalized MKSA system," was the direct ancestor of SI.

meter–kilogram–force–second system

A metric system used by engineers, who are much more concerned with force than with mass as such, and so prefer to work in a system with base units of length, *force* and time instead of length, *mass* and time. Abbr, m-kgf-s. It has the same relation to the meter-kilogram-second system as the British Engineering system of units has to the foot-pound-second system. Such systems are often called technical or gravitational systems.

The unit of force is the *kilogram-force*. Abbr, kgf. It is approximately the weight of a 1-kilogram mass on earth, but the effects of location are eliminated by including a standard value for the acceleration due to gravity (or if you prefer, a standard weight-to-mass ratio). One kilogram-force is the force that a 1-kilogram mass exerts at a place where the acceleration due to gravity is 9.80665 meters per second per second. There is a corresponding *gram-force*. One kilogram-force = 9.80665 newtons.

The unit of mass in the m-kgf-s system is somewhat confused. It was once called the *hyl*, but unfortunately that term has been used in two senses: 1) a mass such that a gram-force acting on it will accelerate it 1 meter per second per second, $\approx 9.80665 \times 10^{-3}$ kilograms; or 2) a mass such that a kilogram-force acting on it will accelerate it 1 meter per second per second ≈ 9.80665 kg (the term *kilohyle* always applies to this second sense). To avoid confusion it is best to use the term *metric-technical unit of mass* (abbr, TME), which always has the second meaning.

It has also been called the *metric slug*, alluding to the unit of mass in the British gravitational system.

Kilopond. A name given the kilogram-force in Germany and Eastern Europe. Symbol, kp. Thus instead of a meter–kilogram-force–second system, they had a m-kp-s system.

metric system

Various systems of units that have the ☞meter as the unit of length, the ☞kilogram as the unit of mass and the second as the unit of time and that employ only decimal multiples and subdivisions of those units, which are identified by attaching prefixes to the names of the unit. These systems originated in France in the late 18TH C as described in the entries for meter and kilogram. The ☞centimeter-gram-second and ☞meter-kilogram-second systems are examples, now obsolete, of metric systems used in scientific work. The current version of the metric system, used in both science and trade since 1960, is the ☞International System of Units.

micron

An obsolete metric unit, $= 10^{-6}$ meter. Abbr, μ. It was adopted in 1879 by the CIPM and again in Resolution 7 of the NINTH CGPM (1948).

It was often encountered as the millimicron $= 10^{-9}$ meter, or $1/1000$th of a micron. Symbol, $m\mu$. Like the micron itself, it is obsolete. The current SI unit having the same value is the nanometer (symbol, nm).

In 1967 the 13TH CGPM abolished the micron, along with all other special names for decimal submultiples of a unit that aren't formed by attaching an SI prefix to that unit (Resolution 7). The approved SI term for the same length is micrometer (symbol, μm). Nonetheless, "micron" is still the term most commonly used in fields like semiconductor fabrication.

microscope

Objectives. The first to succeed in persuading microscope manufacturers to use the same threads on their objectives was the Royal Microscope Society, which is the origin of the term "society thread," by which the standard is known. The society thread has 36 threads per inch of the 55° Whitworth form; the male thread has an outer diameter of 0.7965" (between 0.7952" and 0.7982"). The female thread, in the nosepiece, has a top-of-thread diameter between 0.8030" and 0.8000".

The RMS standard dealt only with mechanical fit; two more recent national standards also address optical fit: a Japanese Standard, JIS (36 mm), and a German standard DIN (45 mm), the distances referring to the distance between the face of the nosepiece and the plane of focus on the stage. Both have male threads 20.1 mm diameter, 36 threads per inch, 55° Whitworth threads (so, mechanically, they fit the society thread). JIS objectives are designed for a 160 mm mechanical tube length (which was the Leitz standard); DIN objectives for a 170 mm tube length (which was the Zeiss standard).

Objectives are marked with their magnification (in lieu of focal length) and numerical aperture, which is the product of the refractive index of the medium in front of the lens, such as air, water or immersion oil, and the sine of the angle between the optical axis and the most divergent ray that will make it to the image. If the numerical aperture is greater than 0.4, a condenser is needed; very high numerical apertures require the use of immersion oil between the objective and the coverglass.

Eyepieces. The standard eyepiece has an outer diameter of 23 mm. The magnification marked is calculated using the tube length for which the eyepiece was designed; 160 mm for JIS eyepieces and 170 mm for DIN eyepieces.

Two smaller standards are used only for lower quality student microscopes. Both employ a 139 mm tube. One uses 21 mm outer diameter eyepieces and an objective with an outer diameter of 17.5 mm with 42 threads per inch. The other standard uses 19 mm O.D. eyepieces and 15 mm O.D., 42 tpi objectives.

microwave ovens

The power of a microwave oven is given in watts. The magnetron, the part of the oven that makes the microwaves, is unlike a gas flame in that it is either on or off; there are no intermediate stages. The intermediate settings are achieved by cycling the magnetron on and off. For example, at 50% power the magnetron is on half the time and off half the time. The International Microwave Power Institute has standardized the meanings of the words used for the settings: High means on 100% of the time; Medium High, 70%; Medium, 50%; Low, 30%; and Warm, 10%.

Most cookbooks assume an oven with a power of about 650 to 700 watts. (Power and physical size differ; 700-watt ovens are made in a range of cubic inch capacities.) Such an oven boils a cup of water in 2 1/2 to 3 minutes. Unfortunately, there is no trustworthy way of converting cooking times for a 700-watt oven to cooking times for ovens with less power. A 350-watt oven will not take twice as long. For one thing, much of the cooking is done by heat from the already heated parts of the food; the longer the cooking time, the more time this heat has to do its work, even without any further input from the magnetron. So it is best to guess on the low side (you can always zap the food for a few more seconds, but you can't uncook it) and keep good records.

There is a fairly simple way to compare two ovens. Put a liter of room temperature water in a wide microwavable container. Take the temperature of the water in degrees Celsius. (If your thermometer reads in degrees Fahrenheit, use the chart at the back of this book to convert the reading to Celsius.) Microwave for five minutes. Stir the water and take its temperature again. Subtract the first temperature from the second. The result is the number of kilocalories of energy the oven transferred to the water. Repeating the test with the same container in a different oven will provide an accurate comparison of their powers.

In some parts of the country the voltage drops in the evening, when people begin using lights and cooking dinner. The lower the voltage, the lower a microwave oven's power. If your oven seems to take longer to cook at meal time than at other times of day, this could be the reason.

mil

In the United States the mil is a unit of length = 0.001 inch. The thickness of plastic trash bags, for example, is usually given in mils.

mile

In the English-speaking world, 10TH–20TH C, a unit of distance = 8 furlongs = 5,280 feet, ≈ 1.609344 kilometers. Often referred to as the *statute mile*, from its having been established by a statute of Elizabeth I ("An Acte againste newe Buyldinges") which forbade building within 3 miles of the gates of London, and included a definition of this mile (35 Elizabeth I c 6 1592/3).

The word "mile" comes from the Latin *mille passum*, literally "thousand paces," a unit introduced to Britain by the Roman occupation (57 BC–AD 450). Each *passus* consists of five *pes*, the Roman foot, so the *mille passum* was 5,000 *pes*. This distance was also known as a *milliarium*, literally "milestone." The *mille passum* was divided into 8 *stadia*, each of 625 *pes*.

The Roman *pes* was shorter than our foot, and a well-accepted guess at the length of the *mille passum* in Roman Britain is ≈ 1,479.5 meters, about 90% of a statute mile.

The Saxons seem to have retained a 5,000-foot mile (their *mil*), but the Saxon foot was even shorter than the Roman one, closer to the size of a real foot. The Saxon *mil* was probably ≈ 1,257 meters, ≈ 0.78 statute miles.

The question then becomes how the mile grew from "5,000" feet to 5,280 feet. The answer seems to be that the English furlong became confused with the Roman *stade*. In those days legal proceedings, records and other official documents were kept in Latin. "Mile" in English naturally became "mille" in Latin. The nearest equivalent in Latin to the English "furlong" (660 feet), however, was the "stade" (625 *pes*). The educated knew that the Roman *mille passus* contained 8 *stadia*, and continually using "stadia" to stand for "furlongs" planted the idea that a mile contained 8 furlongs, whereas in the past the two units had been used for entirely different purposes and had had no direct relationship. The result was confusion: 5,000-foot miles, 8-furlong miles, and even attempts to redefine the furlong to make 8 of them fit in a 5,000-foot mile. Something had to give. The length of the furlong, the basis of the acre, was not adjustable because the ruling on the celestial sphere that marks where the sphere is cut in half by the plane of the earth's orbit. A tropical month is the average interval between instants when the line through the moon crosses the point on the ecliptic called the vernal equinox.

Sidereal month. The time it takes the moon to return to the same position among the stars.

Anomalistic month. The moon's orbit around the earth isn't circular; the point in the orbit which it is closest to the earth is called the perigee. The anomalistic month is the average interval between successive passages of the moon through its perigee.

Nodical month. The average interval between successive northward passages of the moon across the ecliptic. It is sometimes called a *draconic* or *draconitic month*.

	days	days	hrs	min	sec
Synodic	29.53059	29	12	44	3
Tropical	27.32158	27	7	43	5
Sidereal	27.32166	27	7	43	12
Anomalistic	27.55455	27	13	18	33
Nodical	27.21222	27	5	5	36

In addition to the physical phenomena that show a monthly variation, such as the tides, many biological phenomena have periods of about a month, for example, women's menses.

mortar for brickwork

Five types of mortar are defined. The number is the compressive strength in pounds per square inch.

M — vigorous exposure, load-bearing, below grade, 2,500 psi.
S — severe exposure, load bearing, below grade, 1,800 psi.
N — mild exposure, light loads, above grade, 750 psi.
O — interiors, light loads, 350 psi.
K — non-bearing walls, or very light loads. 75 psi.

motion pictures

B picture. Between about 1932 and 1950, American movie theaters generally showed two feature-length films for the price of admission: a "double feature." One of the films would be a major production; the other, a "B movie," was a cheaply-made filler. "B movies" rented for a flat fee, regardless of ticket sales; "A movies" commanded a percentage of the gate. (Unlike "B movie" and "B picture," the term "A movie" was rarely used, and there was no "C movie.") There was little risk in producing B movies, but little profit, and the major studios soon stopped making them. A number of independent studios specialized in B movies.

classes' rents and revenues were based upon it, but a modest change in the mile would have no great impact. So Elizabeth I ended the confusion by coming down on the side of the 8-furlong, 5,280-foot mile, in effect abolishing the 5,000-foot mile.

Other miles persisted in England for centuries after the statute mile was defined. The distances between English cities given in guidebooks as late as the 17 C use a mile which is longer than the statute mile, probably around 1.3 statute miles. This mile has been dubbed the *old English mile*, 14TH–17TH C, although it is probably no older than the statute mile.

mile, nautical

A unit of length used at sea, in principle the length of 1 mean minute of arc on the meridian. In 1929, the International Hydrographic Conference in Monaco defined the international nautical mile as exactly

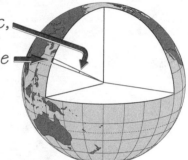

If this angle is 1 minute of arc,

this distance is 1 nautical mile

1,852 meters, ≈ 6,076.11549 feet. Prior to this, a value of 1852.276 meters had been used, based on the International Terrestrial Geoid.

Until July 1, 1954, the United States used the U.S. nautical mile, = 1,853.248 meters, ≈ 6,080.20 feet. Thereafter, by an agreement between the Departments of Commerce and Defense, the international nautical mile has been used. (In the Departments' announcements, the figure 6,076.10333... feet is given as equivalent to 1852 m. It differs from the currently correct figure, given above, because the announcement was made prior to the change to the international foot.)

In the UK, the length of the nautical mile was defined by its relation to the *admiralty knot*, 6,080 imperial feet per hour, so 1 imperial nautical mile ≈ 1,853.181 meters. The imperial nautical mile was often called an *admiralty mile*.

The *telegraph nautical mile* = 6,087 feet.

minim

1) In the USA, a unit of liquid capacity ≈ 0.062 milliliter ≈ 1.041 (British) minims. **2)** In the UK, 19TH–20TH C, a unit of liquid capacity used by druggists. See ☞apothecaries' measure. It was scheduled for abolition by the 1963 Weights and Measures Act, and actually became no longer legal in trade on February 1, 1971, a date set by the 1970 Weights and Measures Act.

minot

In Canada, 20TH C, a unit of capacity ≈ 3,891 liters.

Mohs' scale

A scale of hardness primarily used for minerals, devised around 1812 by Friedrich Mohs (1773–1839), a German minerologist. Mohs' scale consists of 10 common minerals in order of increasing hardness (shown in the second column below). An unknown mineral's place on the scale is determined by what it will scratch and what will scratch it. For example, the average fingernail will scratch gypsum and can be scratched by calcite, so fingernail would be given a rating between 2 and 3. Window glass is about 5.5, which shows ordinary quartz will scratch it. Many minerals show different hardnesses depending on the direction in which they are scratched, due to their crystal structure.

Increasingly sophisticated methods for measuring hardness showed that the steps in Mohs' scale are far from equal, especially at the high end. For example, on an equal-step scale, if diamond is taken as 10, corundum would be 2.5 and topaz 1.6. Taking advantage of very hard synthetic materials that weren't available to Mohs, the top end of the scale has been revised to provide finer (but not equal) gradations, as shown below.

	Original scale	Revised scale
1	talc	talc
2	gypsum	gypsum
3	calcite	calcite
4	fluorite	fluorite
5	apatite	apatite
6	orthoclase	orthoclase
7	quartz	vitreous pure silica
8	topaz	quartz
9	corundum	topaz
10	diamond	garnet
11		fused zirconium oxide
12		fused alumina
13		silicon carbide
14		boron carbide
15		diamond

mole

The unit for amount of substance in SI. One mole is "the amount of substance of a system that contains as many elementary entities as there are atoms in 12 grams of carbon-12". Abbr, mol. When the mole is used, the user must specify what elementary entity is meant, which

may be "atoms, molecules, ions, electrons, other [subatomic] cles, or specified groups of such particles." The mole was defi the CIPM in 1967 and adopted in 1971 by the 14TH CGPM (Reso 3). In 1980, the CIPM added that it is understood the atoms of c 12 referred to are at rest and in their ground state.

Originally, the mole was a unit used by chemists to count th countable, and was also known as *gram molecular weight* or *gram m* One mole of any element or compound was the atomic weigh lecular weight or formula weight, depending on the substance, substance in atomic mass units, expressed in grams. This defi makes the number of molecules in the mole 6.02×10^{23}, wh Avogadro's number.

momme

An old Japanese unit of mass, in the 20TH C ≈ 3.75 grams. In the it became a unit indicating the quality of silk cloth, = the weig pounds of 100 yards of silk cloth 45" wide.

moneyers' weight

In England, a sequence of units supposedly used for medicine precious metals, produced by subdividing the grain alternately l and 24 (continuing the pattern in troy weight). By the middle c 19TH C at the latest these units had been entirely replaced by dec fractions of the grain.

The smaller units in the sequence had to have been purely cor tual. Although the system is described in several old documents, looks like the creation of some monk's overwrought imagina Today, a sophisticated $10,000 laboratory analytical balance we with an accuracy of roughly ± 5 micrograms. The *blank* would I been ≈ 0.28 micrograms.

				grain
			mite	20
		droit	24	480
	periot	20	480	9,600
blank *or* blanc	24	480	11,520	230,400

month

Various periods of time based on the revolution of the moon about earth. All except the calendar month are the intervals of time betwe the instants when the moon passes through some reference point.

Calendar month. A division of the calendar year, of arbitrary leng but roughly equal to the various astronomical months defined bel See ☞calendar.

Synodic month. The average length of time the moon takes to retu to the same position relative to the sun. This is the interval betwe full moons.

Tropical month. Imagine a line from pole to pole on the celesti sphere, passing through the moon. It will cross the ecliptic, the circ

Ratings. The practise of rating motion pictures in terms of their suitability for various audiences first began abroad. In the UK, ratings are assigned by the British Board of Film Censors.

U   Universal admission.
A   Parental discretion advised.
X   Youngsters under 16 not admitted.

On July 1, 1970, the categories were changed to:

U   Universal admission.
A   Parental discretion advised.
AA   Youngsters under 14 not admitted
X   Persons under 18 not admitted.

In the USA, ratings were first introduced in 1968. Ratings are assigned by a private organization, the Code and Rating Administration of the Motion Picture Assn. of America.

G   General audience, anyone admitted.
PG   Parental guidance. Some material may not be suitable for a child under 13. When the system was first introduced this category was called "M." In February 1970 the name was changed to "GP," and then to PG in 1972.
PG-13 Parents are strongly cautioned. Some material may not be suitable for children under 13.
R   Persons under 17 admitted only if accompanied by a parent or adult guardian.
NC-17 No one under 17 is admitted. This category was formerly called X.

motors, electric

In the USA, the National Electric Manufacturers Association (NEMA) establishes standard dimensions for electric motors. The rating plate of a motor will give a "frame size," consisting of a number which may be followed by a letter. In purchasing a replacement motor, it is only necessary to get the same frame size to be sure of a physical fit (horsepower, voltage, type of enclosure, bearings, etc. are another matter). In the home, the most commonly encountered frame sizes are 48 and 56.

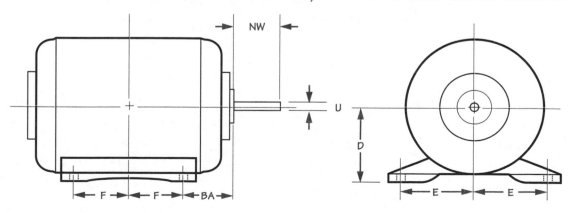

Size	D	2E	2F	BA	Mounting	NW	U
48	2 5/8"	4 1/4"	2 3/4"	2 1/2"	11/32" slot	1 1/2"	1/2"
56	3 1/2"	4 7/8"	3	2 3/4"	11/32" slot	1 7/8"	5/8"

The NEMA standards also describe the way the motor shaft is modified so that pulleys and gears can be securely fastened to it.

a flat

a slot

Size	Key on shaft
48	29/64" flat
56	3/16" wide, 3/16" deep, 1 3/8" long slot

myria- An obsolete decimal multiplier prefix in the metric system, indicating 10^4.

In 1982 the USA, having authorized use of the myriameter and myriagram in the Act of July 28, 1866, declared the terms no longer acceptable (Feb 26, 1982, FR 8399–8400).

nail

In England, 15TH C–20TH C, various units all of which are 1/16th of some larger measure. By far the most common meaning is 2 1/4 inches, 1/16th of a yard; but it also occurs as a synonym for the clove (= 7 lbs, 1/16th of a hundredweight), and as 1/16th of an acrc. The ratio may have come from the Roman *digitus,* (literally, finger, and hence nail) having been 1/16th of a *pes.*

nails

Length. As a rule of thumb, the length of a nail should be three times the thickness of the board being fastened with it. The lengths of nails are usually indicated by their size in pennies (abbr, d); an 8d finishing nail and an 8d common nail are about the same length. A 2d nail is 1" long. Each 1d increase is a 1/4" increase in length up to 10d, and a 1/2" increase after that.

One explanation of the origin of the penny as a nail size is that the size of a nail in pennies was the price in pennies of 100 such nails. Another theory asserts that the pound was once abbreviated "d". The "d" size of a nail was the weight in pounds of 1000 nails; that is, a thousand 2d nails would weigh 2 pounds. Confusion between "d" for penny and "d" for pound did the rest. But R. E. Zupko, who has made an extensive study of records of British weights and measures, makes no mention of "d" as an abbreviation for the pound.

Several types of small nails are now sized by length and wire gauge. The wire gauge used for nails is the steel wire gauge; the bigger the number, the thinner the nail. Brads, which have small diameter heads and look like miniature finishing nails, come from 1/2" to 1 1/2" and in wire gauges from 19 to 16. "Wire nails" have the same dimensions but bigger heads. (In the more general sense of wire nails almost all modern nails are wire nails; see below.) Escutcheon pins, made in brass, are shorter and thicker than brads and wire nails and have round heads.

Cut nails. Most nails made today are wire nails, machine-made from mild steel wire and more or less round. In earlier times the cut nail was more common. Cut nails, which are still made, are cut from a steel or iron plate and so have a rectangular cross section. In most fields they are now a specialty item prized for their quaint appearance. They are not inferior to wire nails, however; in fact their holding power is about 1.5 times greater than that of a wire nail of the same length—even more in end grain—but they are more expensive to manufacture.

Weight. Most nails are sold by weight, usually in 1-lb boxes. Some stores still offer them in bulk, to be bagged by the purchaser. Contractors purchase bulk nails in corrugated cardboard cartons holding 50 lbs, and 5-lb, 10-lb, and 25-lb boxes are also sometimes available. The nail keg of an earlier era, usually holding 100 lbs (but 150 lbs of wrought spikes or 200 lbs of boat spikes) is now rare.

From tables like those on pp. 184 & 185, the user who knows how many nails are needed can calculate the number of pounds required.

Nails for power nailers, the professional's replacement for the hammer, are sold by count not weight. These machines require nails that have been stuck together in coils or sticks (like the staples for an office stapler); a typical coil holds about 100 to 300 nails and a stick about 100. Each machine has particular requirements (for example, in some sticks the nails are tilted at 31°

Wire Gauge for Nails		
Gauge	Inches	mm
7/0	0.490	12.45
6/0	0.462	11.73
5/0	0.430	10.92
4/0	0.394	10.01
3/0	0.362	9.19
2/0	0.331	8.41
0	0.306	7.77
1	0.283	7.19
1 1/2	0.272	6.91
2	0.262	6.65
2 1/2	0.253	6.43
3	0.244	6.20
3 1/2	0.234	5.94
4	0.225	5.72
4 1/2	0.216	5.49
5	0.207	5.26
5 1/2	0.200	5.08
6	0.192	4.88
6 1/2	0.184	4.67
7	0.177	4.50
7 1/2	0.170	4.32
8	0.162	4.11
8 1/2	0.155	3.94
9	0.148	3.76
9 1/2	0.142	3.61
10	0.135	3.43
10 1/4	0.131	3.33
10 1/2	0.128	3.25
11	0.120	3.05
11 1/2	0.113	2.87
12	0.106	2.69
12 1/2	0.099	2.51
13	0.092	2.34
13 1/2	0.086	2.18
14	0.080	2.03
14 1/2	0.076	1.93
15	0.072	1.83
15 1/2	0.067	1.70
16	0.062	1.57
16 1/2	0.058	1.47
17	0.054	1.37
17 1/2	0.051	1.30
18	0.048	1.22
18 1/2	0.044	1.12
19	0.041	1.04
19 1/2	0.038	0.97
20	0.035	0.89

and in others 22°). Nails should be purchased with a specific make and model of nailer in mind, though there is some interchangability.

Finish. "Bright" nails have no finish and can cause rust streaks if they are used in siding or decking, for example. A common way of making nails corrosion-resistant is to coat them with zinc. Hot-dipped (H.D.) nails have been galvanized by dipping them in molten zinc. Electrogalvanized nails are plated with zinc, and are not as corrosion-resistant as hot-dipped nails. A third process peens zinc onto the nail. By roughening the nail's surface all these treatments, but especially hot-dipping, increase the holding power of the nail. Blued nails have very little resistance to corrosion and are intended to be used indoors. Today, nails are also available in types 304 and 316 stainless steel, which, though about three times as expensive as galvanized nails, are much more rust resistant. Aluminum nails are not strong enough for most structural framing and are primarily used to fasten aluminum siding or screening.

There are dozens of different kinds of nails. The apple-box nail differs from the berry-box nail, the cigar-box nail, the fruit-box nail, and the beer-case cleat nail. Even the ordinary hardware store offers more than a dozen types. A few of the less specialized types are described below.

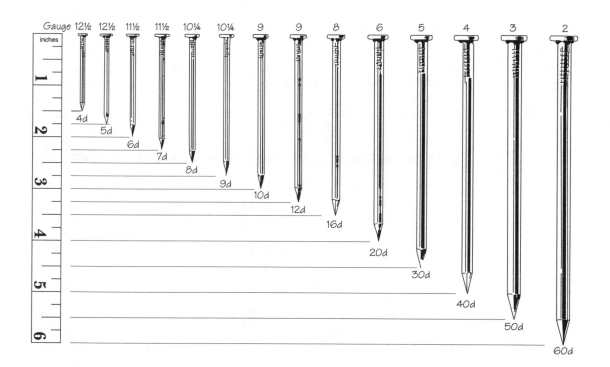

Bright, Common Wire Nails and Common Wire Spikes

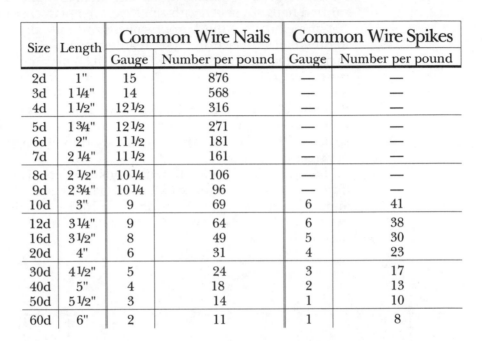

Size	Length	Common Wire Nails		Common Wire Spikes	
		Gauge	Number per pound	Gauge	Number per pound
2d	1"	15	876	—	—
3d	1 1/4"	14	568	—	—
4d	1 1/2"	12 1/2	316	—	—
5d	1 3/4"	12 1/2	271	—	—
6d	2"	11 1/2	181	—	—
7d	2 1/4"	11 1/2	161	—	—
8d	2 1/2"	10 1/4	106	—	—
9d	2 3/4"	10 1/4	96	—	—
10d	3"	9	69	6	41
12d	3 1/4"	9	64	6	38
16d	3 1/2"	8	49	5	30
20d	4"	6	31	4	23
30d	4 1/2"	5	24	3	17
40d	5"	4	18	2	13
50d	5 1/2"	3	14	1	10
60d	6"	2	11	1	8

Formerly 7" wire spikes were 0 gauge (0.3065"), and 8" and 9" spikes were 00 gauge (0.331"). Now 7", 8", and 9" spikes are 5/16" in diameter and 10" and 12" spikes are 3/8".

Finishing and Casing Nails

These nails are used where the nailhead must be hidden. Both types have small heads and smaller diameters than common nails.

Finishing nails, seen in profile, have a barrel-shaped head with a small diameter and a dimple on the top. After the nail is driven almost flush with the surface, the point of a nail set is placed in the dimple and the head driven below the surface. The resulting small hole can be filled with putty. Outdoors, in time the hole will tend to close by itself when the wood fibers swell.

Casing nails have a conical head, sometimes cupped, and are somewhat thicker than a finishing nail. They are sometimes painted and are used to attach trim.

Size	Length	Finishing Nails		Casing Nails	
		Gauge	Number per pound	Gauge	Number per pound
2d	1"	16 1/2	1,351	15 1/2	1,010
3d	1 1/4"	15 1/2	807	14 1/2	635
4d	1 1/2"	15	584	14	473
5d	1 3/4"	15	500	14	406
6d	2"	13	309	12 1/2	236
7d	2 1/4"	13	238	12 1/2	210
8d	2 1/2"	12 1/2	189	11 1/2	145
9d	2 3/4"	12 1/2	172	11 1/2	132
10d	3"	11 1/2	121	10 1/2	94
12d	3 1/4"	11 1/2	113	10 1/2	87
16d	3 1/2"	11	90	10	71
20d	4"	10	62	9	52
30d	4 1/2"	—	—	9	46
40d	5"	—	—	8	35

Smooth Box Nails

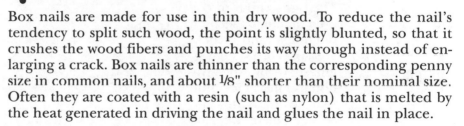

Box nails are made for use in thin dry wood. To reduce the nail's tendency to split such wood, the point is slightly blunted, so that it crushes the wood fibers and punches its way through instead of enlarging a crack. Box nails are thinner than the corresponding penny size in common nails, and about 1/8" shorter than their nominal size. Often they are coated with a resin (such as nylon) that is melted by the heat generated in driving the nail and glues the nail in place.

Size	Nominal length	Gauge	Number per pound
2d	1"	15 1/2	1,010
3d	1 1/4"	14 1/2	635
4d	1 1/2"	14	473
5d	1 3/4"	14	406
6d	2"	12 1/2	236
7d	2 1/4"	12 1/2	210
8d	2 1/2"	11 1/2	145
9d	2 3/4"	11 1/2	132
10d	3"	10 1/2	94
16d	3 1/2"	10	71
20d	4"	9	62
40d	5"	8	35

napkins

In the days of formal dinners, napkins were 22" to 24" square, and this large size is also useful when diners will be using their laps as tables. Ordinary dinner napkins are 16" to 18" square, or similarly sized rectangles.

Cocktail napkins are much smaller: perhaps 10" to 12" square. Paper cocktail napkins are usually in or below the smaller end of this range, often 9 1/2" square.

For the benefit of institutional users, the ASTM divides paper napkins into three classes:

Type	Area	Shortest dimension, unfolded
Cocktail	100 sq. inches or less	5 11/16"
Luncheon	100–183 sq. in.	9 1/2"
Dinner	over 183 sq. in.	11 3/8"

The weight of the paper in paper napkins is the weight in pounds of 500 sheets 24" × 36". The ASTM specification sets the following weights:

1 ply	light weight	11.9 or less
	standard	12.0–13.9
	heavy	at least 14.0
2 ply		at least 19.0
3 ply		at least 28.5

National Fire Rating System

The signs with four colored diamonds seen on buildings and trucks are a part of a system established by the National Fire Prtoection Assn. to warn fire and other emergency response personnel about potential dangers from hazardous materials within the building or vehicle. The

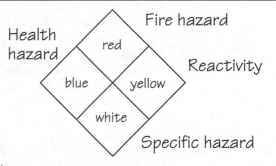

numbers and symbols within the diamonds have the following meanings; complete descriptions are found in the Assn.'s *Recommendations for Identification of Fire Hazards of Materials*:

Flammability (red, top square)
4   Very flammable gases or very volatile flammable liquids.
3   Can be ignited at all normal temperatures.
2   Ignites if moderately heated.
1   Ignites after considerable preheating.
0   Will not burn.

Health (blue, left square)
4   Can cause death or major injury despite medical treatment.
3   Can cause serious injury despite medical treatment.
2   Can cause injury. Requires prompt treatment.
1   Can cause irritation if not treated.
0   No hazard.

Reactivity (yellow, right square)
4   Readily detonates or explodes.
3   Can detonate or explode but requires strong initiating force or heating under confinement.
2   Normally unstable but will not detonate.
1   Normally stable. Unstable at high temperature and pressure. Reacts with water.
0   Normally stable. Not reactive with water.

Specific Hazard (white, bottom square)
OX   Oxidizing agent.
W̶   Water reactive.
☢   Radioactive.
☣   Biohazard.

neckties

Length varies with nationality, because of style and average national physique. Americans generally wear their four-in-hands so that the tip of the apron just reaches the belt buckle, and American ties range from 53" to 57". On the average the British have thinner necks, but also prefer the tip of the apron to reach below the belt, so British ties are somewhat longer, in the range of 55" to 58". Like the Americans, the Italians prefer the tip at the buckle, but on average they need a somewhat shorter tie, perhaps 53" to 56".

Width is the necktie dimension subject to fashion's whims. The "belly warmer" of the 1940s and early 1950s provided ample canvas for exhuberant post-war painting. In the early 1960s the wide (5"–6") tie returned in the form called "kippers." In between, and even simultaneously, ties have been sold that were as narrow as 1 1/2". (The official state tie of Arizona, the bola, doesn't count; it is another form entirely.) Some would say that if a tie's width calls attention to itself, the tie is badly chosen, but obviously width has often been chosen in the hope it would call attention to itself.

needles

Hand Sewing
Needle sizes, numbers from 1 to 24, refer to the needle's diameter. Within any given type, the higher the number the thinner and shorter the needle. The type also determines the size and shape of the eye and the style of the point. Several hundred different types of needles have been made, but a relative few are still manufactured.

Sharps. (Sizes 1–10) The standard needle, sharp, small eyes.

Betweens. (Sizes 3–10) Shorter than sharps, not as short as blunts. Also called quilting needles.

Milliners. These needles are exceptionally long (≈ 1 5/8") with small round eyes. Sometimes called "milliner straw needles."

Crewels. (Sizes 1–10) A sharp, medium long needle with larger eyes than those of sharps. Most embroidery is done with crewels and they are often called embroidery needles.

Chenilles. (Sizes 13–26) These thick, large-eyed needles resemble sharp tapestry needles, and are used for embroidery with heavy yarn.

Tapestry. (Sizes 13–26) These needles have blunt points, large eyes, and are thicker in proportion to their length than most needles. They are used for needlepoint and some types of embroidery.

Cotton Darners. (Sizes 1–5) Long needles with long eyes; besides darning, often used for basting.

Yarn Darners. (Sizes 14–18) Very long, large-eyed needles used with heavy yarn.

Glovers. Heavy sharp needles for sewing leather.

The following special purpose needles are readily available, though usually in sets of "craft needles," but have limited use:

Mattress needles. Heavy semicircular needles, several inches long.

Doll needles. Exceptionally long (3 1/2" to 7") needles for making stuffed animals.

Machine Sewing

Needles for sewing machines sport a lot of numbers. The first is the one that indicates whether the needle will fit a particular machine. For most current home sewing machines, this is "15×1". (The equivalent size in the system used in Europe is "130/705".)

A second number describes the diameter of the needle above the scarf. In the American system this is a number between 6 and 22; the bigger the number the thicker the needle. In the European system, the numbers range from 50 to 130 and are the actual needle diameter in hundreths of a millimeter (that is, a 110 needle is 1.1 mm in diameter). Most packaging gives both the American and metric numbers separated by a slash, for example, "9/65." A designation like "3.0/80", however, indicates the package contains twin or triple needles, and the first number is not the American size but the distance between the needles in millimeters. Twin needles are made in 1.6/70, 2.0/75, 2.0/80, 2.5/75, 3.0/90, 4.0/75, 4.0/100, and 6.0/100 sizes.

The size of the eye is proportional to the thickness of the needle, but certain needle styles (for example, for topstitching) have extra large eyes to accept large thread. The machine won't work properly if the thread doesn't match the needle size, because the mechanism assumes a certain amount of drag created by the fit of the thread in the eye.

Other characteristics of sewing machine needles have no standardized designations. Needle makers usually use a letter code to indicate the type of tip, which may be sharp, ballpoint for knits, wedge-shaped for leather and vinyl, and so on. And finally, there are characteristics which are not indicated at all—such as the length of the scarf— and can only be recognized through familiarity with that maker's product.

needles, knitting

Knitting needles are selected for color (which should contrast with the color of the yarn being knit), length, and size number, the latter indicating the needle's diameter. Choosing the right size number for a project is crucial, because the diameter of the needles is one of the factors that determines the size of the garment.

Unfortunately, needles from different manufacturers that are supposedly the same size may have different diameters. If needles must be changed in the middle of a project, the actual diameters of the old and new needles should be compared rather than relying only on their sizes.

The table below shows the American size numbers with a range of actual diameters that might be encountered. It also shows the standard metric sizes (which are simply the needle's diameter in millimeters) and their equivalents in the old UK sizes. To compare metric or old UK sizes with American sizes, compare the metric size and the American diameter in millimeters.

In knitting, the word "gauge" has a special meaning, the number of stitches in 1½", and so to avoid confusion, we will not refer to knitting needles' size numbers as a gauge.

Single-pointed Needles. Sizes range from 0 to 15, with smaller numbers representing thinner needles. Aluminum needles come in lengths of 7", 10", 12", and 14", and size numbers of 0 to 5 in the short lengths and 0 to 8 in the longer. Plastic needles are made in sizes 0 to 10½, 13, and 15. Wooden needles are 14" long in sizes 10 to 15. Steel needles are now only available in the smaller sizes, 0 to 3.

Double-pointed Needles. Double-pointed needles are made in even inch lengths of 5", 6", 7", 10", and 14". The sizing of double-pointed needles varies with the material from which the needles are made. Plastic needles run from 1 through 10, from fine to thick. In contrast, steel double-pointed needles run from 18 to 8, with the highest number being the thinnest needle. For aluminum needles, some manufacturers use the plastic system and some the steel.

Circular Needles. The smaller sizes, 0 through 3, are usually made of steel.

	Knitting Needle Sizes				
	United States				
Size	Diameter in millimeters	Steel double-pointed	Crochet hook	Metric	Old UK, Australia, etc
0000	1.25			1.25	16
000	1.5–1.75	15		1.5	15
00	1.75–2	14		2	14
0	2.1–2.25	13	4		
1	2.25–2.75	12	3	2.25	13
2	2.75–2.8–3	11	2	2.75	12
				3	11
3	3–3.3	10	1	3.25	10
4	3.5–3.75	9	0		
5	3.8–4	8	00	3.75	9
6	4–4.5		F	4	8
7	4.5–4.6		G	4.5	7
8	5.0		H	5	6
9	5.3–5.5		I	5.5	5
10	5.75–6		J	6	4
				6.5	3
				7	2
10½	6.5–7		K	7.5	1
11	8.0			8	0
13	9.2–10			9	00
15	10.2			10	000
16					
17	12.7				
18	14.3				
19	16.0				
35	19.0				
50	25.4				

newton The unit of force in SI, defined as that force which, applied to a mass of 1 kilogram, gives it an acceleration of 1 meter per second per second. Symbol, N. In terms of SI's basic units, a newton is:

$$\frac{meter \cdot kilogram}{second^2}$$

newton meter

The unit of torque in SI, the torque exerted by a force of 1 meter acting at a perpendicular distance of 1 meter from the specified axis of rotation.

Note that although a joule is a newton meter, a newton meter is not a joule. The force in the definition of a joule acts in the direction along which the meter is measured, not at right angles to it.

noise

Noise is measured because it is annoying and people want to regulate it, for example, in a residential area; because high levels impair performance, as in a submarine; and because high levels can permanently damage hearing, as among rock musicians and jackhammer operators (the latter are now protected and the former aren't).

Sound levels are measured with sound level meters (see ☞decibel), generally with a weighting (the A scale) that mirrors human sensitivity to different frequencies. In most noisy environments, however, the sound level is constantly changing. To describe a sound level that changes over a period of time, acousticians can use the A-weighted noise equivalent level (L_{eq}), which is that level of a steady sound which has the same energy as the actual, ever-changing noise.

More than 22 different noise rating scales have been devised. Perhaps the most widely used, at least in legislation, is the Community Noise Equivalent Level (CNEL), first developed by the California Department of Airports, now incorporated in state (California Administrative Code Title 25 Art. 4, Sec. 1092) and municipal law. CNEL measurements take into account the fact that evening noises annoy people more than daytime noises do, and nighttime noises are worst of all. The CNEL is a 24-hour A-weighted equivalent sound level with a 5-dB penalty applied to sound levels between 7 and 10 PM and a 10-dB penalty applied to sound levels between 10 PM and 7 AM. Another measure, used by the Environmental Protection Agency and many cities, is the day-night sound level (L_{dn}), which is similar to the CNEL, but without the penalty on noises between 7 and 10 PM.

Sound Level in dBA	Examples
200	200 m from Saturn V rocket at liftoff.
160	Peak level at ear of person firing 30-30 rifle.
140	25 m from jet aircraft.
120	Submarine engine room. On stage at a rock concert.
100	Noisy factory. Jackhammer (unsilenced).
90	7 m from large diesel truck.
85	Upper limit of comfort.
80	1 m from ringing alarm clock. Conversation is difficult. After a 1-hour exposure, thought is difficult and the stomach contracts.

Sound Level in dBA	Examples
75	Railroad carriage. Normal conversation not possible. Consensus of experts is that sound levels below 75 dBA "are unlikely to cause permanent hearing damage."
70	Small car at 30 mph; 3 m from vacuum cleaner.
65	1 m from normal conversation. Busy office. About half the people in a large sample will have difficulty sleeping.
55	Recommended upper limit for large open offices, restaurants, gymnasiums, swimming pools.
45	Recommended upper limit for homes, hotels, laboratories, libraries, private offices, court rooms.
40	Quiet office. Recommended upper limit for classrooms, churches, motion picture theaters (without the film soundtrack).
35	Quiet bedroom.
25	Countryside on windless day, away from traffic.

OSHA Noise Standards for Steady-State Noise

To determine whether exposure to steady noise at different levels during the day exceeds Occupational Safety and Health Administration standards, for each noise level make a fraction whose numerator is the total exposure time at that level, and whose denominator is the total permitted exposure time at that level, from the table above. Add the fractions; the total must not exceed 1. For example, exposing a worker to a 90 dBA noise for 4 hours and to 105 dBA for 0.5 hour would be barely permissible ($4/8 + 0.5/1 = 1$).

Permissible Daily Noise Exposure	
Duration in hours	Sound level in dBA
8	90
6	92
4	95
3	97
2	100
1.5	102
1	105
0.5	110
0.25	115

Hearing Protection Devices

The U.S. Environmental Protection Agency has created a Noise Reduction Rating scale for devices like ear plugs, ear muffs, and helmets. The scale runs from 0 to 30, with 30 being best. Devices should have ratings of at least 20 NRR.

numbers, names of big

In the English-speaking world two different systems are used to name numbers larger than a million, which forces writers addressing an international audience to such awkward phrases as "one thousand million," to avoid the ambiguous "billion" (although many non-American writers in the fields of economics and finance have begun to use "billion" in the American sense). In physics, the ambiguity helped lead to the demise of the term "Bev"—a billion electronvolts.

In both systems the names of the numbers are taken from Latin. In the American system, which was taken from the French centuries ago, the Latin prefix represents the number of groups of 3 zeros, not counting the first group of three, which represents a thousand. In the British system, which is also used by the rest of the world including today's French, the Latin prefix refers to a power of a million. For example, "bi-" means two. To the Americans, that means adding 2 more "000" groups to "1,000," so a billion = 1,000,000,000. To the British, a billion is a million to the second power, that is, squared, so a billion = 1,000,000 × 1,000,000 = 1,000,000,000,000. The discrepancy between the two systems grows as the numbers the prefixes represent get bigger. The table below summarizes the result.

# of zeros after 1	# of ,000, groups after 1,000	Name in American English	Power of one million	Name in British English
9	2	billion		milliard
12	3	trillion	2	billion
15	4	quadrillion		—
18	5	quintillion	3	trillion
21	6	sextillion		—
24	7	septillion	4	quadrillion
27	8	octillion		—
30	9	nonillion	5	quintillion
33	10	decillion		
36	11	undecillion	6	sextillion
39	12	duodecillion		
42	13	tredecillion	7	septillion
45	14	quattordecillion		
48	15	quindecillion	8	octillion
51	16	sexdecillion		
54	17	septendecillion	9	nonillion
57	18	octodecillion		—
60	19	novemdecillion	10	decillion
63	20	vigintillion		—
66	21	—	11	undecillion
72	23	—	12	duodecillion
78	25		13	tredecillion
84	27		14	quattordecillion
90	29		15	quindecillion
96	31	—	16	sexdecillion

SIZES

# of zeros after 1	# of ,000, groups after 1,000	Name in American English	Power of one million	Name in British English
102	33	—	17	septendecillion
108	35	—	18	octodecillion
114	37	—	19	novemdecillion
120	39	—	20	vigintillion
303	100	centillion		—
600	199	—	100	centillion

oars

The handles of a pair of oars should overlap by 4", that is, the inboard portion of each is 2" longer than half the distance between the rowlocks. The distance between the rear edge of the rower's seat and the rowlocks should be about the distance between the inside of the rower's wrist and the inside of the elbow.

An oar is a lever with its fulcrum at the oarlock. The oarlock's position relative to the oar is set by the location of the button, the ring that keeps an oar from sliding through the oarlock. Shaw and Tenney (Orono, ME), arguably America's premier maker of oars, recommends a ratio of 7:18 for all boats designed for efficient rowing, from skiffs to shells. To achieve this, the inboard portion of the oar must be 7/25ths of the overall length of the oar. So, for example, if the distance between rowlocks is 42", the distance from the end of the handle to the button should be (42 ÷ 2, + 2 =) 23", and the overall length of the oar

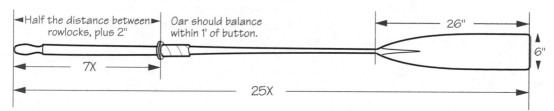

◄Half the distance between► rowlocks, plus 2"
Oar should balance within 1' of button.
26"
7X
6"
25X

$(23 \div 7, \times 25 \approx)$ 82" or 6' 10". Stock oar sizes from 6' to 10' are in 6" increments, so round up to 7'.

For a utility boat not really made for efficient rowing, such as a dinghy, round down instead of up. Longer oars will do no good and just be more cumbersome. But in any boat, if an oar continually pops out of the oarlock, the oar is too short.

The point at which the oar would balance if it were supported on a narrow rail should be on the outboard side, but within a foot of the button.

octane number

Gasoline is not a chemical compound; it is a mixture of many different compounds. Early in the history of the gasoline engine, experimenters noted that engines knocked more on some gasolines than on others.

To select a way of rating the propensity of a gasoline to cause knocking, a Cooperative Fuel Research Committee was set up in 1927 comprising representatives of the American Petroleum Institute, the American Manufacturers Assn., the National Bureau of Standards, and the SAE. In the committee's opinion, no one test was able to give a rating useful over the whole range of operating conditions, and so two methods were defined: the Motor Method (ASTM D 357) and the Research Method (ASTM D 908).

Both methods are based on comparing the performance of the gasoline being tested with the performance of a mixture of 2,2,4, trimethyl pentane (also called iso-octane) and normal heptane. The octane number is the percentage of iso-octane in that mixture whose performance (in regard to knocking) is the same as that of the gasoline under test. For example, if the performance of the gasoline under test is the same as that of a mixture of 80% 2,2,4,trimethyl pentane and 20% normal heptane, the gasoline is 80 octane. Octane numbers above 100 are found by extrapolation.

The two test methods give different results, and the difference in the results differs from gasoline to gasoline. As a broad generalization, the motor method captures the gasoline's performance at high engine speeds and the research method at low speeds. The octane rating on gasoline pumps is usually the average of the research and motor octane numbers.

Fuel is only one of many factors affecting whether an engine will knock. Consequently in any particular engine gasolines with the same octane number but from different blenders may perform differently: one may cause knock and the other may not. Similarly a gasoline that causes knock in one engine model may not in another. This is not proof that the octane rating was inaccurate.

ohm

The unit of electrical resistance in SI; a derived unit. One ohm is the "electrical resistance between two points on a conductor when a constant potential difference of 1 volt, applied to these points, produces in the conductor a current of 1 ampere, the conductor not being the seat of any electromotive force" (CIPM, Resolution 2, 1946). The dimensions of the ohm are $\dfrac{volts}{ampere}$, or in terms of only base units,

$$\frac{meter^2 \cdot kilogram}{second^3 \cdot ampere^2}$$

History

In 1833, Karl Friedrich Gauss showed how all magnetic units could be defined in terms of the "mechanical" units—the meter, kilogram, and second—and 21 years later Wilhelm Weber showed how to define a complete system of electrical units in terms of mechanical units. In 1861 the British Association for the Advancement of Science created a committee to define a unit of electrical resistance. By 1864 this committee created the "B.A. unit" of resistance, an absolute unit, based on a meter-gram-second system of units. In order to give it a useful size, the unit was made 10^7 times bigger than the mgs absolute unit of resistance. The committee also prepared a standard made of wire for the unit. In 1872 a second committee recommended a change to the cgs system and renamed the unit the ohm.

The First International Conference of Electricians (Paris, 1881), accepted the British Assn's definition of the ohm but also sought "reproducible standards." The conference settled on a definition of the "reproducible ohm" as the resistance at 0°centigrade of a column of mercury 106.3 cm in length, having a uniform cross section, and with a mass of 14.4521 grams. That particular mass was chosen to make the cross section 1 square millimeter. The ohm so defined was sometimes referred to as the "mercury ohm." Such units were called "practical units" because they could be fairly easily realized in the average laboratory, which the absolute definitions certainly could not be.

At the International Electrical Congress in Chicago in 1893 it was decided to change the name from "reproducible ohm" to "international ohm." (Public Bill 105, passed by Congress on July 12, 1894, made the international ohm the legal definition of the ohm in the United States.) The next International Conference (London, 1908) confirmed the previous conference's decisions.

As instrumentation improved the need for practical units declined. The CIPM finally did away with the international ohm and all the other practical units in 1946 (Resolution 2), replacing it with the new absolute definition given above. This decision was adopted by the NINTH CGPM in 1948.

oil

Engine Oil Grades

As long ago as 1911 the SAE recognized a need for standardizing grades of oil for automobile engines; today the ratings are provided in collaboration with the ASTM and the American Petroleum Institute

(API). Engine oil ratings are indicated by a trademarked circular design on the package. The mark contains three pieces of information. In the inner circle is a viscosity grade. In the upper part of the outer circle is an API Service Classification, and the bottom of the outer circle may contain an energy conservation rating.

Viscosity

The purpose of the viscosity rating is to assure that, in the climate in which the engine is operated, oil can always flow through the engine's lubrication system. Eleven grades are defined. Six of them end in the letter "W," beginning with "0W" and proceeding in steps of 5 to "25W." The W stands for winter. The remaining five grades go from "20" to "60" in steps of 10, without the W. In general, higher numbers mean higher viscosities.

For all grades the viscosity of the oil at 100°C is measured; it must exceed a minimum specified for that grade. In the grades without a W, a maximum viscosity is also specified. These tests basically ensure the oil will perform in a warm, running engine.

For grades ending in W, an additional low temperature test is required (for the 0W grade, for example, at −35°C). The purpose of these tests is to ensure that if the oil's viscosity is low enough to permit cranking, it will also be low enough to be pumped through the engine. (Those actions involve different kinds of viscosity, so the cranking viscosity is measured in centipoises and the pumpability viscosity in centistokes.) The test temperatures rise by 5°C for each grade; oils with the lower numbers are intended for climates with colder winters. However, to select a viscosity grade for a particular car, consult the owner's manual and not just the thermometer.

Multiviscosity oils, such as "20W–50," must satisfy both the low temperature cranking and pumping test for the grade indicated first, and the 100°C test for the second grade. Such an oil would also pass the tests for all the grades in between.

Service Classification

The original grades were based only on viscosity. In 1947, three service classifications were added: Regular, which was straight mineral oil; Premium, which had added anti-oxidants; and Heavy Duty, with anti-oxidants and detergents. Both engines and the technology of lubrication became increasingly more sophisticated, so these classifications were replaced in 1952 with, in order of increasing quality, ML, MM, and MS classifications for oil for gasoline engines and DG, DM, and DS for diesel engines. After a number of revisions, those classifications were replaced by an entirely new, more easily extended system in 1983.

For gasoline engines, service classifications start with SA and proceed through SH. Classifications SA through SF are considered obsolete, except that SE and SF are needed for certain smog systems which can be poisoned by additives present in later classifications. SA has no requirements at all; while the others are for earlier generations of engine (SC, 1964; SD, 1968; SE, 1972; SF, 1980). SG is suited to a 1989 engine.

A similar set of classifications covers diesel engines. CA, CB, and CC are obsolete; CD, CD-II, and CE are in current use.

Energy Conservation
If present, the marking will be either "EnergyConserving" or "EnergyConserving II." To qualify as "EnergyConserving," an engine oil must improve fuel economy in laboratory tests by at least 1.5% when compared with a reference oil. If the improvement is 2.7% or more, the oil can be labelled "EnergyConserving II." These ratings don't guarantee that switching to "EnergyConserving" oil will improve mileage by 1.5% in a particular car, because of the large number of other factors at work.

Fuel Oil Grades
1   Light domestic fuel oil-distillate.
2   Medium domestic fuel oil-distillate.
3   Heavy domestic fuel oil-distillate.
4   Light industrial fuel oil. Minimum flash point of 150°F.
5   Medium industrial fuel oil.
6   Heavy industrial fuel oil. This is about the consistency of gel toothpaste, and is burned in the boilers of, for example, the liner *Queen Elizabeth.* Sometimes called "bunker C" fuel oil.

olive oil

The most sought-after olive oils come from the first, cold pressing. Such oils are not refined (oils from later pressings usually are). They are divided into four grades based on the oil's free oleic acid content:

Grade:	Virgin	Fine	Superfine	Extra-Virgin
Maximum free oleic acid:	4%	3%	1.5%	1%

olives

Canned whole ripe olives (other than tree-ripened)

Size:	Small	Medium	Large	Extra Large	Jumbo	Colossal	Super Colossal
# per lb:	128–140	106–127	91–105	65–90	47–60	33–46	<33

For a few varieties, the count for Extra Large is 65–75. Tolerances are set by variety of olive.

ounce

Various units of mass in the English-speaking world, 15TH–20TH C. The most common is the *avoirdupois ounce*, 1/16th of the avoirdupois pound,

≈ 28.3495 grams. The *apothecaries' ounce* and the *troy ounce*, $\frac{1}{12}$th of the apothecaries' pound and the troy pound respectively, have identical masses ≈ 31.1035 grams.

ounce, fluid

In the USA, the U.S. fluid ounce, a unit of liquid capacity ≈ 29.5735 milliliters. In British imperial measure the fluid ounce is a unit of capacity ≈ 28.413 milliliters. One U.S. fluid ounce is 1.041 imp. fl. oz.

outdoor advertising

In 1901, Foster and Kleiser saw a business opportunity in erecting signs with standardized sizes in prepared locations. Today, size standards for "out-of-home" advertising are set by the Outdoor Advertising Assn. of America.

Billboards
There are two types of billboards: bulletins, and poster panels.

Bulletins are 14' × 48'. The sign is painted on vinyl in a studio, which takes about two days. A bulletin may have "extensions," elements that stick out of the rectangle,such as the tip of a cigarette. An advertiser buying bulletins specifies locations and the length of time the advertisement is to be displayed. Every 60 days the vinyl is taken down, trucked to a new location, and restretched. Bulletins are sometimes called *rotary bulletins*, because they are rotated from site to site.

A specialized type of bulletin is the *permanent* or *spectacular bulletin*, 20' × 60'. These are painted directly on the wood panels at the site. "Permanent" is a relative term; they are usually contracted for a year.

Poster panels are printed on paper. There are two sizes: *30-sheet*, which is 11' × 23', and *8-sheet*, which is 5' × 11'. Today a 30-sheet poster panel is printed in 6 sheets, but around 1900 it actually was 30 sheets, each the size of a vaudeville poster. Poster panels can be distinguished from bulletins by their frames; bulletins have no frame.

In contracting for poster panels, the advertiser does not select locations, but rather how many cars are to pass the advertisement, by specifying a number of "gross rating points of outdoor." Every three years, an organization called the Traffic Audit Bureau counts the number of cars passing a given billboard location on an average day.

oysters

Shucked Atlantic and Gulf Oysters (*Crassostrea virginica*)

Size	Extra Large or Counts	Large or Extra Select	Medium or Select	Small or Standard	Very Small
No. in a pint	<20	20–26	26–38	38–63	>63

Shucked Pacific Oysters (*Crassostrea gigus*)

Size	Large	Medium	Small	Extra Small
No. per pint	<8	8–12	12–18	>18

pace
A unit of length, in the United States = 30 inches. In England, however, since at least the 12TH C one pace = 60 inches, on the model of the Roman *passus* (which equalled 5 *pes*), and one step = 30 inches. To show that a unit is meant, in Great Britain the pace is sometimes called the geometrical pace.

paddles
For canoes, the rule of thumb for paddle length is that, when the paddler stands upright, the paddle of the person in the bow should reach from the floor to the paddler's chin, while the paddle of the person in the stern should reach that person's nose.

padlocks
Padlocks are usually sized by the width of the case.

The ASTM has defined 6 grades for padlocks, with 1 being the least secure and 6 the most secure. As a very broad generalization, each grade is twice as good as the one before. For each grade, the standard sets minimum performance requirements for various categories of attack. In the "forcing" category, for example, a grade 1 padlock must withstand a pull of 1,000 newtons without opening and a grade 6 padlock 40,000 newtons. In the "surreptitious" category, a grade 1 lock must foil an expert at picking locks for at least 30 seconds, but a grade 6 lock must hold out for at least 15 minutes. A grade 1 combination padlock must remain operable for 1000 cycles; a grade 6, for 100,000 cycles.

Because the value of a lock's performance in a particular category depends on the situation in which the padlock is used, a padlock that offers better than grade performance in some categories may be so marked. A padlock graded "grade 3, F5S3," for example, has passed the forcing tests for a grade 5 padlock, though overall it is a grade 3 padlock.

---

paint brushes

Artists' Brushes

There is no exact standard for the physical dimensions of artists' brushes, although the designations are standardized. The actual size varies with the type of brush (filbert, round, etc.), the quality, and the manufacturer. The usual designations are:

Inch sizes: 1/8, 1/4, 3/8, 1/2, 5/8, 3/4, 7/8, 1, 1¼, 1½, 2, 2½, 3, 3½, 4 inches.

Metric sizes: 10, 20, 30, 40, 50, 60, 70, 80, 90, 100 mm.

Numbered sizes, from smallest to largest: 7/0 (that is, 0000000), 6/0, 5/0, 4/0, 000, 00, 0, 1, 2, 3, 4, 5, 6, 7, 8, 9, 10, 11, 12, 13, 14, 16, 18, 20, 22, 24, 26, 28, 30.

The German numbered sizes tend to resemble the English ones, with the exception of bristle brushes for oils, those German brushes being roughly half the width of an English brush of the same size. French sizes are longer from 000 through 1 and tend to be thinner and shorter after 7, so that a French 12 resembles an English 10. The enormous prices for the larger sizes reflect the fact that, for example, producing a size 12 watercolor round requires hairs from the tails of 50 squirrels.

A special series of sizes is used for quill brushes. In a quill brush the bristles are inserted into the quill of a feather rather than into a metal ferrule; the resilience of the quill gives the brush a special feel. The sizes of quill brushes are named after the birds that originally (supposedly) provided the feathers. From small to large, the sizes are: lark, crow, small duck, duck, large duck, swan, small goose, goose, large goose, condor.

Wall and Trim Brushes

Brushes are sized by width. As a rule of thumb, bristles should be about 50% longer than the brushes' width (and even longer on very narrow brushes).

Brushes with natural bristles should not be used with water-based paints. Before being used for the first time, natural bristle brushes should be soaked in linseed oil (not resting on their ends) for a couple of days in order to swell the bristles inside the ferrule, which helps to prevent their pulling out. Synthetic bristles, good for latex paints, can be destroyed by certain lacquers and other paints containing strong solvents.

There are four main classes of brushes:

Wall. Made in widths from 3" to 6", in ½" steps from ½" to 3", and from 3" to 5" in steps of a whole inch. The 5" and 6" sizes have been almost killed by the rise of the paint roller. It hardly matters for do-it-yourselfers; the wider the brush the greater the demand placed on rarely-used muscles in the hand; the weekend painter is generally more comfortable with a 4" brush, and women often prefer 3". Wall brushes are used for walls, ceilings, siding, and floors. They have a square edge.

Sash and Trim. These brushes are made in three styles: round (½" to 2" in diameter); oval, and flat (1½" to 3"). They often have a chisel edge. A 1" chisel edge brush would be a good choice for trim; a 2" chisel edge could be used for doors, shelving, and window frames.

Varnish and Enamelling. Flat 2" to 3" brushes. Be sure the composition of the bristles is compatible with the varnish.

Stucco and Masonry. Very wide brushes, 5" or 6". Unlike any other type, for this purpose a cheap brush is a good idea.

Paint Rollers

Most rollers are 7" to 9" long, but they are available in lengths from 2" to 18". All have an inner diameter of 1½". The most important dimension, however, is the length of the nap. The smoother the surface to be painted, the shorter the nap should be. A ⅛" nap is suitable for painting drywall; for painting concrete block or wooden shingles a 1¼" nap (the longest made) is not too long.

palm

An English unit of length, originally a body-unit (though influenced by the Roman *palm*, one-fourth of a *pes*, the Roman foot), the breadth of the palm of the hand at the base of the fingers, without the thumb, which was taken to be 4 fingerbreadths, 3 thumbwidths, or 3 inches. By the 17TH C it is always simply = 3 inches.

pans, cake

The table belows shows consumer cake pan sizes commonly available in the United States, with the approximate amount of batter the pan will hold assuming the batter rises 50% during baking. Consumer pans are generally 1½" deep; commercial pans are 2" deep.

Round

8" × 1½"	1¾ cups
9" × 1½"	2⅛ cups
10" × 1½"	2⅔ cups

Rectangular

7¾" × 3⅝" × 2¼"	1½ cups	16" × 5" × 4"	7⅓ cups
8" × 8" × 1½"	2⅛ cups	15½" × 10½" × 1"	3¾ cups

9" × 5" × 2 3/4"	2 3/4 cups	15" × 10" × 2"	7 cups
9" × 9" × 1 1/2"	2 3/4 cups	13" × 9" × 2"	5 1/3 cups
11" × 4 1/2" × 2 3/4"	3 1/8 cups	11" × 7" × 1 1/2"	2 2/3 cups

panties

The table gives a general guide to American panty sizes, in inches, but there are, of course, differences between manufacturers and models.

Size:	5	6	7	8	9	10
Waist:	26–28	28–30	30–32	32–34	34–36	36–38
Hip:	36–38	38–40	40–42	42–44	44–46	46–48

Shops that cater to large women sometimes translate standard sizes to "X" sizes, where 8 = 1X, 9 = 2X, and so on up to 13 = 6X.

paper

See also ☛paper, blotting.

American Printing Papers

Paper sizes are described by weight and type. The number in a paper weight (such as the 20 in "basis 20" or "substance 20" or "20-lb bond") is the weight of 500 sheets of that paper in a standard sheet size whose dimensions are defined for that particular type of paper, regardless of the actual size of the sheets being purchased. For example, a package of 8 1/2" × 11" typing paper might be marked "20-lb." Typing paper is a variety of bond paper, and bond paper weights are based on a 17" × 22" sheet size, so 500 17" × 22" sheets of this paper would weigh 20 pounds. The standardized sizes are as follows:

Bond 17" × 22". Some speculate that this is the size of the largest sheet that could easily be made by one person when all paper was handmade.

Book 25" × 38". Coated, text, book, offset.

Cover 20" × 26".

Bristol 22 1/2" × 28 1/2". Sometimes called printing bristol.

Index 25 1/2" × 30 1/2". Sometimes called index bristol.

Tag 24" × 36". Tag is the stock from which manila folders and shipping tags are made. This size is also used for newsprint.

Like wood, machine-made paper has grain. Folding with the grain produces a smooth fold; folding against the grain causes buckling and cracks. In paper catalogs the direction of the paper's grain is often indicated by underlining the dimension in which the paper grain runs. In a 17 × 22 sheet the grain runs in the direction of the 17" side.

Cotton content papers. "100% cotton content, extra #1" paper has been made entirely of new fibers that have never been dyed or bleached. Paper marked "100% cotton content" may contain bleached fibers. Cotton content decreases in 25% steps over the three remaining grades. The 25% grade is comparable to sulphite #4 bond.

Sulphite. Grades run from 1 through 5, with 1 the best. Grades 3 and 5 are no longer produced. Most of the sulphite paper sold is #4.

Architects' Paper Sizes

A	B	C	D	E
9" × 12"	12" × 18"	18" × 24"	24" × 36"	36" × 48"

International Standard Paper Sizes

The International Standard for trimmed sizes of writing paper for administrative, commercial, and technical use, and for use in forms, catalogs, and so on, does not apply to newspapers, books, posters, and similar printed materials.

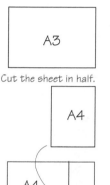

Cut the sheet in half.

The result has the same proportions as the original sheet.

All sizes have the same proportions, $\sqrt{2} : 1$. A rectangle in this ratio has the property that, if it is cut in half, halving the longer dimension, the sides of the resulting rectangles are also in the ratio $\sqrt{2} : 1$.

A Series

This is the main series; the basic size ("A0") has an area of 1 square meter. A4 is used for letters and A5 for postcards. All dimensions are in millimeters.

A0	A1	A2	A3	A4	A5	A6	A7	A8	A9	A10
841 × 1189	594 × 841	420 × 594	297 × 420	210 × 297	148 × 210	105 × 148	74 × 105	52 × 74	37 × 52	26 × 37

A few other sizes sometimes encountered are:

4A0	2A0	⅓ A4	¼ A4	⅛ A4
1,682 × 2,378	1,189 × 1,682	99 × 210	74 × 210	13 × 17

B Series

This is a subsidiary series, "for use only in exceptional circumstances." The sizes are geometric means between sizes in the A series. For example, the width of A1 is 594 mm, of A2, 420 mm. The width of B2 is set at $\sqrt{594 \cdot 420} = 499.47$, which is rounded to 500 mm.

B0	B1	B2	B3	B4	B5	B6	B7	B8	B9	B10
1000 × 1414	707 × 1000	500 × 707	353 × 500	250 × 353	176 × 250	125 × 176	88 × 125	62 × 88	44 × 62	31 × 44

Unless other tolerances are specified, a tolerance of ± 1.5 mm is permitted on dimensions less than or equal to 150 mm; of ± 2 mm on dimensions greater than 150 mm and less than or equal to 600 mm, and ± 3 mm for dimensions greater than 600 mm.

The C Series are envelope sizes designed to fit A series sheets of paper.

The RA and SRA Series describe sizes used by printers.

paper, blotting

Most of the blotting paper sold in the USA today is used in desk pads. Three sizes are available: 19" × 24", 20" × 36", and 24" × 38". In the 19TH C, blotting paper was sold in medium (22¼" × 17¼"), post (21" × 16½"), and foolscap (16½" × 13¼") sizes.

parachutes

Pilots' parachutes are about 28' across, which is big enough to slow a 200-lb person to about 20 feet per second at the time of landing. That speed is considered slow enough to be safe even for an untrained person. A U.S. Army parachute for a paratrooper is about 35' in diameter, which compensates for the heavy load the soldier carries. The reserve chute worn on the chest has a diameter of only about 24', which leads to a landing speed of about 25 feet per second, the highest acceptable level.

parsec

A unit of distance used in astronomy, abbreviated pc. One parsec = 3.26 light-years, or 3.08×10^{13} km.

The parsec is based on the phenomenon called parallax. Close one eye and hold up a finger at arm's length. Note what is behind the finger. Now change eyes. The finger appears to jump against the background; something different is behind it. Now bring the finger closer to your face. Change eyes again. Notice that the nearer your finger is to your face, the bigger the apparent jump.

Parallax can be used to measure the distance to stars that are not too far away. Instead of switching eyes, astronomers photograph the star from opposite sides of earth's orbit, six months apart. As your finger did, a nearby star will appear to jump against the background of very distant stars. The size of the jump can be expressed as the angle between the two positions the star had. Half of this angle is defined as the star's parallax.

In the 2ND C BC, Hipparchus used parallax to measure the distance to the moon (he came within 20%), but not until 1838 did astronomers succeed in measuring the parallax of a star, because the angle is so small; the parallax of the nearest star is only 0.76 seconds of arc. (For comparison, the angle between the sides of a U.S. quarter three miles away is about one second of arc.) In fact, the Greeks took their failure to detect parallax for stars as proof that the Earth didn't move.

So far parallaxes have been measured for about 10,000 stars; the Hubble Space Telescope is expected to measure more.

One parsec is the distance from the earth to a star that shows a parallax of one second of arc; the distance to any star, expressed in parsecs, is the reciprocal of the star's parallax expressed in seconds of arc. (This works only because the distance to the star is so huge compared to the diameter of the earth's orbit that the base of the triangle Earth–star–Earth six months later can be treated as a segment of a circle with the star at its center.) One parsec ≈ 206,265 astronomical units ≈ 3.26 light-years ≈ 3.086×10^{13} km.

pascal

In SI, the unit for pressure and stress, a derived unit. Symbol, Pa. One pascal is the pressure resulting from a force of 1 newton acting uniformly over an area of 1 square meter, or in terms of the base units,

$$\frac{kilogram}{meter \cdot second^2}$$

peck

In the United States, a unit of dry capacity, = 537.605 cubic inches = 8 U.S. dry quarts ≈ 8.80977 liters. Four such pecks make a U.S. bushel. In the United Kingdom, the imperial peck (1824–1976, when the peck was made no longer legal for trade) ≈ 9.09218 liters. The peck is recorded as early as the 14TH C, with the same relation to the quart and bushel that it now has.

Pegboard

Pegboard (a trademark), sheets of hardboard punched with a grid of holes with 1" between their centers and used to hang tools in workshops, is made in 4' × 8' sheets in two thicknesses. One is 1/8" thick with holes 3/16" in diameter. The heavier 1/4" thick type has 1/4" holes. The fittings are not interchangeable.

pencils

Since 1795, pencil leads have been made by combining graphite with clay, extruding the mixture into leads, firing the leads, and then impregnating them with wax. The proportion of clay to graphite and the amount and nature of the wax determine how soft the resulting lead will be.

The pencils used by artists and draftsmen are graded from 9B, the softest, through 8B, 7B, and so on to B, HB, both of medium softness, F, H, 2H, and on to 9H, the hardest. The extremes of the range are little used and difficult to obtain. Probably the most popular grade among artists is 2B.

The standard wooden artists' pencil is 7" long with a lead 2 mm in diameter. Two millimeter leads are also used in lead holders, popular with draftsmen. The point on a 2 mm lead in a lead holder is made with sandpaper or a lead pointer, but leads that do not require sharpening are made in diameters of 0.3, 0.5, 0.7 and 0.9 mm for drafts-men's mechanical pencils.

A close relative of the artists' pencil is the graphite crayon, made in diameters of 7, 8 and 12 mm.

Office pencils are graded on a different scale: 1, very soft; 2, soft; 2½, medium soft; 3, hard; 4, very hard. The number 2 pencil has acquired a certain cachet from being used to darken the bubbles on the answer sheets of machine-scored multiple-choice tests. Today most office-type mechanical pencils accept one of the lead sizes used by draftsmen, usually 0.5 mm, but leads with diameters of 0.2, 3, 3.15, and 5.6 mm have also been used.

pens, technical

Today most pens are manufactured in the ISO sizes given in the last row of the table. Plotters use the same sizes, but usually only to 0.7 mm.

In addition to the point size, actual line widths depend on the nature of the paper or film surface, the ink, and the speed of the pen.

Approximately Equivalent Pen Standards

	6/0	4/0	3/0	00	0	1	2	2.5	3	3.5	4	5	6	7
North American line width (in.)	.005	.007	.010	.012	.014	.020	.024	.028	.031	.039	.047	.050	.055	.079
line width (mm)	.13	0.18	.25	.30	.35	.50	.60	.70	.80	1.0	1.2	1.3	1.40	2.00
European (mm)	0.1	0.2	—	0.3	0.4	0.5	0.6	—	0.8	1.0	1.2	—	1.4	2.0
ISO	.13	.18	.25	—	.35	.50	—	.70	—	1.0	—	—	1.4	2.0

penis, human

The typical limp human penis is about 3 cm in diameter at the base and somewhere between 8.5 and 10.5 cm long (measured along the top)—but fathers have been shorter than 3 cm, and lengths as great as 30 cm are reported. In general, smaller penises lengthen proportionally more than large ones do during an erection, but though the difference between small and large is reduced, the larger remain larger. The erect penis is about 15 to 19 cm long, with, again, many functioning very well outside this range.

As penises go, men's are no great wonders. In many mammals—the raccoon, for example—the penis is stiffened with a bone, something men must pay a surgeon to achieve, and in plastic at that. In size humans are dwarfed: the bull's is 3', the elephant's 5', the blue whale's 7' to 8', and even a small animal like a pig, domestic or wild, has 18".

Counsellors, marriage handbooks, and sensitive females assure us that there is no correlation between penile size and lovemaking ability. Xaviera Hollander, an author who claims professional expertise of a practical sort, agrees about the lovemaking but says size does matter, and comments: "Men worry mainly about length, whereas women care more for girth....If he's all the way in, up against her cervix, yet there are still two inches on the outside, those are two useless inches. Girth is another matter....A penis is hardly ever too thick." (*Xaviera's Su-perSex*, New American Library.)

One of the most curious facts about the human penis is that, of all the organs of the male body, e.g., heart, lungs, brain, liver, and so on, the size of the penis is least related to skeletal size.

pennyweight

A unit of mass, 1/20th of a troy ounce = 24 grains ≈ 1.55517 grams. Abbr, dwt. In the United Kingdom, the pennyweight was made no longer legal for trade after January 31, 1969, by the Weights and Measures Act of 1963.

What penny is the pennyweight the weight of? The first "English" pennies were minted by kingdoms in Kent around 775. At that time the English had close relations with the Franks. The Franks coined *deniers* (from which we get the abbreviation d for the penny) at the rate of 240 coins to the pound. (In those days the value of a coin lay in the actual mass of precious metal it contained, not in the authority of the issuer.) Like earlier English coinage, the new English silver penny was modelled on that of the Franks. Taking the pound to be the troy pound, 1/240th of a pound is 24 grains. Pennies weighing 24 grains were often minted during Saxon times, but so were lighter pennies. The pennyweight is based on the idea that there are 240 pennyweights to the (troy) pound, rather than on the actual weights of the coins.

From the 13TH C on the pennyweight is often described as being the weight of 32 grains of wheat. Since 4 to 3 was the conventional wheat grain-to-barleycorn ratio from ancient Egypt through the Middle Ages, 32 wheat grains are equivalent to 24 barleycorns. The old commentators' repeated description of the pennyweight in terms of grains of wheat suggests its French origins, for the grain of wheat played the same role in French weights that the barleycorn did in the English.

The weight of the real penny was most stable during two centuries shortly after the Norman Conquest, when it weighed 22 1/2 grains. As a result there arose another pennyweight, = 22 1/2 grains, and even a pound consisting of 240 such pennyweights (= 5400 grains) called the Tower pound, used exclusively by the mints to check coinage. The Tower pound was abolished by Henry VIII in 1527, and this second pennyweight is long forgotten.

In the 19TH C a special pennyweight = 30 grains was used for weighing pearls.

perch

One of the terms for the unit of length known in different times and places as the perch, rod or pole, 12TH C–PRESENT. In the United States, 5 1/2 yards, ≈ 5.02920 meters. See ☞acre. In the United Kingdom, it was abolished by the 1963 Weights and Measures Act.

It is natural to wonder how a unit arose having such strange relations with other units in the system: 5½ (yards) and 16½ (feet). R. D. Connor speculates that the perch may be a body-unit, a score of natural feet. Others have suggested it is 15 Drusian feet. However it arose, it probably owes its survival to the convenience of a unit of about this length in primitive methods of surveying.

The perch is also a unit of capacity in masonry work, = 24 ¾ cubic feet.

pH

A measure of the acidity of a solution, devised by the Danish chemist S. P. L. Sørenson in 1909. It is the negative logarithm (base 10) of the hydrogen ion concentration expressed in moles per liter; the lower the number, the more acid the solution is. By convention, pHs outside the range 0–14 are not used.

The concentration of an acid or base in a solution affects the solution's pH; such concentrations are often expressed in terms of normality, which is the number of gram-equivalent weights of solute per liter of solution.

Some Typical pHs

hydrochloric acid (N)	0.1	human saliva	5.8–7.1
sulfuric acid (N)	0.3	cow's milk	6.9
human gastric juice	1.3–3.0	water	7.0
lemon juice	2.1	human urine	7.4
vinegar	2.3	egg white	7.6–9.5
orange juice	3.0	sea water	8.2
wine	3.4	baking soda in water (0.1N)	8.4
sauerkraut	3.5	household ammonia	11.9
tomatoes	4.2	lye (0.1N)	13.0
black coffee	5.0	potassium hydroxide (N)	14.0
rain (unpolluted)	5.7		

pillows

Standard bed pillow sizes in the USA are:
Standard   20" × 26"
Queen   20" × 30" to 22" × 34"
King   20" × 36"

A pillow 26" square is considered "European." Bolsters are the width of the bed, with a diameter of about 9", or if wedge-shaped, are about 12" high. Body pillows, favored by some pregnant women, are 20" × 60" or 72". A wide variety of other pillows are made: neck rolls, bedrests, anti-snore pillows, and so on, but their sizes are not standardized.

Pillowcases
Standard   20" × 30" to 22" × 30"
Queen   22" × 34"
King   20" × 40" to 22" × 40"

Throw Pillows
The typical square throw pillow is about 14" × 14". A floor pillow is larger, perhaps 24" × 24".

pinheads

Although writers are fond of comparing various objects to pinheads, it is a very inexact quantity. Measurements of heads of ordinary pins, (that is, excluding pins whose heads are glass or plastic beads) currently sold shows that diameters vary from 1 mm to 1.9 mm.

In Indian cooking, the amount that can be heaped on a pinhead is a unit of measure for very powerful ingredients, such as camphor.

pins

The number describing a pin size is the length of the pin in sixteenths of a inch. Thus a #17 dressmakers pin is $17/16$, or 1 1/16" long. The diameter of the pin depends on the type of pin.

pint

In the USA, two units: one of dry capacity, the U.S. dry pint, ≈ 0.55061 liters, and the other of liquid capacity, the U.S. liquid pint, ≈ 0.473176 liters. In Britain, the imperial pint ≈ 0.568261 liters. The pint is one of the few non-metric units Britain will retain as a member of the European Community, and then only in pubs and for milk.

pipe, copper

Pipe for Plumbing
Pipe for residential plumbing, or "plumbing tube," is sold in nominal sizes which are 1/8" less than the actual outside diameter. There are three series, K, L and M, with K having the heaviest walls and M the lightest (some plumbing codes do not permit M). Wall thickness varies with nominal size; for example, in the 3/4" size, type K has a 0.065" wall, type L has a 0.045" wall, and type M has an 0.038" wall. The resulting inside diameter is always within a few hundredths of an inch of the nominal size.

Types K and L are available in two tempers: "drawn temper," sometimes called "hard" or "rigid," and "annealed temper", often called "soft." M is available only in drawn temper. In sizes below 8", drawn temper pipe is sold in 20' lengths. Annealed temper pipe is also sold in 60', 100', and 200' coils.

Flare fittings may be installed on annealed temper pipe, but not on drawn temper; both types can be soldered or brazed. Soft pipe is sometimes called "flexible," but it should not be confused with the corrugated copper pipes used, for example, to make connections to water heaters.

A fourth type, DWV (for drain waste vent) is sold only in drawn temper and in sizes from 1 1/4" to 8". It comes in 20' lengths. The sizes usually used are 1 1/4", 1 1/2", 3", and 4".

Pipe for Refrigeration
Copper pipe for use in air conditioning and refrigeration is designated ACR. It is sized by the actual outside diameter and comes in lengths of 20' in hard temper and coils of 50' in soft temper.

pipe threads

Pipe thread sizes are described much as bolt sizes are, although the shapes are different. For example, "1/2–14 NPT" identifies a pipe thread with a nominal outside diameter of 1/2" and 14 threads to the inch, made according to the NPT standard. If "LH" is added, the pipe has a left hand thread. The pipe thread standards are:

NPT   American Standard Pipe Taper Thread
NPSC American Standard Straight Coupling Pipe Thread
NPTR American Standard Taper Railing Pipe Thread
NPSM American Standard Straight Mechanical Pipe Thread
NPSL American Standard Straight Locknut Pipe Thread

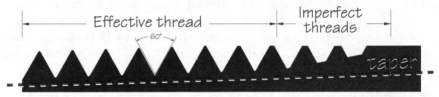

The word "taper" in several of these names points to the big difference between many pipe threads and those on bolts and screws. A pipe thread must make not only a mechanical joint but also a leakproof one. To accomplish this, the threads become shallower the farther they are from the end of the pipe or fitting. The bottoms of the threads aren't on a cylinder, but a cone; they taper. The taper is 1/16" in an inch or 3/4" in a foot.

Because of the taper, a pipe can only screw into a fitting a certain distance before it jams, unlike threading a nut on a bolt. The standard specifies this distance, the "effective thread." It also specifies another distance, the "engagement," the distance the pipe can be screwed in by hand, without much effort. For workers, instead of these distances, it is more convenient to know how many turns to make by hand and how many with a wrench.

The table shows the distances and number of turns called for in the standard. A tolerance of plus or minus one turn is allowed, and in practice threads are often routinely cut shorter than the standard specifies.

American Standard Taper Pipe Threads						
Nominal size	Actual OD	Threads per inch	Length of engage-ment	Hand tight turns	Wrench makeup turns	Length of effective thread
1/8	0.405	27	0.180	4 1/2	2 1/2	0.260
1/4	0.540	18	0.200	4	3	0.401
3/8	0.675	18	0.240	4 1/2	3	0.408
1/2	0.840	14	0.320	4 1/2	3	0.534
3/4	1.050	14	0.340	4 1/2	3	0.546
1	1.315	11.5	0.400	4 1/2	3 1/4	0.682
1 1/4	1.660	11.5	0.420	4 1/2	3 1/4	0.707
1 1/2	1.900	11.5	0.420	4 1/2	3 1/4	0.724
2	2.375	11.5	0.436	5	3	0.756
2 1/2	2.875	8	0.682	5 1/2	3	1.136
3	3.500	8	0.766	6	3	1.200

Note: All measurements in inches. The fourth column contains the normal length of engagement when tightened by hand.

planets

Column 1 is the average diameter at the planet's equator. Column 3 is the surface gravity compared to Earth. Column 4 is the length of the planet's day (the period of rotation, in relation to distant stars) in earth days; planets that spin in the opposite direction from Earth's spin are marked with an asterisk. Column 5 is the length of a year (one trip around the sun, in relation to distant stars) in Earth years. Column 6 is the distance to the sun at the widest part of the orbit, where Earth is 1.

	Diameter (km)	Mass (kg)	Gravity	Length of day	Length of year	Distance to sun
Mercury	4,878	3.30×10^{23}	0.38	58.65	0.24	0.38
Venus	12,104	4.87×10^{24}	0.91	243.01*	0.61	0.72
Earth	12,756	5.97×10^{24}	1	1.00	1.00	1.00
Mars	6,795	6.42×10^{23}	0.38	1.03	1.88	1.52
Jupiter	142,985	1.90×10^{27}	2.53	0.41	11.86	5.20
Saturn	120,537	5.69×10^{26}	1.07	0.44	29.46	9.53
Uranus	51,118	8.66×10^{25}	0.92	0.65*	84.07	19.19
Neptune	50,538	1.03×10^{26}	1.19	0.77	164.82	30.06
Pluto	3,000	1.59×10^{22}	0.09	6.39*	248.6	35.53

plastics

The Plastic Bottle Institute, a division of the Society of the Plastic Industry, has developed a code to be molded onto plastic products so that the resin from which the a bottle was made could be identified easily when the bottle was recycled. A bale of mixed resins is much less valuable than one consisting entirely of bottles made from the same resin. Thirty-nine states have incorporated the code in their waste management legislation.

1, PETE	Polyethylene terephthalate. By far the most valuable of the recycled plastics, and the one most often recycled. It is made into stuffing for pillows, sleeping bags, and quilts, into the fuzz on tennis balls, the tennis ball "can," carpet, twine combs, car bumpers, and many other products. Until recently it was not remade into containers for food, but a new process has been developed which is said to repurify the plastic at reasonable cost.
2, HDPE	High-density polyethylene.
3, V	Vinyl or polyvinyl chloride.
4, LDPE	Low-density polyethylene.
5, PP	Polypropylene.
6, PS	Polystyrene.
7, Other	None of the above. Sometimes the plastic resin is one of those listed above, but it contains an additive which makes it unsuitable for recycling.

play yards

Most are square, 36" by 36" or 40" by 40". Rectangular models are 24" by 36" or a bit larger. If the play yard has slats, the openings between slats should be no wider than 2 3/8". If it is covered in mesh, the mesh openings should be no larger than 1/4".

plywood

Unlike wood, plywood is a manufactured product. Without standards, it would be very difficult for a consumer to judge its quality, a problem that occurs today with imported plywood, some of which is superb and some of which is far below U.S. standards.

Softwood Plywood
In the USA, the standards for most softwood plywood are established by the American Plywood Association in cooperation with the National Institute of Standards and Technology. A Voluntary Product Standard for plywood became effective November 1, 1966, and was revised in 1974 and again in 1983. The mark "PS 1-83" indicates that the panel conforms to the Product Standard published in 1983, which was still in force in 1992.

Panels are stamped with a grade mark, unless such a stamp would deface a high quality surface that might be given a natural finish, in which case the grade is marked on the edge.

Dimensions
Lumber yards usually carry 4' × 8' and 4' × 10' panels, but will cut half and quarter sheets. Other sizes are manufactured, almost always in increments of 12", for example, in widths of 36", 48" and 60", and in 9+ lengths. The exception to the whole feet rule are the panels marked "sized for spacing," which are slightly shorter than normal

panels (e.g., 48" × 95½" instead of 48" × 96") in order to leave space between panels in, for example, sheathing a roof with rafters on 24" centers. The space is necessary to allow for the panels' expansion.

Thicknesses of sanded panels range from ¼" to 1¼" or more, in steps of ⅛". The thickness tolerance is ± 1/64" for panels ¾" or less, ± 3% of specified thickness for thicker panels. Nominal thicknesses of unsanded panels range from 5/16" to 1 ¼" or more, ± 1/32" for panels with a specified thickness of 13/16" or less, and ± 5% for thicker panels.

Veneer Grades

N	A premium grade (N for natural finish), available on special order from some manufacturers. Either 100% heartwood or 100% sapwood. Repairs must be made with well-matched wood parallel to the grain, and only 6 are permitted in a 4' × 8' panel.
A	Smooth, paintable surface. Not more than 18 neatly made repairs parallel to the grain, of the boat, sled, or router types. Repairs with synthetic patching compound are permitted in this as well as all lesser grades.
B	Shims, circular repair plugs, and tight knots as large as 1" measured across the grain are permitted. as well as minor splits.
C plugged	Splits may be no wider than 1/8", and knotholes and borer holes no larger than 1/4" × 1/2". Some broken grain is allowed.
C	In this grade tight knots as large as 1½", discoloration and sanding defects that do not affect strength, and stitching are permitted.
D	Knots and knotholes as wide as 2½" measured across the grain and even larger (within limits) in other directions. Splits and stitching permitted.

Species Group Number

A number from 1 to 5, with wood from the species of trees in group 1 being the strongest and stiffest (such as beech and Douglas fir from certain states), and 5 the least stiff and strong (such as basswood or poplar).

Exposure Durability Classifications

"Exterior". Panels intended for exposure to the weather. D grade veneer may not be used in Exterior panels; contrary to a common misconception, CDX is not an exterior panel. Exterior plywood is not necessarily the best choice where plywood will be constantly exposed to the weather; plywood pressure-treated with preservative would probably be better.

"Exposure 1". The glue is the same as that used for Exterior plywood, but other characteristics that affect bonding are not. These panels are for use in high moisture conditions or where, during construction, long delays may be expected prior to providing protection.

"Exposure 2". Same glue. The wood itself is a bit worse and the panel less rugged.

"Interior". A different glue is used. Plywood in the other exposure classifications can act as a vapor barrier if glued and nailed; interior plywood cannot. For use only in protected areas indoors.

Panel Grade

Panel grade is either a pair of veneer grades, e.g. A-B, C-D, or a name identifying the principal end use, such as : APA Rated Sheathing, APA 303 Siding, or APA Underlayment.

APA Trademarked Panels

Certain designations are trademarked by the APA, such as "APA Rated Sheathing," "APA Rated Sturd-I-Floor," and "APA Rated Siding." These panels are marked with span ratings, which indicate the center to center distance, in inches, of the joists or studs to which the panel is fastened during construction. In the case of sheathing, the span rating is two numbers separated by a slash: the first number is the span rating if the panel is used for roofing, and the second is for subflooring. Both cases assume that the long dimension of the ply-wood crosses three supports.

Hardwood Plywood

Hardwood plywood is usually not grade-stamped, though thicker pieces may be stamped on the edge. The grade is a letter followed by a digit. The letter, from AA to E, refers to the quality of the best side (the face) and the digit, from 1 to 4, to the quality of the other side (the back). A and 1 represent the best quality. D and E are suitable for crates, pallets, and similar uses.

---

point

1) A unit for describing the size of type, = 1/12th of a pica. See ☞type.
2) In describing the thickness of cover stock, board and other heavy papers, 1 point = 1/1000".

---

pools

The Consumer Product Safety Commission recommends 48" as the minimum height of fencing around swimming pools.

---

pound, avoirdupois

A unit of mass = 453.59237 grams (the international pound), now used chiefly in the United States, but formerly the most common unit of mass throughout the English-speaking world. Its value has varied less than 1% since Elizabeth I distributed standards of weight in 1588.

A comparison of the British Imperial Standard Pound and the International Prototype Kilogram made in 1883 led to the equivalence 1 pound = 0.4535924277 kg, which both Great Britain and the USA adopted. In the USA this conversion factor continued in use until 1959, but the British officially rounded it off to 0.45359243 in 1889, after which the two countries' pounds differed.

Effective July 1, 1959, by mutual agreement a new International Pound = 0.45359237 kilogram became effective for scientific and technical work in Australia, Canada, New Zealand, South Africa, the United Kingdom and the United States. In the USA, the new value was accepted as the value of the pound avoirdupois for *all* purposes, as it was in the UK by the Weights and Measures Act of 1963, in which, for the first time, the British government defined the pound in terms of the kilogram. The new International Pound is about 1 part in 10 million smaller than the U.S. pound avoirdupois that it replaced.

imperial pound	$\approx$ 0.453592338 kg
international pound	= 0.45359237 kg
U.S. pound av., 1958	= 0.4535924277 kg

proof

In the USA, the proof of an alcoholic beverage is twice its alcohol content in percentage by volume at 60°F. So an 80-proof whiskey is 40% alcohol. Recently the USA has begun to label bottles containing wine and spirits with percentage alcohol by volume, instead of proof.

A different proof system, called Gay-Lussac, is used in Europe; it is also the percentage of alcohol by volume, which is half the American proof. The European Union has adopted Gay-Lussac proof as its standard.

The situation in Great Britain is much more complicated. A distilled spirit was originally "proved" by dissolving some gunpowder in it and trying to ignite it. If it wouldn't burn, there was too much water. If it burned evenly and steadily, the spirit was "proven."

Early in the 19TH C Bartholomew Sikes determined that proven spirits contained at least 57.1% alcohol by volume. The British proof system is built on this number. "Proof" spirits, or 100-proof spirits, are 57.1% alcohol by volume. Proofs above and below 100-proof are sometimes referred to as so many degrees under proof or over proof. American 100-proof whiskey, for example, might be called either "87.5-proof" or "12.5 under proof." For a quick conversion of British proof to American, multiply the British proof by 8, then divide by 7.

Thus the same beverage could have been 40 proof (Gay-Lussac), 80 proof (American), or 70 proof (British), depending on where you drank it.

pulse

A frequently quoted rule-of-thumb for determining the target pulse rate for aerobic exercise is to subtract age in years from 220, then take 70% of the result.

puttonos

A designation indicating the composition of the mixture of grapes used to make tokay, a Hungarian wine produced in Aszú. (Hungarian tokay is not made with the tokay grape and does not resemble the American dessert wine called tokay.)

The character of the Hungarian wine depends upon the soil and climate of a very small area (smaller than New York City) and on a variety of grape called the Furmint. Furmint grapes are left on the vine when they ripen. In most years, the unpicked, over-ripe grapes are attacked by the "noble rot" that occasionally distinguishes French and German vintages. The berries shrivel and the concentration of sugar soars. The resulting "grapes" are known by the German name trocken-beeren.

In making tokay, the wine is fermented in standardized casks called *gönci hordó* (cask from Gönc), which hold about 120–140 liters. The must, the mass of fermenting grapes, is a mixture of Furmint trocken-beeren and ordinary crushed grapes; the trockenbeeren are measured out in wooden measures called *puttonos* that each hold about 27 liters. A *gönci hordó* that gets 3 *puttonos* of trockenbeeren produces 3-puttonos tokay. The more *puttonos* put into the cask the higher the quality of the resulting tokay; 5-puttonos is the highest quality.

quad

In the USA, 10^{15} (1 quadrillion, American style) British thermal units $\approx$ 1.055×10^{18} joules. This unit is used for such purposes as reporting the total annual energy consumption in the American economy. One quad is roughly the amount of energy in 46 million short tons of coal, 175 million barrels of crude oil, or 1 trillion standard cubic feet of natural gas.

quart

In the USA, the U.S. dry quart, a unit of dry capacity, $\approx$ 1.101221 liters, and the U.S. liquid quart, a unit of liquid capacity, $\approx$ 0.946353 liters. In Britain, the imperial quart, used for both liquid and dry measure, $\approx$ 1.13652 liters. Four of the U.S. liquid quarts or the British imperial quarts make a gallon; half of any of the above quarts is a pint (but different pints!).

quart, reputed

In Britain, 17TH C–20TH C, a unit of liquid capacity, identified with the capacity of the typical glass bottle for wine and spirits, $\approx$ 757.7 milliliters. Sometimes called a whiskey quart. Such bottles began to be made in England in the late 17TH C.

The problem is, what gallon is the reputed quart a quarter of? It is not a quarter of the ale or wine gallon. A statute of 1803 says 5 bottles of wine make roughly 1 wine gallon (the wine gallon legalized by

Queen Anne, of 231 cubic inches). Scholars have suggested that the reputed quart is a quarter of a wine gallon defined as the volume occupied by 8 troy pounds of wine, the sort of measure that might be used in the wine import-export trade. With the introduction of imperial measure in 1824, the reputed quart became 1/6th of an imperial gallon, a very slight change in size. The reputed quart has now been abolished in the UK but is still in use in some former colonies.

In the USA the nationally recognized gallon is actually the wine gallon of Queen Anne. Before 1979, when the USA adopted metric sizes for alcoholic beverage bottles, bottles of whiskey and other spirits contained 1/5 U.S. liquid gallon = 4/5 quart, hence the name *fifth*. The fifth and the reputed quart are therefore the same.

quarter	Various units, all of which are a fourth of some larger unit. Some of the meanings in the USA are ✓ 25 cents, especially the coin, one fourth of a dollar. ✓ a college term approximately 12 weeks long, a fourth of a school year. ✓ a *long quarter*, 1/4th of a long ton, = 560 lbs. ✓ a *short quarter*, 1/4th of a short ton, = 500 lbs. In Britain, the quarter is a unit of mass = 28 pounds, which is a fourth of a hundredweight.
quarter hour	In the USA, a unit of academic credit obtained by satisfactorily completing a course which meets for one hour per week (or in the case of labs, typically for three hours), over an academic quarter. Compare ☞ semester hour.
quarter-section	In the USA and the western parts of Canada, a unit of land area, = 160 acres.

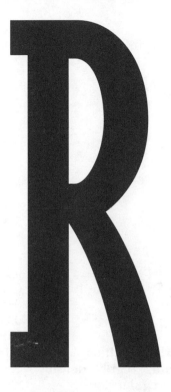

R-value

A measure of how well a building material or structure keeps heat in—or out. The higher the R-value, the better the substance is as thermal insulation.

$$\text{R–value} = \frac{\text{temperature difference} \times \text{area} \times \text{time}}{\text{heat loss}}$$

where the temperature difference is in degrees Fahrenheit, the area is in square feet, the time is in hours, and the heat loss is in Btus. If the R-value of a partition and the temperature difference is known, the formula can be used to find the heat loss.

The reciprocal of R-value is known as the U-value; the higher the U-value the better the conduction of heat. In Europe, the U-value is based on $\frac{watts}{meters^2 \cdot kelvin}$; to obtain it multiply the U.S. U-value by 5.678.

Typical R-values of Building Materials

The R-value of a structure made of layers of different materials can be estimated by adding the R-values of the layers; the R-value of a layer can be estimated by multiplying its thickness in inches by the R-value per inch. These techniques don't give strictly accurate results (among other factors, a layer of air stuck on the surfaces between layers is itself an insulator), but they come close.

Insulation (typical R-value per inch of thickness)

Vermiculite, loose fill	2.08
Perlite, loose fill	2.7
Fiberglass, blankets and batts	3.33
Fiberglass, blown loose fill	2.2
Fiberglass, boards	4.5
Rock wool, batts	3.66
Rock wool, blown loose fill	2.93
Polystyrene boards	3.45
Cellulose, blown loose fill	3.6
Urea-formaldehyde foam	4.48
Urethane foam	5.3

Walls and Siding

Wood bevel siding, 1/2" × 8" lapped	0.81
Wood siding shingles, 16" × 7 1/2" exposure	0.87
Asbestos-cement shingles	0.03
Stucco, per inch	0.20
Building paper	0.06
1/2" nail-base insulation board sheathing	1.14
1/2" insulation board sheathing, regular density	1.32
insulation board sheathing, regular density	2.04
1/4" plywood	0.31
3/8" plywood	0.47
1/2" plywood	0.62
5/8" plywood	0.78
Softwood, per inch	1.25
Softwood board 3/4" thick	0.94
Concrete block with three oval cores	
cinder aggregate, 4" thick	1.11
cinder aggregate, 8" thick	1.72
cinder aggregate, 12" thick	1.89
sand and gravel aggregate, 8" thick	1.11
lightweight aggregate (expanded clay, shale, slag, pumice, etc.), 8" thick	2.00
Concrete block with two rectangular cores	
Sand and gravel aggregate, 8"	1.04
Lightweight aggregate, 8" thick	2.18
Common brick, per inch	0.20
Face brick, per inch	0.11
Sand-and-gravel concrete, per inch	0.08
1/2" gypsum board	0.45

5/8" gypsum board	0.56
1/2" lightweight aggregate gypsum plaster	0.32

Floors

Hardwood finish flooring	0.68
Asphalt, linoleum, vinyl, or rubber floor tile	0.05
Carpet with a fibrous pad	2.08
Carpet with a foam rubber pad	1.23

Roofs

Asphalt roof shingles	0.44
Wood roof shingles	0.94
3/8" build-up roof	0.33

Doors

Solid wood 1" thick	1.56
Solid wood 1" thick with wood storm door	3.3
Solid wood 1 1/2" thick	2.04
Solid wood 1 1/2" thick with wood storm door	3.7
Solid wood 2" thick	2.33
Solid wood 2" thick with wood storm door	4.17

Three-quarter-inch Air Spaces

Heat flow up	0.87
Heat flow up, one surface reflective	2.23

Recommended Levels of Insulation

Building codes specify a minimum level of insulation. The optimum amount of insulation depends on guessing what the cost and availability of heating fuel (or electricity for cooling) will be over the life of the house. The Department of Housing and Urban Development's *Minimum Property Standards for One- and Two-Family Dwellings* (1979) are shown below; many experts would recommend higher levels, especially for a house that will be heated electrically.

	Zone A	Zone B	Zone C	Zone D	Zone E
Ceiling	19	19	26	30	38
Wall	11	11	13	13	19
Foundation walls (heated basement)	none	none	11	11	19
Slab foundation (perimeter insulation)	none	2	5	5	7.5

rad

1) The abbreviation for ☞radian. 2) A unit of absorbed radiation dose (the name comes from **r**adiation **a**bsorbed **d**ose). Abbr, rd. The rad was defined by the International Commission on Radiological Units as the amount of radiation that leads to the absorption of 100 ergs of energy per gram (0.01 joule per kilogram) in whatever substance is being used. The value 0.01 joule was chosen so that absorption of 1 ☞roentgen of X rays or gamma radiation (of energies typically used in medicine) in water or soft tissue would produce an absorbed dose of 1 rad. For soft tissue, a measurement in rads of any dose will closely resemble its measurement in ☞reps; this is not true of exposures to bone.

Unlike the roentgen, the rad can be applied to radiation of any type. Unlike the rep, the amount of energy absorbed is defined, not determined experimentally. However, since different types of radiation differ in the damage they do, another unit, the ☞rem, is required to express a quantity of radiation in terms of biological damage done.

The rad has been replaced by an SI unit, the ☞gray; one rad = 0.01 gray.

radian

The unit used to measure plane angles in SI, equal to the angle between two radii of a circle that cut off a piece of the circumference whose length is equal to the length of the circle's radius. Abbr, rad. One radian ≈ 57° 17' 45".

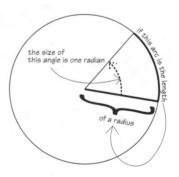

railroads

In railroad track, gauge is the distance between the inside edges of the rails. The standard gauge is 4' 8 1/2". One story has it that this was the distance between the wheels of Roman chariots, which wore permanent ruts in English roads, forcing English wagonmakers to adopt the same spacing, which was adopted in turn by the builders of the first railways. Whatever its origin, standard gauge is now found throughout the world, although many countries also have other gauges.

Why do gauges differ? Sometimes a country has chosen a gauge that differed from that of its neighbors as a security measure. Another reason is money: the narrower the gauge, the cheaper the track and equipment. Sometimes there simply was no sufficiently powerful standards-setting agency, public or private. Lack of a standardized gauge, as occurred in some South American countries, has significantly hindered development.

In North America, narrow gauge railroads have now almost disappeared. In *American Narrow Gauge Railroad*s (Stanford Univ. Press, 1990), George Hilton reports that 95% of all the U. S. narrow gauge mileage was 3', often used in Pennsylvania and the Rocky Mountains. A great deal of 2' gauge was laid in Maine and Massachusetts, however, and 3'6", 3'2", and 2'6" were also used.

Not all narrow gauge is obsolete. Japan National Railways, for example, is mostly 3'6". Many countries have a 1-meter gauge.

Gauges wider than standard gauge include a 5' 6" gauge used in Argentina, India, Portugal, Spain, and Sri Lanka, and a 5' gauge in Finland and Russia.

ratings, audience

A rating is given as two numbers separated by a slash. The first number, the rating, is the percentage of all homes with televisions that were tuned to the program. In 1993, one rating point = 942,000 households. The second number is share, the percentage of all households whose televisions were on that were tuned to the program.

reaction time

Many tests have been done to see how fast people can respond to a stimulus. For example, how much time passes between the moment the brake lights of a car come on and the moment the driver behind slams on the brakes? Some of the results are curious: a right-handed person can respond with the right hand about 3% faster than with the left—and conversely for a left-handed person. It takes about 20% longer to respond with the feet than with the hands.

The most important experimental result is one everyone knows: the older people are, the slower their reactions. The table below compares reaction times in milliseconds to a stimulus that is seen (a light coming on) and one that is heard (a buzzer), by age and gender.

Typical Human Reaction Times in Milliseconds				
Age (years)	Females		Males	
	seen	heard	seen	heard
20	320	310	240	230
30	260	200	220	190
40	340	300	260	240
50	360	300	270	250
60	440	420	380	370

ream

A quantity of paper, 20 quires. Well into the 20TH C a ream of writing or drawing paper contained 480 sheets while a ream of printing paper was 500 sheets. Today the standard ream of all types of paper is 500 sheets.

rebar

These mild steel bars used to reinforce concrete have an interesting series of sizes. Between #2 and #8, the size number is the nominal diameter of the bar in eighths, for example, #5 bar is 5⁄8" in diameter.

Metric designations of reinforcing bars have the form "K" followed by the mass in kilograms of a 1-meter length of the bar. For example, "K3" rebar weighs 3 kg per meter.

Size	Dia.	Lbs/ft
2b	0.250"	0.167
3	0.375"	0.376
4	0.500"	0.668
5	0.625"	1.043
6	0.750"	1.052
7	0.875"	2.044
8	1.000"	2.670
9	1.128"	3.400
10	1.270"	4.303
11	1.410"	5.313

reel

A unit of running time used in the motion picture industry to describe the length of films, ≈ 10 minutes. Early projectors used reels that held a maximum of 1000' of 35 mm film, which at 24 frames per second has a running time of 11.1 minutes. Later reels were physically larger (2000' or more), but the name stuck.

refrigerators

The capacity of refrigerators is usually given in cubic feet, but manufacturers have different ways of calculating the capacity of their models. See the most recent article on refrigerators in the magazine *Consumer Reports* for capacities measured in a consistent way. A rule of thumb for estimating needed capacity, for the USA, is 12 cu. feet for two people plus an additional two cubic feet for each additional person.

rem

A unit of dose equivalent. Abbr, rem. Usually encountered as millirem (mrem). Originally defined by H. M. Parker as the quantity of radiation (of any mixture of types) that would produce the same biological damage in a human being as would result from absorption of 1 ☞rep of X rays or gamma rays (the name comes from **r**oentgen **e**quivalent **m**an). It was subsequently redefined, as described below.

Some forms of radiation are more harmful than others. For example, a dose of 1 rad of alpha particles will do ten to twenty times as much damage as a dose of 1 rad of X rays, even though both exposures would deposit the same amount of energy in the tissue. To describe this a factor called relative biological effectiveness (RBE) is used, which is the ratio of the size in rads of a dose of X rays to the size in rads of a dose of another type of radiation that causes the same amount of damage. Thus the RBE of alpha particles is in the range 10–20 (depending on their energy, among other factors). RBE is determined experimentally.

The rem was redefined by letting a dose in rems = a dose in rads × RBE.

The rem has been replaced by the ☞sievert, 1 rem = 1⁄100 sievert, but the temporarily continued use of the rem was sanctioned by the CIPM.

An example of the use of the rem are the exposure limits for workers set by the U. S. Occupational Safety and Health Administration (29 CFR 1910.96, last amended in 1993). The limits are given as the maximum permissible number of rems accumulated during a calendar quarter, for various parts of the body:

Dose	Portion of Body
1.25	Whole body; head and trunk; active blood-forming organs; lens of eyes; or gonads
7.5	Skin of whole body
18.75	Hands & forearms; feet & ankles

For an employee who is under the age of 18, the limits are 10% of those shown in the above table.

However, doses of up to 3 rems per calendar quarter are allowed, provided adequate records are kept and the dose to the whole body, added to the accumulated occupational exposure to the whole body, stated in rems, isn't more than the person's age minus 18, multiplied by 5.

The above table applies to chronic exposures to low levels of radiation. Exposure to a single powerful dose has different effects:

25–100 rems	Probably no disabling illness.
100–200 rems	Nausea, fatigue, vomiting. An exposure to more than 125 rems causes a 1% reduction in life expectancy.
200–300 rems	Probable recovery in 3 months.
300–600 rems	Nausea, vomiting, diarrhea in first few hours. After a latent period of a week, loss of hair, malaise, fever, progressing to hemorrhage and emaciation in the third week. At about 500 rems, 50% die in 2 to 6 weeks.
more than 600 rems	Almost all die within weeks.

rep

A unit of quantity of radiation, devised by H. M. Parker to fill the need for a unit to be used with types of radiation other than X rays and gamma rays, since the definition of the roentgen restricted its use to X rays and gamma rays. The rep is defined as the quantity of radiation which, absorbed in the body, would liberate the same amount of energy as 1 roentgen of X rays or gamma rays would. The name comes from **r**oentgen **e**quivalent **p**hysical. The value of the rep thus depends on the amount of energy liberated in the body by X rays producing 1 esu of charge, which is determined experimentally. At first it was taken to be 32.5 electron volts per ion-pair in air, and later to be 33.5. The latter value made the rep the amount of radiation which, absorbed in the body, liberated 97 ergs, and this definition was the one generally used.

The rep was never a widely used unit. It was replaced by the SI unit, the gray. One rep ≈ 8.38 milligrays.

resistors, electrical

The value of a resistor, in ohms, is indicated by a series of four or five colored rings or dots. The colors are read from the left when the uncolored end, or, in the case of resistors with 5 colors, the gap, is placed on the right. High-precision resistors may have their value printed on them in numerals.

Color	1st or 2nd Bands	3rd Band (multiplier)	4th Band (tolerance)
black	0	× 1	± 20%
brown	1	× 10	± 1%
red	2	× 100	± 2%
orange	3	× 1,000	± 3%
yellow	4	× 10,000	− 0, + 100%
green	5	× 100,000	± 5%
blue	6	× 1,000,000	± 6%
purple	7	× 10,000,000	± 12.5%
gray	8	× 100,000,000	± 30%
white	9	—	± 10%
silver	—	× 0.01	± 10%
gold	—	× 0.1	± 5%

rings

Size	Inside measurements in inches		Size	Inside measurements in inches	
	diameter	circumference		diameter	circumference
2	0.538	1.690	8 1/2	0.730	2.293
3	0.554	1.740	9	0.746	2.344
3 1/2	0.570	1.791	9 1/2	0.762	2.394
4	0.586	1.841	10	0.778	2.444
4 1/2	0.602	1.891	10 1/2	0.794	2.494
5	0.618	1.942	11	0.810	2.545
5 1/2	0.634	1.992	11 1/2	0.826	2.595
6	0.650	2.042	12	0.842	2.645
6 1/2	0.666	2.092	12 1/2	0.858	2.695
7	0.682	2.143	13	0.874	2.746
7 1/2	0.698	2.193	13 1/2	0.890	2.796
8	0.714	2.243			

The origin of American ring sizes is unknown. A u.s. patent for a ring gauge, issued to F. E. Allen on February 3, 1874, shows ring sizes from 1 to 13 with quarter sizes, so the system was in use by then. In the 1920s the National Bureau of Standards surveyed the ring gauges in use at a nationwide sample of jewellers and discovered the same size numbers were being used for different dimensions.

rivets

The most useful type of rivet for most do-it-yourselfers is the blind rivet, often called a "Pop Rivet," a trademark of USM. Blind rivets come in diameters of 3/32", 1/8", 5/32", 3/16", and 1/4". Most hardware stores carry them in several lengths and in aluminum and steel.

Many other types of blind rivet are available, including ones that leave a threaded hole, ones with large truss heads, ones made of stainless steel, and so on, but these are difficult for consumers to locate.

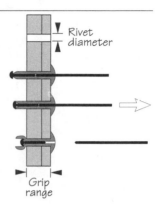

Rivet diameter

Grip range

rod

A unit of length in the English-speaking world, = 5.5 yards, ≈ 5.029 meters. The name rod is commonly used in the USA; it is also called the pole or ☞perch.

roentgen

A unit describing exposure to x-radiation or gamma rays. Symbol, r. It was defined by the 1937 Radiological Congress (Chicago) as the amount of x-radiation or gamma radiation that produces ionization equal to 1 electrostatic unit of charge, either negative or positive, in 1 cubic centimeter of dry air at 0°C and at standard atmospheric pressure.

Although the roentgen has been officially discontinued in favor of expressing such measurements in coulombs per kilogram, the CIPM (1978) sanctioned its continued use for the time being. One roentgen = 2.58×10^{-4} coulombs per kilogram.

rood

In Britain, 10TH C–20TH C, a unit of land area, = 1210 square yards, ≈ 1011.7 sq. meters. Originally a piece of land 1 rod wide and 40 rods long, a quarter of an acre.

rope

In Britain, a unit of distance, = 20 feet.

rubber bands

Size	Length	Width	Number in a pound	Size	Length	Width	Number in a pound
8	7/8"	1/16"	7,000	31	2 1/2"	1/8"	1,420
10	1 1/4"	1/16"	5,780	32	3"	1/16"	1,065
12	1 3/4"	1/16"	4,000	33	3 1/2"	1/8"	880
14	2	1/16"	3,200	62	2 1/2"	1/4"	745
16	1/2"	1/16"	2,655	64	3 1/2"	1/4"	460
17	2 3/4"	3/8"	410	73	3"	3/8"	395
18	3"	1/16"	2,100	84	3 1/2"	1/2"	235
19	3 1/2"	1/16"	1,800	105	5"	5/8"	70
30	2"	1/8"	1600	107	7"	5/8	52

saber

The saber used in fencing competition has a maximum weight of 500 grams (but usually weighs less) and is at most 1,050 mm long, with a blade not longer than 880 mm. The guard must be small enough to pass through a hole 150 mm by 140 mm, keeping the flat of the blade parallel to the 150 mm sides of the hole.

While retaining its general dimensions, the fencing saber has lost weight as fencing has increasingly emphasized speed. In the fencing schools of early 20TH C Vienna, a saber had to weigh *at least* 500 grams.

The last of the working swords were the cavalry saber and the naval saber. The U.S. cavalry saber Model 1840 (first issued in 1840) was so heavy it got the name "Old Wristbreaker." Model 1860 was much lighter; that saber, with a 35 1/2" blade, was the one used in the Civil War.

The ceremonial swords worn by diplomats and military officers are sabers. Because they have been used to differentiate ranks, ceremonial sabers have been made in a bewildering array of sizes.

sack

1) In England, 13TH–19TH C, an important unit of mass used for wool. Thirteenth century documents define the sack as 28 stones each of 12 1/2 pounds avoirdupois, or 350 pounds, but its value was already shifting. Wholesale quantities of wool were weighed on the King's bal-

ance, and it was the custom to add extra wool until the balance tipped in the buyer's favor. Such a procedure is easily abused by a weighmaster who wishes to favor the buyer, since the scales can be as easily tipped by an extra ten pounds as an extra two. So London abolished this practice effective December 6, 1256. To compensate buyers for the use of exact weight, they were given a well-defined extra bit, called *tret* or *cloffe*, which was set at an extra four pounds for every hundred pounds purchased. A 350-pound purchase (the old sack) thus gained 14 pounds (4 lbs × 350/100), becoming 364 pounds. That weight was coincidentally almost the same as 500 *libbrae* of the city of Florence, one of England's most important customers in the wool trade. This new definition of the sack was legalized by Edward III in 1340, when he declared the sack to be 26 stones of 14 pounds each, establishing a value for both the stone and sack that survived for six centuries. But see ☞stone.

	wey	last
wey		6
sack (wool)	2	12

	clove *or* nail	stone	tod	hundredweight	sack (wool)
hundredweight					3 1⁄4
tod				4	13
stone			2	8	26
clove *or* nail		2	4	16	52
pounds	7	14	28	112	364

2) In Scotland, a unit of mass used for wool, 24 stones of 16 pounds each. **3)** In England, a unit of capacity used for coal, described in 1552 as equaling 4 bushels. An act of Parliament in 1730 defined the capacity of the sack as 3 bushels (the bushel had shrunk since 1552), and fixed the dimensions of the physical object: 50" long and at least 20" broad. Twenty-eight years later Parliament lengthened the sack by 2 inches. In the Act of 1824 establishing imperial measure, the sack was set at 3 heaped imperial bushels ≈ 136.3 liters.

For a full discussion of this and other English units, see R. D. Connor, *The Weights and Measures of England* (London: Her Majesty's Stationery Office, 1987).

saddles

Few manufactured objects must fit two creatures simultaneously. E. Hartley Edwards, a noted English saddler, wrote:

"I would regard my saddle both from the horse's viewpoint and my own in much the same light as I would regard my shoes. The latter are a very personal part of my apparel and have taken on the shape of *my* feet; and in the same way my saddle has moulded itself to one horse's back. I would not, therefore, want my saddle or shoes to be used by any other horse or person.

"I know that this is a perfection-ist outlook, but it is the correct one if the saddle is to fit the horse per-fectly. Where a saddle is used on a number of horses, it may initially, if the structure of the backs is roughly similar, fit all of them rea-sonably well, but it will ultimately never fit one of them really cor-rectly and it may even cause trouble in some cases. Many mod-ern saddles are termed 'All Pur-pose' or 'General Purpose.' This

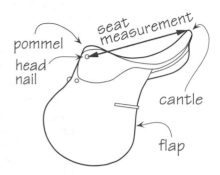

name applies to the variety of equestrian pursuits for which the makers claim the saddle is suitable; it does not mean that it fits all animals as some would-be purchasers think. No saddle yet made will fit *every* type or shape of equine back, just as no one pair of shoes will fit all human feet." (from *Saddlery, Modern Equipment for Horse and Stable* (NY: A. S. Barnes, 1963, by permission of the author).

A saddle takes its shape from a part called the "tree," which is usually made of laminated wood, sometimes combined with fiberglass. At one time all trees were entirely rigid, but in "springtrees" the front and rear of the tree are connected by flat strips of spring steel. An important feature of the tree are the points, rigid projections which extend from the front of the tree down over the horse's withers.

Trees are made in a range of widths to accommodate the broadness of the horse's back; manufacturers sometimes identify these sizes by numbers and sometimes by bloodlines, for example "thorough-bred/cross" will be narrower than "warmblood." Adjustable trees are also made: an Allen wrench inserted in an opening in the head of the saddle can make it broader or narrower.

To check tree sizing, put the saddle on the horse, placing it too far forward. Press down on the pommel and slide the saddle back until you feel it reach the natural resting point determined by the shape of the horse's back. Then check two things. First, the saddle should clear the horse's withers. Edwards suggests a mounted rider should be able to fit three fingers between the head of the saddle and the withers; others say two. Less clearance means the tree is probably too wide. Second, with the horse on level ground, the cantle should be an inch or more higher than the pommel (as much as 3" if the saddle has a deep seat). If it isn't, the tree is probably too narrow. If possible, fit should be checked by an experienced saddler with the rider present.

Beneath the tree are the two panels, a sort of cushion. Between the panels runs a channel which must be wide and deep enough to clear the horse's backbone. The adequacy of the channel should be checked periodically as the saddle ages. The remainder of the panel must contact the back. In many horses, the back under the front portion of the panels falls away from the top of the back in a noticeably concave curve. In such cases the bottom of a long panel will rest on the shoulder, holding the rest of the panel off the back. The solution is a shorter panel. In extreme cases, a ¾ panel may be required.

Although it is possible to adjust fit by adding or subtracting padding, this expedient should be approached cautiously. It is never a substitute for obtaining a saddle that actually fits. The object of the saddle is to distribute the rider's weight *evenly* over the back. Padding used to change the way a saddle sits will almost always result in excessive pressure under the pads.

Seat size, the most commonly given saddle measurement, is the distance in inches and half inches from a head nail to the center of the cantle. This dimension is fitted to the rider. In saddles with rigid trees it may be 14" to 18", sizes below 16" being for children. Springtree saddles are offered in fewer sizes, for example 15", 16½", 17½". The saddle should not, of course, be longer than the horse's back. Seat depth is a matter of personal preference. A rider may find the front-to-back contour of certain seats uncomfortable.

The flap length and position is also chosen to fit the rider. Short riders (under 5'4") may prefer short straight flaps; tall riders, or those with long thighs, long forward flaps.

safety pins

The common safety pin is made in 5 sizes, with the following lengths: #00: ¾"; #0: ⅞"; #1: 1 1/16"; #2: 1 ½"; #3: 2". Size 2 ½ is no longer made. Blanket pins are now 3" long, though they were 4" long in the 1890s.

sand

One definition of sand considers it to be all particles between 1/16 mm and 2 mm in diameter (but see ☞sedimentary particles). In commerce, the size of sand grains is often specified in ☞sieve numbers, for example, a contractor might order "30–200 sand." The source may also be specified. Beach sand, for example, whose grains are usually well-worn and almost spherical, does not make as strong a concrete as river sand does, whose grains are less-worn and have irregular shapes more likely to interlock with the cement matrix. Sand containing a lot of organic matter also makes poor concrete.

sandbag

The U.S. Army Corps of Engineers Standard sandbag is 14" × 26" and is intended to hold 40 pounds of sand. The bag is tested by dropping a filled bag onto a concrete floor from a height of 4 feet: once on its face, once on a side, and once on an end.

Experts recommend that bags used for flood control should be closed simply by folding over the end, so that except for the flat fold the entire inner surface of the bag lies next to sand. Such bags can be stacked like bricks, without hollows that may allow water to flow through. Bags closed with ties cannot be stacked together as tightly.

8 teeth per inch (8 TPI)
7 points per inch (7 PPI)
one inch

saws, saw blades

Two different systems are used to specify the number of teeth per inch. In the USA, the number of teeth in one inch is counted beginning at the bottom of a gullet. The count is either a whole number or, if the count ends on a point rather than a gullet, a whole number plus ½. The result is called teeth per inch, abbreviated TPI. In Europe, the count begins at the point of a tooth, not a gullet, and one counts the number of points within an inch. The result is called points per inch, abbr. PPI. For a circular saw blade, tooth count is simply the number of teeth on the blade.

Tooth count is determined by the use to which a saw will be put, though tooth shape, set, and other factors are also important. Saws for cutting green wood across the grain, such as loggers use, have a very small number of teeth per inch, sometimes less than one. Consumer saws for this purpose have about 3 TPI. Rip saws, for cutting seasoned wood with the grain, have about 4½ TPI, and crosscut saws, for cutting wood across the grain, have roughly 9 to 20 TPI.

Circular Saw Blades. Consumer blades are made in diameters of 4", 5½", 6½", 7", 7¼", 7½", 8", 8¼", 9", 10", and 12", all of the above to fit a ⅝" arbor. The most common size is 7¼" for portable saws, and 10" for consumer table and radial saws.

Scroll Saw Blades. Scroll saw blades are sold in sizes numbered from 0 to 12; the higher the number, the fewer the teeth. The smaller sizes are fragile and are used for veneer and other thin stock; the two largest sizes are typically used on stock ¾" or more thick. Between these extremes, the smaller the size number the smoother the cut.

Hacksaw Blades. The standard hacksaw blade is nominally 12" long (actually 12⅜"), with 11⅞" between the centers of the holes used to mount the blade. Ten inch blades are also made, and power hacksaws take sizes as large as 30".

Blades are made with 14 to 32 teeth per inch. As a rule of thumb, in cutting thin stock at least two teeth should be in contact with the work at all times.

scallops

Intending to protect the scallop fishery by reducing the catch of young scallops, a 1982 federal regulation made any catch that, by random check, contained more than 36.3 scallop meats per pound subject to seizure. The regulation is controversial; scallopers say they have no way of knowing the size of the meat until the shell is opened, at which point it's too late to throw the animal back.

Scallop meats are often treated with sodium tripolyphosphate, which makes them absorb water, and hence gain weight.

scoville unit

A unit used to express the pungency of peppers. Also called the scoville index or scoville heat unit. Abbr, SHU. In Scoville's original test, the substance principally responsible for pepper's bite, capascin, was extracted from a pepper with ethanol. The alcohol solution was then diluted with sweetened water until the pungency could no longer be detected by a human taster; the extent of the dilution gave the scoville unit.

In more modern tests specified by the ASTM, tasters compare a solution made from the pepper under test with standardized solutions of n-vanillyl-n-nonamide.

Another modern test dispenses with tasters and uses a high pressure liquid chromatograph, the results of which are expressed in *ASTA units* (named for the American Spice Trade Assn.).

Pepper type	Scoville units
bell peppers, pimentos	0
long green Anaheim	250–1,400
poblano	3,000
Hungarian yellow	4,000
jalapeño	3,500–4,500
serrano	7,000–25,000
chile de arbol	15,000–30,000
tabasco	30,000–50,000
santaka (Japan)	50,000–60,000
Mexican tabiche	100,000
cayenne	100,000–105,000
birdseye (India)	100,000–125,000
kumataka (Japan)	125,000–150,000
habanero	300,000

The search for a means of describing the hotness of peppers is quite old. Nahuatl, the language of the Aztecs, has six adjectives describing the hotness of peppers, in order of increasing pungency: *coco, cocopatic, cocopetz-patic, cocopetztic, copetzquauitl,* and *cocopalatic.*

screw drive systems

Every threaded fastener requires a means of turning it. It may have a head with a shape that a driver can engage, as a wrench fits a hex-head bolt or a nut, or it may have a shaped hole into which a driver can be inserted (fastener engineers call the hole the "recess").

Slotted
Screws with slotted heads appear in 16TH C illustrations. The advantages of the slotted head are that most people have a screwdriver that more or less fits them, the drivers can be reground easily, and a

hacksaw can easily cut a new slot. Otherwise the slotted head is easily the worst of all drive systems, and generally speaking is obsolete. Some of its deficiencies:

- A slotted screwdriver doesn't automatically line up with the slot; it is easy to get off center. The user gets little help in keeping the axis of the screwdriver aligned with the axis of the screw.
- The driver can engage the head in only two possible positions, at 180° to each other.
- The sides of most slotted screwdriver bits are tapered. Turning the bit in the slot tends to push it up and out of the slot. This is called "camout."

To add to the shortcomings of the slotted head, screwdrivers for slotted screws are usually described by the length of the shaft and the width of the tip—the crucial measurement, the tip's thickness, is not given. Bits are made tapered because each size of machine screw, for example, had its own slot width, and the only way of accommodating all screw sizes with a reasonable number of bit sizes was to taper the bit, so that one size of bit could wedge into several slot sizes. Any given tip width is sold in a range of thicknesses; the longer shafts usually have the thicker blades. Here for example, are some thicknesses found on currently available screwdrivers:

Tip width	Thickness
1/8"	0.012", 0.020"
3/16"	0.031", 0.037"
1/4"	0.030", 0.039", 0.042"
5/16"	0.039"
3/8"	0.055"

A tamper-proof slotted head design is used in low-tech areas where vandalism and theft are feared, such as window fixtures and public toilet stalls. Opposite quarters of the head are cut away so that a flat blade driver rotating counterclockwise has nothing to push against.

Cross Drive Systems

In all cross drive systems the driver will self-align with the fastener. Both the driver and fastener recess are tapered. Camout is possible and can ream the recess and destroy the bit.

Phillips.

The licensor is the American Screw Co. The Phillips system was invented for assembling aluminum aircraft, with the goal of preventing assemblers from tightening screws too much. The driver will cam out before that happens. The driver has a 123° point with a blunt tip and tapered wings.

Consumers are likely to think that any screw head with a cross drive recess is a Phillips. This can lead to problems.

Size	Fits these wood screws	Fits these machine & tapping screws
0	#0, #1	#0 and #1
1	#2–#4	#2–#4
2	#5–#9, some #10	#5–#10
3	some #10, #11–#16	#12, ¼", 5⁄16" if round head
4	#18, #20, #24	3⁄8", 9⁄16", plus 5⁄16" flat head
5	—	5⁄8", 3⁄4"

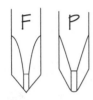

Frearson

A later cross drive system, referred to in ANSI standards as type II recess and sometimes called Reed & Prince, after the firm where the design originated. Today it is found mostly on marine hardware and other special uses, such as the screws that hold inserts in the faces of golf clubs. In the drawing, note the difference between the Frearson and Phillips points: the Frearson has a sharper V (75°) than Phillips. Any Frearson driver fits all Frearson screws.

ISO Metric Cross Drive

A cross drive system found in German and Japanese electronic equipment. Driver sizes are #000, #00, #0, #1, #2, and #3.

Pozidriv®

Identified in ANSI standards as type IA. Because it doesn't cam out, great torque can be applied. Pozidriv screws can be turned by Phillips screwdrivers, but Pozidriv drivers won't turn Phillips screws.

Size	Fits these wood screws	Fits these machine and tapping screws
0	#0, #1	#0, #1
1	#2, #3, #4	#2, #3, #4
2	#5–#9	#5–#10
3	#10–#16	#12 and ¼" 5⁄16" in some head styles
4	#18–#24	5⁄16" to ½"

Supadriv®

Supadriv drivers will turn Pozidriv heads.

Regular Polygons: Square, Hex, etc.

Square Head

Square nuts and four-sided heads are mainly found in farm equipment and on lag screws.

Robertson

A square recess design, invented by P. L. Robertson in 1908, whose advantages are resistance to camout and 4 possible positions for the driver. The Ford Motor Company used Robertson screws in the Model A, but dropped them when Robertson refused to grant exclusive rights to the design. Robertson also refused to license other fastener manufacturers, so the design spread very slowly. Many recreational vehicles built in the 1950s use these screws. In Canada, most wood screws have square recess heads, and in the 1980s they began to catch on in the USA.

Size	Fits these wood screws
0	#3 and #4
1	#5, #6, #7
2	#8, #9, #10
3	#12, #14

Scrulox
Similar to Robertson, and driver sizes fit the same screw sizes.

Five-sided
Five-sided heads are used only in situations in which a fastener that cannot be removed by commonly-available tools is needed, as in the caps and valves of fire hydrants.

Hexagonal head
Probably the most common of all fastener heads, hex heads are also very old. Fasteners with hexagonal heads were used to hold armor together in the fifteenth century.

To find the size of wrench needed to turn a hex head (or hex recess), measure from flat to flat, not from point to point.

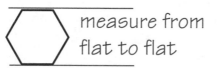 measure from flat to flat 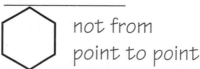 not from point to point

Allen (hex recess)

Sizes are the flat-to-flat dimension. Consumers encounter Allen heads chiefly in set screws and cap screws.

Inch Sizes	Set Screws	Cap Head Socket Screws		Metric Sizes (mm)	Set Screws	Cap Head Socket Screws
0.028"	#0	—		0.7	M1.4, M1.6 M1.7	—
0.035"	#1, #2	—		0.9	M2, M2.3	—

Inch Sizes	Set Screws	Cap Head Socket Screws
0.050"	#3, #4	#0
1/16"	#5, #6	#1
5/64"	#8	#2, #3
3/32"	#10	#4, #5
7/64"	—	#6
1/8"	1/4"	—
9/64"	—	#8
5/32"	5/16"	#10
3/16"	3/8"	1/4"
7/32"	7/16"	—
1/4"	1/2"	5/16"
5/16"	5/8"	3/8"
3/8"	3/4"	7/16"
7/16"	—	—
1/2"	7/8"	5/8
9/16"	1"	—
5/8"	—	3/4"

Metric Sizes (mm)	Set Screws	Cap Head Socket Screws
1.27	M2.5, M2.6	M1.4
1.5	M3	M1.6, M1.7, M2
2	M4	M2.3, M2.5, M2.6
2.5	M5	M3
3	M6	M4
4	M8	M5
4.5	—	—
5	M10	M6
5.5	—	—
6	—	—
8	—	—
10	—	—

Complex Shapes

Clutch Head

Originated by United Screw and Bolt. The recess in clutch heads looks like a bowtie. In a pinch, a clutch head screw can be driven by a slotted screwdriver. A worn tip on a driver can easily be restored by grinding off the end. Clutch head screws were popular in mobile home construction and electric motors. The size is the diameter in inches of the bit point. Sizes are 1/8", 5/32", 3/16", 1/4", 5/16".

Bristol Spline

Originated by the Bristol Co. A recess with 6 flutes (except for 2 sizes that have 4 flutes). Sized in inches: 0.048", 0.060", 0.069" (4 flute), 0.072", 0.076" (4 flute), 0.096", 0.111", 0.145", 0.183".

Torx®

The Torx system was introduced in 1965 by Camcar. This style of head is now very common in trucks and automobiles. The walls of the recess are not tapered and the drivers greatly outlast similar hex head drivers.

Driver size designations for Torx recesses begin with a T; those for the less-common external drivers begin with an E. Tamperproof Torx heads are the same as the internal recess heads, with an added post in the center that prevents ordinary Torx drivers from entering the recess. Tamperproof sizes begin with TT.

The shaded lines in the table indicate sizes whose future use is discouraged.

Size	Most types of inch fasteners	Inch socket set screws	Most types of metric fasteners	Metric socket set screws
T-1	—	#0	—	M1.6, M1.8
T-2	—	#1	—	M2
T-3	—	#2	—	M2.2
T-4	—	—	—	—
T-5	—	#3	—	M2.5
T-6	—	#4	M2	M3
T-7	—	#5, #6	—	M3.5
T-8	—	#8	M2.5	M4
T-10	#4, #5	#10	M2.9, M3	M5
T-15	#6, #8	—	M3.5	—
T-20	#8, #10	1/4"	M4, M4.2	M6
T-25	#10, #12	—	M4.8, M5, M5.5	M7
T-27	—	5/16"	M4.5, M5 cap screws	M8
T-30	1/4"	—	M6, M6.3	—
T-40	5/16"	3/8"	M8	M10
T-45	3/8"	1/2"	—	M12
T-50	—	—	M10	M14
T-55	1/2"	5/8"	—	—
T-60	3/4"	3/4"	—	—
T-70	—	7/8", 1"	—	M22, M24

Line Head

A Japanese system, found in IBM PS/2 computers and Nintendo games. Driver sizes for the internal recess design begin with the prefix ALR. Five sizes are available in the USA: ALR2, ALR3, ALR4, ALR5, and ALR6. There is also a tamper-resistant line head design, with a post in the middle of the recess that prevents an ordinary ALR driver from entering. Available (in the USA) drivers are ALR3T, ALR4T, ALR5T, ALR6T.

Designations of the external head begin "ALH"; driver sizes available in the USA run from ALH2 through ALH6.

Combination Heads

Fasteners are often made with heads that combine two drive systems, usually because the tools of the service people in the field are more old-fashioned than those the factory uses. Examples include hex head cross drive, slotted internal Torx, hex head internal Torx, and so on.

screw thread systems for fasteners

In hardware stores, a machine screw or bolt is described by length, the type of head and the thread. The convention for describing a fastener's threads is to give a gauge number if the bolt is smaller than a quarter-inch in diameter, otherwise by the diameter in fractions of an inch, followed by a hyphen and then the number of threads per inch. So, for example, a "2-inch quarter-twenty bolt" would be 2" long, have a nominal diameter of a quarter of an inch, and have twenty threads to the inch. A typical smaller fastener could be "eight thirty-two" (8-32), "8" being the gauge number and "32" the number of threads per inch.

Knowing a bolt's diameter isn't enough to tell what nut will fit it. A bolt a quarter-inch in diameter might have 20, 27, 28 or 32 threads per inch, and a nut that fit one would not fit another. In a thread series, the relationship between diameter and number of threads per inch is standardized, the two most common series in the USA being Unified National Coarse (UNC) and Unified National Fine (UNF). A more complete sizing of a quarter-inch bolt's thread might be ¼-20 UNC or ¼-28 UNF. A few examples:

UNC	UNF
¼-20	¼-28
5/16-18	5/16-24
3/8-16	3/8-24

A brief history of the origin of these thread series is given below. American thread sizes up to 1 inch in diameter are given in the table that begins on page 248.

Most stores now also sell machine screws and bolts in metric sizes. The metric sizes are described in a different way, for example "M3.5 × 1.2". The number following "M" is the diameter in millimeters; the number following "×" is the pitch (also in millimeters), which is the distance from one thread to the corresponding point on the next thread. Metric sizes are described on page 250.

The thread situation, though complicated now, was much worse in the past. If you deal with imported equipment or anything manufactured before the end of the Second World War, read the sections on national series below.

Tolerance classes. The standards for a thread series include specifications of tolerances. Most specify several different classes, because for some uses a close fit is essential, while achieving it for other uses would be a waste of money. For example, the old American National series had four classes of tolerance: Loose-fit (class 1), Free-fit (class 2), Medium-Fit (class 3), and Close-fit (class 4).

Handedness. Almost all threaded fasteners tighten when the head or nut is rotated clockwise. That is, as a viewer turns a nut clockwise it moves away from the viewer. Such a fastener is said to have a right-hand thread; all screw fasteners are assumed to be right-hand unless otherwise specified. Left-hand threads are usually found only on rotating machinery. For example, the axles of bicycle pedals screw into threaded holes in the cranks. In a pair of pedals one will have a right-hand thread and the other a left-hand thread. That way the rotation of the pedals doesn't tend to un-screw their axles.

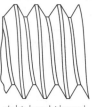 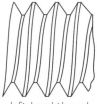

right-hand thread   left-hand thread

To designate a left-hand thread, the letters "LH" are placed after the class of fit. No comment is necessary for a right-hand thread.

Multiple threads. Fasteners can be made with two or three parallel threads instead of the usual one, although no standard series in-cludes such a thread. The advan-tage of multiple threading is that the bolt will be stronger than a sin-gle thread bolt whose nut would advance the same distance in one

single thread   double thread

turn—or conversely, that the nut will advance twice as far in a single turn on a double thread bolt than it would on a single thread bolt with the same root diameter. Double-threading is commonly found on drywall screws (though of course they don't take nuts).

To designate a multiple thread the word "DOUBLE" (or "TRIPLE," and so on) is placed after the class of fit.

British Screw Thread Series

Modern machining was born in the industrial flowering in late 18TH C Great Britain. The modern lathe, capable of cutting threads with great precision, was invented in 1797 by Henry Maudsley. Even today, for most purposes there is no need for any greater precision than that achieved by Maudslay. With the lathe, making threaded fasteners became much easier, but everyone made them to their own pattern. If you lost a nut from a machine and the shop that made it was out of business, a new nut would have to be custom made to match the existing bolt.

Maudslay took on as an apprentice, Jospeh Whitworth, who proved exceptionally talented. While he was with Maudslay, Whitworth in-vented the method for producing a true plane surface in steel, one of the fundamental operations in precision machining. He next worked at Joseph Clements, where they were trying to build Babbage's calcu-lating engine, the first computer, and finally set up shop for himself as a toolmaker. By 1859 he had produced a machine capable of measure-ments to one two-millionth of an inch.

Whitworth set himself the task of devising a standard for threads. He had his own ideas about what would work best, but being a pragmatist he also collected bolts from all over England, noting which sizes experience had shown to be most useful, and the results of various thread forms. In 1841 he proposed as a standard a thread form with an

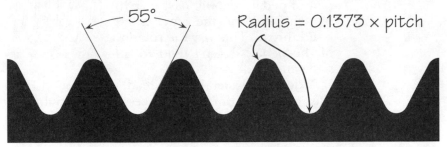

included angle of 55°, and the tops and bottoms of the threads rounded with a radius equal to 0.1373 times the pitch. Due in part to the immense prestige Whitworth gained from the display of his machines at the Crystal Palace Exhibition of 1851, Whitworth's system was in general use in Great Britain by 1860. Later a second series with finer threads (BSF) was added.

In 1884 the British Association for the Advancement of Science adopted a thread form and series, primarily for use in precision equipment. It was inspired by one used in the Swiss watch and clock industry, and was formerly sometimes called the Swiss Small Screw Thread System; but is now just referred to as the BA series. Like the Whitworth thread, it has a rounded root and crest, but the included angle is 47.5° and the radius is 0.1818... times the pitch.

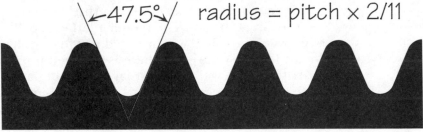

Despite the date and the British sponsorship, the BA is a metric series. Not only is it based on the meter, but the thread frequency is specified in terms of round numbers in the pitch sequence, with threads per meter allowed to fall where it may.

The British Association thread played a role similar to that of the ASME series in the United States, that is, it filled in sizes below a quarter-inch. The sizes most used were the even-numbered ones between 0 and 10, inclusive. The very small sizes, from 17 up, were rarely used. The British Standards Institution discouraged the use of #0 BA in favor of the 7/32" BSF.

British Standard Whitworth			British Association (BA)		
Diameter, inches	Threads per inch BSW	Threads per inch BSF	Gauge Number	Major Diameter, mm	Pitch, mm
1/8	40	—	23	0.33	0.090
3/16	24	32	22	0.37	0.098
7/32	—	28	21	0.42	0.11
1/4	20	26	20	0.48	0.12
9/32	—	26	19	0.54	0.14
5/16	18	22	18	0.62	0.15
3/8	16	20	17	0.70	0.17
7/16	14	18	16	0.79	0.19
1/2	12	16	15	0.90	0.21
9/16	12	16	14	1.0	0.23
5/8	11	14	11	1.5	0.31
11/16	11	14	10	1.7	0.35
3/4	10	12	9	1.9	0.39
13/16	10	12	8	2.2	0.43
7/8	9	11	7	2.5	0.48
15/16	9	—	6	2.8	0.53
1	8	10	5	3.2	0.59
(Additional sizes are defined to 6" in diameter.)		(Defined to 4" diameter)	4	3.6	0.66
			3	4.1	0.73
			2	4.7	0.81
			1	5.3	0.90
			0	6.0	1.00

United States Thread Series

Americans experienced the same problems from lack of thread stand-ardization that Britain did. The challenge was taken up by William Sellers, a member of an eminent family of American "mechanicians" (his grandfather made the plates for the Continental Congress' currency). To William himself we owe, among other things, the color "machinery gray." While others were decorating their machinery, he insisted on painting his a uniform light gray, so as not to obscure the functions of the parts. Sellers specified a thread form and a graded series of nuts and bolts using it.

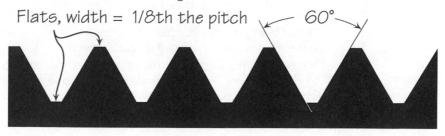

Flats, width = 1/8th the pitch   60°

In 1864, a committee of the Franklin Institute recommended the adoption of Sellers' system of screw threads. The thread form became known as the "Franklin thread," or more commonly, "Sellers' thread," and later as the "United States Standard Thread." It became the basis of the French standard thread, and then of the Système International thread. In May 1924 it was designated the "American Standard Thread."

The differences between Seller's thread and Whitworth's in part reflected the states of the art of machining in their countries: Whitworth's is elegant and Seller's is let's-get-the-job-done. Determining a 55° angle requires good measuring tools; a child with a sharp pencil and a good pair of compasses can create a very accurate 60° angle. The second major difference between the two thread forms is that in Seller's thread the crests and roots (the tops and bottoms of the threads) are flattened. The flattened roots was a bad choice. Such angular joins concentrate stress, and the manufacturing process results in high stresses at the roots of threads anyway. The result is cracks and the failure of the fastener. In Sellers' day this was not much of a problem, for two reasons. One was that most machinery was stationary and the weight of a bolt rarely mattered. If a bolt broke it could be replaced with a larger one. The second reason was that thread roots tend to be rounded anyway as the tools that make the bolts become worn. But later, with airplanes, "just put in a bigger bolt" was not a satisfactory solution, and aerospace engineers finally introduced an American thread form (UNJ) with rounded roots. By changing to a UNJ thread form, for example, an American car manufacturer finally solved a persistent problem with connecting rod breakage.

Manufacturers adopted Sellers' thread form, but rejected other parts of his proposed series, such as his formulas for the size of square and hexagonal nuts and bolt heads, and they chose to use a different number of threads per inch for the 11/16", 13/16", and 15/16" bolts.

In 1907 the American Society of Mechanical Engineers (ASME) defined two additional series that used Seller's thread, numbering the sizes by gauge numbers from 0 to 30. In both series the major diameter increased by 0.013" with each size from 0 to 10, and by 0.026" between gauges above #10. Threads per inch for the ASME Standard Series were calculated from:

$$\text{threads per inch} = \frac{6.5}{\text{diameter} + 0.02}$$

The ASME Standard Special Series used the same major diameters with different numbers of threads per inch, lower in the sizes below #10, sometimes higher in the larger sizes. All the ASME gauges, including the obsolete ones, are included in the table on page 248.

American National Series. When the American Standards Assn. (now ANSI) was formed, one of its first undertakings was to pull together a set of thread standards for the United States that would be consistent and would provide for most needs. The thread form and most sizes were based on the old United States Standard. Sizes below ¼" were added from the 1907 ASME standard. A Fine-thread Series (NF) was taken from the "Regular Screw-Thread Series" of the Society of Automotive Engineers, with sizes below ¼" added from the ASME "Fine-thread Series." Later the SAE Extra-Fine Series was added as the American National Extra Fine Thread Series (NEF).

Fixed Pitch Series. In all the series discussed thus far, the number of threads per inch decreases as the diameter increases. It became obvious to engineers using very large bolts on bridges and similar structures that this practice makes no sense for very large bolts. So for large bolts three series were defined in which the pitch never changes; they are simply lists of standard diameters. All the bolts in the 8N series have 8 threads per inch, all in the 12N series have 12 threads per inch (used in boilers and for thin nuts on shafts), and in 16N, sixteen threads per inch (used where precise positioning of a big nut is required, for example, nuts used to adjust the position of big bearings). These constant-pitch series were later replaced by constant-pitch Unified Thread series (see below), which have the Unified thread form and are designated 4UN, 8UN, and so on.

Other. In addition to series standardized by national organizations, other series enjoyed a long life as manufacturers' standards. As late as 1950, manufacturers made a stovebolt series that ran ⅛-32, 5/32-28, 3/16-24, 7/32-22, ¼-18, 5/16-18, ⅜-16, 7/16-14, ½-13.

Unified Thread Series. The differences between the American and British thread forms became a painful problem during the Second World War, especially in manufacturing and repairing airplane engines. In 1948, representatives of Britain, Canada and the United

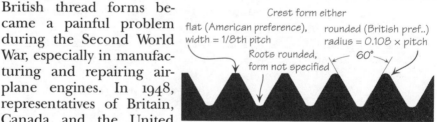

States agreed on a Unified Standard. In the compromise, the British accepted the 60° thread angle, and the Americans accepted rounded roots and optionally rounded crests. Five classes of fit were defined. For most practical purposes, the new fasteners were interchangeable with those manufactured under the old American National Standards.

In 1955, the same countries met to agree on a standard for miniature threads, an issue the Americans had left to individual manufacturers. The Waltham Watch Co. had a metric series of 12 screws peculiar to itself, and the Elgin National Watch Co. produced 27 miniature screws based on the inch, replete with sizes with left-hand threads.

The scheme adopted for the Unified Miniature Threads was based on the meter and on the recommendations of the ISO regarding sizes.

Unlike the designations for other metric screws, the designation is the major diameter of the screw followed by UNM.

Unified Miniature Threads (UNM)			
Size designation (diameter in mm)		Threads per inch	Pitch (millimeters)
1st pref.	2nd pref.		
0.30 UNM		318	0.080
	0.35 UNM	282	0.090
0.40 UNM		254	0.100
	0.45 UNM	254	0.100
0.50 UNM		203	0.125
	0.55 UNM	203	0.125
0.60 UNM		169	0.150
	0.70 UNM	145	0.175
0.80 UNM		127	0.200
	0.90 UNM	113	0.225
1.00 UNM		102	0.250
	1.10 UNM	102	0.250
1.20 UNM		102	0.250
	1.40 UNM	85	0.300

To summarize the recent American inch thread series, with their symbols:

NC   American National Coarse Thread (obsolete)
NF   American National Fine Thread (obsolete)
NEF   American National Extra Fine Thread (obsolete)
8N   American National 8 Pitch (obsolete)
12N   American National 12 Pitch (obsolete)
16N   American National 16 Pitch (obsolete)
NS   Special Threads of American National Form (obsolete)
SB   Manufacturers Stovebolt Standard Thread (obsolete)
UNC   Unified Coarse Thread
UNF   Unified Fine Thread
xUN   Unified diameter-pitch combination (x = 8, 12, 16 etc., e.g, 8UN)
UNS   Unified threads of special diameters, pitches, and length of engagement
UNM   Unified Miniature
UNR   UN with a mandatory rounded root on external threads
UNJ   UNR with a larger rounded root, internal threads with increased minor diameter

The sizes in the first column that are not followed by an inch mark are American Standard Screw gauges. Shading indicates sizes no longer in use or whose use is discouraged by standards organizations.

The obsolete constant-pitch series 8N, 12N etc. and the current 8UN, 12UN, etc series are not shown. Up to 1 inch they included 9/16-12N, 5/8-12N, 11/16-12N, 3/4-12N, 3/4-16N, 15/16-12N, 15/16-16N, 7/8-12N, 7/8-16N, and 1" in 8N, 12N, and 16N.

The NS series is a catch-all category for threads which have the American Standard form, but whose pitches are not in the National Coarse or National Fine series. The tap drill sizes are listed in the order in which the tpi are listed in the previous column.

American Screw Thread Series

Gauge and fractional sizes	Major diam.	Clearance Drill	NC & UNC tpi	Tap drill for UNC	NF & UNF tpi	Tap drill for UNF	NEF	NS	Tap drill for NS	Nut Size
0000		#73	160	1/64"	—	—	—			
000		#63	120	#71	—	—	—			3/32"
00		#55	90	#65	—	—	—			3/32"
0	0.060	#52	—	—	80	3/64"	—			5/32"
1	0.073	#48	64	#52	72	#53	—	56	54	5/32"
2	0.086	#43	56	#50	64	#50	—	—	—	3/16"
3	0.099	#38	48	#47	56	#45	—	—	—	3/16"
4	0.112	#33	40	#43	48	#42	—	32, 36	45, 44	1/4"
5	0.125	#30	40	#39	44	#37	—	36	40	1/4"
6	0.138	#28	32	#36	40	#33	—	36	34	5/16"
7	0.151	#24	—	—	—	—	—	30, 32, 36	31, 31, 1/8"	5/16"
8	0.164	#19	32	#29	36	#29	—	30, 40	30, 28	11/32"
9	0.177	#15	—	—	—	—	—	24, 30, 32	29, 27, 26	11/32"
10	0.190	#11	24	#25	32	#21	—	28, 30	23, 22	3/8"
12	0.216	#2	24		28		—	32	13	7/16"
14	0.242	D					—	20, 24	10, 7	7/16"
1/4"	0.250	1/4" or E	20	#7	28	#3	32	24, 27, 32	4, 3, 7/32"	7/16"
16	0.268	I	—	—	—	—	—	18, 20, 22	7/32", 2	1/2"
18	0.294	M	—	—	—	—	—	18, 20	B, D	9/16"
5/16"	0.3125	O	18	F	24	I	32	20, 27, 32	17/64, J, 9/32	9/16"
20	0.320	P						16, 18, 20	G, 17/64, I	5/8"
22	0.346	S						16, 18	9/32, L	5/8"
24	0.372	V						16, 18	5/16, O	5/8"

American Screw Thread Series

Gauge and frac- tional sizes	Major diam.	Clear- ance Drill	NC & UNC tpi	Tap drill for UNC	NF & UNF tpi	Tap drill for UNF	NEF	NS	Tap drill for NS	Nut Size
3/8"	0.375	V	16	5/16"	24	Q	32	20, 27		5/8"
26	0.398	Y						14, 16	21/64, R	11/16"
28	0.424	7/16"						14, 16	T, 23/64	11/16"
7/16"	0.4375	7/16"	14	U	20	25/64"	28	24, 27		
30	0.450	29/64"						14, 16	V, 25/64	7/8"
1/2"	0.5000	1/2"	13†	27/64"	20	29/64"	28	12, 24, 27		
			12							3/4"
9/16"	0.5625	9/16"	12	31/64"	18	33/64"	24	27		
5/8"	0.6250	5/8"	11	17/32"	18	37/64"	24	12, 27		
11/16"	0.68753	11/16"					24			
3/4"	0.7500		10	21/32"	16		20	12, 27		1 1/8"
7/8"	0.8750		9	49/64"	14		20	12, 18, 27		1 5/16"
1"	1.0000		8	7/8"	14		20	12, 27		1 1/2"

† In the Unified Series the 1/2" size has 12 threads per inch, but the American Standard retains 13 threads per inch.

Metric Thread Series

Since the meter was intended as a global standard from its conception, one might expect that thread series based on the meter would be fewer and more standard than those based on the inch. That isn't the case; there have been many metric thread standards.

A metric thread designation is something like "M12 × 1.75". The "M" identifies a metric screw. The "12" is the diameter of the screw in millimeters, and the "1.75" is the pitch, the distance from any thread to the corresponding part of the next thread.

Most present day metric threads are based on a series of ISO standards. The thread profile is defined in ISO 68, tolerances in ISO standard 965/1, and so on. National organizations then define national metric thread series conforming to the ISO standards, but sometimes with local additions and amendments. In the USA, ANSI has defined M-Profile screws (ANSI B1.13M-1983). Finding there was no ISO standard for carriage bolts, the ANSI committee specified a metric carriage bolt. In the USA, an M10 hex head screw measures 15 mm across the flats, while the ISO standard calls for 16 mm. Despite such small differences, for practical purposes recently manufactured metric screws can be interchanged successfully regardless of where they were made.

In addition to the threads shown in the following table, there are metric constant-pitch series, with pitches of 6, 4, 3, 2, 1.5, 1, and 0.75 mm.

Spark plugs, even currently manufactured ones, use some metric threads not in the ISO series.

Metric Screw Thread Series

(All dimensions in millimeters.)

Major Diameter				Pitch (distance from thread to thread)								
ISO 1st pref.	ISO 2nd pref.	ISO 3rd pref.	Non-ISO	French[1]	old metric fine[2]	old metric coarse[3]	Löwenherz[4]	ISO Coarse	ISO Fine	JIS	DIN Fine	DIN Standard
1				(0.25)	0.2		0.25	0.25	0.2			
	1.1			—	—		—	0.25	0.2			
1.2				(0.25)	0.2		0.25	0.25	0.2			
	1.4			(0.3)	0.2		0.30	0.30	0.2			
1.6				(0.3)	—		—	0.35	0.2			
			1.7	—	0.2		0.35	—	—			
	1.8			(0.4)	—		—	0.35	0.25			
2				(0.4)	0.25		0.40	0.40				
	2.2			(0.45)			—	0.45	0.35			
			2.3	—	0.25		0.40	—	—			
2.5				(0.45)	—		—	0.45	0.35			
			2.6	—	0.35		0.45					
3				0.5 (0.6)	0.35		0.50	0.5	0.35	0.6	0.35	0.5
	3.5			—	0.35		0.60		0.35			
4				0.75	0.5		0.70	0.70	0.5	0.75	0.5	0.7
	4.5			—	0.5		0.75		0.5			
5				0.75 (0.9)	0.5		0.80	0.80	0.5	0.9	0.5	0.8
		5.5		—			0.90	—	0.5			
6				1	0.75	1	1.00	1.00	0.75	1	0.75	1
	7			1	0.75	1	1.10	1.00	0.75			
8				1	1	1.25	1.20	1.25	1	1.25	1.0	1.25
		9		1	1	1.25	1.30	1.25	—			
10				1.5	1	1.5	1.40	1.5	1.25	1.25	1.0	1.5
		11		—			—	1.5	—			
12				1.5	1.5	1.75	1.60	1.75	1.25	1.5	1.5	1.75
	14			2.0	1.5	2	1.80	2	1.5	1.5	1.5	2.0

Metric Screw Thread Series

(All dimensions in millimeters.)

Major Diameter				Pitch (distance from thread to thread)								
ISO 1st pref.	ISO 2nd pref.	ISO 3rd pref.	Non-ISO	French[1]	old metric fine[2]	old metric coarse[3]	Löwenherz[4]	ISO Coarse	ISO Fine	JIS	DIN Fine	DIN Standard
		15					—					
	16			2.0	1.5	2	2.00	2.0	1.5	1.5	1.5	2.0
		17					—					
	18			2.5	1.5	2.5	2.20	2.5	1.5			
20				2.5	1.5	2.5	2.40	2.5	1.5			
	22			2.5	1.5	2.5	2.80	2.5	1.5			
24				3.0	2	3	2.80	3	2			
		25					—					
		26		3.0			3.20					
	27				2	3	—	3.0				
		28		3.0			3.20					
30				3.5	2	3.5	3.60	3.5				

1. French Standard Thread, which has been superseded by the ISO series. The values in parentheses belong to a second, more recent French series which conformed to international metric specifications except for screws with a diameter of less than 6 mm. One peculiarity of this series is that screws under 3 mm in diameter were allowed to have a thread angle of either 50 or 60 degrees.
2. The fine pitch thread series that complemented the series in column 3.
3. The thread series adopted in 1898 by an international congress held at Zurich (the Congrès International pour l'Unification des Filetages). The thread form is similar to the United States Standard thread, except that the roots are rounded. An ancestor of the present ISO series.
4. The Löwenherz thread series was used by instrument makers, mainly in Germany.

Future Threads

One might expect that after 150 years so seemingly simple a thing as the bolt would have been brought to perfection, but that is not the case. All the thread forms mentioned so far share one characteristic: they are symmetrical. But when a bolt is tightened, the forces on the two sides of the thread differ. That alone suggests that an asymmetrical thread form might be better, and tests show that some asymmetrical thread forms are stronger. The U.S. Space Shuttle, for example, uses bolts with an asymmetric thread form. In time all threaded fasteners may have forms subtly different from those we use today.

screws, wood For many years American wood screws were made to two different standards, one a series that originated with the American Screw Co., and the other from the Asa I. Cook Co. In both series, sizes were indicated by gauge numbers, which went up to #30. The overall dimensions in the two series were the same, but the number of threads differed slightly. When an American Standard for wood screws was adopted, most of the diameters were within a few thousandths of an inch of the old dimensions, but the sizes extended only to #24.

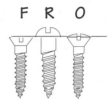

Lengths. The length of a wood screw is measured from the tip of the point to the surface of the material into which the screw is driven, which is the head's widest part. So the length of a flat head wood screw is measured from the tip to the top of the head, but the length of a round head screw is measured from the tip to the bottom of the head. The thread extends 2⁄3rds the length of the screw.

In the table below, the unshaded area indicates commonly available sizes. Letters within the cells indicate which head styles are made in that gauge and length: "F" for flat head, "O" for oval head, and "R" for round head. The last two columns indicate matching screwdriver sizes. The Phillips sizes are exact. For slotted screws the width of the tip is given; because a given tip width is often made in several thicknesses, these are only a rough guide.

American Wood Screws
Length in Inches

	$\frac{1}{4}$	$\frac{3}{8}$	$\frac{1}{2}$	$\frac{5}{8}$	$\frac{3}{4}$	$\frac{7}{8}$	1	$1\frac{1}{4}$	$1\frac{1}{2}$	$1\frac{3}{4}$	2	$2\frac{1}{4}$	$2\frac{1}{2}$	$2\frac{3}{4}$	3	$3\frac{1}{2}$	4	$4\frac{1}{2}$	5	Min. slot width	Slot. tip	Ph. bit #
0	FR	FR																		0.016	3/32	0
1	FR	FR	FR																	0.019	1/8	0
2	FR	FR	FR	FR	FR															0.023	1/8	1
3	FR	FRO	FR	FR	FR	FR	FR	FR												0.027	1/8	1
4	FR	FRO	FRO	FRO	FRO	FR	FR	FR	FR											0.031	3/16	1
5		FR	FRO	FRO	FRO	FR	FRO	FR	FR											0.035	3/16	2
6		FR	FRO	FRO	FRO	FR	FRO	FRO	FRO	FRO	FR	FR	FR							0.039	3/16	2
7		FR	FRO	FRO	FRO	FRO	FRO	FRO	FRO	FRO	FR	FR	FR							0.039	3/16	2
8		FR	FRO	FRO	FRO	FRO	FRO	FRO	FRO	FRO	FR	FR	FR	FR						0.045	1/4	2
9			FR	FR	FRO	FRO	FRO	FRO	FRO	FRO	FR	FR	FR	FR	FR					0.045	1/4	2
10			FR	FR	FRO	FRO	FRO	FRO	FRO	FRO	FRO	FR	FR	FR	FR	FR				0.050	5/16	2, 3*
11			FR	FR	FR	FRO	FRO	FRO	FRO	FRO	FR	F	F	F						0.050	3/8	3
12				FR	FR	FRO	FRO	FRO	FRO	FRO	FRO	FRO	FR	FR	FR	FR				0.056	3/8	3
14					FR	FRO	FRO	FRO	FRO	FRO	FRO	FRO	FR	FR	FR	FR	F	F		0.064	3/8	3
16						FR	FR	FRO	FRO	FRO	FR	FR	F	FR	FR	FR	F	F		0.064	3/8	3
18								F	FRO	FRO	FRO	F	FR	F	FR	F	F	F	F	0.072	3/8	4
20									FRO	FRO	FRO	F	FR	F	F	F	F	F	F	0.072	3/8	4
24														F	F	F	F	F	F	0.081	3/8	4

*Some head styles in this size take a #2 Phillips and others a #3.

Pilot Holes for American Standard Wood Screws

Screw gauge	Body dia. (inches)	Shank pilot hole (inches)	Pilot hole in softwood (inches)	Pilot hole in hardwood (inches)
0	0.060	1/16	1/64	1/32
1	0.073	5/64	1/32	1/32
2	0.086	3/32	1/32	3/64
3	0.099	7/64	3/64	1/16
4	0.112	7/64	3/64	1/16
5	0.125	1/8	1/16	5/64
6	0.138	9/64	1/16	5/64
7	0.151	5/32	1/16	3/32
8	0.164	11/64	5/64	3/32
9	0.177	3/16	5/64	7/64
10	0.190	3/16	3/32	7/64
11	0.203	13/64	3/32	1/8
12	0.216	7/32	7/64	1/8
14	0.242	1/4	7/64	9/64
16	0.268	17/64	9/64	5/32
18	0.294	19/64	9/64	3/16
20	0.320	21/64	11/64	13/64
24	0.372	3/8	3/16	7/32

scruple

A unit of mass in the USA, 18TH C–20TH C, and in the UK, = 20 grains = 1/3 drachm ≈ 1.2959782 grams. See ☞apothecaries weight. In the UK, use of the scruple in trade ended on January 1, 1971 (Weights and Measures Act, 1963, reaffirmed in the Weights and Measures Acts of 1976 and 1985).

The symbol for the scruple is Э, which is very ancient, appearing in manuscripts of the Roman era. It is sometimes followed by an S, which stands for the Latin *semis*, half. So ЭS is half a scruple.

second

The unit of time in SI, the duration of 9,192,631,770 periods of the radiation corresponding to the transition between two hyperfine levels of the ground state of the cesium-133 atom (13th CGPM, 1967). In scientific work it is abbreviated "s", but often "sec" in other contexts. Formerly 1/86,400 of the mean solar day. See ☞time for a discussion of changes in the definition of the second.

section

In the USA and the prairie provinces of Canada, 19TH–20TH C, a unit of land area, = 1 square mile = 640 acres ≈ 259 hectares.

sedimentary particles

One well-known classification of "detrital particles" was published by C. K. Wentworth in 1922:

Name	Particle diameter
boulder	over 256 mm
cobble	64–256 mm
pebble	2–64 mm
sand	1/16–2 mm
silt	1/256–1/16 mm
clay-sized particle	less than 1/256 mm

The Udden system is a refinement of Wentworth's:

boulder	over 256 mm
cobble	64–256 mm
pebble	4–64 mm
granule	2–4 mm
very coarse sand	1–2 mm
medium sand	0.5–1 mm
fine sand	0.125–0.5 mm
very fine sand	0.0625–0.125 mm
silt	0.0039–0.0625 mm
clay	0.00024–0.0039 mm
colloid	less than 0.0024 mm

In the phi grade scale, particles are sized by the negative logarithm to the base 2 of the particle diameter in millimeters. So, for example, a particle 256 mm in diameter would have a phi value of minus 8, and one 1/16 of a mm in diameter would be 4.

serving

In November 1991 the U.S. Food and Drug Administration defined for the purpose of package labeling, standard serving sizes for 131 categories of food. Any package that contains less than 2 servings is considered a single-serving container. The serving size is part of a system for giving consumers nutrition information in a consistent fashion. The size of a serving is not meant to suggest how much of the food ought to be consumed at a meal. For example, a typical portion of spaghetti at dinner might consist of 2 or 3 servings.

Breads, cereals, rice & pasta (6–11 servings each day)

bread	1 slice
rice, cooked	1/2 cup
pasta, cooked	1/2 cup
cereal, cooked	1/2 cup
cereal, ready-to-eat	1 cup

Vegetables (3–5 servings each day)

vegetables, chopped, cooked or raw	1/2 cup
vegetables, leafy raw	1 cup

Fruits (2–4 servings each day)

apple, banana, orange	1 medium-sized fruit
melon	1 wedge
fruit juice	¾ cup
fruit, dried	¼ cup

Milk, yogurt and cheese (2–3 servings each day)

milk	1 cup
yogurt	1 cup
cheese	1½ oz (2 oz if processed cheese)

Meat, poultry, fish, dry beans, eggs, nuts (2–3 servings each day)

meat, lean	2½ to 3 ounces
fish	2½ to 3 ounces
poultry	2½ to 3 ounces
egg	2
beans (cooked dry beans)	1 cup
peanut butter	4 tablespoons

shake

A unit of time, one hundred millionth of a second.

shakes

American shakes are made from western redcedar, either handsplit or handsplit and then resawn. They are longer and thicker than shingles, so the exposure (the part that shows) of a shake is greater than that of a shingle. Thickness ranges from ⅜" to 1 ¼". Widths may be random, Standard lengths are 18" and 24", with a special 15" length for starter-finish courses, and a very large 32" length.

There are three styles of shake. Shake making begins by cutting a blank the length the shakes will be. Pieces are split off this blank using a mallet and a kind of wedge called a froe; it is the splitting that gives shakes their attractive texture. If the blank is turned end for end after a shake has been split off, the resulting shakes will be tapered. They are "Taper-split." If all the splitting is done from the same end of the blank, the shakes have no taper and are "Straight-split." The taper of "Hand-split and Resawn" shakes comes from sawing straight-split shakes in half diagonally.

There is only a single grade of shake, #1: they must be 100% clear. Hand-split and Resawn shakes are graded from the split face; Handsplit shakes are graded from the best face.

Like shingles, shakes are sold by the square, enough for 100 square feet of finished roof, but whereas a square of shingles consists of 4 bundles, a square of shakes may contain 5 and even, for the 32" length, 6 bundles. It's easy to see why; such a square weighs 450 pounds.

sheets

Fitted sheets are sized by the name of the size of mattress they are intended to fit (for convenience, USA mattress sizes are listed below). In recent years mattresses have become increasingly deeper, and more people are using thick mattress pads of sheepskin, down, and so on. Many fitted sheets are not deep enough to fit these newer styles.

The "height" of a fitted sheet is determined by the depth of what makers call the "pocket." Pockets are usually shallower on fitted sheets for twin beds (say, 8 1/2") than for the larger sizes (say, 10 1/2"). Fitted sheets are available with pockets as deep as 12" or even 14".

Flat sheet dimensions given below are after hemming; some packages are marked with the size before hemming. The table shows for each size the dimensions of a typical sheet of that size followed by the dimensions of the largest marketed sheet of which we're aware. All measurements are in inches.

	Fitted	Flat
twin	39" × 75" or 76"	70" × 100", 76" × 106"
long twin	39" × 80"	70" × 106", 76" × 114"
full or double	54" × 75" or 76"	80" × 100", 85" × 106"
queen	60" × 80"	90" × 100", 94" × 114"
king	78" or 79" × 80"	100" × 104", 110" × 114"
California king	72" × 84"	

See also ☞crib.

sheet metal

Sheet metal differs from "plate" in being less than 1/8" thick (some say less than 1/4"). Sheet metal is also expected to have a much better surface finish than plate.

Sheet metal is usually purchased by thickness. With the building of the first rolling mills (Wales, 18TH C), manufacturers had to decide what series of thicknesses to offer. Some took their series from the series of diameters in wire gages; others made up their own gages. The use of many different gages lead to confusion.

Iron and steel sheet. By 1877, the American Institute of Mining Engineers was recommending a Standard Decimal Gauge, in which the gauge numbers were simply the thickness of the sheet in thousandths of an inch. The series ran 2, 4, 6, 8, 10, 12, 14, 16, 18, 20, 22, 25, 28, 32, 36, 40, 45, 50, 55, 60, 65, 70, 75, 80, 85, 90, 95, 100, 110, 125, 135, 150, 165, 180, 200, 220, 240, and 250.

An act of Congress on March 3, 1893, established the U.S. Standard Gauge for sheet iron and steel for the purpose of levying taxes and duties. This series was not based on thickness but mass. The mass of a cubic foot of wrought iron was taken to be 480 pounds avoirdupois. A sheet 1 foot by 1 foot by 1 inch thick will then weigh 40 pounds, or 640 ounces, so a sheet 1/640" thick should weigh 1 ounce per square foot. The gauge numbers started at 7/0, which was set at 320 ounces per square foot (and thus 320/640 = 1/2" thick). From #7/0 to #0 the gages differed by 20 ounces (so in thickness by approximately twenty 640ths); from #0 to #14, ten ounces (and ten 640ths); from #14 to #16, five ounces; from #16 to #20, four; from #20 to #26, two; #26 to #31, one; #31 to #36, half an ounce, and #36 to #38, a quarter of an ounce.

This proved unsatisfactory, not least because it was based on wrought iron and not rolled steel, whose weight is nearer 501.84 pounds per cubic foot. In 1895 the ASME and the American Railway Master Mechanics Assn. jointly called for the use of the decimal gauge and "the abandonment and disuse of the other gauges now in use, as tending to confusion and error." Thereafter the decimal gauge was often referred to as the "Master Mechanics Gage." Westinghouse Electric & Mfg. made the best-known attempt to abandon gauge numbers (*American Machinist* April 14, 1904).

But gauge numbers would not die. The steel manufacturers redefined the U.S. Standard gauge numbers, retaining the weights per square foot, but correcting the thickness for the weight of continuously rolled steel. This became known as the Manufacturers' Standard Gauge, in which #16 sheet, for example, still weighed 40 ounces per square foot, but was 0.0598" thick instead of the 1/16" (= 40/640" = 0.0625") expected by the U.S. Standard Gauge. (The actual specification includes a tolerance of ± 0.005 to 0.007", depending on the width of the roll and whether it was hot rolled or cold rolled.)

Aluminum, copper, magnesium. In the USA the Brown and Sharpe Gauge, also called the American Wire Gauge, is used for most nonferrous sheet metal, including aluminum, brass, German silver, magnesium, and phosphor bronze sheet.

In England the Imperial Wire gauge was used for aluminum (or should we say aluminium) sheets and the Birmingham Metal Gauge (not to be confused with the Birmingham Gauge or the Birmingham or Stub's Iron Wire Gauge) for brass sheets.

Zinc has a gauge all its own.

Sheet Metal Gages

Gauge No.	Manuf. Standard Gauge	Brown & Sharpe Gauge	Birmingham Wire Gauge	Birmingham 1914 Gauge	Imperial Wire Gauge	Zinc Gauge
7/0	—	—	—	0.6666	0.5000	—
6/0	—	0.5800	—	0.6250	0.4640	—
5/0	—	0.5165	0.500	0.5883	0.4320	—
4/0	—	0.4600	0.454	0.5416	0.4000	—
3/0	—	0.4096	0.425	0.5000	0.3720	—
00	—	0.3648	0.380	0.4450	0.3480	—
0	—	0.3249	0.340	0.3964	0.3240	—
1	—	0.2893	0.300*	0.3532	0.3000	0.002
2	—	0.2576	0.284	0.3147	0.2760	0.004
3	0.2391	0.2294	0.259*	0.2804	0.2520	0.006
4	0.2242	0.2043	0.239	0.2500	0.2320	0.008
5	0.2092	0.1819	0.220*	0.2225	0.2120	0.010

	Sheet Metal Gages					
Gauge No.	Manuf. Standard Gauge	Brown & Sharpe Gauge	Birmingham Wire Gauge	Birmingham 1914 Gauge	Imperial Wire Gauge	Zinc Gauge
6	0.1943	0.1620	0.203*	0.1981	0.1920	0.012
7	0.1793	0.1443	0.180*	0.1764	0.1760	0.014
8	0.1644	0.1285	0.165*	0.1570	0.1600	0.016
9	0.1495	0.1144	0.148*	0.1398	0.1440	0.018
10	0.1345	0.1019	0.134*	0.1250	0.1280	0.020
11	0.1196	0.09075	0.120*	0.1113	0.1160	0.024
12	0.1046	0.0808	0.109	0.0991	0.1040	0.028
13	0.0897	0.0720	0.095	0.0882	0.0920	0.032
14	0.0747	0.0641	0.083	0.0785	0.0800	0.036
15	0.0673	0.0571	0.072	0.0699	0.0720	0.040
16	0.0598	0.0508	0.065	0.0625	0.0640	0.045
17	0.0538	0.0453	0.059*	0.0556	0.0560	0.050
18	0.0478	0.0403	0.049	0.0495	0.0480	0.055
19	0.0418	0.0359	0.042	0.0440	0.0400	0.060
20	0.0359	0.0320	0.035	0.0392	0.0360	0.070
21	0.0329	0.0285	0.032	0.0349	0.0320	0.080
22	0.0299	0.0253	0.028	0.0312	0.0280	0.090
23	0.0269	0.0226	0.025	0.0278	0.0240	0.100
24	0.0239	0.0201	0.022	0.0247	0.0220	0.125
25	0.0209	0.0179	0.020	0.0220	0.0200	0.250
26	0.0179	0.0159	0.018	0.0196	0.0180	0.375
27	0.0164	0.0142	0.016	0.0174	0.0164	0.500
28	0.0149	0.0126	0.014	0.0156	0.0148	1.000
29	0.0135	0.0113	0.013	0.0139	0.0136	—
30	0.0120	0.0100	0.012	0.0123	0.0124	—
31	0.0105	0.0089	0.010	0.0110	0.0116	—
32	0.0097	0.0080	0.009	0.0098	0.0108	—
33	0.0090	0.0071	0.008	0.0087	0.0100	—
34	0.0082	0.0063	0.007	0.0077	0.0092	—
35	0.0075	0.0056	0.005	0.0069	0.0084	—
36	0.0067	0.0050	0.004	0.0061	0.0076	—
37	0.0064	0.0045	—	0.0054	0.0068	—
38	0.0060	0.0040	—	0.0048	0.0060	—
39	—	0.0035	—	0.0043	0.0052	—
40	—	—	—	0.0048	—	—
41	—	—	—	0.0044	—	—
42	—	—	—	0.0040	—	—
43	—	—	—	0.0036	—	—
44	—	—	—	0.0032	—	—
45	—	—	—	0.0028	—	—
46	—	—	—	0.0024	—	—
47	—	—	—	0.0020	—	—
48	—	—	—	0.0016	—	—
49	—	—	—	0.0012	—	—
50	—	—	—	0.0010	—	—

* In the 19TH C, several different tables defining the "Birmingham Wire Gauge" were in circulation. For the sizes marked with an asterisk, Molesworth's *Engineering Formulae* gives: 1 = 0.312", 3 = 0.261", 5 = 0.217", 6 = 0.208", 7 = 0.187", 8 = 0.166", 9 = 0.158", 10 = 0.137", 11 = 0.125", 17 = 0.056".

shelving, metal

In the USA, commercial and industrial sheet metal shelving is manufactured with shelf depths of 12", 15", 18", or 24" and widths of 36" and 48". Units are typically 75" or 85" high. In wire shelving, shelves 36", 48", 60" and 72" wide are available.

Still larger sizes are offered in the type of shelving in which the shelves are particleboard or plywood decks supported by metal angles: shelf depths of 12", 18", 24", 36", and 48", and lengths of 4', 6', and 8'. Typical height is 84".

shingles

Regardless of their type or size, shingles are sold by the ☞square, which is enough material to cover 100 square feet of roof. A square typically contains 4 bundles.

Wooden shingles. Wooden shingles should not be confused with ☞shakes. Shingles are sawn; shakes are split.

In the USA, available lengths are 16", 18", and 24", referred to as fivex, perfections, and royals, respectively. The length is the side of the shingle that runs downhill when the shingle is installed. Widths are usually random but can be specified ("dimension shingles") for a few species. Just as with wood flooring, narrow shingles are less likely to warp than wide ones.

Thickness is based on the average thickness of the thick end (the "butt") of the shingle. Nowadays, thickness is often given as a decimal fraction of an inch, but it used to be specified by a fraction: 4/2, for example, means the butts of 4 of the shingles put together measure 2 inches (so they average 0.50"). The two other standard thicknesses are 5/2¼ (0.45") and 5/2 (0.40"). Thickness is proportional to length; 16" shingles average 0.40" thickness; 18", 0.45"; and 24", 0.50". Shingles with thick butts are less likely to warp than thin ones.

The direction in which the grain runs also affects the quality of a shingle. Edge-grained shingles, in which the surface of the shingle is perpendicular to the direction of the grain, are less likely to warp than flat-grained shingles, in which the surface is tangent to the rings. And finally, heartwood is less likely to decay than sapwood.

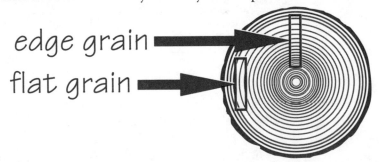

Wooden shingles are sawn from western redcedar, northern white-cedar, redwood, and sometimes cypress, each with its own grades. In western redcedar, the grades are No. 1 Blue Label, No. 2 Red Label,

No. 3 Black Label, and No. 4 Undercoursing; in northern white cedar, Extra, Clear, 2nd Clear, Clear Wall, and Utility; and in redwood, No. 1, No. 2 VG, and No. 3 MG. The top grade of wood shingle is 100% clear (that is, free of knots), edge-grain heartwood. As an example of definitions of lower grades, in No. 2 grade, 10" of a 16" shingle must be clear, 11" of an 18" shingle, and 16" of a 24" shingle. For No. 3, a utility grade, 6" of a 16" shingle and 10" of a 24" shingle must be clear. Flat grain and some sapwood are allowed on grades below No. 1.

Rebutted-Rejointed grades are the same as the ordinary numbered grade except that special care has been taken to make them exactly rectangular, which is useful when shingling sidewalls.

Since shingles are overlapped, only a portion shows, which is called the "exposure". The longer the shingle and the steeper the slope, the greater the exposure can be. For example, on a roof that rises 5" in a foot, 7 1/2" of a 24" shingle would show, but on a roof that rises 3" in a foot, only 3 3/4" of a 16" shingle would show.

English wooden shingles of the early 1700s were much smaller than ours: 6"–8" broad and 12" long.

Asphalt shingles. The most common size is the "strip shingle," 12" by 36", with either 2 or 3 tabs.

shirts, men's

In the USA, men's shirts are sized by the circumference of the neck in inches and additionally, if it is a long-sleeved shirt, the length of the sleeves. To measure sleeve length, raise an arm to shoulder level, bending the elbow a bit, and measure from the center of the back of the neck to the wrist bone. Measure both arms; they may be different.

In the 1950s, the U.S. Dept. of Commerce defined a standard for men's dress shirt sizes. A shirt with a 14" neck had a 42" chest and was 19 1/2" around the armholes and 14 3/4" around the sleeves. For each 1/2" increase in neck size, the chest increased by 2", and the armhole and sleeve diameters by 1/2". The length, front and back, was 33" for all sizes.

shoelaces

Approximate lengths are:

Infant's Shoes		**Children's Shoes**	
Oxfords, sizes 3 to 12	18"	Sizes 12 1/2 to 8	24"
High shoes	24"	Sizes 8 1/2 to 12	27"

Adults' Shoes:	Dress	Casual
1 or 2 pairs of eyelets	18"	18"
3 or 4	24"	27"
5 or 6	27"	36"
7 or 8	36"	

Boots and Work Shoes	
Oxford	27"
6" to 8" high	40"

8" to 10" high	54"
over 10" high	72"

Sport Shoes

Golf	27"
Low cut (boys, girls, ladies)	36"
Low cut (men's)	40" or 45"
Hightop (men's)	54"
Ice Skates	72" or 81"

shoes

Shoe sizes primarily reflect the length of the foot. Even a tracing of a foot, however, may not provide enough information for a good fit, for the foot is three-dimensional. Footprints of wet bare feet capture some of this three-dimensionality. A person whose wet foot makes a print outlining the entire foot needs a shoe different from that needed by one whose footprint, while the same length and width, shows no connection between the forefoot and heel.

In the USA sizing systems, whole sizes differ by one-third of an inch in length, the length being that of the last, the form on which the shoe is made. Infant's size 0 is $3^{11}/12$" long; all other sizes differ in length from this by the addition of a multiple of $1/6$" (because there are half sizes). There are different numberings for girls', boys', women's, and men's sizes, shown in the chart.

In the U.K., whole sizes also differ by $1/3$", but size 0 is 4" long. Numbering begins again after size 13, 1 being $8^2/3$". In France, the size increment is $2/3$ cm, which is called a Paris point. Size 0 is a length of 0 cm. The table on page 264 compares the various sizing systems, but it should only be taken as a starting point. Even within one country, shoes of the same size can have different dimensions. Width, sized in letters, also affects length. A 10 EEE shoe is wider than a 10 D, but it is also longer.

High heels. This form of foot destruction first appeared in England between 1570 and 1580. In a survey conducted in the 1980s by Dr. Carol Frey, an orthopedic surgeon at UCLA, 88% of the women wore shoes smaller than their feet and 75% had not had their feet measured in the last five years. Eighty per cent of the women with shoe sizes of 8 or larger suffered from foot pain.

High heels double the pressure on the forefoot, throw the back out of line, stress the knee, and make the ankle more vulnerable to twists and turns.

Dr. Frey recommends never wearing heels higher than 2 inches, and never wearing any high heels for more than 3 hours at a stretch.

Buying the right size. Shop for shoes at the end of the day, when your feet are largest. Have both feet measured. Old measurements may no longer apply; adult's feet, like children's, change with age and activity.

In the USA, shoe fittings are usually made with an tool called the Brannock Device, made since the 19TH C by a company of the same name in Syracuse, NY. The person being fitted should sit and keep his or her socks on. If a fitting stool is available, the fitter puts the measuring device on the inclined ramp of the stool, otherwise on the floor. Either way, the measuring device must be positioned so that the leg is perpendicular to the foot.

arch length

The fitter first measures the distance from the heel to the ball of the foot, taken as the outermost point of the bone. Call this the arch length. On the Brannock Device, this measurement is read from a scale marked in shoe sizes. Then the distance from the heel to the toes is measured. In doing so the sock is drawn against the ends of the toes so that only two layers of cloth (at heel and toe) are included in the measurement, and the toes are gently pressed down. Call this measurement the toe length; it is also read off a scale marked in shoe sizes.

If the arch length size is the same as the toe length size, the arch length size is the correct size *for that foot*. If the toe length size is larger than the arch length size, the toe length size is the correct size. If the arch length is half a size larger than the toe length, the arch length is the correct size.

Having the size, the width can now be determined. Some judgment is called for. Very fleshy feet or ones with very high insteps may need a width one size larger than the measuring device indicates, while if the foot is thin it's considered proper to apply a bit of pressure with the bar used to measure width, to see if the foot compresses to a smaller width. Widths are designated by letters. The average man takes a C or D width, but shoes are made up to EEEEEE. (Nowadays persons with exceptionally wide feet who can't get such sizes locally have mail order resources such as Hitchcock Shoes in Massachusetts.)

Now the whole procedure must be repeated with the other foot. Always insist on having both feet measured.

A competent fitter may also examine the shoes you were wearing, especially if they are the same style as the ones you are purchasing, because the ways in which they are worn can reveal how well that size fit you. Just as an auto mechanic can look at a tire and know whether the alignment is off or the shocks need replacing, an experienced fitter can read signs of the quality of the fit in the sweat line, bumps in the innersole, and the wrinkles in the vamp.

Real feet only approximate standard sizes. Real shoes also only approximate standard sizes. Shoes are made on forms called lasts. Two lasts may be the same size but quite different shapes, and the shoes made on them may fit quite differently. That is why it is essential to try shoes on.

Try on both shoes in the size from the measurement of the larger foot. If you wear orthotics, insert them. Before tying the laces, stand up, put your weight on the shoes and wiggle your feet around a bit. Otherwise, tightening the lacing may clamp your foot into an unnatural position.

Make sure there is 1 cm between your longest toe and the inside front of the shoe. The sides of the throat-line, where the shoe is laced, should not meet. When walking about, be aware that most shoe stores install extra-thick carpeting.

Leather may stretch, but synthetic materials won't. If such a shoe doesn't fit when you buy it, it never will. Don't buy shoes that don't fit.

Preserving the fit. Use shoe trees. Don't wear the same pair day after day. Replace worn heels promptly; walking in worn heels can permanently deform a shoe's counter, the part that cups the back of the foot.

Approximately Equivalent Shoe Sizes (Lengths)

U.S. inch	Infants' U.S.	Infants' Euro	U.S. boys'	U.S. girls'	Euro	Women's U.S.	Women's Euro	Women's U.K.	Men's U.S.	Men's Euro	Men's U.K.	cm size
3.92	0	15	—	—	—	—	—	—	—	—	—	9
4.08	1/2	15.5	—	—	—	—	—	—	—	—	—	9.5
4.25	1	16	—	—	—	—	—	—	—	—	—	10
4.42	1 1/2	17	—	—	—	—	—	—	—	—	—	10
4.58	2	17.5	—	—	—	—	—	—	—	—	—	10.5
4.75	2 1/2	18	—	—	—	—	—	—	—	—	—	11
4.92	3	19	—	—	—	—	—	—	—	—	—	11.5
5.08	3 1/2	19.5	—	—	—	—	—	—	—	—	—	12
5.25	4	20	—	—	—	—	—	—	—	—	—	12.5
5.42	4 1/2	20.5	—	—	—	—	—	—	—	—	—	13
5.58	5	21	—	—	—	—	—	—	—	—	—	13
5.75	5 1/2	22	—	—	—	—	—	—	—	—	—	13.5
5.92	6	22.5	—	7	—	—	—	—	—	—	—	14
6.08	6 1/2	23	—	7 1/2	—	—	—	—	—	—	—	14.5
6.25	7	23.5	—	8	—	—	—	—	—	—	—	15
6.42	7 1/2	24	—	8 1/2	—	—	—	—	—	—	—	15.5
6.58	8	25	8	9	—	—	—	—	—	—	—	15.5
6.75	8 1/2	25.5	8 1/2	9 1/2	—	—	—	—	—	—	—	16
6.92	9	26	9	10	—	—	—	—	—	—	—	16.5
7.08	9 1/2	27	9 1/2	10 1/2	—	—	—	—	—	—	—	17
7.25	10	27.5	10	11	—	—	—	—	—	—	—	17.5
7.42	10 1/2	28	10 1/2	11 1/2	—	—	—	—	—	—	—	18
7.58	11	29	11	12	—	—	—	—	—	—	—	18.5
7.75	11 1/2	29.5	11 1/2	12 1/2	—	—	—	—	—	—	—	19

Approximately Equivalent Shoe Sizes (Lengths)

U.S. inch	Infants' U.S.	Infants' Euro	U.S. boys'	U.S. girls'	Euro	Women's U.S.	Women's Euro	Women's U.K.	Men's U.S.	Men's Euro	Men's U.K.	cm size
7.92	12	30	12	13	—	—	—	—	—	—	—	19
8.08	12½	—	12½	13!/2	30.5	—	—	—	—	—	—	19.5
8.25	13	—	13	1	31	1	31	—	—	—	—	20
8.42	13½	—	13½	1½	32	1½	32	—	—	—	—	20.5
8.58	—	—	1	2	32.5	2	32.5	—	—	—	—	21
8.75	—	—	1½	2½	33	2½	33	1	—	—	—	21
8.92	—	—	2	3	34	3	34	1½	—	—	—	21.5
9.08	—	—	2½	3½	34.5	3½	34.5	2	—	—	—	22
9.25	—	—	3	4	35	4	35	2½	—	—	—	22.5
9.42	—	—	3½	4½	36	4½	35.5	3	—	—	—	23
9.58	—	—	4	5	36.5	5	36	3½	—	—	—	23.5
9.75	—	—	4½	5½	37	5½	37	4	—	—	—	24
9.92	—	—	5	6	*	6	37.5	4½	—	—	—	24
10.08	—	—	5½	6½	*	6½	38	5	5½	—	5	24.5
10.25	—	—	6	7	*	7	39	5½	6	39	5½	25
10.42	—	—	6½	7½	*	7½	39.5	6	6½	39.5	6	25.5
10.58	—	—	7	8	*	8	40	6½	7	40	6½	26
10.75	—	—	7½	8½	*	8½	40.5	7	7½	41	7	26.5
10.92	—	—	8	9	*	9	41	7½	8	41.5	7½	27
11.08	—	—	8½	9½	*	9½	42	8	8½	42	8	27
11.25	—	—	9	—	*	10	42.5	8½	9	43	8½	27.5
11.42	—	—	9½	—	*	10 1/2	43	9	9½	43.5	9	28
11.58	—	—	10	—	*	11	44	9½	10	44	9½	28.5
11.75	—	—	10½	—	*	11½	44.5	10	10½	44.5	10	28.5
11.92	—	—	11	—	*	12	45	10½	11	45	10½	29
12.08	—	—	11½	—	*	12½	—	11	11½	46	11	30
12.25	—	—	12	—	*	13	—	11½	12	46.5	11½	30
12.42	—	—	—	—	—	13½	—	—	12½	47	12	30.5
12.58	—	—	—	—	—	14	—	—	13	48	12½	31
12.92	—	—	—	—	—	15	—	—	14	49	13	32
13.25	—	—	—	—	—	16	—	—	15	50	14	33
13.58	—	—	—	—	—	17	—	—	16	—	—	33.5
13.92	—	—	—	—	—	18	—	—	17	—	—	34.5
14.25	—	—	—	—	—	19	—	—	18	—	—	35

* For these boys' and girls' sizes, use the adult conversions.

Approximately Equivalent Shoe Sizes (Widths)			
U.S.	U.K. Men	U.K. Women	German Children's
AAAAAA			
AAAAA			
AAAA			
AAA		A	
AA		B	
A	1	C	
B	2	D	I
C	3	E	II
D	4	EE	III
E	5		IV
EEE	6		V
EEEE			
EEEEE			

shot

1) The round pellets fired from guns, generally made of lead, are sized by numbers:

Gauge	Diameter (inches)	Number in a pound
12	.050	2,385
11	.060	1,380
10	.070	868
9	.080	585
8	.090	409
7½	.095	350
6	.110	299
5	.120	223
4	.130	172
2	.150	136
air rifle	.175	88
BB	.180	50

• #12
• #7½
• #4
• BB

Buck
#4
#1
OO

(The following are the so-called "Eastern" buckshot sizes. There used to be a second series called "Western.")

#4 Buck	.24	340
#3 Buck	.25	300
#1 Buck	.30	175
#0 Buck	.32	142
#00 Buck	.33	130
#000 Buck	.36	103

Shot sizes in other countries, though often using the same numbers, are not the same diameter. An extensive table comparing American and other shot sizes is given in *Gunsmithing* by Roy F. Dunlap (Harrisburg, PA: Stackpole Books, 1963).

2) A unit of liquid capacity used for alcoholic drinks, typically whiskey, = 1 or 1½ u.s. fluid ounces. The capacity of a shotglass.

3) A unit of length used for anchor chain on ships = 15 fathoms = 90 feet. Anchor chains for ships are made up of 15-fathom lengths of chain joined by detachable links. The joins are distinctively marked so a ship's officer can estimate at a glance how much chain is out. In the merchant marine, the detachable links are painted red. At 15 fathoms, the end of the first shot, the two links on either side of the detachable link are painted white, and one turn of wire is wound around the stud of the link on either side of the detachable link. At 30 fathoms, two links on either side of the detachable link are painted white, and two turns of wire are put on the second stud on either side of the detachable link, and so on for the remaining shots.

In the command to let go the anchor in the merchant marine, the amount to be played out is given in shots; in the navy it is given in fathoms.

shotguns

The gauge of a shotgun was originally based on round lead balls just big enough to fit the gun's bore; the gun's gauge was the number of such balls needed to make up one pound. Cannons were similarly sized. (These hypothetical balls should not be confused with the "pumpkin balls," formerly used with modern guns and now replaced by rifled slugs. Pumpkin balls had to be smaller than the gun's bore in order to get past the choke in modern barrels.) Besides the gauges shown below, 11-, 13-, 14-, 15-, and 19-gauge shotguns were once made in the usa, and 14-, 24-, and 32-gauge guns are still manufactured in Europe. The bore diameters given below are nominal; actual size varies from maker to maker.

4	0.935" (cartridges this size were sold within living memory!)
6	0.919"
8	0.835" (became illegal for waterfowl just before World War II)
10	0.775"
12	0.729"
16	0.662"
20	0.615"
28	0.550"
.410	0.410" (actually a caliber, not a gauge)

Cartridges and loads. Most American shotguns are now chambered for 2¾" shells. In Europe, 65 mm (2½") cartridges are standard.

Weight of Rifled Slugs			
Gauge	12	16	20	.410
Weight in grains	415	350	282	93

shot put

The men's shot has a mass of 7.62 kg and a diameter between 110 and 130 mm; the women's is 4 kg, and 95–110 mm.

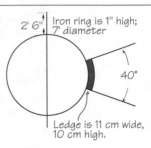

2' 6"   Iron ring is 1" high; 7" diameter

40°

Ledge is 11 cm wide, 10 cm high.

showerheads

In the USA, the standard showerhead has a 1/2" female NPT thread (see ☞ pipe threads).

shuffleboard

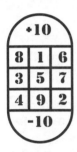

The ancestors of shuffleboard were board games in which coins were shoved onto a scoring pattern. Ocean liners enlarged these games into a deck game for passengers. The typical scoring pattern to the left shows that the game emphasized luck as much as skill.

In the USA it became a not-too-strenuous game of skill for landlubbers. On land, permanent lanes, with drains, gutters, bumpers, and so on were possible. The rules and dimensions of the lanes were standardized in 1924.

Discs. According to National Shuffleboard Assn. rules, the disc shall be 6" in diameter, 9/16" to 1" thick, and weigh 15 ounces when new. Friction with the concrete surface of the lane takes its toll; a disc may no longer be played when its weight drops below 11 1/2 ounces. Brand

Shuffleboard Courts

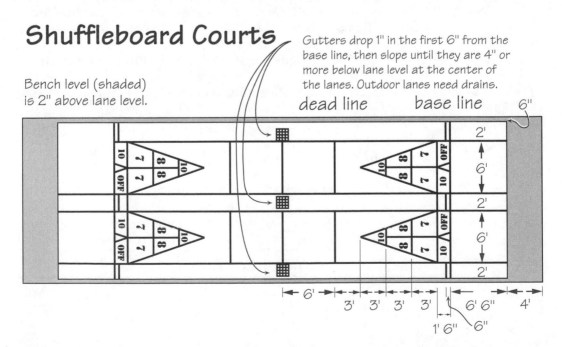

Gutters drop 1" in the first 6" from the base line, then slope until they are 4" or more below lane level at the center of the lanes. Outdoor lanes need drains.

Bench level (shaded) is 2" above lane level.

new discs are not permitted in tournament play; they must be broken in first.

Cue. The cue may not be longer than 6' 3".

shutters, photographic

Camera lenses have f/stops marked on their diaphragm ring, and usually click-stop detents to hold the ring at an f/number setting. The marked f/stops are chosen so that each lets through the lens half as much light as the f/stop before it (or twice as much, reading from the other end of the scale). When a photographer changes either the f-stop setting or the shutter speed setting for aesthetic reasons, it is convenient to be able to keep the exposure the same by changing the other setting by the same number of steps. Ideally, then, each shutter speed should be half the duration of the preceding one.

Current shutters are designed to operate at a series of speeds that begins with 8 seconds and proceeds by halving down to 1/2048th of a second. Although the shutters actually operate at these speeds, plus or minus the tolerance, by international agreement a slightly different set of numbers is used to mark speeds shorter than 1/8th of a second:

Actual:	1/16	1/32	1/64	1/128	1/256	1/512	1/1024	1/2048
Marked:	1/15	1/30	1/60	1/125	1/250	1/500	1/1000	1/2000

A pattern often found on older leaf shutters is 1, 1/2, 1/5, 1/10, 1/25, 1/50, 1/100, 1/200, 1/400.

SI

Official abbr. for the International System of Units, from the French "Système International d'Unités."

siemens

1) In SI and in the meter-kilogram-second system, the unit of electrical conductance, admittance, and susceptance. Abbr, S. "Siemens" is the singular and plural; "1 sieman" is not correct.

A conductor has a conductance of 1 siemens if an electrical potential difference of 1 volt produces a 1-ampere current in it. The conductance of a conductor in siemens is the reciprocal of its resistance in ohms, and the siemans was formerly known as the *mho* or *reciprocal ohm*. In equations, conductance is represented by G.

The dimensions of the siemans are $\dfrac{amperes}{volts}$ or, in terms of base units only, $\dfrac{second^{3} \cdot ampere^{2}}{meter^{2} \cdot kilogram}$

2) In the 19TH C, "Siemens' unit" referred to a unit of electrical resistance proposed and used by Siemens himself, the resistance of a meter of pure mercury with a square cross section 1 millimeter on a side. For practical purposes, the standard was realized as a German silver wire 3.8 meters long and 0.9 mm in diameter, ≈ 0.9534 ohm.

sieves

Sieves are an ancient tool, at least as old as the open weave baskets used to separate grain from chaff, the earliest example of a go/no-go gauge. A later, more sophisticated sieve was the medieval miller's bolting cloth. Even more precise sieves began to be made during the Industrial Revolution. In 1800, for example, to extend the supply of grain during an agricultural crisis, the king of England forbade the baking of bread with flour that would pass through a sieve with 13 wires on each side of a square inch.

Many occupations are concerned with the size of large numbers of small objects, such as grain, seeds or soil particles. If a graded series of sieves is available, a batch can be shaken through a stack of sieves with increasingly smaller holes. Weighing the amount left behind in each sieve gives a series of masses which is a size distribution for the particles in the batch. In such situations, it is more accurate to describe the sizes of the particles in sieve numbers, rather than as particle diameters. For an example of how sieve numbers are used to grade a commercial product, see ☛abrasives.

The sieves used in industry and the laboratory are precision products. The smaller the particle that is not to pass through the sieve, the finer the wires of the sieve—but despite that, the smaller the proportion of the sieve's area which is hole.

Standard[1]	U.S. Alternate[2]	Tyler Screen Scale Equivalent Designation
25.0 mm	1"	—
19.0 mm	3⁄4 "	0.742"
16.0 mm	5⁄8 "	0.624"
12.5 mm	1⁄2 "	—
9.5 mm	3⁄8 "	0.371"
8.0 mm	5⁄16 "	2 1⁄2 mesh
6.3 mm	1⁄4 "	—

Fine Sieves

5.6 mm	3 1⁄2 mesh	3 1⁄2 mesh
4.75	4	4
4.00	5	5
3.35	6	6
2.80	7	7
2.36	8	8
2.00	10	9
1.70	12	10
1.40	14	12
1.18	16	14
1.00 mm	18	16
850 µm	20	20

Standard[1]	U.S. Alternate[2]	Tyler Screen Scale Equivalent Designation
710	25	24
600	30	28
500	35	32
425	40	35
355	45	42
300	50	48
250	60	60
212	70	65
180	80	80
150	100	100
125	120	115
106	140	150
90	170	170
75	200	200
63	230	250
53	270	270
45	325	325
38	400	400

Shaded lines identify sizes in common use in the USA that are not in the ISO series.

1. The first column of the table gives test sieve apertures in millimeters or micrometers (μm) as recommended by the ISO. The ratio between adjacent sizes is the fourth root of 2, so the aperture size doubles every 5th size.

2. The second column shows "U.S. Alternate" sieve designations, a survival of an older system, which are roughly the number of openings per inch.

sievert

A special unit in ☞SI, the unit of "dose equivalent," used by health physicists in protecting people from overexposure to radiation such as X rays and gamma rays. Abbr., Sv. It has the dimensions joules per kilogram, or, in base units, $\dfrac{meter^2}{seconds^2}$.

When anything absorbs radiation, energy is deposited in it. The amount of energy deposited can be measured; the amount of energy deposited in tissue by an exposure to ionizing radiation (a "dose") can be expressed in joules per kilogram. Health physicists give 1 joule per kilogram a special name, a ☞gray.

A measurement of the amount of energy tissue has absorbed from exposure to ionizing radiation is not all that is needed to predict the amount of harm done. There are different kinds of ionizing radiation, including alpha, beta, and gamma rays. Experience has shown that a 1-gray dose of alpha rays, for example, is about 10 to 20 times more harmful than a 1-gray dose of gamma rays, depending on the energy of the alpha ray. Beta rays and X rays are about as harmful as gamma rays. Slow neutrons are about 5 times as harmful, and fast neutrons 10 times as harmful.

To express the size of an exposure in terms of biological damage, which is what health physicists need to do, a measurement of the absorbed dose in joules per kilogram (hence in grays) is multiplied by a "quality factor" for that type of radiation. The quality factor is in part determined experimentally and in part based on expert judgment. These dimensionless quality factors are maintained by the International Commission for Radiation Protection.

The quality factors are chosen so that 1 sievert of radiation is the amount of any kind of radiation which would cause the same amount of biological damage in a human being as would result from absorbing 1 gray of X rays. The sievert is said to measure "dose equivalent" because it indicates, for a dose of any kind of radiation, what dose of X rays or gamma rays would produce the same amount of damage. It is intended to be used at the sort of radiation levels encountered in medicine or the workplace; it "should not be used in assessing the effects of high-level, accidental exposures."

The sievert was recommended by the ICRU and the ICRP in 1977, and adopted by the General Conference on Weights and Measures in October of 1979. It replaced the ☞rem, although continued use of the rem was sanctioned for the time being. One hundred rem = 1 sievert.

signs, exit

According to the 1985 version of the National Fire Protection Assn. code, the letters on every exit and directional exit sign must be not less than 6" high, and the "principal strokes" must be at least 3⁄4" wide. A new requirement was that the letters (except "I") had to be at least 2" wide, and spaced at least 3⁄8" apart.

Early versions of the Life Safety Code required green letters on exit signs. In 1949, the Fire Marshall's Assn. asked for red. At present the NFPA makes no recommendation, but some local codes require exit signs be green while others require red.

The 1985 code also introduced requirements for the "no exit" signs to be placed on interior doors and in other locations that might be mistaken for an exit in an emergency. The letters in "NO" are to be at least 2" high with the principal strokes at least 3⁄8" wide, and the letters in "EXIT" are to be at least 1" high. "NO" is to appear above "EXIT."

singers

The table gives the typical range for various types of singer. The notes in parentheses are those reached by exceptional singers.

soprano	B_3–C_6
mezzo-soprano	A_3–A_5 (B_5)
contralto	G_3–G_5
alto	E_3–E_5 (F_5)
tenor	C_3–B_4 (C_5)

baritone	F₂–G₄ (A₄)
bass	(G₁) E₂–F₄

baritone F$_2$–G$_4$ (A$_4$)
bass (G$_1$) E$_2$–F$_4$

skateboards

Decks. Increased emphasis on freestyle tricks has led to a narrowing of the deck. A typical deck in the early 1990s was 8" or 8¼" wide and 31" to 32" long.

Trucks are described by the length of the axle in millimeters. The range is from 130 mm to 156 mm.

Each truck is held to the deck by 4 bolts, generally with centers on the corners of a rectangle 1 5/8" by 2 1/2".

Wheels. The diameter of the wheels has shrunk in order to lower the center of gravity and facilitate tricks. A very wide range of diameters are offered, including (in mm) 37, 37.5, 38, 38.5, 39, 40, 40.5, 41, 42, 42.3, 42.5, 43, 44, 45, 46, 50.5, 52.5, 54.5.

The hardness of the wheels, which are urethane, is given in durometer ratings; the higher the number, the harder the wheel. Typical values are 92 for ramp wheels and 99 for street wheels. Wheels with ratings over 100 have been offered.

skeet

Skeet began as a variation on short-range trapshooting that provided a greater variety of shooting angles. Originally, the trap and shooting stations were on a circle with a 25-yd radius (reduced to 20 yards in 1923). The modern form with two traps originated around 1925; it takes less space and provides the same types of shots as the circle did, as well as affording a safe area for spectators.

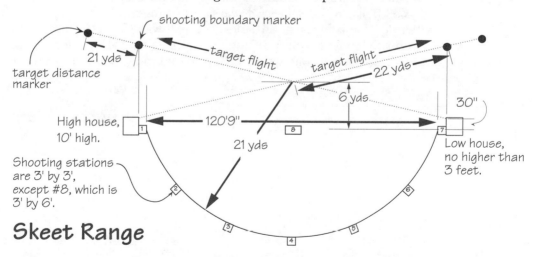

Skeet Range

skis, snow

To estimate the length of ski required, measure in centimeters from the floor to the wrist with the arm extended above the head. If the skier is heavier than average, add 5 cm.

For pole length, measure from the floor to the palm of an outstretched arm at chest level.

slippers

Size	Men's shoe size	Women's shoe size
XS		5–5½
S		6–7½
M	7–8½	8–9½
L	9–10½	10–12
XL	11–13	

snap fasteners

Size	0000	000	00	0	1	2	3	4
Diameter	0.235"	0.27"	0.287"	0.35"	0.4"	0.45"	0.5"	0.6"

soccer

Field. The dimensions of the playing field are not fixed. The original (1863) association rules said only that the field couldn't be bigger than 100 yds by 200 yds; in 1875 they added that it couldn't be smaller than 50 yds by 100 yds. The present dimensions were laid down in 1897; 100–130 yds by 50–100 yds for domestic matches; 110–120 yds by 70–80 yds for international matches.

Balls. The ball is between 27" and 28" in circumference. Its mass at the start of a game must be between 14 and 16 ounces, inflated at a pressure between 0.6 and 1.1 atmospheres (≈ 8.8–16.2 pounds per sq. inch).

For younger players, balls are made in various sizes. Size #5 is suited to players 13 years old and above; #4 is best for players from 9 to 12; and #3 balls are for players 8 years and younger.

Under the original 1863 rules, the ball was 13 to 15 ounces; it was given the modern weight in 1937. In 1905, a rule was added requiring a leather cover; nowadays other "approved materials" are permitted.

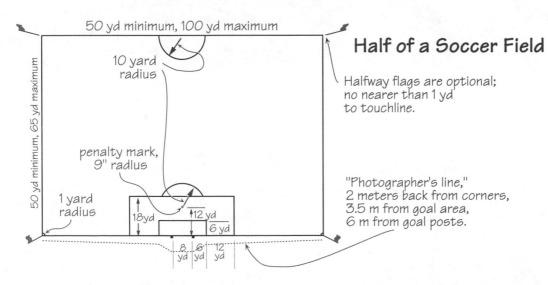

50 yd minimum, 100 yd maximum

50 yd minimum, 65 yd maximum

10 yard radius

penalty mark, 9" radius

1 yard radius

18yd

12 yd

6 yd

8 yd | 6 yd | 12 yd

Half of a Soccer Field

Halfway flags are optional; no nearer than 1 yd to touchline.

"Photographer's line," 2 meters back from corners, 3.5 m from goal area, 6 m from goal posts.

socks

Shoe size		1	2	3	4	5	6	7	8	9	10	11	12	13	14
	Men	1	2	3	4	5	6	7	8	9	10	11	12	13	14
	Women	2	3	4	5	6	7	8	9	10	11	12	13	14	—
Sock sizes		8	8	8–9	9	9	9	10	10–11	11	11–12	12	12–13	13–14	14
		S	S	S	S	M	M	M	L	L	L	L	L	XL	XL

softball

Bat. Not more than 2 1/4" in diameter at the thickest part; no longer than 34".

Ball. Circumference between 11 7/8" and 12 1/8"; mass between 6 1/4 ounces and 7 ounces.

Fielder's Glove. Not more than 13 1/4" from the tip of the longest finger to the back edge. The web between the thumb and first finger must not be longer than 5", measured along the top.

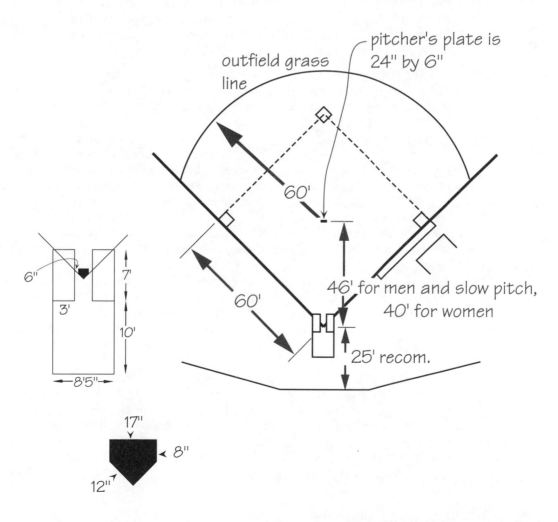

solder

Most hardware stores carry a variety of solders—metal alloys with low melting points—for different purposes, together with the fluxes needed to keep the surfaces to be soldered clean during the soldering process. The solder and flux must be suited to the job and to each other. For example, using fluxes other than rosin on electronic circuit boards will lead to corrosion that destroys the boards.

Solder for Electronics
The composition of tin-lead solder is sometimes shown in the form "Sn60". "Sn" is the chemical symbol for tin; this designation means the solder is 60% tin and the balance lead. When the alloy designation contains a slash, e.g., "40/60", the first number is the per cent tin and the second the per cent lead. (In a lead-free solder, the first number is percent tin and the second the percent antimony.)

An important tin/lead solder alloy is 63/70, called "eutectic," meaning it goes directly from solid to liquid without a pasty stage. This alloy melts at 361° F, the lowest melting point of any tin-lead alloy.

Almost all the solder sold for hobbyist use in electronics is in the form of wire with cores of rosin flux.

Solder for Plumbing
Solder used on copper pipes is no longer permitted to contain lead; it is more than 90% tin with the rest antimony.

sound

The magnitude of a sound can be measured in two distinct ways. One is purely physical, without any reference to a listener. Loudness, however, is the perceived magnitude of a sound, which is different, for people are more sensitive to some frequencies than others. See ☞decibel; loudness as perceived by people is measured in phon and sone.

sound transmission class (STC)

A system devised by the ASTM in 1961 to describe how well various types of interior walls, floors, doors, etc., prevent sound in one room from reaching another.

To assign an STC rating to a barrier separating two rooms, a sound is generated in one of the rooms, the sound power is measured on the two sides of the barrier, and the ratio between the two (the transmission loss) is stated in decibels. Measurements are made at different frequencies, a total of 16 in all at $\frac{1}{3}$ octave intervals from 125 Hz to 4000 Hz.

The standard specifies a transmission loss curve having the 16 points on the same $\frac{1}{3}$ octave intervals. From 125 to 40 Hz, the curve slopes 9 dB per octave; from 400 Hz to 1250 Hz, 3 dB per octave, and it is flat from 1250 Hz to 4000 Hz. The curve is moved up and down until the sum of all 16 differences between the curve's value and the measured values for the barrier is less than 32 dB. The rating is then the curve's loss in decibels at 500 Hz (providing no single difference is more than 8 dB).

Typical STC Ratings

Type of Construction	STC
2 × 4 studs on 16" or 24" centers, 3/8"–5/8" wall-board, rock wool or fiberglass batting	30 to 42
Same as above with plaster instead of wallboard	40 to 54
Staggered stud 2 × 4's on 2 × 6 plate, 2 sheets of 5/8" plasterboard on each side, 2" fiberglass inside	51

The STC system is useful for comparing different ways of building a partition, but it is not a guarantee that a barrier, once built, will achieve a certain level of isolation. It tends to give too much credit to materials which absorb high frequencies, such as sheetrock, and too little to materials and forms of construction which absorb the lower frequencies.

span

In the USA, a unit of length, = 9 inches.

spark, electric

The length of a spark depends not only on voltage, but also on a host of other factors, including the nature of the gas, the shape and composition of the electrodes, the temperature, and the presence of other ionizing agents. In fact, the whole phenomenon is not well-understood.

To give an idea of the relation of spark length to voltage in air (at room temperature and pressure), 5000 volts will produce a spark between needlepoints 0.42 cm apart; 20,000 volts, 1.75 cm; and 100,000 volts, 15.5 cm.

species

In *The Diversity of Life* (Belknap Press of Harvard University), Edward O. Wilson takes a stab at estimating the number of known species:

Insects	751,000, of which	
		112,000 are butterflies or moths
		103,000 are bees or wasps
		290,000 are beetles
Protozoa	30,800	
Higher plants	248,400	
Viruses	1,000	
Algae	26,900	
Fungi	69,000	
Bacteria, etc	4,800	
Mammals	4,000	
All else	281,000	

Which brings to mind the reply of the eminent biologist J. B. Haldane, when he was asked what he had learned in a lifetime of research: "God must have loved beetles; He made so many of them."

spirits

Bottle Sizes

The USA began converting to metric sizes on October 1, 1976, completing the conversion by January 1, 1980. Unlike earlier regulation of bottle sizes for spirits, this applied also to liqueur and cordial bottles, which formerly had been unregulated (leading to at least 39 bottle sizes).

New size	Old size	Capacity
Miniature	miniature	50 mL
Small	half pint	200 mL
Medium	pint	500 mL
Regular	fifth	750 mL
Large	quart	1 L
Extra Large	half gallon	1.75 L

square

In the USA, 18TH–20TH C, a quantity of roofing material, such as shingles or slates, sufficient to cover 100 square feet of roof.

stairs

The most critical characteristic of stairs, even more important than the size of any of the parts, is that every step be the same. In fact, building codes enforce this rule. Fire and building codes devote a lot of space to stairs; falls on stairs kill 4,000 people a year in the USA and another 2 million are seriously injured.

Many different terms have been used in describing stairs; we will use those defined in the illustration below. The ratio of unit rise to unit run determines the angle of the stairs.

Rules of thumb for determining satisfactory rise/run ratios have existed at least since Classical times. In *De Architectura*, Vitruvius suggests a unit rise of between 9 and 10 inches, and a unit run between 18 inches and 24. To modern tastes, this proportion would create a very stately stair. Sir Henry Wooten (1568–1639) suggested that the unit rise not exceed 6 inches and that the unit run be between 1 and 1 1/2 feet. Both authors, however, are describing public buildings or grand houses.

Jacques-Francois Blondel (1705–74) argued in his *Cours d'Architecture* that the rise/run ratio should

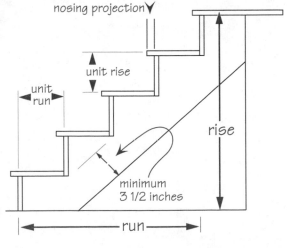

be based on the length of the human pace, which he took to be 25.5 inches. Since in one step on a stair, a foot travels by two risers and a tread, Blondel arrived at the formula two times the unit rise, plus the unit run = 25.5", or unit rise = (25.5" − unit run) over 2. This formula works well only for moderate values for unit rise (or unit run). It is, nonetheless, enshrined in the National Fire Code. Among American architects, an old rule-of-thumb is that the sum of the unit rise and the unit run should be about 17½". Common practice is to make the unit rise about 7½", and the unit run 9" for interiors and 11" for exteriors.In modern times, stair researchers have gone beyond observing which existing stairs cause the most accidents. Using tools like endless mechanically driven staircases with variable unit rise and unit run, they have been able to experiment with many combinations of unit rise and unit run, and to capture in stroboscopic photography how missteps occur. The results largely confirm the rules of thumb, but some interesting results emerge, such as that the optimal rise/run ratio for descent is not the same as the one for ascent. Several researchers feel that for descent the unit run should be at least 11".

But requiring an 11" unit run is controversial. Increasing the unit run even an inch or two can greatly increase the size of the staircase. With a rise of 12' and a unit rise of 7.2", increasing the unit run from 9" to 11" makes the staircase two feet longer—probably an extra 6 square feet of floor area carved out of the living room. When a "7-11" requirement was added to a building code in the Northeast, the National Assn. of Home Builders succeeded in having it removed, with the argument that it increased costs without proof that it was safer.

Alternate Tread Stairs. Imagine climbing a staircase in which alternate halves of the treads have been removed. A foot moving to the next empty tread does not need to clear the tread on which the other foot stands. Such staircases exist. Their great advantage is that they can be very steep (up to 70°, compared to up to 50° for normal stairs) and still be safe and comfortable. The great disadvantage is that they can accommodate only one person at a time.

Width. Again, this is probably specified in the local building code. Typically the minimum width permitted in residences is around 2'8". Three feet is better, and 3'6" is the standard for normal occupancy.

Landings. Most fire codes do not allow stairs to rise more than 12' without providing a landing. The length of the landing should be at least equal to the width of the stair tread.

stars

The best known star, the sun, has a mass of 1.989×10^{30} kilograms, and a radius of 6.96×10^8 meters.

The masses of a few hundred other stars have been found directly. Unlike the sun, most stars have one or more companion stars, all revolving about their common center of mass. If their orbits can be calculated from observations, their masses can be estimated. Masses of other stars are estimated from their luminosity.

Stellar radiuses must also be determined indirectly, since even in the most powerful telescope, no star looks like a disc. If two stars in a binary system happen to eclipse

Radiuses of Some Objects with the Same Mass as the Sun	
red giant	90,000,000 km
sun	696,000 km
white dwarf	10,000 km
neutron star	10 km
black hole	3 km

one other as seen from earth, the radiuses of the stars can be calculated from the durations of the eclipses. Some stars' radiuses can be estimated by the way the star's rotation affects the light it is emitting.

From a star's mass and radius its density can be estimated. Many stars with great mass have very low densities. A red giant star, such as Betelgeuse, has an average density about that of earth's air at sea-level. Red supergiants, like Antares, have an average density less than a ten-thousandth that of sea-level air; they have been called "red-hot vacuum."

The range of masses of stars is limited—between a tenth and sixty times the sun's mass—because an agglomeration with too little mass (say, the planet Jupiter) does not compress under its own weight enough to ignite, while one with too much mass soon explodes. In between, the more massive a star is the faster it ages. Stars are like laboratory rats; the fatter they are, the sooner they die.

steel wool

USA grades are listed below by number and name, together with some typical uses. Regardless of advice given on the packaging, steel wool should not be used to clean stainless steel, as it leaves behind microscopic steel particles which can eventually become centers for rusting.

0000. Super Fine. Polishing furniture finishes before applying top coat. Applying wax to furniture, buffing finishes. Cleaning windows. Cutting gloss on painted wood.

000. Extra Fine. Removing rust from chrome (with kerosene). Surface preparation between intermediate coats of varnish.

00. Fine. Cleaning wood floors. Polishing aluminum windows. Polishing copper and brass. Buffing burns, etc., from furniture and leather.

0. Medium Fine. Cleaning metal before soldering. Cleaning grouting between tiles. Cleaning aluminum pots and pans.

1. Medium. Preparing walls, wood for painting with water-free finishes. Cleaning resilient flooring. Removing rust from cast iron (with turpentine).

2. Medium Coarse. Rough cleaning jobs, for example on masonry. Not usually used for finishing.

3. Coarse. Removing paint and varnish.

4. Extra Coarse. Removing rust from metal and (using turpentine as a lubricant, with gloves) tile. Engine cleaning. Heavy duty stripping of finishes.

steradian

The unit of solid angle in SI, equal to the solid angle which cuts off, on the surface of a sphere, an area equal to the area of a square having the radius of the sphere as its side. Abbr., sr.

stère

A metric unit of capacity for wood, = 1 cubic meter of wood, adopted by the CIPM in 1879. At that time the abbreviation was s; in 1948 the 9TH CGPM changed it to st (Resolution 7). The décastère (= 10 cubic meters) and décistère (= 100 cubic decimeters) have been used in the last half century in the tropical hardwoods trade.

The stère was approved for use in the USA by Sec. 2 of the Act of July 28, 1866. In 1982 it was declared no longer acceptable (*Federal Register* Feb 26, 1982 (47 FR 8399-8400)).

stocks

In the American and New York Stock Exchanges, any fractional portion of a stock's price must be a multiple of 1/8th of a dollar. Some trace the choice of this module to the young United States' reliance on Spanish "dollars" for currency, which were gold pesos worth 8 reals, "pieces of eight," from which we get both the expression "two bits" for a quarter-dollar and the symbol $, from the symbol p^s for pesos.

In 1994, Nasdaq, the computerized exchange on which over-the-counter stocks are traded, proposed allowing stock prices to quoted in 1/16ths, 1/32nds and 1/64ths of a dollar.

stone

Various units of mass formerly used in Britain.

1) From at least 1340, "stone" has usually referred to a unit of mass = 14 pounds. For a discussion of the origin of this stone, see ☞sack. As late as 1862, however, over a dozen other definitions of the stone were in use in various trades and locations in the UK. Use of the stone in trade was abolished by the Weights and Measures Act of 1985.

Some of the other stones:

2) A stone of 5 pounds used for glass, mentioned in a document of 1302.

3) A stone of 8 pounds. In the 13TH C it was used for spices and pharmaceuticals, "wax, sugar, pepper, cinnamon, nutmegs and alum." By 1496, it was already referred to as being "of old time called the stone of London." In the 1600s the 8-lb stone was still used for spices, but by 1700 it had become associated with butchers. The Weights and Measures Act of 1834 mentions it in passing as a unit to be suppressed in favor of a universal 14-lb stone. In 1934, 582 years after Edward III specified "every stone to weigh 14 lb," the Board of Trade was writing its inspectors about "the old London or butcher's stone," advising them "New machines [i.e., scales] graduated in 8 lb units will be

accepted for verification and stamping until 31 January 1935 it being understood…that after that date no new machines so graduated are to be stamped."

straws

The standard length of drinking straws in the USA is 7¾". Sizes are named, in order of increasing diameter: Cocktail, slim, jumbo, super jumbo, and giant.

suits, men's

The technology of fitting has kept garments like men's suits affordable; if all suits were made to measure, as they were in the Middle Ages, few could afford them.

Men vary greatly in stature but the ratio of part to part varies much less, a fact iconized in Leonardo's man-in-a-circle. From that recognition it was a short and potentially profitable leap to the idea that men can be sorted into a small number of groups such that a single garment could fit any man in the group fairly satisfactorily. Figuring out how to make patterns with this property began in the early days of factory production; *The Mathematical Art of Cutting Garments According to the Different Formation of Men's Bodies*, by Henry Wampen, appeared in 1834. It is interesting that this work began with *men's* garments.

In the United States, standard ready-to-wear suits are sized by a chest measurement in inches. Of all the measurements of a jacket, the chest is the one on which the largest number of other significant dimensions depends. A typical full line is made in all whole number sizes from 33 to 44, then even sizes to 50. Sometimes 45 is also offered, especially in "portly" fittings. Sizes to 60 are regularly made, but are carried only by shops catering to large men.

In addition to the chest measurement, a suit size also includes a "fitting." Common fittings are regular, long and short; on labels these are often abbreviated, e.g., "40L." For a Long fitting, for example, a jacket might be made an inch longer than a Regular, the pockets and buttons would be lowered half an inch, and the lapels lengthened. Other fittings sometimes made include Portly, Short Portly, and Long Portly; Stout (symbol ST), Short Stouts and Long Stouts, Extra or Double Shorts, and Double Longs.

In any particular line the difference between the chest and waist measurements in a suit is kept the same from size to size, decreasing an inch or two in the larger sizes. This difference is called the "drop." A typical drop in the USA for the Regular and Long fittings is 4". (In sport coats, it was 6" to size 39, 5" to size 48, and 4" for size 50.) Thus the pants that came with a size 36R suit would have a 30" waist; those in a size 42R would have a 38" waist, and so on. For the Stout fittings, the drop for sizes through 48 is zero; the chest and waist measurements are the same. For 50 and 52 the waist is 1" larger than the chest, and 2" larger for 54 and up. Manufacturers produce trousers in waist sizes as large as 80", but such sizes are only available in large men's shops.

Like everything to do with fashion, the drop is subject to change. In the 1980s some manufacturers got the idea that men were becoming more athletic (bigger chests, smaller waists) and increased the drop to as much as 8". In England in the 1940s, the drop was 4".

The idea that one is a particular size should not be held too rigidly. Much depends on style and manufacturer. If a size 36 doesn't fit, another 36 from a different manufacturer, or even one from another line of the same manufacturer, may.

Shopping. Wear a suit whose fit pleases you and a shirt and shoes you expect to wear with the new suit. If you usually wear a sweater or vest, wear one. If you habitually carry junk in your pockets, bring it along. In the dressing room, transfer your wallet, pens and other paraphernalia to the pockets of the new suit.

In front of the mirrors many men take a stance they otherwise assume only while being awarded the Presidential Medal of Freedom. Avoid this. If the tailor asks you to empty your pockets and stand up straight, explain that that is not how you expect to wear the suit. Do not inflate your chest to the maximum while it is being measured.

Manufacturing grades. Within the trade, grades are used to indicate the amount of hand labor that went into a suit, a system that originated in union contracts. In a suit, jacket, trousers and vest (if any) must be the same grade. The grades run from 1 to 6. In grade 1, only the felling of the armholes and the sewing of buttons may be done by hand; in grade 2 the undercollar and cuffs may be felled by hand, and so on to grade 6, which "has all the features associated with British handicraft bespoke tailoring," according to a British report. An additional grade, "X," has no hand tailoring.

sunglasses

The comfort sunglasses provide, aside from anonymity, comes from their absorbing visible light; most also absorb invisible ultraviolet light, and a few absorb infrared light. Long-term exposure to ultraviolet light is thought to increase the risk of cataracts and damage to the retina. Wearing sunglasses that absorb visible light but not ultraviolet is probably more damaging than wearing no sunglasses at all, because it makes the wearer less conscious of the dose of ultraviolet he is receiving.

The ultraviolet spectrum is divided into bands. The UVB band includes light with wavelengths between 290 and 315 nanometers, and UVA, from 315 nm to 400 nm. Of the two, the UVB is the more harmful; the shorter the wavelength, the more energetic the radiation.

Various standards have been set for how much of the ultraviolet light a pair of sunglasses has to block, and most standards describe different classes of sunglass. The British standard of 1987, for example, said that General Purpose sunglasses had to block 97.1% of UVB and 92.75% of UVA, while Special Purpose sunglasses had to block 99.82% of UVB and 95.5% of UVA. The British also used *shade numbers:* cosmetic glasses having shade numbers from 1.1 to 2, general purpose glasses from 2.5 to 3.1, and special purpose glasses from 3.1 to 4.1.

The American National Standards Institute also defined three classes.

Cosmetic sunglasses must let through
- at least 40% of the visible light
- at most the same percentage of UVA as they do visible light
- half the percentage of UVB as of visible light, but in no case more than 30%.

General Purpose sunglasses must let through
- 8 to 40% of the visible light
- at most the same percentage of UVA as they do visible light
- half the percentage of UVB as of visible light, but in no case more than 5%.

Special Purpose sunglasses must let through
- at least 3% of the visible light
- no more than 1% of the UVB
- half the percentage of UVA as of visible light.

For the first two CLASSES ANSI included provisions for letting through enough red, yellow, and green light that traffic signals could be read, but this is not required of Special Purpose sunglasses.

In 1978, the U.S. Food and Drug Administration published a monograph on sun protection in the Federal Register. The Sunglass Assn. of America voluntarily adopted the standards in the FDA monograph, asking members to label all sunglasses as "Cosmetic," "General Purpose," or "Special Purpose," with transmittance limits. Unfortunately, many sunglasses sold in the USA, particularly cheap imports, are outside the SAA's program.

On the basis of animal tests, some researchers believe blue light also has harmful long-term effects, but this remains controversial. The British standard provides that no particular wavelength in the blue-green may exceed overall transmittance by more than 20%.

The Future. In June 1992, the FDA proposed a revised voluntary standard by which all sunglasses would block 99% of the UVB. Sunglasses advertised as UV-blocking would have to block 99% of UVA and UVB, and 60–90% of the visible light. Sunglasses sold for extreme conditions, like skiing, would block 92–97% of the visible light and have side shields.

sunscreens

The protection given by sunscreens is rated in SPF numbers (for sun protection factor). If a person's skin would redden after 10 minutes' exposure to the sun under a particular set of conditions, protected by a suntan lotion with an SPF of 15 it would not redden until it had been exposed for (10 min. × SPF 15 =) 150 minutes. SPF numbers for products are determined experimentally, by exposing patches on people's arms to UV from sunlamps with and without the sunscreen, which is applied in a rigorously-controlled way. This method of rating sunscreens was chosen because it was felt it would be more meaningful to users than transmittance/absorbance numbers. For comparison, SPF 2 blocks 50% of UVB; SPF 15 blocks 93%. The typical dry white cotton T-shirt has an SPF of about 7.4 (wet it is 5.5).

The biggest catch in this system for rating sun protection products is that the wavelengths that cause reddening are not the only damaging ones. Ultraviolet light is divided into three bands: UVA, UVB, and UVC. UVC (below 290 nm) is mainly encountered from germicidal lamps; in sunlight, the shortest ultraviolet wavelengths that reach earth's surface are about 286 nm.

UVB, which runs from 290 to 320 nm (definitions vary), is the band that causes sunburn. The most damaging wavelengths are in the range from 300 to 307 nm, although tests with artificial ultraviolet sources showed that 297 nm and 254 nm have the greatest reddening effect.

UVA (320 to 400 nanometers) is less energetic than UVB but more penetrating. UVA is generally considered nonreddening, although long exposures to UVA (e.g., 2 hours of midday sun on a fair-skinned person) can cause sunburn. Because UVA is nonreddening, SPF numbers do not take into consideration a sunscreen's ability to block this radiation. Ten to 15 per cent of UVA passes through the epidermis to the dermis in fair-skinned people, 5% to 10% in dark-skinned persons. UVA does cause degenerative skin changes; to a greater extent than UVB, it is responsible for aging effects.

Another cautionary note is that a sunscreen, even one with a very high SPF number, may not prevent serious damage from UVB itself. Some researchers have found that sunlight suppresses the immune system, and that this may be the result of the action of UVB on a substance found in the uppermost surface of the skin, while sunscreens tend to be absorbed into a lower layer.

The old regulations allowed a product with an SPF of 8 to say it provided "maximal protection." It is now realized this is not true, but such a label continues to be permitted. Of two preparations with the same SPF number, it is probably best to pick the one that claims its protection extends into the UVA.

supplementary units

In ☞SI, a class of units created in 1960 by the 11TH CGPM (Resolution 12) to cover those units which are neither ☞base units nor derived from base units (☞derived units). Then as now, the only supplementary units were the ☞radian and ☞steradian, both measuring angles. In 1969 the CIPM, "considering that Resolution 12...has provoked discussions," formally declared that "the name 'supplementary units' is given to SI units for which the General Conference declines to state whether they are base units or derived units."

In 1980, taking into account the advice of two committees, the CIPM refined the concept of supplementary units (Resolution 1, CI-1980), deciding "to interpret the class of supplementary units in the International System as a class of dimensionless derived units for which the CGPM allows the freedom of using or not using them in expressions for SI derived units."

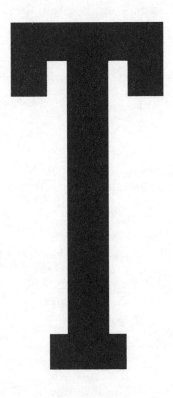

tablecloths

At a formal dinner, the tablecloth is expected to overhang the table edge by 15" or more. An overhang of 9" is more practical and appropriate to everyday dinners, but when the "drop" shrinks to a few inches the table looks peculiar. The chart below shows how large a table can be, with three different depths of overhang, for sizes in which tablecloths are commonly sold today.

Tablecloth size	Maximum table size at various drops		
	6" drop	9" drop	15" drop
52" × 52"	40" × 40"	34" × 34"	22" × 22"
Oblong and Oval Tables			
52" × 70"	40" × 58"	34" × 52"	22" × 40"
60" × 84"	48" × 72"	42" × 66"	30" × 54"
60" × 102"	48" × 90"	42" × 84"	30" × 72"
60" × 120"	48" × 108"	42" × 102"	30" × 90"
60" × 142"	48" × 130"	42" × 124"	30" × 112"
70" × 64"	58" × 52"	52" × 46"	40" × 34"
70" × 72"	58" × 60"	52" × 54"	40" × 42"
70" × 96"	58" × 84"	52" × 78"	40" × 66"
70" × 114"	58" × 102"	52" × 96"	40" × 84"

Tablecloth size	Maximum table size at various drops		
	6" drop	9" drop	15" drop
70" × 126"	58" × 114"	52" × 108"	40" × 96"
70" × 144"	58" × 132"	52" × 126"	40" × 114"
Round Tables			
60" round	48" diameter	58" diameter	78" diameter
70" round	42" diameter	52" diameter	72" diameter
90" round	30" diameter	40" diameter	60" diameter

tables, dining
A formal place setting is about 24" wide; an informal, 18". Restaurant designers allow a minimum of 29" from an adult diner's nose to his neighbors', and 12" between chairs.

Card tables, to 40" x 40", seat 4 persons.

Size of oblong or oval tables	28" × 46" to 42" × 54"	36" × 56" to 42" × 64"	42" × 72" to 42" × 84"	42" × 90" to 42" × 96"	42" × 100" to 42" × 120"
Persons seated	4 – 6	6 – 8	8 – 10	10 – 12	12 – 16

Diameter of round tables	36" – 44"	44" – 54"	60" – 70"
Persons seated	4	4 – 6	6 – 8

tables, typing
The surface is typically 29 1/2" above the floor; however, this should be adjustable to fit the typist.

table tennis
Ball. Of celluloid, 4 1/2" to 4 3/4" in circumference with a mass of 37 to 39 grams, except in the USA, where it is 37 to 41 grams.

Table and net. The net is 6" high and 6' long. The playing surface is 30" above the floor, 9' long, and 5' wide.

Racket. It may be any size, shape, or weight. Any racket surface may be used to hit the ball. If the surface is covered with dimpled rubber, which is usual, the layer of rubber must be no more than 2 mm thick. If a layer of foam rubber is used beneath the dimpled rubber, their combined thickness may be no more than 4 mm.

tacks
Cut tacks are made in a variety of metals (blued steel, copper, aluminum); tacks used to hold metal screening should be made of the same metal as the screening, to prevent galvanic corrosion.

Size	2	4	6	8	10	12	14	16
Length	1/4"	7/16"	1/2"	9/16"	5/8"	11/16"	3/4"	13/16"

tatami
In Japan, a traditional unit measuring the area of a domestic room. The tatami is a woven straw mat used as floor covering; its size became standardized in the Muromachi Period (1338–1573) at one *ken* long

and half a ken wide. The ken, however, has varied. It is now ≈ 1.82 meters (1.97 m in the Kansai area, including the cities of Kyoto, Osaka, and Kobe). Thus 1 tatami ≈ 1.66 square meters ≈ 1.99 sq. yards.

telephone, modems

If you are planning to use your modem on an overseas trip, you may have a problem, and not just with the connectors. For example, in some countries telephone use is metered by sending impulses over the phone line. These impulses interfere with modem operation and must be filtered out.

A company called TeleAdapt, Inc. (51 East Campbell Ave., Campbell, CA 95008) sells adapters, filters, testers, and other types of hardware needed to connect modems to the telephone systems of various countries. They have extensive information about what is to be expected in various countries, emphasizing what is found in major hotels.

telescopes

Refractors

A refractor's size is given as the aperture, which is the diameter of the lens at the front of the telescope, and the f/stop. Multiplying the f/stop by the aperture gives the focal length in whatever units were used for the aperture. So a 4" f/9 refractor would have a focal length of 36".

The magnification of a refractor depends on its focal length, the focal length of the eyepiece, and the magnification of any barlow lens inserted between the eyepiece and the telescope. To find the system magnification, divide the focal length of the refractor by the focal length of the eyepiece measured in the same units). If a barlow is used, then multiply by the magnification number marked on the barlow. For example, a 60 mm f/8 refractor with a 12 mm eyepiece would have a system magnification of 40× (60 × 8, ÷ 12). With a 2.5× barlow added, the magnification would be 100×.

Reflectors

A reflector's size is specified by the aperture, which is the diameter of the primary mirror, and the focal length. Dividing the focal length by the aperture, when both are expressed in the same units, gives the f/number. So the f/number of a reflector with a 48" focal length and a 6" aperture would be f/8.

A larger aperture is a mixed blessing, because the effects of air turbulence are more pronounced.

The quality of a reflector depends on the quality of the mirror. In 1879, Lord Rayleigh observed that an optical instrument was as good as perfect if the difference between the longest and shortest optical paths to the focus did not differ by more than 1/4 wavelength. Reflectors that meet this criterion have become known as "diffraction-limited." But there are different ways of expressing this tolerance. If the difference in optical paths is really to be no greater than 1/4 wave, the highest zone on the mirror cannot be more than 1/8 of a wave higher than the lowest zone. Instead of highest peak-to-lowest valley error, most makers give a root-mean-square average for the mirror's entire surface. The R.M.S. value for a mirror is typically four to six times smaller than the peak-to-valley error.

Trials have shown that beginning observers can easily detect improvements in image quality up to 1/4 wave; improvement beyond that is more apparent to observers with extensive training and experience.

Eyepieces

Eyepieces for consumer refractors are interchangeable with those for reflectors. They are sized by focal length (of the eyepiece, not the telescope) and outer diameter. Standard outer diameters are 0.965" (mostly found on economy imports), 1 1/4" (the most common) and 2" (mostly found on premium low-power or wide-angle eyepieces). Adapters are sold which make it possible to put 1 1/4" eyepieces in focusing mounts made for 2" eyepieces. To use 1 1/4" eyepieces in an 0.965" mount, a "hybrid star diagonal" can be used, which inserts a mirror between the focusing mount and the eyepiece.

Available focal lengths range from 2.5 mm to 80 mm, with 5 to 40 a normal range. An eyepiece's focal length will always be marked on it (in a marking like "AH20", the letters indicate the optical construction and the numbers are the focal length in millimeters).

Most users have a set of eyepieces to enable them to change the telescope's magnification. The shorter the focal length of the eyepiece, the greater the magnification. However, beyond a certain point increasing the magnification by using a shorter focal length eyepiece produces only "empty magnification": the image is bigger, but also fuzzier, so that no additional detail can be seen. As a rule of thumb, the greatest useful magnification will be 50× to 60× per inch of aperture. So a four-inch telescope would have a maximum usable magnification of about 200× to 240×. If the telescope had a focal length of 1200 mm, the shortest sensible focal length eyepiece would be (1200 ÷ 200 =) 6 mm.

Eyepieces with the same focal length but different optical designs may have different apparent fields of view. The apparent field of view is expressed as an angle in degrees. To find the actual field of view with any particular eyepiece, divide the apparent field by the telescope's magnification.

A characteristic of eyepieces which is important to eyeglass wearers is eye relief, the maximum distance an eye can be from the outer lens of the eyepiece and still see the entire field. When manufacturers provide this information, it is usually given in millimeters.

temperature

To convert between Celsius and Fahrenheit, see the appendices.

People are very interested in how hot or cold substances are, but human perception of temperature is notoriously inaccurate. (See

☛temperature, sensible.) Techniques for measuring temperature depend on finding something whose changes, as it warms or cools, can be observed. Mercury, for example, expands as it becomes warmer, and confining the expansion in a narrow tube makes this change observable. The electrical resistance of platinum wire changes with temperature, and that resistance can be measured with great precision. Different temperatures call for different methods of measurement. A mercury thermometer cannot be dipped into a vat of molten steel.

Scales. Observations of temperature-sensitive changes in substances led to the construction of temperature scales. Defining a temperature scale (or any other kind of scale) requires specifying 1) the size of the interval between points on the scale and 2) a fixed point. A typical fixed point on a temperature scale is a temperature at which some dramatic change takes place, such as the melting of a metal. Historically, the most commonly-used fixed points have been the melting and boiling points of water, but such melting points as those of gold, silver, and antimony, and the boiling points of oxygen and sulfur, have also been used. A special fixed point is the triple point of water, the temperature at which water vapor, liquid water, and solid water exist simultaneously, which occurs only at a unique pressure (611 pascals, or 0.00603 atmospheres, or 4.58 millimeters of mercury) and temperature. The triple point temperature of water is used as a fixed point in defining most current temperature scales.

Absolute Zero. Scientists exploring temperature turned to the gas-filled thermometer, because as gases are heated they expand far more evenly than liquids and solids do. If the volume of the gas is held constant, changes in temperature can be measured as changes in pressure. Experiments with gas-filled thermometers revealed something very interesting: measurements of the pressure, volume and temperature of gases, extrapolated, showed that at a temperature of about −273° centigrade, pressure should be zero. Of course, no one was able to reach such a low temperature. This point was named absolute zero; it doesn't get any colder than absolute zero. Once it was thought that all molecular motion stops at absolute zero; now physicists don't think so. (Temperatures below absolute zero are used by physicists to describe certain situations involving spins in magnetic fields, but this is not temperature as most people think of it.)

Thermodynamic Temperature Scales. In the 19TH C, scientists were leary of any definition of a fundamental unit that depended upon the behavior of some particular substance, such as mercury or platinum (although that was acceptable in a "working definition"). They preferred being able to measure everything in terms of mass, length and time. A way of measuring temperature that didn't depend on using any particular substance, and that directly related temperature to mass, length and time, came from attempts to improve steam engines, studies which evolved into the science of thermodynamics. The steam engine was seen to be an example of a general class of machines that change heat to work. In any such engine, heat, Q_{high}, is taken from a high temperature source such as a fire (at temperature T_{source}) and a portion of it, Q_{low}, transferred to a low temperature sink, usually the atmosphere. The rest of the heat is converted to work, W. The maximum percentage of Q_{high} that can be converted to work depends solely on the difference between the source and sink temperatures.

$$\frac{W}{Q_{high}} = \frac{1 - T_{sink}}{T_{source}} \quad \text{and} \quad \frac{T_{source}}{T_{sink}} = \frac{Q_{high}}{Q_{low}}$$

William Thomson (Lord Kelvin) saw that this relationship offered a way of defining temperature that had nothing to do with the properties of any particular substance. In principle, a heat engine could be operated with a sink at some known temperature (say, the triple point of water) and the source at a temperature to be measured, and the temperature of the source calculated from the ratio of the heat supplied to the heat exhausted. In this way temperature could be defined entirely in terms of mass, length, and time, creating what is called a thermodynamic temperature scale.

Thomson and J. P. Joule conducted a long series of experiments comparing temperature ratios from heat to work conversions with those taken with a gas thermometer, and determined that they agreed, so far as it was possible to tell.

The temperature scales defined in SI and other recent systems of units are all thermodynamic scales in which 0 is at absolute zero. Other scales, like the Celsius scale, are defined in terms of a thermodynamic scale.

Temperature from Radiation. High temperatures are usually measured by analyzing the radiation given off by the object whose temperature one is taking. All objects give off electromagnetic radiation, whether light bulb filaments, stars, or people, and the hotter they are the more radiation they give off. In 1900 Max Planck deduced the relationship between the temperature of an perfect emitter—a "black body"—and the amount of energy given off at any wavelength in its spectrum. In practice, real objects behave much like black bodies, so from the spectrum of the radiation they emit we can infer their temperature.

Some Temperature Scales

The Fahrenheit scale became popular through its use on the first reliable, commercially-available, mercury-in-glass thermometers. Gabriel Daniel Fahrenheit manufactured thermometers in Amsterdam from about 1717 until his death in 1736. As the zero point on his scale he chose the temperature of a bath of ice melting in a solution of common salt, a standard 18TH C way of getting a low temperature in the laboratory (and in the kitchen, as in an old-fashioned ice cream churn). For a consistent, reproducible high point he chose the temperature of the blood of a healthy person (his wife), which he called 96°. (The scales of the first thermometers had been divided into 12 intervals. When they became a little more precise, the size of the steps was cut in half, making 24 of them, then 48, and finally 96.) Fahrenheit's successors changed the upper fixed point to the boiling point of water, which they set at 212° in order to avoid changing the size of Fahrenheit's degree. The Fahrenheit scale of temperature remains in use in the USA, but it is now defined in terms of the Kelvin scale.

The Rankine scale is a thermodynamic scale formerly used by engineers in English-speaking countries. The degrees in the Rankine scale are the same size as Fahrenheit degrees, but 0 is set at absolute zero, −459.67°F. This scale is obsolete.

The Réaumur Scale. In 1739, R. A. F de Réaumur proposed a scale in which 0 was the freezing point of water and 80 degrees the boiling point. Thus one Réaumur degree is 4/5ths of a centigrade degree. This scale was used in France and several other countries prior to the metric system.

The Centigrade and Celsius Scales. In 1741 Anders Celsius, professor of astronomy at the University of Uppsala, Sweden, introduced a temperature scale with 0° at water's boiling point and 100° at freezing. Shortly after his death, the fixed points were reversed and the scale became known as the centigrade scale, in which 0° is the freezing point of water and 100° its boiling point at atmospheric pressure. In 1887 the International Commission on Weights and Measures adopted "as the standard thermometric scale for the international services of weights and measures the centigrade scale of the hydrogen thermometer, having as fixed points the temperature of melting ice (0°) and the vapor of distilled water boiling (100°) at standard atmospheric pressure, the hydrogen being taken at an initial manometric pressure of one meter of mercury."

The Celsius scale is the centigrade scale with a difference. Defined in 1954 at the 10TH CGPM, temperature on the Celsius scale is the temperature on the Kelvin scale minus 273.15. This made the Celsius scale's values almost the same as those of the centigrade scale (they differ by less than 0.1 degree).

Why was the centigrade scale abandoned? The problem is that the "temperature of melting ice…at standard atmospheric pressure" cannot be measured with enough precision. Ideally one takes the temperature of a bath of pure, air-saturated water containing pure melting ice. But as ice melts it surrounds itself with an insulating layer of meltwater that is not air-saturated. The bath cannot be stirred because that would heat it. In contrast, the Kelvin scale has a nearby set point, measurements of which are reproducible with an accuracy of a ten-thousandth of a degree: the triple point of water, by definition 273.16 K. Replacing the hard-to-measure ice point with the triple point made possible more precise measurements, but to indicate the change required giving the "zero is freezing, 100 is boiling" scale a new name.

The Kelvin Scale. In 1848, Lord Kelvin himself proposed a thermodynamic temperature scale using a constant volume hydrogen-filled gas thermometer, and this scale was accepted by international agreement in 1887. In 1948, the NINTH CGPM took the triple point of water as the fixed point for the thermodynamic scale in the metric system, and in 1954 assigned this temperature the value 273.16 kelvin. The 13TH CGPM (1967) made the kelvin "the fraction 1/273.16 of the thermodynamic temperature of the triple point of water" and stated that "the unit of thermodynamic temperature and the unit of temperature interval are one and the same unit." In 1980, the CIPM decided the word "degree" and the degree symbol should not be used in connection with the kelvin.

The International Practical Temperature Scale

Constant-volume gas-filled thermometers are not everyday instruments, and in fact over limited temperature ranges their readings are not as reproducible as those of thermometers especially suited to that range, such as platinum resistance thermometers. For practical purposes, a temperature scale is needed that has many reference points whose thermodynamic temperature is known from laboratory investigations with gas thermometers, so that other kinds of thermometers can be calibrated whatever form they take or temperature range they cover. A series of such temperature scales has been defined by the CIPM:

✓ International Temperature Scale of 1927 (ITS-27)
✓ International Practical Temperature Scale of 1948 (IPTS-48)
✓ International Practical Temperature Scale of 1968 (IPTS-68) (amended 1975)
✓ 1976 Provisional 0.5 K to 30 K Temperature Scale (EPT-76)
✓ International Temperature Scale of 1990 (ITS-90)

These temperature scales use the kelvin as their interval and consist of reference points with their thermodynamic temperature, so readings on the practical scales closely approximate the true thermodynamic temperature. Different measurement techniques are assumed for different parts of the scale; for example, in ITS-90, Planck's radiation law has been used to define temperatures of 773.15 K and above, while temperatures near absolute zero are measured by the vapor pressure of helium isotopes. Some examples of the fixed points, from IPTS-68:

Hydrogen boils	20.28 K
Oxygen boils	90.188 K
Ice point	273.15 K
Boiling point of water	373.15 K
Freezing point of zinc	692.73 K
Freezing point of silver	1235.08 K
Freezing point of gold	1337.58 K

temperature, sensible

The measured temperature is often a poor gauge of how cold or warm the air feels to people. Temperature as it is perceived is often called the sensible temperature, and various measures have been invented to convey it.

In cold weather, wind makes it feel colder than it is. The National Weather Service describes this effect by the windchill factor, a method based on heat-loss measurements made in Antarctica. For a particular combination of temperature and wind speed, the windchill factor is that temperature of still air in which a person walking would experience the same sensation of cold.

The dotted lines show how the graph is used. A horizontal dotted line is drawn for a temperature of 10°F, and a vertical one for a wind speed of 20 mph. They meet halfway between the -20°F and −30°F curves, indicating a windchill factor of about −25°F.

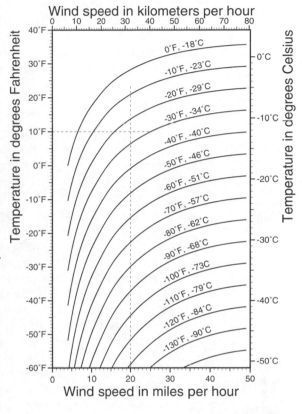

tennis

The sport Americans call tennis is called lawn tennis in Great Britain, to distinguish it from court tennis. In the USA, the regulations are set by the United States Tennis Association.

Ball. Stitchless, either white or yellow. It weighs more than 2 ounces but less than 2 1/16 ounces; its diameter is between 2 1/2" and 2 5/8". Dropped from a height of 100" to a concrete surface, it bounces more than 53" but less than 58". Limits are also placed on how mcuh the ball can deform under pressure, which is measured with an 18-pound load coming from three different directions.

For play at altitudes above 4000', two additional types of balls are permitted. One, called a "pressurized ball," has an internal pressure greater than the surrounding atmospheric pressure and, dropped from a height of 100", bounces higher than 48" but not as high as 53". The second type is called a "zero pressure" or "non-pressure ball." It

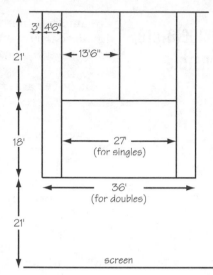

must be allowed to acclimatize at the altitude at which it will be played for at least 60 days before being put into play, and the standards for the height of its bounce are the same as for the regular ball.

Racquet. The maximum length is 32" and the maximum width 12 1/2". The string surface has a maximum length of 15 1/2" and a maximum width of 11 1/2".

Grip sizes, from 1 to 5, indicate the circumference of the grip in increments of 1/8", starting with 4 1/8" (so 5 is 4 2/8"). "String" is sold in 5 gauges: 15, 15L, 16, 16L, and 17, with the higher numbers indicating thinner string. As a rule of thumb, a tennis racquet will require restringing as many times per year as it is used each week.

Court. The cord or wire supporting the net must be no more than 1/3" in diameter. The posts support the ends of net at a height of 3'6". The band along the top of the net extends down each side at least 2", but no more than 2 1/2". The center line is 2" wide; the baseline may be as much as 4" wide; all other lines must be not less than 1" wide nor more than 2" wide. The center mark is 4" long and 2" wide.

ten pin bowling

Ball. Diameter: 8 1/2" Weight: no more than 16 pounds. The lighter balls are used by women and juniors.
Pin. Weight: between 3 lb 2 oz and 3 lb 10 oz. Height: 1'3". They are set in a triangle 3' on a side.
Lane. 3' 6" wide and 60' long. A minimum approach area of 15' is required. Guide marks are placed on the lane 7' from the foul line, and 12'–16' from the foul line.

tesla

The unit of magnetic flux density in SI. Abbr., T. One tesla is one weber of magnetic flux per square meter of circuit area. Its dimensions are $\frac{weber}{meter^2}$ or, in terms of base units only, $\frac{kilogram}{second^2 \cdot ampere}$

test scores

Many of the terms used in describing test scores, such as stanine and percentile, are used in two senses. Statisticians use them to refer to points dividing the scores into groups, but counsellors often use the words to describe the group rather than its boundaries, e.g., "Johnny is in the fifth stanine."

Because scores on standardized tests depend on comparing an individual's score with the scores of a large group of test-takers, it is important to know what group is being used for the comparison. For example, if Johnny scored in the fifth stanine, is that in relation to everyone who took the test in his school, in the community, in the state, or nationally? He might be in the ninth stanine locally and the fifth nationally.

In grading many standardized tests, the raw scores are normalized: points are added to or subtracted from the raw scores, according to the size of the score, until their distribution fits a symmetrical, bell-shaped curve. For scores expressed in stanines, normalizing will put 4% of the testees in the first stanine, 7% in the second, and so on through 12%, 17%, 20%, 17%, 12%, 7%, and 4%. Having the scores fit a normal curve is very convenient for statistical purposes, but it assumes that whatever ability the test measures is evenly distributed around a central peak, which is questionable.

Median. The median score divides the group in half, with as many scores below the median as above it. Note that this is probably not the arithmetic average (the mean) of all the scores. For example, the average of the set of scores 2, 4, 4, 9, and 9 is 5.6, but the median score is 4.

Quartile. The three points that divide the scores into four groups each with the same number of testees. The first quartile contains the lowest 25% of the scores.

Stanine. The raw scores are normalized and placed on a scale with 9 intervals, from 1 (lowest) to 9. The median falls in stanine 5. It is thought that the difference in ability between the students in any two adjacent stanines will be about the same, that is, a student in stanine 7 and a student in stanine 8 differ about as much as a student in stanine 3 does from one in stanine 4.

Percentile ranks. Scores are normalized as for stanines but instead of being sorted into nine groups they are sorted into 99, which gives a more precise picture of the test-takers's relative standing than a stanine would. The raw scores are processed so that the median falls in the 50th percentile rank. If a raw score of 88 puts the testee in the 65th percentile, 65% of the raw scores were below 88.

Percentiles are frequently reported in percentile bands, which take into account the test's measurement error. Usually the band is one standard error below the score to one standard error above it. There is a 68% chance that if the student took this test an infinite number of times, his or her average score would fall within the band.

Grade Equivalent. When a third-grader gets a grade equivalent score of 5.4 on a third -grade math test, it does not necessarily mean the student has mastered any fifth-grade math; it means that the student's score is what the average 5th grader in the fourth month of the school year would score *on this test for third-graders.*

therm 1) In the USA, one thousand cubic feet of natural gas.   2) 100,000 Btu.

thimbles Standardized sizes began to be made around the middle of the 19TH C. The size is often marked on what thimble collectors call the "apex," the inside top of the thimble.

Origin	Small	Medium	Large
USA	6, 7, 8	9, 10, 11	12
British	9, 8, 7	6, 5	4, 3
French	8	9, 10	11, 12
German & Dutch	3, 4	5, 6, 7	8, 9, 10
Norwegian	1, 2	3, 4	

American ring and thimble sizes correspond approximately as follows:

Ring	3	3 1/2	4	4 1/2	5	5 1/2	6	7	7 1/2	8	8 1/2
Thimble	6	7	8	9	10	11	12	13	14	15	16

Very small thimbles were made for children, but salesmen's samples were also sometimes deliberate miniatures.

thread, sewing Thread sizes are called "ticket numbers." "A multiple number of undefined and unrelated ticketing systems," as the ASTM puts it, have been used for assigning ticket numbers. The table gives some approximate equivalents. Many of these systems are no longer in use—nor is the thread itself, for in natural threads today's home seamstress has a narrower range of choice than her mother did.

Approx. Equivalent Ticket Numbers

Regular cotton and core spun	Mercerized cotton	Polyester and nylon	Silk
16	F	105	
20	E	90	E
24	D	69	
30	C	61	D
36	B	53	
40	A	42	C
50	0	38	
60	00	32	B
70	000	30	A
90	0000	21	0
100	—	18	
120	00000	14	
150			00

In studying the problem, the ASTM subcommittee concluded that ticket numbers should reflect the actual content of raw fiber in the thread, but that finishing operations (such as bleaching, dyeing, mercerizing, application of waxes and silicones, and so on) made it impossible to determine fiber content from the weight or diameter of the finished thread. In their system, the ticket number is based on the yarn number of the unfinished thread, measured in tex (see ☞ yarn), before bleaching, dying, mercerizing, the addition of lubricants, and so on. Such a ticket number would be a better indicator of actual fiber content (not to mention being better defined) than the older systems. The ticket is, roughly, the tex value, but only certain values are permitted, and for each of these the standard specifies a range of tex.

ties, railroad

The usual lengths in the USA are 8', 8 1/2', or 9', with a cross section between 6" × 7" and 7" × 9". Treated ties can last an average of 25 to 40 years, although they may have a much shorter life due to mechanical wear.

tights, women's

Typical USA Sizing

| | Hips | | | |
Height	34"–37"	37"–41"	41"–44"	44"–48"
5'0"–5'2"	S	S	M	—
5'3"–5'4"	M	M	M	—
5'5"–5'6"	L	L	L	L
5'7"–5'8"	L	XL	XL	XL
5'9"–5'10"	XL	XL	XL	XL

tile

Ceramic Tile

Ceramic mosaic tile is made in a wide range of sizes, from less than 1 square inch to as large as 6". The most common sizes are 1" × 1", 1" × 2", and 2" × 2" rectangles, and 1" and 2" hexagons (measured from flat to flat). Usually the tile is nominally 1/4" thick. Smaller tiles are sometimes "unitized" by adhering their faces, with the proper spacing, to paper or plastic backing. Such units are usually 12" × 12". Slip-resistant surfaces are available only in the 1" × 1" size.

Glazed wall tile has a nominal thickness of 5/16". Common square sizes are 4 1/4" × 4 1/4", 6" × 6", and 8" × 8". Oblong rectangles are 6" × 4 1/4" and 8" × 4 1/4". A wide variety of matching trim pieces are available, such as inside and outside corners, beads, counter trim and cove bases.

Non-rectangular shapes include hexagons (5" between flats) and octagons (4 1/4" between flats, with a matching 1 3/8" square). Spanish 5 7/16" × 5 5/16".

Unglazed tile is generally square, 4" to 12" on a side, and 3/8" to 7/8" thick.

Quarry and paver tile comes in nominal thicknesses of 1/2" and 3/4" for quarry tile, and 3/8" and 1/2" for paver tile. Typical sizes 4" × 4", 6"

× 6", and 4" × 8" for squares; 6" and 8" between flats for hexagons, and 4" × 8" for rectangles. Special shapes like 3 × 9 lozenges, Spanish, and elongated hexagons are also available.

Resilient Tile
Vinyl tile is 12" × 12"; some asphalt tiles are 9" × 9".

Stone Tile
Dimensioned stone tiles are cut in squares or rectangles, 12" to 18" on a side, and ¼" to ⅜" thick.

time

Two measures are taken of time: of the duration of an interval ("she lived for 100 years"), and of an instant, labeling it in a way that permits sequencing ("she was born at 6:01 a.m. on July 29, 1943"). Both measurements are made using regularly repeating phenomena as a standard: the recurring seasons mark the passing of years, and the days are separated by the rising and setting of the sun.

Observation of the night sky, with its regular motion and a surface infinitely subdivided by the fixed stars, makes possible more precise measurements of time. The stars around the pole, for example, form a clock. In the northern hemisphere, at midnight on March 5, the pointer stars point directly down at the Pole Star. At midnight two months later, they will be at the 2 o'clock position, and so on around the clock during one year.

The precision with which time could be measured increased greatly when astronomical observations began to be made with naked eye instruments, and recorded. Such observations were made in all inhabited continents.

The system of time units now used throughout the world can be traced to the Sumerians, who around 3000 BC devised a base-60 system of numeration later refined by the Babylonians. The system was taken up by the Egyptians, who divided the night into ten hours and the day into twelve, with an additional two hours of dusk. The Egyptian 24-hour day was adopted by the Greeks. In the words of Otto Neugebauer, "Our present division of the day into 24 hours of 60 minutes each is the result of a Hellenistic modification of an Egyptian practice combined with Babylonian numerical procedures." From prehistoric times until the adoption of atomic time in 1958, the measurement of time was essentially a province of astronomy.

Human Time
Most cultures with units of time smaller than a half day arrived at them by subdividing a day by astronomical observation. The derivation of units from the human body, common in measures of length (fingerbreadth, span, foot, etc) was used for time in only one system I know of, in Tibet. Perhaps reflecting that culture's interest in meditation, the smallest time interval, the *dbug*, was the average length of time a healthy person took to exhale and inhale. Six *dbugs* = 1 *chu-*

srang; 60 *chu-srang* = 1 *chu-tshod;* 60 *chu-tshod* = 1 *zhag,* which was a 24-hr day. (Currently in spoken Tibetan a *chu-tshod* is the same as an hour.) The pulse rate never became the basis of a time system.

Like many other animals, humans have an internal clock whose ticking establishes their circadian rhythm of hormone ebb and flood. Experiments with people in underground bunkers, deliberately deprived of all clues to the time of day, show that the ungoverned body's natural day is about 25 hours long.

Decimal Time?

At least two attempts have been made to establish decimally-related time units, the first by the ancient Egyptians. The second, almost identical to the Egyptian's, was voted in by French revolutionaries on April 7, 1795. The French system comprised a 10-day week, a 10-hour day, a 100-minute hour, and a 100-second minute. The system was repealed on December 31, 1805. Ten-hour days and 100-minute hours were possible, but the French public couldn't cope with a 10-day week.

Apparent Time and Mean Time

By the Middle Ages, days were divided into 24 hours; hours into 60 minutes (*minutiae prima*); and minutes into 60 seconds (*minutiae secundae*). But hour did not mean a fixed length of time. The period from sunset to sunrise was divided into 12 equal hours, and the period from sunrise to sunset was also divided into 12 equal hours. This is time by sundial, time told in *temporal hours.*

A night hour in the winter was much longer than a night hour in the summer, and so with the minute and second—which few could measure anyway. For people who can only work by sunlight, using temporal hours has the advantage that the hour tells what part of the work day remains. But there is another problem in getting to equal hours, as the

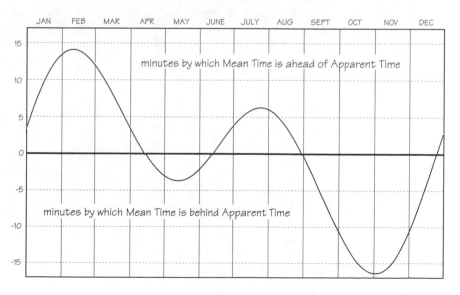

ancient Greeks realized.

Because the Earth's orbit is not circular, and because the Earth's axis is not perpendicular to the plane of its orbit (it's "tilted"), the sun appears to move more quickly during some parts of the year than others. Thus some 24-hour days are longer than others, and so even if we divide each day into 24 equal hours (which is *apparent solar time)*, some hours in a year will be longer than others. An alternative to apparent solar time is *mean solar time*: average the lengths of all the days in a year to obtain a *mean solar day*, and divide that day into 24 equal *mean solar hours.* The difference in minutes between apparent solar time and mean solar time is given by the so-called equation of time, shown in the chart.

Water clocks, the most common type of clock in ancient and medieval times other than candles, could easily be built to accommodate apparent time. Instead of a single mark on the side of a container to indicate the depth of an hour's worth of dripping water, a series of lines could be ruled, one for the length of the hour in each month. It is much harder to make a mechanical clock tell hours whose length varies over the year, but such clocks, called equation clocks, have been built.

As mechanical clocks became more plentiful and accurate, mean time became more important. By the end of the 18TH C, mean time was replacing apparent time in Europe. It was adopted in 1780 in Geneva, in 1792 in England, in 1810 in Berlin, and in 1816 in Paris. Technical advances such as the invention of the pendulum clock by Huygens in 1657 made clocks and watches more accurate. The industrial revolution made them available to more people, a process of commercial diffusion still going on in poorer nations at the close of the 20TH C.

Modern Times

The second has been the unit of time from the beginning of the metric system, but originally its meaning was understood rather than defined. In 1820, a committee of French scientists recommended that it be 1/86,400 of the mean solar day (86,400 = 60 seconds × 60 minutes × 24 hours). Increasingly precise measurements of time made this definition inadequate.

If the time scale's interval was uncertain, the fixed points were pandemonium; there were thousands of them. Every town kept its own time. The improvement of transportation, especially the introduction of railways running on a schedule, led to a need for predictable relationships between the time kept in different localities. For countries spread over many degrees of longitude, like the United States, Canada, and Russia, ☛time zones were essential.

In October 1884, the International Meridian Conference voted that the prime meridian, 0° of longitude, would run through the Royal Observatory in Greenwich, England. This choice was almost forced by the universal use of Greenwich as the prime meridian by marine navigators, thanks to the effort the seafaring British had put into developing the tools navigators needed. (The French did not agree; they wanted the prime meridian to run through Paris, and held out until 1911.) The choice of the prime meridian was in effect a choice of noon for the world, and Greenwich Civil Time (GCT) became the time from which other times were calculated. Thereafter, most of the world's clocks have been an even number of hours ahead of or behind the time in Greenwich.

So that all of a night's observations would have the same date, astronomers had always reckoned a day as beginning at noon. They used a time scale based on Greenwich, so that it was "midnight" when the mean sun crossed the prime meridian. They called this scale Greenwich Mean Time (GMT).

In the 1920s, the IAU instituted a series of changes that created a standard solar mean time with noon at the moment when the mean sun passed the prime meridian. They first decided that after 1925, the day should begin at midnight. This new time scale was first called UT, Universal Time, but in 1935, responding to the zeitgeist, the IAU named this time scale TU (temps universel, for France), UT (universal time, for UK and the USA) and WZ (Weltzeit, for Germany). Day-begins-at-noon-in-Greenwich time was renamed Greenwich Mean Astronomical Time (GMAT). Navigators continued to use what they call GMT, Greenwich Mean Time.

Meanwhile, as clocks continued to become more precise, it became clear that the rotation of the earth was not constant, as Flaamsted thought he had shown (Kant thought it wasn't). By 1950, improvements in clocks made possible a precision greater than the variations in the rotation of the earth (see ☞day). A second found by subdividing the day was no longer suitable, since the day itself varied irregularly.

Ephemeris Time

To escape the variations in the earth's rotation, the astronomers decided to create a time standard based on the length of a particular year, rather than on the mean solar day. The IAU introduced such a scale, Ephemeris Time, in 1952; in 1956 the CIPM recommended adoption of the ephemeris second; and in 1960 the 11TH CGPM abandoned the second as a fraction of the mean solar day in favor of the ephemeris second, defined as "the fraction 1/31,556,925.9747 of the tropical year for 1900 January 0d 12h ephemeris time." A tropical year is the interval between two successive passages of the sun through the vernal equinox.

Ephemeris time had two shortcomings. One was that the ephemeris second was based on a standard that could never be measured again. Current years are not the same length as the year in 1900, since years are getting shorter by about 1/2 second a century. But the variation in the rotation of the Earth was more of a problem. Some people who used time measurements—physicists, say—needed every second to be just as long as every other second. But other users—navigators, for example—needed, in crude terms, the sun to be overhead at noon. In the USA, for example, the National Bureau of Standards' stations WWV and WWVB broadcast a time based on ephemeris seconds, while the U.S. Naval Observatory station (NSS) broadcast time based on the earth's rotation for the use of navigators.

Atomic Time

A more precise way of defining a second appeared with the development of the atomic clock. The stability of an atomic clock is based on a behavior of atoms: they must absorb radiation of a precise frequency to pass from one energy state to another. In the type of clock adopted as a standard, the isotope cesium-133 is heated in a vacuum to produce a gas. Magnetic fields separate the atoms in the gas that are in a high energy state from those in a lower energy state, and those in the lower state are directed toward detectors some distance off. On the way, they pass through a beam of radio frequency radiation from an oscillator controlled by a quartz crystal. If the oscillator is running at the frequency cesium-133 atoms can absorb, the atoms pass to the higher energy state. If the frequency of the oscillator drifts, the number of higher energy atoms reaching the detectors drops sharply. The oscillator frequency is constantly and automatically adjusted to maximize the number of high energy atoms reaching the detectors, and that stabilizes the frequency of the oscillator. The best clocks of this type lose or gain less than one second in several million years.

In 1955, the National Physical Laboratory in Britain built such a clock and over the next three years compared its time with astronomical observations made by U.S. Naval Observatory in Washington, D.C. From the comparison, they concluded that the clock mechanism was keeping the oscillator's frequency tuned to 9,192,631,770 cycles per ephemeris second. Turning this relation around, one could say that 9,192,631,770 cycles of the oscillator constituted 1 atomic second.

In 1964, the CGPM recognized the atomic second as the way to get the duration of the ephemeris second, and in 1967, at the 13TH CGPM, the second based on astronomical observations was abandoned. It was resolved: "That the unit of time in the International System of Units shall be the second, defined as follows:

The second is the duration of 9,192,631,770 periods of the radiation corresponding to the transition between the two hyperfine levels of the ground state of the cesium-133 atom."

With the atomic clocks of that time, the new definition increased the precision of the second's definition by about four orders of magnitude. Meanwhile the builders of atomic clocks had been using them to keep time at national services. The U.S. Naval Observatory, for example, started an atomic time scale it named A.1 in 1959. In 1961, the USA and UK synchronized their clocks, making the same step corrections. Two years later the BIH adopted the USA/UK system.

On the basis of this work, in 1971 the 14TH CGPM approved a time scale to be based on the atomic second and called International Atomic Time (abbreviated TAI, from the French), leaving the definition of the scale to the CIPM, who had already prepared it. By definition, TAI equalled UT at 0h 0m 0s on January 1, 1958. Currently the BIH determines TAI by comparing the time on 80 cesium-beam clocks in 24 nations.

The Astronomers and Atomic Time

The astronomers stuck with ephemeris time until 1979, when they defined two new time scales which used the atomic second and which took into account relativity (velocity affects time). Terrestrial Dynamical Time, (TDT) views time from the earth's position and motion. Barycentric Dynamical Time (TDB, from the French) is time at the center of mass of the solar system. From January 1, 1984, these systems have been used in preparing publications like the *Nautical Almanac*. TDT was defined as being equal to TAI plus 32.184 seconds at the instant beginning January 1, 1977. TDB has various forms depending on the theory of relativity adopted.

Coordinated Universal Time

For daily life, as well as surveying and navigating, time based on the earth's rotation, mean solar time, is more useful than the more absolute time provided by TAI or Ephemeris Time.

The IAU decided that as of January 1, 1956, there would be three versions of Universal Time (adopted in 1960 by the CGPM):

UT0: Mean solar time at the prime meridian, obtained by direct astronomical observation.

UT1: UT0 corrected for the observed effects of the wobbling of the Earth's axis (maximum of about 0.035 seconds). This time was used for celestial navigation.

UT2: UT0 corrected for polar motion (maximum of 0.035 seconds) and also for variations in the earth's rotation rate (maximum of 0.035 seconds). UT2 was the basis of the time signals broadcast by most national services.

As the national timekeeping services began to make atomic clocks their primary reference, the broadcast services sought a uniform way of relating atomic time to the time broadcast. The Consultative Committee on Radiocommunications of the International Telecommunications Union developed a scale for broadcast time signals, known as Coordinated Universal Time (UTC), which was broadcast starting January 1, 1972. At the beginning of that day, UTC was to be exactly 10 seconds behind TAI. Previously broadcast time services had kept in step with the earth's rotation by subtly varying the frequency they broadcast; now the frequency was held constant and corrections were made only by adding or subtracting a whole number of seconds, to prevent UTC from differing by more than 0.9 seconds from UT1. The BIH announces when a leap second is to be added to or subtracted from UTC, usually at the end of June or December, but if necessary a change may also be made at the end of March or September. Since the Earth is slowing, a leap second is usually added. In 1975 the CGPM endorsed UTC and recommended that clock time be based on it.

time, daylight saving

Benjamin Franklin seems to have been the first to propose transferring hours of early morning daylight, which is little used by a modern, late-rising, industrial society, to the evening. Today the chief benefit is savings in electric power for lighting. Countries in the earth's middle latitudes are the main users of daylight saving time, since nearer the poles the summer day is so long that the evening is daylit anyway, and in the tropics the length of the day varies very little during the year.

Germany adopted daylight saving in 1915 as a wartime conservation effort, followed by Great Britain in April 1916 (where it was at first called Willett Time, after William Willett, a proponent). In World War II, Britain advanced the clock one hour during the winter (BST, for British Summer Time); and two hours during the summer (DBST, for Double British Summer Time), first for five months, then seven, and finally year round between 1941 and 1944. From 1968 to 1971, Britain tried keeping BST (now standing for British Standard Time) year round, so that it would be the same time in Britain as in Western Europe. It was abandoned because the west and north complained that winter mornings were too dark.

The United States adopted daylight saving time as an energy conservation measure during both world wars. In 1917, Congress called for adding one hour from the last Sunday in March to the last Sunday in October. In 1922, the period was changed to the Sunday following the third Saturday in April (unless it was Easter) to the Sunday following the third Saturday in September. In 1919, daylight saving was repealed, largely at the insistence of farmers. From February 9, 1942, to September 30, 1945, all clocks were advanced one hour year round; there was no summer addition. In 1966, the Uniform Time Act established daylight saving time nationwide as of April 1, 1967. A state can opt out, but only if the entire state does so. Clocks are advanced one hour from the last Sunday in April to the last Sunday in October. The changeover is made at 2 AM. "Spring ahead, fall behind" has become perhaps the best-known mnemonic in the USA.

time, sidereal

A system of timekeeping used by astronomers, useful because a star rises and sets at the same sidereal time every day, but not at the same solar time.

References such as star charts and tables give a star's right ascension and declination. Adding the right ascension to the local sidereal time gives the hour angle. Adjusting the telescope's mount so that its setting circles indicate the hour angle and the declination from the table should point the telescope at the star's present position.

time zones

If our clocks were really set by the sun, all places—and only those places—lying on a particular line of longitude would have the same time. A variety of local times was not much of a problem when even a east- or west-bound traveller might require several days to reach a location where the time was an hour different. The railroad and telegraph, however, required activities in different locations to be synchronized fairly precisely.

Time differences were particularly a problem in North America, where transcontinental railways crossed many degrees of longitude. A clergyman named C. F. Dowd proposed a scheme in which local times were to differ only by a whole number of hours. Since the earth spins 360° in 24 hours, each 15° of longitude is an hour's difference in time. Taking 0° at the meridian through Greenwich, England, every meridian whose longitude was evenly divisible by 15 would be the basis of a time *zone*, an area in which clock time would be uniform. Allowing for political boundaries, each zone was roughly all the land within 7½° on either side of the meridian.

Dowd lobbied the railroads to adopt his scheme, and in 1883 they did, acting independently of the government. Individual communities themselves then began to adopt "railroad time."

The biggest time change is that made at the International Date Line, a change of 1 day at roughly 180° of longitude. Despite the name it was not determined by an international convention, but by the countries in the region deciding what day it was in their country.

Over larger distances, clock time in the summer in a temperate location will tend to differ by an hour from times in tropical locations, because the tropics generally don't adopt daylight saving time. See ☛time, daylight saving.

tipi

Before the Spanish brought the horse to the New World, these hide-covered shelters of the Plains Indians were seldom more than 5' to 6' high, because bigger ones were too difficult to move from one camp to the next. (The Plains Indians carried tipis, like all their goods, on travois, an A-shaped frame dragged by a person or dog.) With the horse, it became possible to transport larger tipis, and they grew. A typical tipi might be 12'–15' high, made of a dozen or so poles 20'–25' long. The tipi of a wealthy chief might be 30' high with 30 poles, requiring several horses. (The poles came from lodgepole pines growing in the Rocky Mountains, which is how the tree got its name.)

R. and G. Laubin, *The Indian Tipi*, Univ. of Oklahoma, 1957.

tires, automobile

A typical tire sold in the USA today might be marked as shown in the illustration:

P185/70HR13 contains six significant sections:
- Any letters at the beginning:
  "P": the tire is meant for a Passenger car.
  "LT": meant to be used on a Light Truck.
- The first number, in this case "185," is the nominal width of the tire in millimeters, from sidewall to sidewall, when it is properly mounted on a wheel and inflated (but not supporting a car).
- The number after the slash, in this case "70," is a percentage; the distance from the rim to the tread, again in a properly mounted and inflated tire not supporting a car, is 70% of the width of the tire. So 70% of 185 = 129.5; from the rim to the road is 129.5 mm (≈ 5.1"). Basically, the number tells you how tall the tire is; it is sometimes called the *aspect ratio* or the *profile* of the tire.

Letters following the first group of numbers describe the construction of the tire and the type of compound:
- The first letter is a performance rating, indicating the range of sustained speeds at which the tire can be safely used, i.e., how fast you can safely go *as far as the tires are concerned.*
  "R": indicates the tire must not be run at speeds over 106 mph.
  "S": 106 mph to 112 mph.
  "T": 112 mph to 118 mph
  "H": 118 mph to 130 mph
  "V": 130 mph to 149 mph
  "Z": 149 mph plus.
- The second letter describes the way the tire cords are laid:
  "R": the tire is a radial, that is, the cords of the belting are at about 90 degrees to the tread.
  "D": a diagonal ply tire; the cords are about 45 degrees to the edge (the D stands for diagonal).
  "B": bias belted.
- The last number, in this case "13" is the diameter of the rim in inches.

radial

diagonal

bias-ply

The Uniform Tire Quality Grading System

In the example illustrated, 200 AB is a designation from the Uniform Tire Quality Grading system developed by the U.S. Department of Transportation. The actual ratings are determined by the manufacturer of the tire, not the Department. These ratings are most useful in comparing different models of one maker rather than models from different makers.
- The number "200" in the example is the treadwear index. The tread of a tire with a treadwear index of 200 should last twice as long as one with a treadwear index of 100. The life of the "reference tire," the one

with an index of 100 to which all others are compared, is determined by convoys of 4 cars driving for 6,400 miles over public roads near San Angelo, Texas. Because tire life depends on many factors other than the tire, such as the weight of the vehicle, how it is driven, tire pressure, and so on, there is no accurate way of determining from the treadwear index how many miles you'll get. However, under the highly controlled test conditions, a tire with a treadwear index of 100 lasts for about 30,000 miles. In practice, treadwear indexes below 200 are low, over 400 high. Some tires with indexes in the 500s are available, while the special tires for the rear wheels of the Acura NSX are rated 120 (the rubber compounds that give the best traction also wear the fastest).

Following the treadwear index number are two letters, either A, B, or C, with A the highest rating.
- The first letter is a traction score that rates the tire's ability to stop on wet pavement.
- The second letter is a temperature grade that rates the tire's resistance to the generation of heat and its ability to dissipate heat.

Manufacturer Code

B9PA B55X 101 is a number assigned by the Department of Transportation, indicating who manufactured the tire, where, and when. The last three digits tell when; the first two are the month (01 = January) and the third the year (1 = 1991). To decipher the rest of the code, see *Who Makes It and Where Directory* (Boca Raton, FL: Tire Guides, Inc.).

Other Markings

The maximum load and pressure ratings are also usually indicated on the sidewall, as well as information on the number of plies.

Some tires have an arrow molded into the sidewall to show the direction the tire must rotate when the car is moving forward. Such a tire has a tread pattern designed to be especially effective in wet weather. To achieve this, the tread is not symmetrical front to back, so, unlike most tires, it makes a difference which way the tire is rolling.

Older Tire Sizing Systems

The tire sizing system described above, known as P-Metric, came into use around 1976. Various systems were used before that, and tires are still manufactured to fit earlier designations.

Alpha-Numeric. This system was used between roughly 1968 and 1976. A typical designation was "GR78-14." The first letter could be anything from A to N and indicated the tire's size and load carrying ability. "A" was a big tire and "N" a small one. The second letter was present only if the tire was a radial, and could only be R. The first number was the aspect ratio and the one after the hyphen the rim diameter in inches.

Numeric. Before the 1960s, a typical American tire size would be something like "8.00-14". The first number, "8" in the example, was the nominal width of the mounted, inflated, unloaded tire in inches. The "14" was the diameter of the rim in inches. The two digits after the decimal point were a code for the aspect ratio. "00" was the code for an aspect ratio of about 92, which covered most of the day's tires.

In Europe similar designations were used, except that the tire's width was given in millimeters. An "R" was inserted to indicate a radial tire, for example, "185R15".

In the early days of motoring, tire sizes were given as the nominal rim diameter in inches × the nominal rim width in inches. In the late 1920s, the order was inverted; but because the larger number is always the rim, the change caused little confusion.

ton

See also ☛tun.

There are many different kinds of tons. Here they are presented in four groups, according to what they measure:

✓ mass
✓ capacity
✓ refrigeration
✓ explosive power

Tons That Are Units of Mass

Ton. In Great Britain and Pakistan, 2,240 pounds, = 20 hundred-weights, each of 112 pounds. In the USA, Canada and South Africa, "ton" usually refers to 2000 lbs av., sometimes called a "short ton" to distinguish it from the 2,240-pound ton, which is then called a "long ton."

Assay ton. In the USA, a unit of mass, ≈ 29.167 grams. The number of milligrams of precious metal in one assay ton of ore will be numerically equivalent to the number of troy ounces of the metal in one 2000-pound av. ton of ore.

Deadweight ton. A measure of the carrying capacity of a ship, the number of long tons (of 2240 lbs av.) it can float. Abbr, DWT.

Long ton. The American term for the British ton, 2,240 pounds. Sometimes called a gross ton. In the United States, the long ton is primarily used for coal.

Short ton. In the United States, 2,000 pounds. Sometimes called a net ton.

Metric ton. 1000 kilograms. Symbol, mt.

Tons That Are Units of Capacity

Most of these arise from the way carriers bill for the transport of goods.

Register ton. 1) A unit used in describing the cargo capacity of a ship, = 100 cubic feet ≈ 2.83 cubic meters. Called a *tonneau de mer* in Belgium. **2)** The volume occupied by a long ton of seawater, about 35 cubic feet.

Shipping ton. In Britain, 42 cubic feet.

Freight ton. In the USA, 40 cubic feet. A common practice is to bill for shipping by volume unless a freight ton of the product shipped weighs more than 1 short ton, in which case the shipping charge is based on weight. Also called a measurement ton or shipping ton.

Water ton. In the UK, 224 imperial gallons.

Tons That Are Units of Refrigeration

In the USA, two units used in refrigeration and air conditioning:

One **commercial ton** of refrigeration is a rate of extraction of 200 Btu_{IT} per minute (3516.857 joules per second), or in other terms, the rate that will make one short ton of ice of specific latent heat 144 Btu_{IT} per pound in 24 hours from water at the same temperature.

The **U.S. standard ton of refrigeration** describes an amount of cooling, not a rate. One standard ton = 288,000 Btu_{IST} removed ≈ the cooling provided by melting 2009.1 pounds of ice.

The Ton as a Measure of Explosive Power

A unit of energy used to describe the explosive power of weapons, equal to the energy released by the explosion of 1 ton of TNT (trinitrotoluene), ≈ 4.18×10^9 joules. Usually expressed as kilotons (1 kiloton ≈ 4.18 terajoules) or megatons (1 megaton ≈ 4.18 petajoules).

torr

A unit of atmospheric pressure, = $1/760$ atmosphere = $101325/760$ or ≈ 133.322 pascals. To within 1 part per million, it is equal to the pressure of a column of mercury 1 millimeter high, at 0° Celsius, when the acceleration due to gravity has the standard value $g_n = 9.80665$ m/s².

towels

Terry Cloth Towels

Bathroom towels are generally of terry cloth ("Turkish towelling"), a looped cotton fabric. For the ground fabric, a higher number of yarns per inch generally means a higher quality towel. For the pile, the less twisted the yarn and the longer the loops, the softer and more absorbent the towel will be. Unfortunately, the longer the loop and the less twisted the yarn, the less durable the cloth, which is why towels in cheap motels are scratchy. In advertisements for towels, the weight of the cloth (in ounces per square yard) is sometimes given to indicate quality. Good towelling often has a weight of around 20 ounces.

Typical Dimensions

Wash cloth. Always square within a half inch or so. Sizes range from 12" × 12" to 14" × 14".

Fingertip or guest towels. Almost always 11" wide, with lengths between 18" and 21".

Hand towel. 16" × 28" to 18" × 32".

Bath towel. 25" × 48" to 30" × 52".

Bath sheet. The least standardized towel size. Some dimensions of towels advertised in the 1990s as "bath sheets" were: 35" × 60", 35" × 65", 35" × 72", 36" × 70", 40" × 72", and 40" × 75".

township

In the USA, 19TH–20TH C, an area of land equal to 36 square miles, 36 sections, or 23,040 acres.

trailer hitches

The SAE has defined four classes of trailer hitch, based on the weight of the trailer and its cargo (the Gross Towed Weight Rating, GTWR).

Class	GTWR	Ball	Receiver	Chain
I	<2000 lbs	17/8"	2 × 5/8" bar	2000
II	<3500		11/4" × 11/4"	3500
III	<5000	2"	2" box	5000
IV	<10,000		2" box	

The standard applies to all types of hitches, ring and pintle as well as ball and socket, but the latter is by far the most common type.

Ball size	Bolt diameters
17/8"	3/4";1"
23/4"	1"; 13/8"
25/6"	1"; 11/4"

The weight a vehicle can tow is not determined by the class of the hitch attached to the vehicle, but by the vehicle's suspension, the horsepower of the engine, and so on. Simply attaching a class IV hitch to a passenger car will not make it capable of towing 9,999 pounds. To determine a vehicle's towing capacity, consult its manual or call the vehicle's manufacturer.

trees

In the USA, the American Forestry Assn. maintains a National Register of Big Trees. Periodically it publishes a listing of the location of the largest known living specimen of each species. The size is determined by a point system in which one point is given for each foot of the average crown spread, each foot of height, and each inch of girth.

Perhaps the tallest tree whose height has been recorded was a Douglas fir felled in British Columbia in 1902. It was 417' high with a circumference of 45' at chest level. The tallest living tree in 1994 was a Coastal redwood in California, 363' high.

triple jump

The runway is 1.22 m wide. A takeoff board like those used in the broad jump is located 45 m from the start of the runway. The board is 10 cm thick, 1.22 m laterally, and 20 cm wide. It is followed by a strip of an indicator such as Plasticene modeling clay, 1.22 m laterally and 10 cm wide. Another 42 m of runway follows, followed by a landing area 8 m long by 2.75 m wide.

troy weight

One of the principal systems of weight in the English-speaking world, 9TH C?–20TH C, the other being avoirdupois weight. The two systems share one unit, the grain, the smallest unit of mass in everyday use. A third system, apothecaries' weight, is grain for grain, ounce for ounce, and pound for pound the same as troy weight, but below the ounce it is subdivided somewhat differently.

		troy ounce	troy pound
			12
	pennyweight	20	240
grain	24	480	5760
64.8 mg	1.555 g	31.104 g	373.248 g

Troy weight is very old, and was certainly in use before the Norman Conquest. Like the Roman *libra*, which was subdivided into 12 *unciae*, the troy pound (≈373.242 g) contains 12 ounces. The origin of the name is controversial; one of the best guesses is that it comes from the French city of Troyes, where major annual trade fairs were held.

Troy weight has always been connected with precious substances. The more recent avoirdupois weight arose in dealing with large bulky goods that were weighed on the king's great beam, a large balance in the care of the Guild of Pepperers, sort of the truck scales of its day. Troy weight was reserved for gold, silver—and bread, which gives some idea of the importance attached to bread. Such items could be weighed in a much smaller device, probably a balance.

Today only the troy ounce is widely used, for trade in precious metals. In the UK, the troy pound was abolished by the Weights and Measures Act of 1878. The 1963 Act restricted use of the troy ounce to trade in precious metals and abolished the pennyweight, effective in five year's time.

t-shirts

As with other garments, the less expensive the t-shirt, the less generous the cut is likely to be.

	S	M	L	XL	XXL
Men	34–36	38–40	42–44	46–48	50–52
Women	6–8	10–12	14–16	18–20	

tubes, collapsible

Collapsible tin tubes were originally invented to hold artist's oil paints, which had previously been stored in animal intestines, like sausages. Some art historians say the availability of paint in tin tubes contributed to a gradual revolution in landscape painting. Only later was the collapsible tube extended to toothpaste.

Size	Capacity
#2	5 mL
#3	8 mL
#5	14 mL
#14	37 mL (1.25 U.S. fluid oz.)
2 oz	60 mL (2.03 U.S. fluid oz.)

#40	122 mL (4.12 U.S. fluid oz.)
#28	150 mL (5 U.S. fluid oz.)

tuffet

A English unit of capacity, equal to 2 pecks, or half a bushel. So Miss Muffet sat on a 1/2-bushel basket.

tun

1) In England, a measure of capacity for wine and ale, originally 256 gallons. Prior to the 14TH C the tun for wine lost 4 gallons, becoming 252 gallons. With the introduction of imperial measure in 1824, the tun became 210 imperial gallons. See ☞barrel.   **2)** In the USA, a unit of liquid capacity, = 252 U.S. gallons ≈ 953.92 liters.

twist drills

The table below shows the sizes of the most generally useful U.S. straight shank drills. Other shanks (i.e., taper shanks) and larger and smaller sizes are mostly used in an industrial setting. For information on them, see the latest edition of *Machinery's Handbook* (NY: Industrial Press).

In the USA, four different systems are used for designating twist drill sizes: fractional inches, letters (Morse gauge), numbers (with higher numbers representing smaller drills), and millimeters.

Lengths. The lengths given in the table below are "jobber's lengths." For some purposes they are too short. Very long twist drills, often called "aircraft drills," sometimes "electrician's drills," are available in 6" and 12" lengths, and sometimes even longer

Points. Ideally the point should be suited to the material to be drilled. (A completely different style of point, the brad point, is designed for wood and will make a cleaner hole in softwood.)

Material	Point Angle	Chisel Angle	Drill Dia.	Lip Relief*
aluminum	118°–130°	125°–130°	#80–#61	24°
brass	118°–125°	125°–135°	#60–#41	21°
bronze (hard)	118°	115°–125°	#40–#31	18°
copper	100°–130°	125°–135°	#30–1/4"	16°
plastic	60°–118°	125°–130°	F–11/32"	14°
stainless steel	118°–140°	115°–125°	S–1/2"	12°
cast iron	90°–118°	115°–125°	33/64"–3/4"	10°
cast steel	118°	125°–235°	49/64" up	8°

* Can be increased slightly for soft materials and reduced for hard ones.

Some Twist Drill Bit Sizes

Abbr: C.H. = clearance hole; P.H. = pilot hole; WS = wood screw

Size	Diameter inch	Diameter mm	Length in inches	Good For
1/64	0.0156	0.3969	3/4	P.H. in softwood for #0 WS.
71	0.0260	0.660	1 1/4	Tap for 000-120.
1/32	0.0312	0.792	1 3/8	P.H. in softwood for #1 & #2 WS and in hardwood for #0 and #1 WS.
65	0.0350	0.889	1 1/2	Close fit C.H. for #000 screw; tap for 00-90.
62	0.0380	0.965	1 1/2	Free fit C.H. for #000 screw.
3/64	0.0469	1.191	1 3/4	Close fit C.H. for #00 screw; tap for 0-80; P.H. in softwood for #3 & #4 WS and in hardwood #2 WS.
55	0.0520	1.321	1 7/8	Free fit C.H. for #00 screw.
53	0.0595	1.511	1 7/8	Tap for 1-64, 1-72.
1/16	0.0625	1.588	1 7/8	C.H. for #0 WS; P.H. in softwood for #5.
52	0.0635	1.613	1 7/8	Close fit C.H. for #0 screw; tap for M2.
50	0.0700	1.778	2	Free fit C.H. for #0 screw; tap for 2-56, 2-64.
48	0.0760	1.930	2	Close fit C.H. for #1 screw.
5/64	0.0781	1.984	2	C.H. for #1 WS; P.H. in softwood for #8 & #9 WS and in hardwood for #5 & #6 WS.
46	0.0810	2.057	2 1/8	Close fit C.H. for M2 screw; free fit C.H. for #1 screw; tap for M2.5.
44	0.0860	2.184	2 1/8	Free fit C.H. for M2 screw; tap for 4-36.
43	0.0890	2.261	2 1/4	Close fit C.H. for #2 screw; tap for 4-40.
42	0.0935	2.375	2 1/4	Tap for 4-48.
3/32	0.0938	2.383	2 1/4	C.H. for #2 WS; P.H. in softwood for #10 & #11 WS, in hardwood for #7 & #8 WS.
41	0.0960	2.438	2 3/8	Free fit C.H. for #2 screw.
40	0.0980	2.489	2 3/8	Tap for M3.
38	0.1015	2.578	2 1/2	Tap for 5-40.
37	0.1040	2.642	2 1/2	Tap for 5-44.
36	0.1065	2.705	2 1/2	Close fit C.H. for M2.5 screw; tap for 6-32.
7/64	0.1094	2.779	2 5/8	C.H. for #3 & #4 WS; P.H. in softwood for #12 & 14. WS; P.H. for #9 & #10 WS in hardwood.
33	0.1130	2.870	2 5/8	Tap for 6-40.
32	0.1160	2.946	2 3/4	Close fit C.H. for #4 screw.
31	0.1200	3.048	2 3/4	Close fit C.H. for M3 screw; free fit C.H. for M2.5 screw.
1/8	0.1250	3.0175	2 3/4	C.H. for #5 WS; P.H. in hardwood for #11 & #12 WS.
30	0.1285	3.264	2 3/4	Close fit C.H. for #5 screw; free fit C.H. for #4 screw.
29	0.1360	3.454	2 7/8	Tap for M4, 8-32, 8-36.
9/64	0.1406	3.571	2 7/8	Free fit C.H. for M3 screw; C.H. for #6 WS; P.H. in softwood for #16 &#18 WS, in hardwood for #14.
27	0.1440	3.658	3	Close fit C.H. for #6 screw; free fit C.H. for #5 screw.
25	0.1495	3.797	3	Free fit C.H. for #6 screw; tap for 10-24.

Some Twist Drill Bit Sizes

Abbr: C.H. = clearance hole; P.H. = pilot hole; WS = wood screw

Size	Diameter inch	Diameter mm	Length in inches	Good For
5/32	0.1562	3.967	3 1/8	C.H. for #7 WS; P.H. in hardwood for #16 WS.
21	0.1590	4.039	3 1/4	Tap for 10-32.
18	0.1695	4.305	3 1/4	Close fit C.H. for M4, #8 screws; tap for M5.
11/64	0.1719	4.366	3 1/4	C.H. for #8 WS; P.H. in softwood for #20 WS.
16	0.1770	4.496	3 3/8	Free fit C.H. for #8, M4 screws; tap for 12-24.
14	0.1820	4.623	3 3/8	Tap for 12-14.
3/16	0.1875	4.762	3 1/2	C.H. for #9 & #10 WS; P.H. in hardwood for #18 WS, in softwood for # 24 WS.
9	0.1960	4.978	3 5/8	Close fit C.H. for #10 screw.
7	0.2010	5.105	3 5/8	Free fit C.H. for #10 screw; tap for 1/4-20.
13/64	0.2031	5.159	3 5/8	C.H. for #11 WS; P.H. in hardwood for #20 WS.
6	0.2040	5.182	3 3/4	Tap for M6.
4	0.2090	5.309	3 3/4	Close fit C.H. for M5 screw.
3	0.2130	5.410	3 3/4	Tap for 1/4-28.
7/32	0.2188	5.558	3 3/4	C.H. for #12 WS; P.H. in hardwood for #24 WS.
1	0.2280	5.791	3 7/8	Free fit C.H. for M5 screw.
E, 1/4	0.2500	6.350	4	Close fit C.H. for M6 screw and for #14 WS.
F	0.2570	6.528	4 1/8	Close fit C.H. for 1/4" screw; tap for 5/16-18.
G	0.2610	6.629	4 1/8	Free fit C.H. for M6 screw.
17/64	0.2656	6.746	4 1/8	C.H. for #16 WS.
H	0.2660	6.756	4 1/8	Free fit C.H. for 1/4" screw.
I	0.2720	6.909	4 1/8	tap for 5/16-24, M8
J	0.2770	7.036	4 1/8	Free fit C.H. for M6 screw.
19/64	0.2969	7.541	4 3/8	C.H. for #18 WS.
5/16	0.3125	7.938	4 1/2	Tap for 3/8-16.
P	0.3230	8.204	4 5/8	Close fit C.H. for 5/16", M8 screws.
21/64	0.3281	8.334	4 5/8	C.H. for #20 WS.
Q	0.3320	8.433	4 3/4	Free fit C.H. for 5/15", M8 screws; tap for 3/8-24.
11/32	0.3438	8.733	4 3/4	Tap for M10.
3/8	0.3750	9.525	5	C.H. for #24 WS.
W	0.3860	9.804	5 1/8	Close fit C.H. for 3/8" screw.
X	0.3970	10.084	5 1/8	Free fit C.H. for 3/8" screw.
13/32	0.4062	10.317	5 1/4	Close fit C.H. for M10 screw.
Z	0.4130	10.490	5 1/4	Tap for M12.
27/64	0.4219	10.716	5 3/8	Free fit C.H. for M10 screw; tap for !/2-13.
29/64	0.4531	11.509	5 5/8	Tap for 1/2-20.
31/64	0.4844	12.304	5 7/8	Close fit C.H. for M12 screw.
1/2	0.500	12.700	6	Free fit C.H. for M12 screw.

type

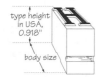

type height in USA, 0.918"

body size

All measurements of type originally referred to the dimensions of a cast piece of metal bearing a character.

The width depends on which character the piece of type will print. A width with a special name is the *em*, the width of a piece of type with a square face, as wide as it is long. The name comes from its typically being the body of the capital letter "M." When type was set by hand in America, the quantity set was measured in ems. In England it was billed in ens, an *en* being half the width of an em. The exact dimensions of the em or en depends, of course, on the size of the type.

The length of the type determines how high the printed character can be, and this is the body size. It is usually measured in points, a unit of length in use with various meanings since 1735. In the USA it was formerly 0.013837 inch (72 points = 0.996"), but with the rise of digital typesetting the value 0.013888..., that is 72 points = 1", has become more usual. Twelve points = 1 pica; 6 picas = 1".

Until 1886, in North America the height of the type or plates, from the surface of the platen to the face of the type, was $^{11}/_{12}$" = 0.9166.... In that year the U.S. Type Founders Assn. adopted a new type height when it adopted the point system. Having decided that the pica would be defined by 83 picas = 35 cm, it decided to let 15 type heights = 35 cm. So type height became 23.333... mm ≈ 0.918". Although only 0.002" higher than the old standard, this difference is great enough that old and new type could not be mixed in the same line. This value was adopted in Britain in 1898.

unit

A unit is a definite quantity—of length, mass, time or whatever—defined in such a way that a count can be made by some process that compares the defined quantity with an actual object or phenomenon. The count and the name of the unit express the object's or phenomenon's amount, value, magnitude, etc. The definition of a unit must allow it to be reproduced with whatever precision is needed for the uses to which the unit is put. The inch, volt, liter, pound, bushel, pint, and second are all units.

Formerly the most common way of defining a unit was a physical standard. The yard was once defined by the length of "the king's iron rod." Metal expands; the yard was longer in summer than winter, but no one cared or could even tell if the yard of cloth he bought in December was a thread's thickness shorter. Later such distances did matter and it was realized that the definition must also include a set of specifications of the conditions under which the standard is to be compared with whatever it measures. The yard was then defined by the distance between lines on a bar at a certain temperature. Later it was realized that the bar had different lengths depending on how it was supported, so that was added to the conditions. The main reason definitions of units are changed is that new technologies create a need for more precision. Measurements (except for those of count, such as "three dozen") are never exact; they are good enough.

The word "unit" is also the name of a number of units, including: **1)** A unit of credit for course work at the collegiate level. **2)** A unit indicating the number of multiples of 1 ¾" in the height of the front panel of rack-mounted electrical equipment. Variously abbr, U or RU. **3)** In the southern USA, a unit of volume used for pulpwood, a stack 8' long, 5' wide, and 4' high, so containing 160 cubic feet.

United States, history of weights and measures

Almost all the customary units used in the United States today began as English units during colonial times. Units of dry capacity, for example, are based on the bushel of William III of 1696–7, and units of liquid capacity on the wine gallon of Queen Anne of 1707 (231 cubic inches). The chief exceptions are land measures such as the ☞vara of Texas and the ☞arpent of Louisiana.

The situation at independence was similar to that in Europe, namely, the definitions of units varied from place to place; a bushel in one county might well be smaller than the bushel in another.

Both the Articles of Confederation (article 9, para. 4) and the Constitution (article 1, sec. 8) gave the central government the power "to fix the Standard of Weights and Measures." George Washington mentioned the subject in his first message to Congress (January 8, 1790): "Uniformity in the currency, weights, and measures of the United States, is an object of great importance, and will, I am persuaded, be duly attended to." He was wrong.

Congress's response was to ask the Secretary of State, Thomas Jefferson, to prepare a report on the matter. Jefferson had been a prime mover behind the already enacted replacement of pounds, shillings, and pence with a decimal currency, and his response was bound to be innovative. Jefferson's report (July 1790) proposed two options: Keep the existing ratios between English units, redefining the inch in terms of a pendulum's period, the gallon as 270 cubic inches (with a bushel of 8 gallons), and the ounce as "the thousandth part of a cubic foot of rainwater", or strike out afresh by "reducing every branch to the same decimal ratio already established in their coins, and thus bringing the calculation of the principal affairs of life within the arithmetic of every man who can multiply and divide plain numbers."

No action had been taken on the report by the time Washington delivered his second message to Congress (December, 1790), and he raised the subject again: "The establishment of the militia, of a mint, of standards of weights and measures, of the post office and post roads, are subjects which (I presume) you will resume of course, and which are abundantly urged by their own importance."

The House thereupon sent Jefferson's report to the Senate, where it was referred to a select committee. Two months later the committee reported that, as both Britain and France were considering establishing new standards of weights and measures "with the avowed object of…uniformity in the measures and weights of the commercial nations," it would be best to wait for them to reach agreement, and not at this time alter the weights and measures in use in the United States. So the matter was dropped.

In his third message to Congress (October 5, 1791) Washington repeated his injunction: "A uniformity of weights and measures is among the important objects submitted to you by the Constitution and, if it can be derived from a standard at once invariable and universal, must be no less honorable to the public councils, than conducive to the public convenience."

In response the Senate appointed a select committee, which in April 1792 recommended adoption of a decimal system of weights and measures. Consideration was postponed to the next session of Congress, and though the subject was later discussed on the floor, no action was taken.

In 1795 Washington tried for the last time, sending Congress information on the metric system in response to a French overture. The House formed a select committee; but this time the committee report advocated retaining the pound and foot and basing everything else on them. A bill to this effect, complete with an appropriation, was passed in May 1796. It died in the Senate.

On March 2, 1799, Congress finally passed the first U.S. weights and measures law—one that was meaningless and unenforceable. It dealt with the collection of customs duties and called for the surveyor of each port to periodically test the weights, measures, and instruments used in collecting duties on imports, using standards to be provided by the collector of customs at that port. Of course, there were no such standards; none had been adopted.

In the meantime, as commerce abhors a metrological vacuum, individual states began to pass laws establishing all sorts of values for the customary units, even importing their own physical standards from England.

In December 1816 James Madison raised the subject again in another Presidential message to Congress: "Congress will call to mind that no adequate provision has yet been made for the uniformity of weights and measures, also contemplated by the Constitution. The great utility of a standard fixed in nature, and founded on the easy rule of decimal proportions, is sufficiently obvious. It led the government at an early stage to preparatory steps for introducing it; and a completion of the work will be a just title to the public gratitude." In response Congress asked another Secretary of State, John Quincy Adams, to prepare another report.

Adams submitted his report on February 22, 1821. Even today, it is an impressive piece of work, an "inquiry into the theory of weights and measures, as resulting from the natural history of man." Although predicting that "the meter will surround the globe in use as well as in multiplied extension; and one language of weights and measures will be spoken from the equator to the poles," Adams called for standardization without innovation, then "to consult with foreign nations, for the future and ultimate establishment of universal and permanent uniformity." No action was taken.

In one area, however, the government was forced to act: money. In minting gold pieces it is wise to know their mass, and that required some standard of weight. At the request of the Director of the U.S. Mint, in 1827 Albert Gallatin, Minister of the United States in London, purchased a brass troy pound. Through connections with the Vice President of the Royal Society, he managed to have the prototype of the British parliamentary troy pound of 1758, then in the keeping of the Clerk of the House of Commons, turned over to Captain Kater, a prominent British metrologist. Kater took the prototype home, where he compared it with the weight Gallatin had purchased, adjusting the latter until the correspondence was "exact." Transported with elaborate care to America, this weight was installed in the mint in Philadelphia as its standard of weight. When Adams, now President, reported this *fait accompli* to Congress, it passed an act (May 19, 1828) adopting the above mentioned weight as the "standard Troy pound of the mint of the United States." The country had its first standard.

At that time customs duties provided most of the national government's revenues, and in the discussion of standards it had emerged that duties in some states might be smaller than those in others because the customs standards in those states were bigger. Using a bigger bushel or a longer yard gave a port an economic advantage, by reducing duties on imports. On May 29, 1830 Congress directed the Treasury to compare the standards then in use at the different ports, without saying what the standards should be. The Secretary of the Treasury, S. D. Ingham, delegated this task to a man he knew to be conversant with metrology, the Superintendent of the Coast Survey, a Swiss immigrant named Ferdinand Rudolph Hassler. It was an inspired choice, for Hassler picked up the ball and ran with it.

Hassler's survey disclosed that there were large differences between the standards of the various ports, although the average values were close to the pre-independence values of British measures. In order to make the weights and measures of the ports uniform, some standards would have to be adopted. Hassler recommended, and the Treasury Department adopted in 1832, the following definitions for four customary units:

- the 36-inch yard, to be based on the distance between the 27th and 63rd inch marks engraved on a 82-inch brass bar made by Troughton, a well-known firm of English instrument makers. Hassler had brought this bar from London in 1815 for the use of the Coast Survey.

- an avoirdupois pound of 7000 grains, based on the Troy pound standard in the mint, that is $7000/5760$ of that standard.
- a gallon of 231 cubic inches, which is the old English wine ☞gallon.
- a bushel of 2,150.42 cubic inches.

These definitions were not and never have been authorized by Congress; the Treasury Department acted on its own on the principle that it was carrying out its responsibility under the Constitution to ensure that duties were uniform throughout the United States. It is also clear that Hassler's intention was to base the American yard and pound on the British prototypes, the Troughton scale and the Mint's troy pound simply being the closest he could come to those prototypes under the circumstances. The selected gallon and bushel, however, were already obsolete in the UK, but were chosen because they most accurately matched the average gallon and bushel then in use in U.S. ports. Thus from the beginning, U.S. dry and liquid measure have been differed from each other, and neither has conformed to Britain's system of units of capacity.

With the approval of the President, Hassler set up shop in the United States Arsenal in Washington and began to manufacture standards of length, weight, and capacity for distribution to the custom-houses. In 1832, the new Secretary of the Treasury, Louis McLane, apprised the Senate of this development when he submitted Hassler's report on the discrepancies between custom-houses.

On June 14, 1836, Congress adopted a joint resolution directing the Secretary of the Treasury to deliver a complete set of weights and measures to the governor of each state (in addition to the customs houses). As it turned out, a set consisted of 33 avoirdupois weights, from 50 lbs to 0.0001 ounce; 28 troy weights, from 1 lb to 0.0001 ounce, a brass yard, and 5 capacity measures, from 1 gallon to 1/2 pint. Two years later (July 7, 1838) Congress also authorized "one standard balance for each state." Hassler, knowing that a single balance could not provide sufficient accuracy over all ranges, and adhering as he said to the law's spirit, instead delivered small, medium, and large balances, with capacities of about 1, 10 and 50 pounds respectively. On receiving the standards, most of the states passed legislation adopting them as the standard for the state. In this roundabout and characteristically American way the Constitution's call for uniform weights and measures was finally realized. The last of these sets to be presented was received by the State of Hawaii in 1960. "To fix the Standard of Weights and Measures," the federal government still recalibrates these standards for the states every ten years.

Hassler's brass bar and the Mint's troy pound standard weren't used very long. In 1834 a fire destroyed the British prototypes. The British government made new ones and in 1845 presented copies of the prototypes for the pound and yard to the United States. Again by administrative action, not by Act of Congress, these standards became the *de facto* basis of the U.S. yard and pound, illustrating the policy of basing U.S. units on the British prototypes. For their subsequent histories, see ☞ yard and ☞ pound.

The Metric System in the United States

Ever since the United States was created it has been considering adopting a decimal system of weights and measures. With the spread of the French metric system, the decimal reformers took up the cause of the meter, liter and kilogram. The struggle between the decimalists and the defenders of customary measure has been going on for two centuries. For example, as small standard weights Hassler provided only ounce weights, and only in decimal fractions. But after 1857, the standards supplied to the states were in common fractions of ounces, not decimal fractions, and weights in grains were also supplied.

A second wave of interest occurred after the Civil War, when reform was urged by state legislatures and taken up by some eminent national figures, including Senator Charles Sumner. On July 28, 1866, Congress adopted legislation defining the meter as 3937/3600 yards and legalizing the metric system: "It shall be lawful throughout the United States of America to employ the weights and measures of the metric system; and no contract or dealing, or pleading in any court, shall be deemed invalid or liable to objection because the weights or measures expressed or referred to therein are weights and measures of the metric system." Thus use of the metric system became permissible, but not obligatory.

The day before, Congress had authorized distribution of metric standards to all the states. These standards were based on some already in the possession of the Office of Weights and Measures. The "Committee meter," a copy of the "mètre des Archives," had been given to Hassler by a friend who had been the Swiss member of the international committee that rubber stamped the metric system. When Hassler emigrated to the United States in 1805 he brought the "Committee meter" with him; all the baselines measured by the Coast Survey before 1890 were based on this meter. The other standard was the "Arago kilogram," a platinum cylinder Gallatin had purchased in 1821 when he was Minister to France, which had been certified as being within 1 mg of the prototype kilogram by the prominent French physicist Arago. (It was actually over 4 mg light.)

Adoption of the metric system continued to be pushed, mainly by commercial interests. The Committee on Coinage, Weights and Measures of the House of Representatives urged adoption of the metric system in 1879, 1896, 1897, 1898, 1901 and 1902, but it never got to a vote on the floor.

The United States participated in the series of conferences on the metric system held by the French beginning in 1870, was a signatory to the Treaty of the Meter (May 20, 1875, ratified by the Senate and proclaimed September 27, 1878), and subsequently contributed annually to the maintenance of the BIPM. As a result, when the new standards called for by the conferees were ready, the United States received prototype meters numbers 21 and 27 and kilograms numbers 4 and 20 (which nation got which standard was determined by lottery). In a White House ceremony on January 2, 1890, meter no. 27 and kilogram 20 were unwrapped and adopted as the National Prototype Meter and Kilogram.

Coming into possession of these state-of-the-art physical standards, the Office of Weights and Measures proceeded to derive the yard from the National Prototype Meter and the pound from the National Prototype Kilogram, by reversing the definitions in the Act of July 1866. Instead of a meter defined from the yard, the yard was now defined by the meter. The resulting change in the size of the units was much too small to have any commercial effect. Three years later Thomas Corwin Mendenhall, the Superintendent of Standard Weights and Measures, got around to reporting what had happened (Bulletin 26 of the Coast and Geodetic Survey, approved by the Secretary of the Treasury on April 5, 1893): "Indeed, this course has been practically forced upon this Office for several years, but it is considered desirable to make this formal announcement for the information of all interested in the science of metrology or in measurements of precison."

The Office's action was fully justified. A lot of progress had been made in metrology since 1815. As Mendenhall said, the Troughton scale was "quite unsuitable for such use [as a national prototype], owing to its faulty construction and the inferiority of its graduation." Moreover, Gallatin's troy pound, in law though not practice still the standard for the coinage, was made of brass of unknown density; had a screwed-on knob that made weighing in water impossible; was not plated, so that oxidation was changing its weight; and in other respects was thoroughly obsolete.

Ever since Mendenhall's order—throughout the 20TH C—all U.S. weights and measures have been based on the metric prototypes or on the definitions adopted by the CGPM. Since the British continued for some time to use their own prototype yard and pound, British and American units inevitably diverged.

The United States is currently in the process of adopting the metric system, not through legislation—none of the significant developments in American weights and measures have originated in legislation—but through the choices of consumers buying in a world market and manufacturers competing in one, and, to a lesser extent, administrative action in the government. No one today expects the focal length of a camera lens to be marked in inches, though they were as recently as the Second World War. No one is surprised to find metric bolts in their American-made car. No law mandated these changes. Commerce and the calculator have changed the balance of advantage between the customary and metric systems.

Modern Times

An act of March 3, 1901 created the National Bureau of Standards (NBS)and assigned the work of the Office of Weights and Measures to it, effective July 1901, together with many additional duties. When the Department of Commerce and Labor was created by the act of February 14, 1903, the NBS was transferred from Treasury to the new department. On March 4, 1913, Commerce and Labor was split into two separate departments; NBS went with Commerce. In 1990, the name of the agency was changed to the National Institute for Standards and Technology (NIST).

NBS and now NIST has always been one of the leading scientific laboratories, responsible for major developments in such fields as atomic timekeeping. It is also, however, involved in the most mundane aspects of everyday life, such as what constitutes a full measure of cornflakes in your box of cereal. Every year since 1905 (except for war and other national emergencies), metrologists from all the states have assembled at a National Conference on Weights and Measures. Most state laws concerning weights and measures began as model laws framed in these conferences. The techniques for ensuring consumers aren't short-weighted are devised and disseminated by NIST.

vacuum cleaners

The ASTM has been developing tests of vacuum cleaner performance for industry for many years. The Subcommittee on Consumer Information of their Committee on Vacuum Cleaners decided that a standardized way of communicating test results to consumers would be useful, so they devised a "Buyer's Guide." The Buyer's Guide is to be used on labels, tags, handouts and other materials available where vacuum cleaners are sold—no additions or deletions permitted. In the Guide, various test results are reported on a scale from 1 to 10, with 10 being best. The tests are performed by the manufacturer; the ASTM only defines the test procedures.

Embedded dirt removal. A "10" represents removal, during a particular test, of 100% of the dirt in a level loop carpet, 75% in a multi-level carpet, 60% in a plush carpet, and 25% in a shag carpet. For all types of rug the increment between steps on the scale is one-tenth of the value for 10.

Ease of moving nozzle on carpet. A "10" means less than 8 foot-pounds of force are required; a "1" means 72 foot-pounds or more of force were required. The increment is 8 foot-pounds.

Durability of motor. A "10" means the motor can be expected to last more than 720 hours; "1" means less than 80 hours.

Maximum air power. A "10" represents 225–250 airwatts; a "1" is anything below 25 airwatts. The increment is 25 airwatts.

Quietness. A "10" means the noise level is less than 75 dB; a "1" means it is higher than 91 dB. Each increment is 2 dB. Three dB is a perceptible difference.

vanity

Standard sizes in the USA for vanity tops incorporating a bowl are:

Depth	Length						
	25"	31"	37"	43"	49"	61"	73"
19 1/2"	•	•	•				
22"	•	•	•	•	•	•*	•*

* Tops in these sizes are available with one or two bowls.

Prefabricated base cabinets for vanities are usually 21" deep, and come in widths from 12" to 48" in steps of 6". Typically bases with three drawers are 12", 15", or 18" wide; drawer-and-door cabinets are 24" wide, and bases for sinks run from 30" to 48".

vara

A unit of length in Texas, Central and South America, and Spain, where it originated. The square vara was an important land measure, and in some areas the vara itself became a unit of area.

The Mexican Imperial Colonization Act of January 4, 1823, Art. 5 and 7, defined a series of land measures: the vara as 3 "piés geométricos," the *legua* as a straight line of 5000 varas, the *sitio* as an area one legua on a side, the *hacienda* as five sitios, and the *labór* as one million square varas. Subsequent laws authorized the states to establish further regulations, providing they did not conflict with existing law. The Mexican states of which present-day Texas formed a part confirmed the units given above, and the Land Law of the State of Coahuila and Texas (March 26, 1834), Section 1, Art. 2) added the *millionada* = a million square varas, thus equivalent to a labór, and (Art. 34) the *ayuntamiento* (a township) = 4 square legua.

The Mexican Ordinance for Land and Sea (September 15, 1837) adopted a value of 837 millimeters for the vara. A regulation of February 20, 1896, implementing metric land measures under the law of June 19, 1895, gives the vara the value 0.838000 meter.

When Texas became independent of Mexico the vara remained a legal unit through a provision of the Constitution of the Republic of Texas (March 17, 1836, Sec.1) that laws then in effect and not inconsistent with the Texas Constitution would remain in effect. The vara was legally set at 33 1/3" (≈ 84.667 cm) in Art. 5730, Acts of 1919, revised 1925.

As a 20TH C unit of length in South America and Spain, the vara varies from 83.5 to 86.66 cm, depending on the country.

volt

The unit of electric potential, potential difference, and electromotive force in SI. Abbr., V. If you think of your house wiring as plumbing, volts measure the water pressure. One volt is the potential difference between two points on a conductor when the current flowing is 1 ampere and the power dissipated between the points is 1 watt (definition adopted by the CIPM in 1946, Resolution 2). The volt is a derived unit; its dimensions are

$$\frac{watt}{ampere} \quad \text{or in terms of base units only,} \quad \frac{meter^2 \cdot kilogram}{second^3 \cdot ampere}$$

The cgs unit of electromotive force (e.m.f.) was based on an idea of F. E. Neumann in 1825. One cgs unit of e.m.f. was produced in any electric circuit cutting 1 magnetic line of force per second. But the e.m.f. people were accustomed to working with was that produced by batteries, which was millions of the cgs unit. To meet the need for a unit large enough for practical use, the volt was defined at the First International Conference of Electricians (Paris, 1881) as 10^8 cgs units of e.m.f.

However, establishing the value of the volt by using Neumann's equations was far beyond the capabilities of most laboratories. They got their standard voltage from special batteries (properly speaking, cells). Cells can be made in a variety of ways, from different materials, and each type has a characteristic voltage. A carbon-zinc flashlight battery, for example, produces 1.5 volts no matter what size it is. Unlike flashlight batteries, some types of cell are able to maintain an unvarying voltage for years. No power is drawn from such "standard cells"; they are simply a voltage reference.

The Fourth Congress (Chicago, 1893) met the need for a volt defined by a standard cell by defining the international volt (symbol, V_{int}). A Clark cell (a kind of cell that uses mercury and zinc) at a temperature of 15° centigrade would by definition have an e.m.f. of 1.434 international volts. (See ☞ohm and ☞ampere for the definitions of their international versions.) The value of 1.434 was chosen to make the international volt equal to 10^8 cgs units of e.m.f. within the limits of experimental error of the day.

Later work by national standards laboratories with the international ohm, volt, and ampere soon showed that these definitions were inconsistent with the relationship ampere equals volts over ohms. To scotch this problem, the International Conference on Electrical Units and Standards (London, 1908) dropped the "reproducible" definition of the international volt, deriving it instead from the international ampere and international ohm: 1 international volt is the potential difference between the ends of a conductor having a resistance of 1 international ohm, when the steady current through it is 1 international ampere. When the international units were abandoned in favor of absolute ones in 1948, the international volt was determined to be ≈ 1.00034 V. (If you're counting, so far we've been through three different definitions of the volt, all leading to more or less identical values in everyday life, and still haven't reached the current one.)

In the reforms that led to the replacement of the ☞centimeter-gram-second system of units with the ☞meter-kilogram-second-ampere system in scientific work, and then to SI, the ampere was introduced as a base unit (at one time the ohm had been considered for this role). It therefore became necessary to define the volt in terms of the ampere and power, in this case watts, which leads to today's definition, given above.

Some voltages in daily life: flashlight battery 1.5 v d.c.; car battery, 12 v d.c. (before about 1960, 6 v). Household current is 117 v a.c.; distribution lines 240 v a.c.; and transmission lines typically are 69 kV, 138 kV, 230 kV, 345 kV, 500 kV, 700 kV, or 1,000 kV. A 69,000-volt line only carries 15 megawatts; a 1,000,000-volt line carries 5,000 megawatts. Underground transmission lines are typically 345,000 v (500,000 in Europe).

volt-ampere

The unit of apparent power in SI. Symbol, VA. The product of the root-mean-square values of voltage and current in an alternating circuit current.

VU

A unit used for the scale of meters ("VU meters") used to monitor audio power levels in recording and broadcast studios, so that the signal can be weakened or amplified to bring it within the optimal range for recording or broadcast. VU is short for volume unit, a term rarely heard; readings are usually described as, for example, "minus 4 VU".

The VU meter was developed in the late 1930s as a joint project of Bell Labs, CBS and NBC. Its response was intended to approximate the response of the human ear to complex, changing waveforms, and its readings lie somewhere between the peak and average values. The specifications cover the meter's ballistics (how fast and far the needle moves when various signals are applied) as well as frequency response. In May of 1939, a reference power level of 1 milliwatt into 600 ohms was adopted, and readings on the VU scale are roughly log to the base 10 of the power ratio referred to that reference level. For a pure sine wave, 1 VU = 1 dB, but the value of the "volume unit" for real world audio signals is embodied in the unique characteristics of the meter itself.

Many inexpensive meters, though marked in VU, do not meet the standard. A VU meter is not suitable for monitoring during digital recording; peak-reading meters are used instead.

wallcoverings Wallpaper is sold in bolts containing one to three rolls. The roll is a somewhat variable unit of surface area and not necessarily an actual roll of paper. If the paper is American-made, the standard single roll is 36 square feet. The most usual widths are 20" and 27", but wallpaper is also made in widths of 18", 20 1/2", 24", 26", 28", and so on up to 54". The length is whatever brings the surface area to 36 square feet, so a single roll 18" wide is 24' long, one 20" wide is 21' long, and so on. Most vinyl wallcovering is 27" wide.

Historical American wallpaper and current wallpapers from Europe are usually narrower than today's American papers. A single roll is usually not 36 square feet, but about 28 square feet. Physically, English wallpaper is typically 22" wide and 36' long and French paper 18" wide and about 27' long.

To estimate the number of rolls required for a room, assume that each standard roll will cover 30 square feet (22 if the paper is European). Multiply the room's perimeter by its height, divide by 30 (or 28), and round up. Subtract 1 roll for every 50 square feet of door or window opening.

The ASTM sets certain quality requirements for wallcoverings, such as that no piece shorter than 9' is allowed in split bolts and that the total area should be at least 10% larger than specified on the label. It allows no more than an 1/8" variance in pattern match at eye level between two 8' strips.

The ASTM also defines tests of colorfastness, washability, scrubability, and abrasion resistance, on the basis of which a wallcovering is placed in one of six categories. The higher the category, the more colorfast the wall covering; under the exposure specified for the test, II only needs to show no fading after 23 hours, but VI must show no fading at 200 hours. There is no scrubability requirement for categories I and II; no abrasion resistance requirement for I, II, and III.

I   Decorative only
II   Decorative with Medium Serviceability
III   Decorative with High Serviceability
IV   Type I Commercial Service
V   Type II Commercial Service
VI   Type III Commercial Service

Only the last three categories meet Federal Specification CCCW-408C.

watches

The size of a watch is measured as the shortest distance across the dial side of the main plate (also called the lower or pillar plate), measured through the center. Today this measurement is made in millimeters. Until recently, in Europe it was made in lignes. One ligne = 1/12 pouce ≈ 2.25583 mm ≈ 0.088814". The thickness of the movement is measured in douzième. One douzième = 1/12 ligne = 1/144 pouce.

Until well into the 20TH C, the USA used a system of pillar plate sizes based on steps of 1/30th of an inch. A size 0 watch had a pillar plate 1 5/30" in diameter; a size 1, 1 6/30", and so on. For sizes smaller than 0 (00, 000, etc), a thirtieth is subtracted.

watches, ships'

The shipboard day is divided into 6 watches, each 4 hours long. The traditional names of the watches are:

Midwatch *or* middle watch   Midnight to 4 AM
Morning watch   4 AM to 8 AM
Forenoon watch   8 AM to noon
Afternoon watch   Noon to 4 PM
Evening watch   4 PM to 8 PM
(The evening watch was formerly divided into the *first dog watch,* from 4 PM to 6 PM, and the *second dog watch,* from 6 PM to 8 PM.)
First watch   8 PM to midnight

water heaters

Some home water heaters have tanks and some don't; the latter are more expensive and are now uncommon in the United States, except among the energy conscious.

The size of water heaters with tanks is usually the capacity of the storage tank. Capacities of home water heaters range from about 10 to

80 gallons. More important than the tank's capacity, however, is the *recovery rate*, which is the number of gallons of water the heater can raise in temperature by a certain number of degrees Fahrenheit in one hour, usually 100°F, but sometimes 60°F. Beginning with a full tank of hot water, a heater with a storage tank can deliver in one hour roughly the number of gallons given as its recovery rate plus about 70% of its tank capacity.

In the past it was sometimes recommended that a water heater thermostat be set to 140°F. There is one reason for doing this and two compelling reasons not to. The 140°F setting is for old-fashioned automatic dishwashers that required this temperature for proper operation. Most modern dishwashers, however, have built-in water heaters. Even though these heaters provide heat in a very costly way (electric resistance), they heat so little water that on balance energy (and money) can be saved by using them and turning down the water heater thermostat. The two reasons not to use a high thermostat setting are: The bigger the difference between the temperatures of a hot object and its surroundings, the faster the object will lose heat; the hotter the water in the pipe, the more heat is lost on the way to the faucet. Also, thermostat settings above 125°F increase the risk of scalding, especially for the very young and the very old.

watt

The unit of power in SI. Abbr., W. Power is a rate, the rate at which energy is expended or work done. The watt is defined as "the power which in one second gives rise to energy of 1 joule" (Resolution 2 of the CIPM, 1946, ratified by the NINTH CGPM in 1948). In mechanical terms, 1 watt is one meter-kilogram per second. In an electric circuit, 1 watt is a current of one ampere at a pressure of one volt. The watt's dimensions are joules per second, or in terms of base units only,

$$\frac{meter^2 \cdot kilogram}{second^3}$$

The watt was introduced at the Second International Congress of Electricians (Paris, 1889), where it was defined as 10^7 ergs per second. (The same conference introduced the joule, defining it as 10^7 ergs.)

weber

The unit of magnetic flux in SI. Abbr., Wb. One weber is "the magnetic flux which, linking a circuit of one turn, would produce in it an electromotive force of 1 volt if it were reduced to zero at a uniform rate in 1 second" (Resolution 2, CIPM, 1946, ratified by the CGPM in 1948). Its dimensions are volts per second or, in terms of base units only,

$$\frac{meter^2 \cdot kilogram}{second^2 \cdot ampere}$$

The weber was introduced as a practical electromagnetic unit = 10^8 maxwells in 1933, but was not much used until the meter-kilogram-second system was generally adopted.

week

The week is the only unit of the calendar whose length is not determined by the motion of the earth or the moon. It has been suggested that the length of the week reflects the interval between market days. In the West, the seven-day week is long established (the first chapter of the first book of the Old Testament). For many families, it is still the interval between major trips to the market.

weight, human

The most widely circulated tables of recommended weights in the USA are those issued by the Metropolitan Life Insurance Company in the 1950s. They are now generally discredited. The guide below is more modern, taken from the U.S. Department of Health and Human Services' publication *Nutrition and Your Health: Dietary Guidelines for Americans*. The weights given are in pounds, without shoes. Women's weights will fall toward the lower end of the range given and men's toward the upper.

Height	Age	
	19 to 34	35 & older
5'0"	97–128	108–138
5'1"	101–132	111–143
5'2"	104–137	115–148
5'3"	107–141	119–152
5'4"	111–146	122–157
5'5"	114–150	126–162
5'6"	118–155	130–167
5'7"	121–160	134–172
5'8"	125–164	138–178
5'9"	129–169	142–183
5'10"	132–174	146–188
5'11"	136–179	151–194
6'0"	140–184	155–199
6'1"	144–189	159–205
6'2"	148–195	164–210
6'3"	152–200	168–216
6'4"	156–205	173–222
6'5"	160–211	177–228
6'6"	164–216	182–234

welding glasses

The rectangular $2" \times 4\frac{1}{4}"$ filters in welder's helmets that protect their eyes from the intense light of welding are sold in different degrees of "darkness," to suit different jobs. In the USA, welder's glasses are assigned *shade numbers*, which can be calculated from

$$\text{shade number} = \frac{7(-\log_{10} T)}{3} + 1$$

where T is transmission, the fraction of visible light transmitted.

Welding produces hot metal, and hence a lot of infrared radiation, and arc welding produces large amounts of ultraviolet. For that reason, welding glasses are made to absorb not just visible light, but also infrared (unlike sunglasses) and ultraviolet. Amateur astronomers typically use a shade 14 welding glass to view the sun with the naked eye. When a total eclipse of the sun is imminent, that shade sells out.

wheelbarrows

A typical wheelbarrow holds about 5 1/2 cubic feet.

wheelchairs

The typical wheelchair is 25" wide, about 36" high, and 42 1/2" long. Making a 180° turn requires a space of about 60" by 60". For a person in a wheelchair to be able to turn around in a corridor, it must be at least 54" wide, and 60" is needed to permit two wheelchairs to pass each other.

An entry door must have a minimum width of 36", but is preferably 38". Interior doors can be narrower: 30"–32", but doors in corners can be a problem. Thresholds higher than 1/2" are serious obstacles.

In fitting homes for those living in wheelchairs, particular attention should be paid to the height of controls, such as light switches, thermostats, drapery pulls, intercoms, fire alarms, telephones, air conditioners, window latches, and so forth. All of these should be somewhere between 30" and 40" from the floor. It may even be desirable to raise the electric outlets, or perhaps install extras, if the existing outlets are beyond the person's reach.

wheels

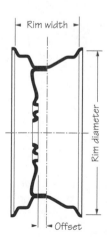

Automobile wheels are described by a designation like "15-6J." The first number is the rim diameter, which is measured across the wheel inside the flange. Rim diameters are in whole inches usually between 12" and 17". (Some English minicars had 10" wheels.) The second number is the rim width in inches, which is measured between the inside surfaces of the flanges. Rim widths run from 5.5 to 12 inches, in half-inch steps in the smaller sizes and whole inch steps in the larger. The letter (or letters) refer to the shape of the rim. Rim contours are standardized by the Tire and Rim Assn., so that tires will fit.

Another important characteristic of a wheel is its offset: the distance between the rim centerline (midway between the flanges, in the center of the tire tread) and the mounting surface (the part of the wheel that sits against the brake housing when the wheel is mounted). If the rim centerline is outboard of the mounting surface, the offset is negative, for example, "minus 1"." If the rim centerline were 1" inboard of the mounting surface, the wheel would have an offset of plus 1". Unfortunately, in some writing the designations are exactly reversed; inboard is negative and outboard is positive.

The wheel's bolt circle is described by a designation like "4-5 1/2." The first number is the number of lugbolts or studs. The second is the diameter in inches of the circle on which the centers of the bolts or studs lie.

whitewater
The American Whitewater Affiliation publishes guidelines for a scale used to rate the difficulty of rapids, reproduced here with their permission. The Affiliation cautions paddlers using ratings based on this scale in deciding whether to run a river that:

- Regional, local, and personal interpretations of the scale may differ from those the paddler is accustomed to. A scale for rapids cannot be as objective as, say, the Richter scale for earthquakes.
- Changes in water level can affect difficulty.
- Last year's rating may no longer apply, due to downed trees, earthquakes, or other changes.
- "There is a difference between running an occasional Class IV rapid and dealing with an entire river of this category."
- Be conservative in cold water.
- Be conservative if the river is inaccessible.

International Scale of River Difficulty

Class I. Easy. Fast moving water with riffles and small waves. Few obstructions, all obvious and easily missed with little training. Risk to swimmers is slight; self-rescue is easy.

Class II. Novice. Straightforward rapids with wide, clear channels which are evident without scouting. Occasional maneuvering may be required, but rocks and medium sized waves are easily missed by trained paddlers. Swimmers are seldom injured and group assistance, while helpful, is seldom needed.

Class III. Intermediate. Rapids with moderate, irregular waves which may be difficult to avoid and which can swamp an open canoe. Complex maneuvers in fast current and good boat control in tight passages or around ledges are often required; large waves or strainers may be present but are easily avoided. Strong eddies and powerful current effects can be found, particularly on large volume rivers. Scouting is advisable for inexperienced parties. Injuries while swimming are rare; self-rescue is usually easy but group assistance may be required to avoid long swims.

Class IV. Advanced. Intense, powerful but predictable rapids requiring precise boat handling in turbulent water. Depending on the character of the river, it may feature large, unavoidable waves and holes or constricted passages demanding fast maneuvers under pressure. A fast, reliable eddy turn may be needed to initiate maneuvers, scout rapids, or rest. Rapids may require "must" moves above dangerous hazards. Scouting is necessary the first time down. Risk of injury to swimmers is moderate to high, and water conditions make self-rescue difficult. Group assistance for rescue is often essential but requires practiced skills. A strong Eskimo roll is highly recommended.

Class V. Expert. Extremely long, obstructed, or very violent rapids which expose a paddler to above average endangerment. Drops may contain large, unavoidable waves and holes or steep congested chutes with complex, demanding routes. Rapids may continue for long distances between pools, demanding a high level of fitness. What eddies exist may be small, turbulent, or difficult to reach. At the high end of the scale, several of these factors may be combined. Scouting is mandatory but often difficult. Swims are dangerous, and rescue is difficult even for experts. A very reliable Eskimo roll, proper equipment, extensive experience, and practiced rescue skills are essential for survival.

Class VI. Extreme. One grade more difficult than class V. These runs often exemplify the extremes of difficulty, unpredictability and danger. The consequences of errors are very severe and rescue may be impossible. For teams of experts only, at favorable water levels, after close personal inspection and taking all precautions. This class does **not** represent drops thought to be unrunnable, but may include rapids which are only occasionally run.

American Whitewater Affiliation, P. O. Box 85, Phoenicia, NY 12464.

wigs

The finest wigs and hairpieces are individually fitted or made to measure, with the fitter making at least seven measurements of the head and often a plaster mold of it. Actually making such a wig takes a week; knots are tied in 50,000 to 150,000 hairs. At the other end of the scale are one-size-fits-all wigs sold in many wig and costume shops.

In between are ready-to-wear wigs that are altered to fit by opening and adjusting a tape that is part of the wig's net. Head size is measured with a string or tape measure, starting from the center of the hairline above the forehead, down over the ear around the back, over the other ear and up to the starting point. Typical head sizes are 19" to 23". To preserve their size and shape, wigs should be stored on blocks of the person's head size; block size is usually indicated on the base of the block.

wind

See also ☛hurricanes.

The Beaufort Scales

The best known scale for wind speed is that of Sir Francis Beaufort (1774–1857), an admiral in the British navy who drew up the first version in 1806. The Beaufort scale was adopted by the admiralty in 1838 and by the International Meteorological Committee in 1874. Beaufort's original scale (from 1 to 12) was made for use in the open sea and based upon the amount of sail a man-of-war could carry (Force 12 was a wind "no canvas could withstand"). With the passing of military sail, later revisions focused on other phenomena observable in the open sea and added correlated wind speeds. The scale is presently maintained by the British Meteorological Office, who publish a version illustrated with very instructive photographs.

A version currently used by mariners is shown below. Column (1) is the Beaufort Number or Force Number. Column (2) is the range of wind speeds in knots, measured at a height of 33 feet above sea level; (3) is the standard description; (4) is the probable height of waves in feet; and (5) the probable maximum wave height in feet; in both cases, in the open sea, remote from land. In enclosed waters, or when near land with an offshore wind, wave heights will be smaller and the waves steeper.

Beaufort Wind Scale

(1)	(2)	(3)	Sea Criteria	(5)	(6)
0	<1	Calm	Sea like a mirror.	—	—
1	1–3	Light air	Ripples with the appearance of scales are formed but without foam crests.	1/4	—
2	4–6	Light breeze	Small wavelets, still short but more pronounced. Crests have a glassy appearance and do not break.	1/2	1
3	7–10	Gentle breeze	Large wavelets. Crests begin to break. Foam of glassy appearance. Perhaps scattered white horses.	2	3
4	11–16	Moderate breeze	Small waves, becoming longer; fairly frequent horses.	3 1/2	5
5	17–21	Fresh breeze	Moderate waves, taking a more pronounced long form; many white horses are formed. (Chance of some spray.)	6	8 1/2
6	22–27	Strong breeze	Large waves begin to form; the white foam crests are more extensive everywhere. (Probably some spray.)	9 1/2	13
7	28–33	Near gale	Sea heaps up and white foam from breaking waves begins to be blown in streaks along the direction of the wind.	13 1/2	19
8	34–40	Gale	Moderately high waves of greater length; edges of crests begin to break into spindrift. The foam is blown in well-marked streaks along the direction of the wind.	18	25
9	41–47	Strong gale	High waves. Dense streaks of foam along the direction of the wind. Crests of waves begin to topple, tumble, and roll over. Spray may affect visibility.	23	32
10	48–55	Storm	Very high waves with long overhanging crests. The resulting foam in great patches is blown in dense white streaks along the direction of the wind. On the whole the surface of the sea takes a white appearance. The tumbling of the sea becomes heavy and shocklike. Visibility affected.	29	41
11	56–63	Violent storm	Exceptionally high waves. (Small and medium-sized ships might be for a time lost to view behind the waves.) The sea is completely covered with long white patches of foam lying along the direction of the wind. Everywhere the edges of the wave crests are blown into froth. Visibility affected.	37	52
12	64+	Hurricane	The air is filled with foam and spray. Sea completely white with driving spray; visibility very seriously affected.	45	—

Note:
Estimating wind force by the sea criteria is difficult at night.
An increase of wind does not immediately produce an increase of sea.
Fetch, depth, swell, heavy rain and tide effects should be considered when estimating the wind force from the appearance of the sea.
WARNING: For a given wind force, sea conditions can be more dangerous near land than in the open sea. In many tidal waters wave heights are liable to increase considerably in a matter of minutes.

In June, 1939 the International Meteorological Committee adopted a correlation with wind speeds measured at a height of 6 meters. Great Britain and the United States, however, had already standardized on measuring the wind speed at 11 meters above ground level, which is shown in column 2 below, in miles per hour.

Beaufort Wind Scale on Land

(1)	(2)	American (British) description	Land Criteria
0	<1	Light (Calm)	Smoke rises vertically.
1	1–3	Light (Light air)	Direction shown by smoke but not by wind vanes.
2	4–7	Light (Light breeze)	Wind felt on face; leaves rustle; ordinary vane moved by wind.
3	8–12	Gentle (Gentle breeze)	Leaves and small twigs in constant motion; wind extends light flag.
4	13–18	Moderate (Moderate breeze)	Raises dust and loose paper; small branches are moved.
5	19–24	Fresh (Fresh breeze)	Small trees in leaf begin to sway.
6	25–31	Strong (Strong breeze)	Large branches in motion; umbrellas used with difficulty.
7	32–38	Strong (Near gale)	Whole trees in motion; inconvenience felt when walking against the wind.
8	39–46	Gale (Gale)	Breaks twigs off trees; generally impedes progress
9	47–54	Gale (Strong gale)	Slight structural damage; chimney-pots and slates removed.
10	55–63	Whole gale (Storm)	Trees uprooted; considerable structural damage.
11	64–72	Whole gale (Violent storm)	Widespread damage; very rarely experienced.
12	73–82	Hurricane	Countryside is devastated.
13	83–92		
14	93–103		
15	104–114		
16	115—125		
17	126—136		

Fujita Scale for Damaging Wind
In 1971, T. T. Fujita proposed a wind scale to cover the range from the top of the Beaufort scale to Mach 1, the speed of sound in air, in 12

equal steps. The equivalent on the Fujita scale, or F-scale, of any wind speed M (in meters per second) can be found from the equation

$$F = \sqrt[1.5]{\frac{M}{6.3}} - 2$$

In practice, however, only whole numbers are used. Like the Mercalli Scale for earthquake intensity, ratings on the Fujita scale are usually assigned in the aftermath by observing the nature of the damage done.

F0. 18–32 meters per second, 40–72 miles per hour, 35–62 knots. Light damage. Some damage to chimneys; break branches off trees; push over shallow-rooted trees; damage sign boards.

F1. 33–49 m/s, 73–112 mph, 63–97 knots. Moderate damage. The lower limit is the beginning of hurricane wind speed. peel surface off roofs; mobile homes pushed off foundations or overturned; moving autos pushed off the roads.

F2. 50–69 m/s, 113–157 mph, 98–136 knots. Considerable damage. Roofs torn off frame houses, mobile homes demolished; boxcars pushed over; large trees snapped or uprooted; light-object missiles generated.

F3. 70–92 m/s, 158–206 mph, 137–179 knots. Severe damage. Roofs and some walls torn off well-constructed houses; trains overturned; most trees in forest uprooted; heavy cars lifted off ground and thrown.

F4. 93–116 m/s, 207–260 mph, 180–226 knots. Devastating damage. Well-constructed houses leveled; structure with weak foundation blown off some distance; cars thrown and large missiles generated.

F5. 117–142 m/s, 261–318 mph, 227–276 knots. Incredible damage. Strong frame houses lifted off foundations and carried considerable distance to disintegrate; automobile-sized missiles fly through the air in excess of 100 m; trees debarked; incredible phenomenon will occur. [Steel-reinforced concrete structures damaged.]

F6–F12. 142 m/s, 319 mph, 277 knots to Mach I. Not expected to occur on Earth.

Applied to tornadoes, F0 is a gale tornado; F1, a moderate tornado; F2 a significant tornado; F3 a severe tornado; F4 a devastating tornado; and F5 an incredible tornado.

T. T. Fujita, "Tornadoes and Downbursts in the Context of Generalized Planetary Scales," *J. of the Atmospheric Sciences*, **38**(8),(Aug 1981).

wine bottles

See also ☛champagne.

The U.S. Bureau of Alcohol, Tobacco and Firearms formerly recognized 16 bottle sizes for domestic American wine and 27 sizes for imports. That ended when metric sizing was introduced on January 1, 1975, becoming mandatory on January 1, 1979. Except for "magnum," the names of the sizes are not allowed to appear on the label.

New size	Corresponds to old size	Capacity
Miniature	miniature	100 mL
Small	split	187 mL
Medium	tenth	375 mL
Regular	fifth	750 mL
Large	quart	1 L
Magnum	magnum	1.5 L
Extra Large	jeroboam	3 L

Some of the traditional names for wine bottle sizes are given below. The larger sizes, especially those with the biblical names, are mostly a novelty produced in very small numbers.

Bordeaux

Fillette	half a bottle
Magnum	2 bottles
Marie-Jeanne	3 bottles
Double magnum	4 bottles
Jeroboam	6 bottles
Imperial	about 8 bottles

Port

Quart	757.5 mL (☞quart, reputed)
Magnum	2 bottles
Tappet hen	3 bottles
Jeroboam	4 bottles

wire

The way wire is made leads to a "natural" sequence of sizes. A rod (made in a rolling mill) is heated and pulled through a hole whose diameter is slightly smaller than the rod's. This process is repeated through ever-smaller holes until the wire is as fine as desired. To reduce the number of steps for economy's sake, the manufacturer would like the change in size at each drawing to be as large as possible; on the other hand if the change in size is too great the wire will break while being drawn. Older wire gauges like the Birmingham, Washburn & Moen, and Lancashire came from calling the wire from the first drawing #1, from the second drawing #2, and so on. Note that the higher the number, the finer the wire.

Brown & Sharpe. Also known as the **American Wire Gauge**, and used in the USA since at least the 1880s for wires in all metals but iron and steel. Number 0000 wire is 0.4600" in diameter, and the diameter of each succeeding size is 0.890525 times the size before it. This gauge is included in the table on pp. 258–259.

Washburn & Moen. Also called the **Steel Wire Gage**, the **Roebling Gauge**, and the **American Steel and Wire Co. Gauge**. Established about 1830 and named after Washburn and Moen Manufacturing Company, which later merged with the American Steel and Wire Co. A partial table of this gauge appears on page 182.

Morse Twist Drill Gauge. A copy of the **Lancashire gauge,** the sizes being taken from wire and rod imported from Britain.

Stub's Steel Wire Gauge. Used for drill rod and tool steel wire.

Birmingham Wire Gage. The steps are irregular. Departmental sanction by the U.S. government ended in 1914. This gauge is included in the table on pp. 258–259.

Standard Wire Gage, also known as the **British Standard Wire Gauge** or the **Imperial Wire Gauge**. It was constructed by improving the Birmingham Wire Gage. Fixed by Order of Council August 23, 1883, and made a legal standard in the U.K. March 1, 1884. This gauge is included in the table on pp. 258–259.

Needle Wire Gauge. Derived from the Birmingham Wire Gauge: #1 = 18 1/2 B.W.G.; #2 = 19 B.W.G., and so on to #14 = 31 B.W.G.

Old English wire gage, also called the London Gage. A 19TH C gauge used for brass and copper wire, mainly brass wire for weaving.

Whitworth's Wire Gauge, also known as **Cocker's Wire Gauge**. The gauge number is the diameter of the wire in thousandths of an inch; for example #1 has a diameter of 0.001".

Edison Standard. A gauge used in the 19TH C by the Edison Electrical Light Company to describe wires for carrying electric current. The gauge number is the number of thousand of circular mils in the wire's cross section.

Music Wire
Music wire is used for musical instruments, such as pianos, but it is also used to manufacture springs and for many other purposes. Many different music wire gauges exist; two of the more important are:

Music Wire (Brown and Sharpe). Derived from the Washburn and Moen gauge; #12 = 22 W&M, #13 = 21 W&M, and so on.

Music Wire (English). Derived from the Birmingham Wire Gauge. #6 = 26 B.W.G.; #7 = 25 1/2 B.W.G.; #8 = 25 B.W.G. and so on up to #20 = 19 B.W.G.

wire cloth

The materials called wire cloth are usually used as fencing. They are sold cut to length or in 100' rolls.

Poultry netting, also called chicken wire. It is made with either 1" or 2" hexagonal holes, of 20-gauge (0.035") galvanized wire. Available in widths of 12", 24", 36", 48", 60", and 72".

Aviary netting. A smaller version of poultry netting, with 1/2" holes, made of 22-gauge (0.028") galvanized wire in widths of 36" and 48".

Hardware cloth, also called wire cloth. A stronger and stiffer material than poultry netting, made of heavier wire. The openings are square. Often galvanized after weaving. Hardware cloth is available in widths of 24", 36", and 48". It is used, for example, to make sieves for garden soil and to cover entrances to crawlspaces.

Nominal hole size	Actual hole size	Gauge
1/8"	0.109"	27 (0.0173")
1/4"	0.226"	27 (0.0173")
1/2"	0.460"	19 (0.041")

Welded wire fabric. Stronger than hardware cloth, usually used as fencing. The openings are usually rectangular. Instead of being woven, all the wires running in one direction lie on top of and are welded to the wires running in the other direction.

Nominal hole size	Gauge	Available widths
1/2" × 1"	16 (0.0625")	24", 36"
1" × 1"	16 (0.0625")	24", 36", 48"
1" × 2"	14 (0.080")	24", 36", 48"
2" × 4"	12 1/2 (0.097")	36", 48", 60", 72"

Field fencing, also called *hog fencing mesh*. In this type of welded wire fabric the size of openings changes from one edge of the fabric to the other. When the fabric is erected as a fence, the fence has small holes at the bottom and big ones on top. The wire is 12 1/2" gauge; available widths are 26", 32", 39", and 47".

---

wire connectors

Often called "wire nuts," these insulated connectors usually contain a small metal coil. Wires to be connected electrically are stripped of a specified length of insulation, held together, and the connector twisted on by hand. (Connectors that don't contain a metal coil may be used to connect fixtures, but not for branch wiring.)

As pressure-type wire connectors, wire nuts may be used in branch circuit electrical wiring—house wiring, for example. But each size is tested and approved by Underwriters Laboratories and the CSA for certain specific combinations of wire, which are listed on the packaging. Code prohibits a connector's use for any other combinations. To illustrate the differences between sizes, here are the specifications for two sizes in a popular brand. The gauge numbers in the given combinations apply to both stranded and solid wire.

#3 connector	#4 connector
Strip stranded wire 5/8"	Strip stranded wire 3/8"
Strip solid wire 1/2"	Strip solid wire 3/8"

Approved combinations

two to five #18	four to six #18
two to four #16	three to five #16
two #14	two or three #14 (continued)

#3 connector	#4 connector (continued)
one #14 + one to three #18	two # 12
one #14 + one or two #16	one #12 + one #14
two #14 + one #18	one #12 + one to three #16 or
one to three #16 + one #18	#18
one #16 + four #18	one #14 + one to four #16 or
one or two #16 + one to three #18	#18
	one #14 + five #18
	two #14 + one to three #16 or
	#18
	three #14 + one #18
	three to five #16
	four to six #18

Old packaging may say the connectors are approved for aluminum or copper-clad aluminum wires, but this hasn't been true since January 2, 1987. Twist-on wire connectors should not be used with aluminum wires; at the time of writing, UL has approved only the special Copalum system made by AMP, whose use requires more equipment and skill than most homeowners have.

wire rope

Wire rope, often called cable, is sized by diameter (not circumference, as large fiber rope is). The diameter is measured across the rope, not from flat to flat. The rope's construction is described by a designation like "6 × 17". In the designation, the first number is the number of strands and the second is the number of wires in the strand. Most wire rope is made with six strands. Although wire rope can be made with a wire core, most have a fiber core which is saturated in oil and helps to

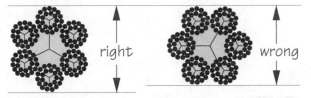

right   wrong

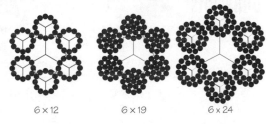

6 × 12   6 × 19   6 × 24

keep the rope lubricated. Seven strand rope is the same construction as six strand but with a wire core; aircraft cable is an example.

It is also necessary to specify the rope's lay, which describes how in which the wires are twisted to make the strands, and the strands to make the rope. There are several different types of lay.

In *regular lay* rope, the strands are twisted in one direction and the strands are laid into the rope in the opposite direction. In *lang lay* rope, the strands of the rope are twisted in the same direction as the wires are twisted in the strand. Lang lay wire rope is uncommon; although it resists wear better than regular lay rope does, it also untwists more easily.

The twist in *right hand lay* rope resembles the twist on an ordinary screw. *Left hand lay* rope twists in the opposite direction; it is used, for example, in well drilling. A very unusual type of wire rope is *right and left lay* rope, which combines 3 regular lay strands and 3 lang lay strands.

The word lay is also used to describe the distance, measured along the rope, required for one strand to make one complete turn around the rope, for example, an "18" lay."

Most wire rope is made entirely of wire of the same gauge, but a few types combine wires of diffferent gauges, and these are also described as lays. *Seale lay* strands have a large inner wire, surrounded by 9 smaller wires, surrounded by 9 large wires. *Warrington lay* strands have 7 inside wires surrounded by 12 wires that are alternately large and small.

The usual sizes of wire rope are:

Size	Use
6×7	haulage rope, transmission, standing rope, aircraft cable
7×7	aircraft cable
6×12	running rope
6×19	hoisting rope
7×19	aircraft cable, often used in automotive winches
6×24	
6×37	special flexible
8×19	extra flexible
$6 \times 6 \times 7$	tiller or hand rope, whose wires are themselves made of wires. Not strong, but very flexible.

Breaking Strength in pounds of 7×19	
3/32"	2,800
3/16"	4,200
7/32"	5,600
1/4"	7,000
5/16"	9,800
3/8"	14,400

Wire rope can be damaged by being bent too sharply, so the diameter of the sheave in pulleys or of windlass drums is important. Manufacturer's recommendations regarding proper sheave size differ. The Coast Guard's rule of thumb is that the diameter of the sheave should not be less than 20 times the diameter of the wire rope. The stiffer the rope, the larger the sheave must be. One manufacturer, for example, suggests that for 1/4" wire rope, 6×19 rope requires a sheave 6" in diameter; 6×37 requires 4 1/2"; and 8×19 requires 5".

Wire rope is available in galvanized steel. Galvanizing the rope stiffens it and helps it to resist corrosion. Such rope is best used in stationary applications—as guy wires, for example. Running it through pulleys cracks the zinc coating and the rope will corrode even faster than nongalvanized rope.

As wire rope wears, individual wires break, often forming "fish-hooks." If 4% of the individual wires in the length of one lay have broken, the U.S. Navy considers the rope unsafe.

word

Sometimes used as a unit of digital computer memory = 16 bits or 2 bytes. More accurately, when a computer is designed so that address-able memory is divided into fixed length chunks, the chunks are called words. Different machines had different word lengths: the IBM 360/370 systems had a 32-bit word length, Burroughs' were 48-bit, and the CDC Cyber systems used 60-bit words. Many minicomputers have had 16-bit words, and many computers have no fixed-length word at all.

XYZ

yard

A unit of length in the English-speaking world, = 0.9144 meter (exactly) by an international agreement effective in 1959. This value has been used for all purposes since 1959 in the USA and since 1963 in the UK. Abbr, yd. Since at least the 12TH C the yard has been subdivided into 3 feet and 36 inches. It was formerly (BEFORE 15TH C) also subdivided in a binary fashion, mainly by clothmakers, the chief divisions being 4 quarters and 16 nails (nayles).

History in Great Britain

In his *Chronicles* William of Malmesbury (1095–1143?) tells how the "false yard" was corrected by referring it to the length of King Henry I's arm. The story is not just a legend—William's descriptions of contemporary events are reliable—but William does not say this was the origin of the yard; it existed before Henry I was born. The yard was in the keeping of the guilds that dealt in cloth.

On November 20, 1196, Richard I proclaimed an Assize of Measures, and afterwards had yard standards in the form of iron rods distributed throughout the country. The expression "by the King's iron rod," referring to the yard, appears frequently in records.

The yard standard of Elizabeth I, made in 1588, is now in the Science Museum in London. It consists of an iron bar with a square cross section, about 1/2" on a side. The yard is the distance between the ends of the bar. Although it was broken and repaired sometime between 1760 and 1819, it is only about 0.01" shorter than today's yard.

From Elizabeth I to the 18TH C not much was done about the British standards of length and mass because not much needed to be done. Then the emergence of new science and technologies (in iron and textiles, for example) began to create an awareness of the possible effect of "high-tech" measurement on national well-being.

In 1742 the Royal Society in London arranged an exchange of standards with the Royal Academy of Sciences in Paris. To accomplish this, two identical brass bars were made and ruled lengthwise with three lines. The length of the yard, taken from a yard measure made in 1720 and based on that of Elizabeth I, was marked off on one of the lines and the line labelled "E" (for English). The bars were then sent to the French, who marked off the length of half a toise on one of the other lines, labelled it "F", kept one bar and sent the other back. The following year the Society decided to compare a number of the existing yard measures, and in the process of doing this the length of Elizabeth's yard was engraved on the third line and marked "EXCH" for Exchequer. The E length turned out to be 0.0075" longer than the EXCH length. This bar is known as Royal Society bar No. 41.

About a decade later the government itself decided to look into the status of the country's weights and measures, and set up a 63-member committee under Lord Carysfort to do so. They rejected Elizabeth's standards as "very coarsely made...bent...very bad standards" but approved of the more modern design of Royal Society bar No. 41, and on the advice of experts decided to make a standard to an even more modern design, taking its length from the "E" line on the Royal Society bar. The standard was duly made by a Mr. Bird, an instrument maker, in 1758 and deposited with the Clerk of the House of Commons. None of the Carysfort Committee's recommendations were acted upon. At the request of a successsor committee, Bird made a second similar yard in 1760.

There followed a succession of committees making various recommendations and suggesting various standards, culminating in the act establishing imperial measure from May 1, 1825. This act declared the yard Bird made in 1760 to be the prototype of the imperial yard. All linear measures were to be based on it. Less than ten years later, in October 1834, the Houses of Parliament burned down, destroying both of Bird's yards.

The government then appointed a committee (1838) to oversee the construction of new standards of a yet more modern nature. The task of constructing the new yard was given to Francis Baily (1744–1844), who conducted extensive research on the best choice of alloy for the bar, and designed its form before dying. The task passed to the Reverend Sheepshanks.

By this time, it was possible to measure a standard's length with a precision of one part in ten million. To give some idea of the care taken in constructing the new yard standards: to account for expansion of the metal, new thermometers were constructed accurate to a hundredth of a degree. To eliminate the effect of bending, the standards were measured floating on a pool of mercury.

Sheepshanks began by constructing some prototypes which he compared with existing yard standards that had been compared with the Bird yard. He concluded that his bar no. 2 was 36.00025" of the average value of those yards, and hence of the true yard, and the commission agreed. Forty new standards were then made to Baily's design and meticulously compared both with bar no. 2 and to one another, to find one that would be $3600000/3600025$ths of bar no. 2. This task took years. Finally one was selected to be the prototype. The four next best became "Parlimentary standards," and the remaining 35 were distributed to various cities and friendly powers. In 1855 the selected bar was made the legal standard (18 and 19 Victoria, c 72 s 2). Sheepshanks had died the day before.

History in the United States
The yard was recognized as the fundamental standard of length in the USA when it was adopted for customs purposes by the Treasury Department in 1832. For the circumstances, see ☞United States, history of weights and measures.

In 1856 the British Government gave the United States two of the new English prototypes (see above) of the imperial yard, one of bronze (Bronze Yard No. 11) and one of iron (Low Moor Iron Yard No. 57). Comparison of Bronze Yard No. 11 with the standard the United States had been using (the Troughton scale) showed that the latter was 0.00087 inch longer than the British imperial yard. Following the policy of trying to keep U.S. measures on British prototypes, the United States began to base its yard on Bronze Yard No. 11.

On April 5, 1893, T. C. Mendenhall, Superintendent of Weights and Measures, announced with the approval of the Secretary of the Treasury that U. S. standards of length would henceforth be based on the international meter. ("Fundamental Standards of Length and Mass," Bulletin 26 of the Coast and Geodetic Survey). In the Act of July 28, 1866 that made use of the metric system permissible in the USA, Congress had defined the meter in terms of the yard, 1 meter = $3937/3600$ yards. To base the yard on the meter Mendenhall turned this relation around, making the yard equal to $3600/3937$ meter, or approximately 0.91440183 meter. Thereafter the U.S. yard was based on prototype Meter No. 27, which the United States had received in 1889 from the BIPM. Meter No. 27 served as the U.S. standard of length until 1960, when the CGPM made all prototypes of the meter obsolete by redefining the meter in terms of the wavelength of light from krypton-86 (and later, in 1983, in terms of the distance light travels in 1/299,792,458th of a second).

After Mendenhall's 1893 order basing the yard on a prototype meter instead of a British prototype yard, the lengths of the British and U.S. yard, (and hence foot and inch) were different. As machining became more precise the difference between the British and U.S. inch became a problem. During the Second World War, for example, it was readily apparent to aircraft machinists using gauge-blocks from different countries. To eliminate such problems, the national standards laboratories of Australia, Canada, New Zealand, South Africa, the United Kingdom, and the United States agreed that effective July 1, 1959, for scientific and technical purposes 1 yard = 0.9144 meter exactly, which was named the International Yard. The United States immediately adopted this value for all purposes. This new value for the U.S. yard was about 2 parts per million smaller than the 1893–1959 U.S. yard.

yarn

Systems for assigning sizes to yarn can be divided into two basic types. In the first, the yarn number is based on the length of yarn needed to make up a specified weight. Cotton, wool and linen are numbered with such systems, in which the finer the yarn, the higher the number. In the second type, the yarn number is the mass of a specified length of yarn. In such a system, used, for example, with silk, synthetic fibers and jute, the higher the yarn number, the thicker the yarn.

Wool

Two systems have been in common use in the USA. The cut system was used around Philadelphia, where it originated; other parts of the country used the run system.

In the cut system, the yarn number is the number of 300-yard hanks needed to make up a pound. Thus 600 yards of 2-cut yarn weigh a pound. In practice coarse yarns are typically five-cut to seven-cut; medium, 18-cut to 21-cut; and fine yarns, 30-cut to 35-cut.

In the more common run system, the yarn number is the number of 1600-yard hanks needed to make up a pound, or in other words, the length of one pound of the yarn divided by 1,600. So one pound of number 1 run yarn is 1,600 yards long, a pound of number 2 run yarn is 3,200 yards long, and so on. Numbers 1 through 3 are coarse, 3½ to 5 are medium, and numbers 6 to 8 runs are fine.

A fraction is used to convey both the weight of the yarn and the number of plies. The numerator is the number of plies and the denominator is the yarn number of the yarn as a whole, not of the plies separately. So, for example, 2/30s cut yarn would have two plies, and 30 hanks would weigh a pound. In other words, the plies individually would be 60-cut yarn; it would take 60 hanks of such yarn to weigh a pound.

Worsted yarns have a system of their own, called "count," similar to the above, but with 1-count yarn having a length of 560 yards to the pound. A pound of 2-count yarn is thus 1,120 yards long.

Futures trading in wool is based on 64's. Counts of 44 and below are used for carpet, not clothing.

Cotton

In the USA, the yarn number for cotton yarns is based on the number of 840-yard hanks in a pound. The convention for indicating plies resembles that for wool. Two-ply 20s would be written 2/20s or 20/2, and would be twice the weight, length for length, of single ply 20s yarn.

Linen, Jute, Hemp, and Ramie

In England and the USA, yarns made of these fibers are counted by the number of leas in a pound, each lea of 300 yards.

Linen has been spun as fine as 400s and even 600s, which are used in making fine lace. To achieve such fineness, Belgian hand spinners worked only in damp basements.

Silk and Synthetic Fibers

Synthetic yarns other than glass and raw and thrown silk yarns are sized by the metric or denier systems.

The metric yarn number is the mass in grams of a 450-meter length of the yarn divided by 0.05, or, another way of saying the same thing, the mass in grams of a 9000-meter length.

The denier was a French coin, = $1/12$ of a sou, whose mass was used as a weight in calculating yarn numbers. In Great Britain and the USA, denier was originally applied only to raw silk. A yard number in "international" deniers is the mass in grams of a 500-meter length ÷ 0.05. Being a natural product, silk varies in thickness, so the size is usually given as a range, for example, "13/16 denier." There were numerous local deniers, among the more prominent:

Turin denier	mass in grams of a 474-meter length ÷ 0.05336
Milan denier	mass in grams of a 476-meter length ÷ 0.0511
Old Lyonese denier	mass in grams of a 476-meter length ÷ 0.5311
New Lyonese denier	mass in grams of a 500-meter length ÷ 0.05311

The Manchester dram system was formerly used for thrown silk, the yarn number being the weight of a 1000-yard skein in drams. It was replaced by the denier.

Spun silk yarn, which is made from leftovers after filament silk has been produced, is numbered by a different system in the USA and the UK, one like that used for cotton. The yarn number is the number of 840-yard lengths (a hank) in a pound. The smaller the number, the heavier the yarn.

In the fractional notation describing the weight and number of plies, the yarn number is based on the weight of the finished yarn, not the weight of the individual plies.

Modern Systems

A unit called the tex has been introduced in an attempt to replace the welter of historical units. The yarn number in tex is the mass in grams of a 1-kilometer length of the yarn. Unlike most yarn number systems, this one is intended to be applied to every type of fiber, internationally. In the USA and Canada, the drex is also used, the yarn number in drex being the mass in grams of a 10-kilometer length of the yarn. One drex = 10 tex.

The following table gives some very approximate equivalents, by weight, for the various systems.

Denier	Worsted	Cotton	Woolen (run)	Linen (lea)	Tex	Metric
50	160	106	56	298	5.6	180
75	106	71	37	198	8.3	120
100	80	53	28	149	11.1	90
150	53	35	19	99	16.6	60
200	40	27	14	74	22.2	45
300	27	18	9.3	50	33.4	30
400	20	13	7.0	37	44.4	22.5
500	16	11	5.6	30	55.5	18
700	11.4	7.6	4.0	21	77.7	12.9
1000	8.0	5.3	2.8	15	111	9
1500	5.3	3.5	1.9	10	166	6
2000	4.0	2.7	1.4	7	222	4.5

year

Various intervals of time based on the earth's revolution about the sun. The meanings of the various years are presented first, their lengths in days (= 86,400 seconds as defined in SI) for the year 1990 are given in the table that follows.

Calendar year: A period of time consisting of an arbitrary number of whole days; in some calendars it consists of a whole number of lunations. In most calendars today the year is 365 days, with a 366-day year roughly every four years. See ☞calendar. However, years as short as 260 days have been used, and in some calendars some years are longer than 366 days. Perhaps the longest calendar year ever was the one Julius Caesar decreed for 46 BC: 445 days, to bring the equinoxes back to their traditional dates in the Roman calendar.

Tropical year: The period of time from one vernal equinox to the next. The tropical year is the interval at which seasons repeat, and is one of the bases of the calendar. Its only connection with sunny beaches and banana farms is that on the vernal and autumnal equinoxes, the sun at noon is directly overhead at the equator.

Sidereal year: The average length of time required for the Earth to make one revolution about the sun with respect to a fixed direction in space, which is determined from distant stars. See ☞time, sidereal.

Anomalistic year: At one point in its orbit the Earth is closest to the sun and at one point farthest away. The anomalistic year is the period of time between the annual closest approach of the Earth to the sun, which, incidentally, occurs during the Northern Hemisphere's winter.

	days	days	hrs	min	sec
Julian	365.25	365	6	0	0
Tropical	365.2421897	365	5	48	45.19
Sidereal	365.25636	365	6	9	10
Anomalistic	365.25964	365	6	13	53
Eclipse	346.62005	365	14	52	52
Gaussian	365.25690	365	6	9	56

yocto-

A decimal submultiplier prefix in SI, indicating 10^{-24}. The name comes from "octo," Latin for eight, because the prefix represents the eighth power of 10^{-3}. The "y" was added to avoid the use of the letter "o" in abbreviations, because it might be confused with the numeral for zero. The yocto- was proposed by the CIPM in 1990 and approved by the 19TH CGPM in Sept–Oct 1991. Compare ☞yotta-.

yotta-

A decimal multiplier prefix in SI, indicating 10^{24}. The name comes from "octo," from the Latin for eight, because the prefix represents 10^3 to the eighth power. The "y" was added to avoid the use of the letter "o" in abbreviations, because it might be confused with the numeral for zero. The yotta- was proposed by the CIPM in September 1990, and approved by the 19TH CGPM in Sept–Oct 1991. Compare ☞yocto-.

zepto-

A decimal submultiplier prefix in SI, indicating 10^{-21}, or one sextillionth (American system) of the unit modified. The name is derived from "septo," from the Latin for seven, because the prefix represents 10^{-3} to the seventh power. Since "s" was already an abbreviation for a unit (the second), the abbreviation for a septosecond would have been "ss". To avoid this typo-prone outcome, "z" was substituted for "s;" hence "zepto." The prefix was proposed by the CIPM in 1990, and adopted by the 19th CGPM in 1991. Compare ☞zetta-.

zetta-

A decimal multiplier prefix in SI, indicating 10^{21}. It was proposed by the CIPM in 1990, and adopted by the 19th CGPM in 1991. For the origin of the term see ☞zepto-.

Conversion Factors

These conversion factors are based on the international (or "unified") pound and yard, used since 1959 in the USA (Federal Register, July 1, 1959). The imperial measures are based on the metric equivalent for the imperial gallon adopted in the Weights and Measures Act of 1985, even applying it to imperial measures that were dropped by or before the Act. For all nontechnical purposes, the difference between the 1985 factor and earlier ones (e.g., the one in the 1963 Act) is insignificant. The liter is taken as equivalent to a cubic decimeter (adopted by the CGPM in 1964).

Round off the conversion factor as appropriate to the datum you're converting. Sometimes an alternate procedure is given in square brackets [] for calculators that accept exponential (or scientific) notation. Conversion factors for some other units can be found in the main entries; the factors for the various metric prefixes are given in the entry on the metric system.

Angles

To convert	To	Enter the number, then do this
degrees	radians	× 0.017 453 293
	quadrants	÷ 90 (exact)
	seconds	× 3600 (exact)
minutes	radians	× 0.000 290 888 208 666
seconds	radians	× 0.000 004 848 136 811
radians	degrees	× 57.295 779 513
grads	degrees	× 9 (exact)

Areas

To convert	To	Enter the number, then do this
sq. inches	sq. centimeters	× 6.451 6 (exact)
sq. feet	sq. meters	× 0.092 903 04 (exact)
sq. yards	sq. meters	× 0.836 127 36 (exact)
sq. centimeters	sq. inches	÷ 6.451 6
sq. meters	sq. feet	÷ 0.092 903 04
	sq. yards	÷ 0.836 127 36

Astronomical Distances

To convert	To	Enter the number, then do this
astronomical units	miles	× 92,955,807 [× 9.3E7]
	kilometers	× 149,597,870
light-years	astronomical units	× 63,279.5
	kilometers	× 9,460,550; shift the decimal point in the result 6 digits to the right [× 9.46055E12]
	miles	× 5,878,510; shift the decimal point in the result 6 digits to the right [× 5.87851E12]
	parsecs	× 3.262
parsecs	astronomical units	× 206,265
	lightyear	÷ 3.262
	miles	× 19,173,800; shift the decimal point in the result 6 digits to the right [× 1.917E13]
	kilometers	× 30,857,200; shift the decimal point in the result 6 digits to the right [× 3.086E13]

Capacity

Some units of capacity, such as liters and the British imperial units, are used for both liquid and dry measure. In the United States, liquid and dry capacity measures differ.

Beware of records, especially those made before the 20TH C, that do not indicate whether a particular measurement was striken or heaped: the difference between a level teaspoon and a heaped teaspoon. No ratio of striken to heaped measure is universally applicable because it depends on the proportions of the container and the nature of the substance being measured. The conversion factors assume striken measure.

From Units Used for Both Dry and Liquid Capacity		
To convert	To	Enter the number, then do this
cubic inches	cubic feet	÷ 1,728 (exact)
	liters	× 0.000 163 870 64
cubic yards	cubic meters	× 0.764 554 860
cubic meters	cubic yards	× 1.307 950 619
liters	cubic centimeters *or* milliliters	Move decimal point 3 digits to the right.
	cubic meters	Move decimal point 3 digits to the left.
	cubic inches	× 61.025 45
	cubic feet	× 0.035 315 66
	U.S. gill	× 8.453 506 568
	U.S. liquid pint	× 2.113 376 419
	U.S. liquid quarts	× 1.056 688 209
	U.S. gallons	× 0.264 172 052
	U.S. dry pint	× 1.816 165 968
	U.S. dry quarts	× 0.908 082 984
	U.S. peck	× 0.113 510 373
	U.S bushels	× 0.028 377 593
	imperial quarts	× 0.879 876 993
	imperial gallons	× 0.219 969 248
	imperial bushels	× 0.027 496 156
milliliters *or* cubic centimeters	cubic inches	× 0.061 023 744 09
	U.S. minim	× 16.230 73
	U.S. fluidram	× 0.270 512
	U.S. fluid ounce	× 0.033 814
imperial gallons	cubic inches	× 277.419 4
	cubic feet	× 0.160 543 6
	cubic centimeters *or* milliliters	× 4,545.596 459 1
	liters	× 4.546 09 (exactly)
	cubic meters	× 0.004 546 09
	U.S. dry quarts	× 4.128 226 974
	U.S. gallons	× 1.200 949 925

From Units Used for Both Dry and Liquid Capacity

To convert	To	Enter the number, then do this
imperial quarts	u.s. liq. quarts	× 1.200 949 925
	u.s. dry quarts	× 1.032 056 743
imperial gills	u.s. gills	× 1.200 949 925
imperial fluid ounces	u.s. fluid ounces	× 0.960 759 4

From Units Used Only for Liquid Capacity

To convert	To	Enter the number, then do this
u.s. minims	milliliters	× 0.061 611 520
u.s. fluidram	milliliters	× 3.696 691 195
u.s. fluid ounces	milliliters	× 29.573 529 563
u.s. liquid pints	liters	× 0.473 176 473
u.s. liquid quarts	cubic inches	× 57.75 (exact)
	cubic feet	× 0.033 420 136
	liters	× 0.946 352 946
	imperial quarts	× 0.832 674 742
u.s. gallons	cubic inches	× 231 (exact)
	cubic feet	× 0.133 680 55
	acre-feet	÷ 325,851.4
	liters	× 3.785 411 8
	cubic meters	× 0.003 785 411 8
	imperial gallons	× 0.832 674 742
acre-feet	gallons	× 325,851.4

From Units of Dry Capacity

To convert	To	Enter the number, then do this
u.s. dry pints	cubic inches	× 33.600 312 5
	liters	× 0.550 610 471
	cubic cm	× 550.610 471
u.s. dry quarts	u.s. bushels	÷ 32 (exact)
	imperial bushels	× 0.030 227 343
	liters	× 1.101 220 943
	cubic inches	× 67.200 63 (exact)
	cubic centimeters or milliliters	× 1,101.220 943

From Units of Dry Capacity

To convert	To	Enter the number, then do this
u.s. bushels	cubic inches	× 2,150.42
	pecks	× 4 (exact)
	imperial bushel	× 0.968 939 5
	cubic centimeters	× 35,239.07
	liters	× 35.239 070 167

Distances

To convert	To	Enter the number, then do this
miles	kilometers	× 1.609 344
kilometers	miles (statute)	× 0.621 371 19
	nautical miles (int.)	× 0.539 956 80
nautical miles (int.)	miles	× 1.150 779 4
	kilometers	× 1.852

Energy

To convert	To	Enter the number, then do this
ergs	joules	Move decimal point 7 places to the right.
British thermal units (Btu)		× 1054.35
calories		× 4.184
kilocalories		× 4,184
watt-hours		× 3,600
kilowatt-hours	kilojoules	× 3,600
horsepower-hours		× 2,684.520
megatons of TNT equivalent		× 4,184,000,000,000

Land Area

To convert	To	Enter the number, then do this
sq. miles	hectares	× 258.998 811 033
	sq. kilometers	× 2.589 988 110
sq. kilometer	hectares	× 100 (exact)
	sq. miles	× 0.386 102 158
acres	sq. meters	× 4,046.856 422 4 (exact)
	square miles	÷ 640
	hectares	× 0.404 685 642
hectares	acres	× 2.471 053 8
	square miles	÷ 258.998 813

Land Area

To convert	To	Enter the number, then do this
sections	acres	× 640 (exact)
townships	acres	× 23,040

Large Masses

To convert	To	Enter the number, then do this
metric tonnes	long tons (2240 lbs)	× 0.984 206 53
	short tons	× 1.102 311 3
long tons	metric tonnes	× 1.016 046 9
short tons	metric tonnes	× 0.907 184 74
	long tons	× 0.892 857 14

Length

From	To	Enter the number, then do this
inches	centimeters	× 2.54 (exact)
feet	meters	× 0.304 8 (exact)
yards	meters	× 0.914 4 (exact)
centimeters	inches	÷ 2.54 (exact)
meters	feet	÷ 0.304 8 (exact)
	yards	÷ 0.914 4 (exact)
angstroms	nanometers	÷ 10

Paper Weights

In the United States, paper weights are based on the weight of 500 sheets of a standard size that depends on the type of paper. In the rest of the world, the weights of all types of paper are given in grams per square meter (referred to as grammage). The factors below convert U.S. basis weights to grammage.

17" × 22" (bond, ledger)   × 3.759 7
20" × 26" (cover)   × 2.704 1
24" × 36" (kraft, tag, newsprint)   × 1.627 5
25 1/2" × 30 1/2" (index)   × 1.808 0
25" × 38" (book paper)   × 1.480 1
25" × 40"   × 1.406 1

Pressure

From	To	Enter the number, then do this
pounds per square inch	kilopascals	× 6.894 76
millibars	pascals	× 100 (exact)
inches of mercury (60°F)	kilopascals	× 3.376 85
atmospheres	kilopascals	× 101.325
technical atmospheres	kilopascals	× 98.066 5

Power

From	To	Enter the number, then do this
horsepower	kilowatts	× 0.745 7
kilowatts	horsepower	× 1.341 02

Small Masses

To convert	To	Enter the number, then do this
grains	milligrams	× 64.798 91
drams	grams	× 1.771 845 195
ounces avoirdupois	grams	× 28.349 523 125
	pounds	÷ 16 (exact)
	troy ounces	× 0.911 458 333
pennyweights	grams	× 1.555 173 84
troy ounces *or* apothecaries' ounces	ounces av	× 1.097 142 9
	grams	× 31.103 486
carats	grams	÷ 5 (exact)
grams	ounces av.	× 0.035 273 961
	troy or apothecaries' ounces	× 31.103 476 8
pounds av.	kilograms	× 0.453 592 37
pounds troy	kilograms	× 0.373 241 72
kilograms	pounds av.	× 2.204 622 6
	pounds troy	× 2.679 228 9

Temperature

To convert	To	Enter the number, then do this
degrees Celsius	degrees Fahrenheit	× 1.8; + 32
	Kelvin	+ 273.15
degrees Fahrenheit	degrees Celsius	− 32; =; ÷ 1.8
	Kelvin	− 32; =; ÷ 1.8; + 273.15
Kelvin	degrees Celsius	− 273.15
	degrees Fahrenheit	− 273.15; =; ×1.8; + 32
degrees Rankine	degrees Celsius	÷ 1.8; =; − 273.15
	degrees Fahrenheit	− 459.67
degrees Réaumur	degrees Celsius	× 1.25
	degrees Fahrenheit	× 2.25; + 32

Graphical Conversions

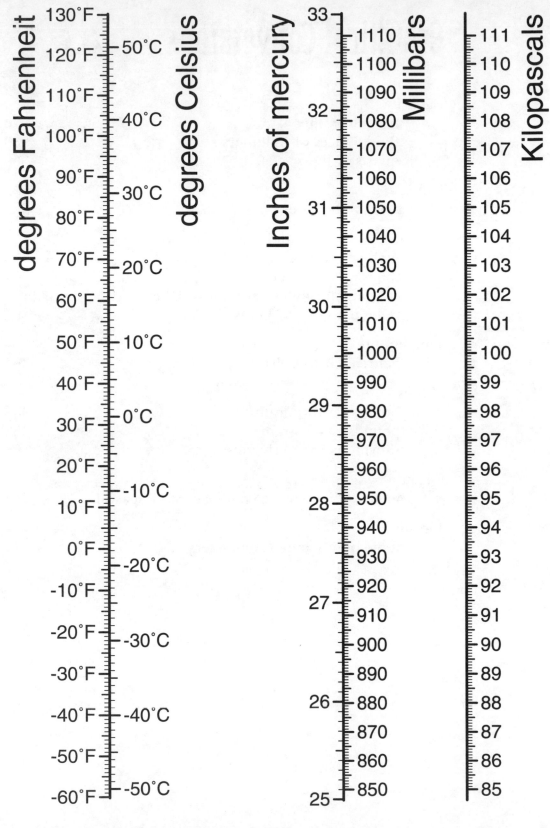

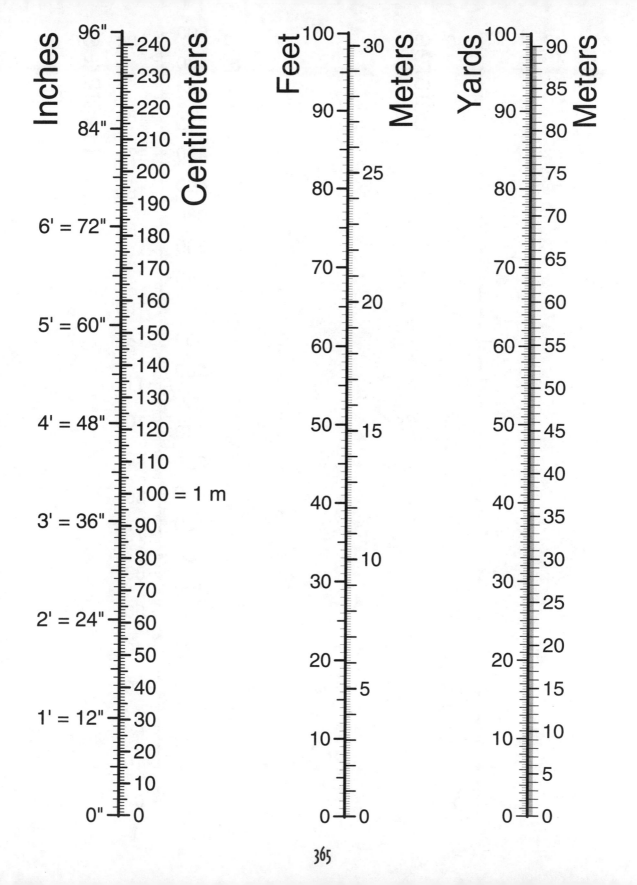

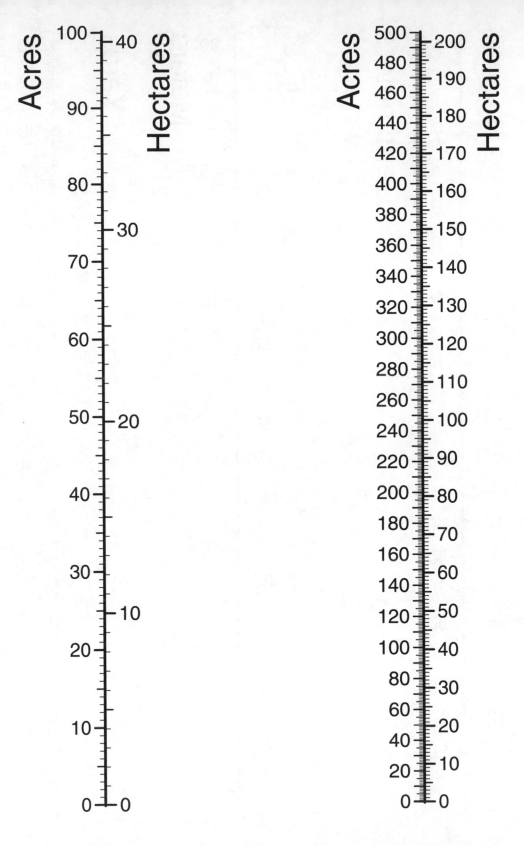

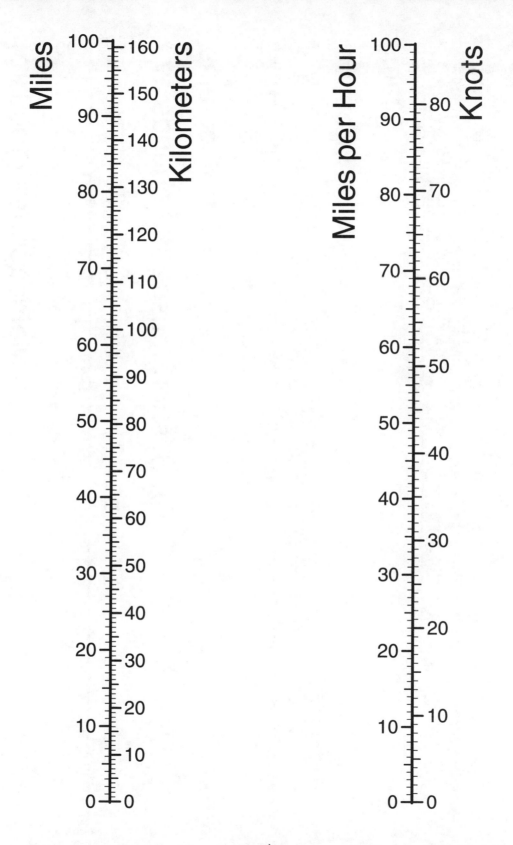

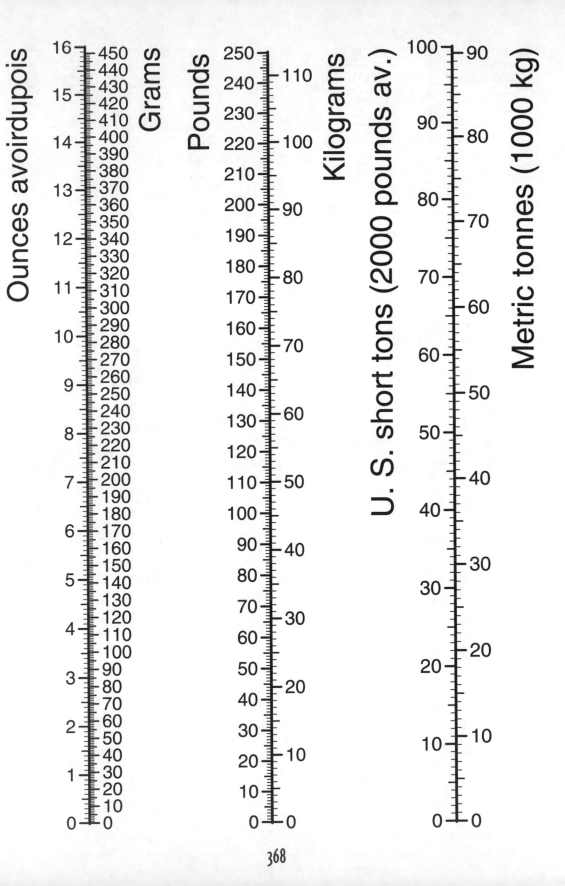

Ounces avoirdupois

Grams

Pounds

Kilograms

U. S. short tons (2000 pounds av.)

Metric tonnes (1000 kg)

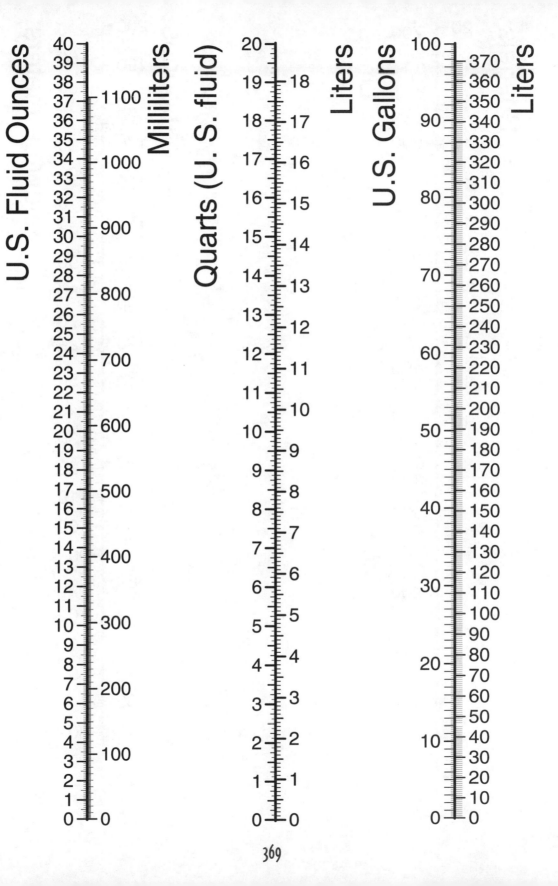

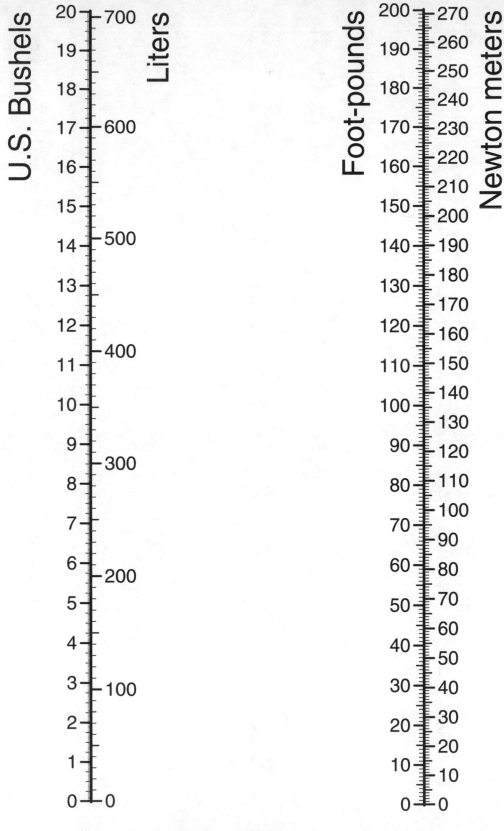

Index

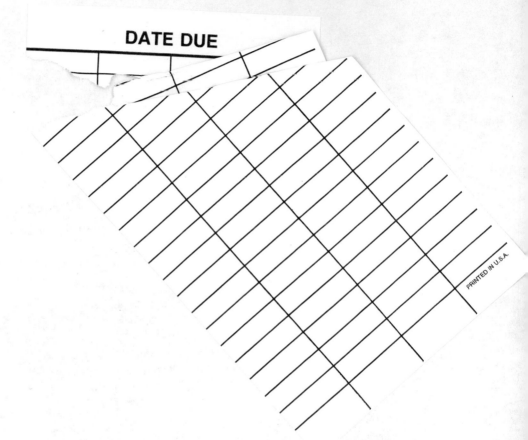

DATE DUE

PRINTED IN U.S.A.